Also by VINCE WALDRON
Classic Sitcoms: A Celebration of the Best
in Prime Time Comedy

With RONNIE SPECTOR:
Be My Baby: How I Survived Mascara, Miniskirts,
and Madness or My Life as a Fabulous Ronette

THE OFFICIAL
DICK VAN DYKE SHOW
BOOK

THE OFFICIAL
DICK VAN DYKE SHOW
BOOK

The Definitive History

and Ultimate Viewer's Guide

to Television's

Most Enduring Comedy

BY

VINCE WALDRON

Library of Congress Cataloging-in-Publication Data

Library of Congress Card Number: 00-108806

British library Cataloging-in-Publication Data
A catalogue record of this book is available from the British Library

APPLAUSE THEATRE BOOKS
151 W46th Street, 8th Floor
New York, NY 10036
Phone: (212) 575-9265
FAX: (646) 562-5852
email: info@applausepub.com

COMBINED BOOK SERVICES LTD.
Units I/K, Paddock Wood Distribution Centre
Paddock Wood, Tonbridge, Kent TN 12 6UU
Phone: (44) 01892 837171
Fax: (44) 01892 837272

SALES & DISTRIBUTION
HAL LEONARD CORP.
7777 West Bluemound Road
P.O. Box 13819
Milwaukee, WI 53213
Phone: (414) 774-3630
Fax: (414) 774-3259
email: halinfo@halleonard.com
internet: www.halleonard.com

10   9   8   7   6   5   4   3   2   1

This book is dedicated to Carl Reiner, who, with his cast and crew of collaborators, conjured magic each week on the set of *The Dick Van Dyke Show.*

And to Frank Adamo, Ruth Burch, Ross Elliot, Jerry Hausner, Ronny Jacobs, Harald Johnson, Marge Mullen, Jim Niver, Ken Reid, Doris Singleton, Tom Tuttle, and all the other unsung grips, gaffers, and bit players who gave substance to that magic for five unforgettable years,

And to my brother, Robert, whose bright idea it was to write about *The Dick Van Dyke Show* in the first place.

CONTENTS

INTRODUCTION

by Dick Van Dyke

IT'S A LITTLE HARD TO BELIEVE THAT IT'S BEEN more than thirty years since we filmed the first episode of *The Dick Van Dyke Show*. After all these years, people still ask me what made our show so special—what was that secret ingredient in our success? I always answer that our show represented a perfect marriage of players and playwright. We had that great, great cast; and Carl Reiner understood exactly how to write to every one of our strengths.

Unlike a lot of writers, Carl never wrote a character and expected the actor to come in and play it as written. Carl is a student of human nature—before he'd write a script, he'd have his eye on us. He'd watch us on the set; he'd listen to us as we talked. Then he'd filter those observations through his own unique comic genius and out would come one of those terrific scripts he wrote for the show. I think that's why, with Carl's scripts, the words always seemed to fit you so perfectly that you almost didn't have to memorize them. *That's* good writing.

And I don't suppose it hurt that we had actors like Morey Amsterdam, Rose Marie, and Mary Tyler Moore around to speak Carl's lines once he'd written them. None of us had ever met before that first day of rehearsal, but after Carl and Sheldon Leonard brought us all together for that very first show, it really was love at first sight. Gosh, they were just so good—all of them. Morey, who walked around with a Rolodex of jokes in his brain; Rosie, with her flawless sense of timing; and, of course, Mary, who had absolutely no background in comedy when she came to us—a serious young actress who was still in her early twenties. But boy did she learn fast! In no time at all, Mary was holding her own with old pros like Rosie and Morey and Richard Deacon.

And it didn't take me very long to figure out how good I had it on that series, either. After all, I wasn't a kid when we started—I'd already been knocking around the business for about fifteen years. So I was acutely aware, every minute that I was on that show, that it just didn't get any better than that. We had so much fun—we had so much latitude to be creative—that I knew even then that things would never get any better. And, as a matter of fact, they didn't!

I suppose the funniest part of it all is that if someone had walked on to our set in 1964 and told us that people would someday be writing entire books about our show, we probably would've had a good laugh. And then we would've very politely shown them the door! Who would have thought our show would still be around thirty years later? We all figured we had an entertaining series, but, I can tell you, nobody thought in terms of posterity back then. We were so busy working every day for the five years that our show was in production that I don't think any of us had any real idea of the impression we were making outside of that studio.

It reminds me of something that the great movie comedian Stan Laurel told me not long after I first came out to California. Stan must've been in his late sixties then—not much older than I am now, come to think of it. And I remember asking him what it had been like making all those classic Laurel and Hardy comedies. "But, Dickie," he said—that's what he called me, Dickie—"we had no idea how successful those old films would be while we were making them." He and Ollie were so busy working in the confines of the studio every day, he told me, that they just lost touch with the outside world. It wasn't until much, much later that Laurel and Hardy realized what a deep and lasting effect their comedies had had on the entire world. And then Stan said something I'll never forget. "The nicest thing," he told me, "is knowing that you were part of something that has stood the test of time."

And, I guess, after thirty years of having people come up and tell me how much our show has meant to them over the years, I think I finally understand what Stan meant. And, looking back now on those five magical years I spent in the company of that wonderful group of people, I must say that I agree with Stan completely. It is nice to know that you were a part of something that has stood the test of time.

Very nice.

Dick Van Dyke
February 1994
Malibu, California

The Official
DICK VAN DYKE SHOW
Book

PROLOGUE:
Inauguration Day

BY SIX O'CLOCK ON THE EVENING OF JANUARY 20, 1961, THE line of people waiting outside Hollywood's Desilu Cahuenga studios was already more than two hundred strong. At a quarter past the hour, a phalanx of fresh-scrubbed CBS Network pages began to herd the curious crowd through the sturdy metal doors that provided direct access from a quiet Hollywood side street called Lillian Way onto the lot's soundstage 5, where, in just under an hour, the pilot episode of a new comedy called *The Dick Van Dyke Show* was about to go before the cameras for the very first time.

It would be a momentous night. And yet, there's little reason to believe that many of those in the Van Dyke show's opening night crowd had even the slightest inkling that they were about to witness television history in the making. As hard as it might be to conceive of today, few of the tourists, idle shoppers, and other curiosity seekers who made up much of *The Dick Van Dyke Show*'s first-night audience had ever heard of the star, whose fame at that time had yet to travel much beyond the East Coast, where he'd been wowing Broadway audiences for the past nine months as the star of *Bye Bye Birdie*. But if Dick Van Dyke seemed a relatively obscure choice to headline a new TV series, it's a cinch that even fewer of those assembled to watch the filming of the show's pilot episode recognized the actress who would be playing Van Dyke's wife that night, a slightly nervous twenty-four-year-old starlet-to-be named Mary Tyler Moore.

Not that many of those in the house that night were overly concerned about the identity of the show's stars; a far more pressing topic of conversation in the moments before the filming began that evening was almost certainly the inauguration of John F. Kennedy, who'd taken the oath of office as the nation's thirty-fifth president just a few hours earlier that day in Washington, D.C. Though he'd only been in office for less than a single day, political pundits on both coasts were already predicting that John F. Kennedy's arrival would mark the dawn of a new era in American politics and culture. And yet, it's doubtful that even the most prescient member of the Van Dyke show's opening night crowd could have predicted that *The Dick Van Dyke Show* itself would be viewed by future generations as a primary icon of its age—one of a small handful of cultural artifacts that would come to define the start of the turbulent decade of the sixties.

By 6:25 P.M., the efficient CBS pages had already seated most of the crowd in a dozen or so rows of stadium-style bleachers that lined one wall of the soundstage. A few feet in front of the grandstands were parked three mammoth 35mm movie cameras, a trio of wheeled behemoths that sat in drooped repose in the narrow limbo that separated the audience from the stage's main playing area. But while they might have appeared cumbersome at first glance, under the stewardship of the show's director of photography, Robert DeGrasse, and his able camera coordinator, Jim Niver, those three cameras would soon prove quite nimble in their ability to chronicle the evening's comic action with an almost surgical precision. Beyond the cameras lay the stage itself, which was, for the time being, masked from the audience's gaze by a matched set of four long wooden flats that had been set end-to-end at the foot of the stage. This makeshift curtain, such as it was, was sufficient to provide the show's stagehands, prop assistants, makeup artists, carpenters, and gaffers with a semblance of privacy as they attended to all the last-minute activities that were necessary to prepare the stage for the filming that lay ahead.

As was customary for the various live shows that were filmed on the nine soundstages at Desilu Cahuenga, *The Dick Van Dyke Show* pilot would be played on only four standing sets. In this case, those four sets included a convincing replica of a cluttered writers' office, the spacious living room of Alan Brady's penthouse apartment, a full kitchen, and a small boy's bedroom. Because the Van Dyke show was at that point still no more than a pilot film for an as-yet-unscheduled series, the evening's standing sets were constructed in a temporary fashion, using lumber, set pieces, and even a few props that had been borrowed from *The Danny Thomas Show*, which was stage 5's usual tenant. At the conclusion of that evening's shoot, it had been arranged that the show's four makeshift sets would be quickly dismantled and their component pieces put into storage or recycled back to *The Danny Thomas Show*, which was scheduled to return to production on soundstage 5 the following Monday morning. This highly efficient—and rigidly economical—production arrangement was the brainchild of *The Danny Thomas Show*'s producer/director, Sheldon Leonard, who would serve as executive producer on *The Dick Van Dyke Show* pilot and the series it would eventually spawn.

At 6:30 P.M., eight or nine members of a small orchestral combo ambled up and took their places behind a small bandstand that had been set up at the far end of the soundstage. There, under the direction of Earle Hagen, the studio's resident composer and conductor, the band struck up the first in an eclectic repertoire of dance numbers and hit-parade selections that had been specially chosen to boost the studio audience's energy level in the last few minutes before show time. Meanwhile, onstage, executive producer Sheldon Leonard—who would also direct the Van Dyke show pilot—huddled for one last powwow with his camera and lighting technicians before the cameras were moved into their starting formation. Farther behind the scenes, makeup man Lee Greenway and his assistants were busy dabbing Mary Tyler Moore, Rose Marie, Morey Amsterdam, and the other members of the show's cast with one last touchup of the heavy reddish pancake makeup that was used to make the performers' skin tones appear normal under the harsh lights that were required in the days of black-and-white television broadcasts. The makeup artists paid particular attention to Dick Van Dyke, who would need a heavier than normal application of pancake that evening to cover a cold sore that had erupted on the star's upper lip earlier in the week—the most visible manifestation of the actor's opening night jitters.

At a few minutes past 7:00, the band ended its final number with a stirring crescendo, and Sheldon Leonard introduced the show's producer, Carl Reiner, who had volunteered to deliver a few informal opening remarks before the filming began. Reiner's entrance was greeted by a generous round of applause from the audience, many of whom recognized the popular character actor from his long stint as one of Sid Caesar's second bananas on *Your Show of Shows* and other variety shows of the 1950s. As the applause subsided, Reiner spoke to the crowd from a spot at the foot of the bleachers, a vantage point from which he would continue to regale the audience with spontaneous jokes and off-the-cuff patter throughout the evening. The ebullient producer began his remarks by identifying himself as the show's writer and creator, which, he explained, meant that he could—and should—be held fully responsible for anything that might go wrong that night. However, he cautioned, if the audience ended up having a good time, they were instructed to give due credit to his utterly resourceful director and executive producer, Sheldon Leonard, as well as the members of his gifted acting company, who were then introduced, one by one.

Richard Deacon. Larry Mathews. Mary Tyler Moore. Morey Amsterdam. Rose Marie. And, of course, Dick Van Dyke. As the players were introduced, each of them stepped out onto the stage for the briefest of curtain calls, before they vanished back behind the scenes to prepare for their initial entrances. After the curtain calls, Carl Reiner tossed a few more wisecracks to the audience as the camera operators wheeled their rigs into place for the first shot of the night. Meanwhile, behind the flimsy plywood partitions that continued to mask the stage from the audience's sightlines, assistant director Jay Sandrich cued Mary Tyler Moore to take her place on the show's first set, a convincing mockup of a modern suburban kitchen, complete with working range and Formica-covered counter. An instant later, Sandrich ducked behind the set to make sure that five-year-old Larry Mathews was standing on his own backstage mark, ready to make his entrance a few lines into the opening scene.

Back on the set, Mary Tyler Moore found herself struggling briefly to get a solid fingerhold on a slippery potato—the so-called practical prop that her character was supposed to be peeling at the top of the show. After a couple of false starts, the actress finally got her potato well in hand, and Sandrich issued a signal to director Leonard that all was well and ready to go on the stage. Suddenly, like magic, the long wooden flats that lined the foot of the stage were pushed aside, and the studio audience got their first lingering glimpse at the kitchen of Rob, Laura, and Ritchie Petrie of New Rochelle, New York, where, at that precise moment, a somewhat jumpy young actress stood behind the Formica counter, waiting breathlessly for her impending moment of truth.

From behind the cameras, character-actor-turned-television-producer/director Sheldon Leonard barked out a few final commands to his crew in a booming baritone that carried easily to the last rows of the bleachers, ending with the single word that would instantly transform the chaos around him into a few privileged moments of magic.

"Action!"

And with that command, a sudden and startling metamorphosis took place on the stage, where the anxious young actress who'd been standing there not two minutes earlier vanished; in her place, the crowd saw only a confident suburban housewife standing behind the counter of a modern suburban kitchen, humming softly to herself as she deftly peeled a potato.

It was show time.

For the next ninety minutes, Dick Van Dyke, Mary Tyler Moore, Rose Marie, Morey Amsterdam, Larry Mathews, Richard Deacon, and the rest of the show's capable cast and crew would perform their chores with effort that would seem almost invisible to the show's studio audience, who were completely charmed from the show's opening moment on. But it's unlikely that anyone in the thoroughly delighted crowd that night was quite so pleased by the evening's progress as Carl Reiner himself, who watched the show unfold from his discreet vantage point just beyond the harsh glare of the arc lamps that bore down on the stage.

To the uninitiated, Carl Reiner's decision to remain on the sidelines throughout much of the evening might have seemed an odd choice, especially considering the character actor's well-established reputation as a scene stealer par excellence on *Your Show of Shows*. But, though Reiner was clearly more than happy to surrender the spotlight to Dick Van Dyke and the rest of his merry band of players for the night, there could be little doubt among those in the know that the triumphant evening belonged to Carl Reiner—regardless of where he happened to be standing while the cameras were rolling.

CHAPTER 1
One Man's Reality

"ANY GOOD SHOW THAT YOU see on television is going to reflect one person's reality," says Carl Reiner, whose work as writer, producer, and creative conscience of *The Dick Van Dyke Show* certainly bears proof of his premise. If anything, Reiner's axiom can be seen as an understatement when applied to *The Dick Van Dyke Show*, a series that reflected the real-life events of its creator's life so closely that it can be viewed practically as a comic memoir of Reiner's early years in show business. Nor was *The Dick Van Dyke Show* Carl Reiner's first attempt to refine the details of his life into comic fodder for his work; almost four years earlier the writer had published *Enter Laughing*, a short comic novel that provided an only slightly fictionalized look at Reiner's early days as an actor. Is it any wonder then that the events depicted in *The Dick Van Dyke Show* pick up almost precisely where the narrative thread in *Enter Laughing* leaves off?

Of course, it probably didn't hurt that the details of Reiner's childhood already read like the treatment of some corny old Hollywood show-biz saga. Born on March 20, 1922, to a Bronx watchmaker named Irving Reiner and his wife Bessie, Carl Reiner was raised on the streets of New York at the very height of the Great Depression. According to a rather colorful account of those years that appeared in Reiner's late fifties studio biography, the man who would grow up to create one of the most enduring popular entertainments of his era had almost no interest in show business as a child. In those days, according to the studio bio, Reiner dreamed only of a career in major league baseball, a fantasy that had been fueled by a few thousand games of stickball played on the streets of the Bronx. "I was what we called a 'three sewer hitter,'" Reiner told his publicist in 1959. "I could belt that ball three sewer covers away—which is quite an accomplishment when you're playing ball on a Bronx street."[1]

It wasn't until he was sixteen, and his parents began urging him to find a trade, that Carl Reiner finally glimpsed his horizons in show business. In fact, Reiner had already landed a job as an assistant machinist in a shop that repaired sewing machines for New York's then-thriving millinery trade when his older brother Charlie urged him to look into a drama course that was being sponsored by the federal Works Progress Administration program. Once enrolled, the younger Reiner found himself bitten by the theatrical bug, and it wasn't long before he found himself abandoning his plan to enter the machinist's trade to embark on a career in the theater.

Once he'd committed to the actor's life, Carl Reiner trod a well-worn path to stardom that began with bit parts and summer stock. An extended apprenticeship at New York's Gilmore Theatre led to a few seasons of summer stock in Rochester, New York, where the young actor landed roles in dozens of venerable melodramas and light comedies of the era, including a lead role in a stock production of Philip Barry's *The Philadelphia Story*. Not long after that, Reiner embarked on a memorable ten-week tour with a traveling Shakespeare troupe, where the fledgling thespian got his first—and last—taste of the classics. "I was never comfortable as a serious actor," Reiner recalled some years later. "I felt silly cavorting about in pink tights, masquerading as a Danish King."[2] And so, in the early 1940s, Reiner made his way to the Catskills, where he found more suitable employment as a sketch comedian in a Borscht Belt resort. "I fell right into the work," he recalled. "Although I hadn't been able to accept myself—a watchmaker's son from the Bronx—as a King of Denmark, I was perfectly at ease kidding kings and generals."[3] It was a quality that producer Max Liebman would admire when he later cast the young comic to play Sid Caesar's foil on *Your Show of Shows*. Notes Reiner, "He used to call that sort of performance 'stinky acting.' It's good bad acting. You make fun of the character and yourself at the same time."[4]

It was also during that eventful stint in the Catskills that Carl Reiner met the woman with whom he would share his life, a pretty young scenery painter named Estelle Lebost. The pair were brought together by the resort's set designer, who carefully took the young actor aside for a few words of sage advice shortly before the introductions were made. "He told me, 'Be nice to her,'" says Reiner. It was a request with which the actor would have little difficulty complying, as he later recalled. "I took her to dinner. I took her dancing. I took her to the theater. I asked her to marry me."[5]

The couple were finally wed about a year later, in 1943, a few months after Reiner had been recruited for his most important engagement yet— an extended tour with Uncle Sam. Drafted into the armed services shortly after the outbreak of World War II, Reiner found himself stationed at Camp Crowder, near Joplin, Missouri, the real-life military installation that would also serve as the setting for some of Rob Petrie's more memorable exploits some twenty years later. After Reiner was eventually assigned to a base in Hawaii, he continued to hone his comic skills in a series of army revues that were designed to boost the sagging morale of GIs stationed in the South Pacific. It was there, Reiner would later recall, that he first discovered his uncanny knack for comic improvisation. "I created my own theater by standing in front of a microphone in rec halls, telling stories and doing Hitler routines," Reiner

During WWII, Reiner did his bit to boost morale as a performer in the army's special services branch. "I created my own theater by standing in front of a microphone in rec halls,' he recalls, "telling stories and doing Hitler routines."

would write.[6] "When I got out, I discovered that comedians were paid four times as much as actors and worked more often—so I gravitated toward comedy."

After the war, the actor and his bride made their way to New York City, where Reiner—at the ripe old age of twenty-three—landed the lead in the national touring company production of *Call Me Mister*, a role that he would eventually assume in the Broadway production. That prestigious booking led to a steady stream of stage and TV assignments throughout the late forties, including work as a sketch comedian on an early TV variety series called *The Fifty-Fourth Street Revue*, as well as a prominent role in the Broadway musical comedy revue *Alive and Kicking*. It was in that show that Reiner first caught the eye of Max Liebman, the Borscht Belt impresario who would revolutionize television comedy in 1950 when he married Broadway revue and Borscht Belt musical comedy styles in a prime-time variety series called, appropriately enough, *Your Show of Shows*.

Back from the war at the ripe old age of twenty-three, Reiner soon landed his first Broadway lead in the road company of *Call Me Mister*. Pictured with Reiner are costars Peter Turgeon and Alan Dreeben, in the sailor suit.

There's no question that Max Leibman's recruitment of Carl Reiner to join the cast of *Your Show of Shows* in 1950 represented a major turning point in the young actor's career. Almost immediately upon its premiere broadcast, on February 25, 1950, the innovative ninety-minute variety show became an institution on NBC, the network that aired the series live from New York each Saturday night. And though the versatile Sid Caesar and his rubber-faced costar Imogene Coca were the show's undisputed headliners, *Your Show of Shows* also provided Carl Reiner and his fellow second banana Howard Morris with more than ample opportunity to add their own comic contributions to a weekly format that somehow managed to embrace the disparate styles of silent comedy, rollicking musical numbers, and exacting social parody with equal fervor. In fact, the show's brash, rapid-fire, musical comedy approach seemed ideally suited to the talents of Carl Reiner, who would go on to lend Sid Caesar comic support through nine television seasons—five years of *Your Show of Shows* and four additional seasons on a pair of variety shows that came in its wake, *Sid Caesar Invites You* and *Caesar's Hour*—for which Reiner would earn two successive Emmy Awards as a supporting actor, in 1955 and 1956.*

But despite the acclaim that Reiner derived from his work as a performer on *Your Show of Shows*, it wasn't long before he began to grow impatient with his somewhat limited role as a supporting actor on the show. "Even though I acted once a week on Saturday and rehearsed all week," Reiner would later complain, "I didn't feel like an actor."[7] Finally, to break the monotony of his long rehearsals as a performer, Reiner cautiously poked his head into the show's noisy writers' room, where the roster on any given day might include Mel Brooks, Lucille Kallen, Mel Tolkin, Tony Webster, and, on occasion, Neil Simon and his brother Danny. Naturally, with some of the sharpest comic minds in America stuck in a single room for as many as eight or ten hours a day, the actor soon discovered that things were rarely dull in the writers' office, and within a matter of weeks, Rein-

---

*Though *Your Show of Shows* actually broadcast its final episode on June 5, 1954, Carl Reiner would rejoin Caesar the following September on *Caesar's Hour*, an NBC variety series that borrowed heavily from the *Show of Shows* format, though without the support of Imogene Coca, who had by that time gone her separate way. A few months after *Caesar's Hour* completed its three-year run on May 25, 1957, Reiner would be reunited with Sid Caesar in the cast of *Sid Caesar Invites You,* a half-hour version of the star's variety show that ran on ABC for a scant three months in early 1958.

er himself became a fixture at the show's daily writing sessions, where his keen wit and gregarious nature soon earned him the respect of the show's writers. Before long, Carl Reiner found himself functioning as an active participant in the show's writing sessions—though it was clearly understood that his contributions were to be made strictly without attribution.

"I was a writer without portfolio," explains Reiner. "I was in on all the sessions, and I contributed as a writer. But I didn't get my name in the credits, because actors didn't do that in those days. The writers were very solicitous of their credits." And with good reason, as he explains. "I didn't blame them, because as actors, we got all the credit anyway. Everybody thought we made the lines up." And, as Reiner soon discovered, this tendency—coupled with the writers' own naturally aggressive personalities—often made for an intensely competitive environment in the writers' room. "If you got your joke in—fine," says Reiner. "But you knew somebody was always gonna try to improve it."

Reiner recalls a particularly vexing session at which one of the show's writers managed to blurt out no more than the first three words of a comic premise before his idea was seized upon by his colleagues and offered up for extended comic debate. "The guy started out saying, 'So, it's Thursday—'" recalls Reiner. But then, before the hapless scribe could even stammer out the rest of his sentence, one of the show's other writers had already decided that the idea was ripe for improvement. "Somebody else said, 'Not Thursday—make it Friday! Friday's funnier.'" And, of course, the kibitzing didn't stop there. "Then somebody else says, 'Why not make it a Saturday? Isn't Saturday funnier?'" And, as Reiner quickly discovered, as a lowly performer he was at a decided disadvantage during such debates. "When they'd fight you for a joke," he recalls, "some writer would always say, 'What the hell do you know? You're an actor!'"

Though his colleagues' frequent putdowns were invariably offered as good-natured jibes, Reiner finally came to view their barbed accusations of his own lack of writerly credentials as a challenge. And he was determined to meet that challenge head-on. After a time, whenever things got hot in the writers' office, Reiner would simply slip out of the room and retire to a vacant office down the hall—a quiet sanctuary that just happened to come equipped with an old manual typewriter. And it was there, in the relative solitude of this unclaimed office, that the novice scribe began to practice his craft in earnest. "I'd learned to type on a teletype in the army," Reiner explains, "so I used to go to that office, just to see if I could still type. And I found out that I could."

In no time at all, Reiner had graduated from simple typing exercises to composing short humorous pieces for his own amusement. For his ear-

Sid Caesar, Imogene Coca, and Carl Reiner in a publicity still from
Your Show of Shows, the groundbreaking early fifties series that would provide
Reiner with comic fodder for five seasons of *Dick Van Dyke Show* storylines.

liest comic exercises, Reiner would frequently contrive to create the cast, characters, and setting for short comic plays that he had absolutely no intention of ever writing. "I would write a little one-page cast of charac-

ters for a play," he recalls, "that's all. Just the cast of characters— what they do, where the play is set. A lot of them were satires of some play that already existed." Then, having created the characters and setting for an imaginary play of his own design, Reiner would simply move on to the next. "You knew from the description alone that you were going to see a crazy play," he explains. "That was all you needed. I thought they were hilarious. I wrote dozens of them. I think I might still have them someplace."

From those humble beginnings Carl Reiner's literary career began to bloom. As his confidence grew, the writer soon moved from one-page play

Carl Reiner in a publicity pose taken in the late fifties, when the future writer, creator, and producer of *The Dick Van Dyke Show* was still best known to television audiences as Sid Caesar's second banana on *Your Show of Shows*.

descriptions to three-page character studies. "Vignettes, really," as he describes them today. From there, it was just a matter of time before he started composing full-blown short stories. One of the most memorable of them was "Fifteen Arthur Barringtons," a tale that concerned the anxieties of a young actor named Arthur Barrington who finds himself sitting at a casting call with fourteen other young actors of his exact age, weight, and physical type, any one of whom could just as easily be he. Through an odd chain of coincidence, that story finally ended up in the hands of a Simon & Schuster editor named Jack Goodman, who suggested that the fledgling writer develop the piece into a longer and more ambitious work about the struggles that face a young actor in the early years of his career.

But, according to Reiner, the editor's pep talk had not been the only factor that spurred him to develop his latent literary ambitions. Far more compelling was an epiphany that struck him in the late spring of 1957, as he watched his two kids—Robbie, who was then ten, and Annie, who was eight—frolic in the sand outside the family's Fire Island summer home. "The kids were getting older," explains Reiner, "and all of a sudden they were big enough to run around by themselves. So one day I said, 'Gee, I'm thirty-five years old. I'd better do something with my life.'" Though the actor could hardly have been described as lazy—he'd just completed three seasons in the cast of *Caesar's Hour*—Reiner nonetheless felt himself trapped by a vague feeling of creative fatigue, a trap from which he could see only one means of escape. "It took five years of going to Fire Island and doing nothing but sifting sand until I finally wrote a novel."

By the middle of August 1957, Reiner had completed *Enter Laughing*,* his fictional memoir of one David Kokolovitz, a struggling actor trying to break into show business despite his family's insistence that he continue to pursue a trade in the millinery business. Though the book draws liberally from the writer's own early show business experiences, Reiner prefaced the work with a somewhat tongue-in-cheek disclaimer. "David Kokolovitz is a fictitious character," the author writes in the book's introduction. "I strongly believe I am not."[8]

Interestingly, Reiner originally planned *Enter Laughing* as a far more encompassing work. "I intended to record the life of a Bronx-born person like myself," the writer told a reporter in 1964,[9] "from his entry into the theater at the age of 17 to his mature years as an actor and writer and husband and father." But, Reiner notes, once he'd completed 250 type-

---

*In 1963, *Enter Laughing* would be adapted for the Broadway stage by playwright Joseph Stein, who had contributed scripts to *Caesar's Hour*. The Broadway show, which starred Alan Arkin, would eventually inspire a 1967 film of the same title, which featured Reni Santoni in the leading role, and was directed by Carl Reiner from his own screenplay, co-written with Stein.

written pages and discovered that he'd barely covered a single year in his young protagonist's life, he "decided it was time to stop."[10]

Even so, the economical writer had no intention of letting the rest of that vast backlog of personal history go to waste. And so, when he began work on a new autobiographical work the following summer, Reiner instinctively picked up his story almost exactly where he'd left it at the end of

The series may have borne the name of its leading man, but to those in the know, there was little doubt that creator/writer/producer Carl Reiner was *The Dick Van Dyke Show*'s real star. Pictured with the proud producer (seated) on the night they filmed the show's pilot episode are Dick Van Dyke, Mary Tyler Moore, Sheldon Leonard, Rose Marie, Morey Amsterdam, and associate producer Ron Jacobs.

Enter Laughing. For the television scripts that would eventually be filmed as *The Dick Van Dyke Show*, the writer chose to draw inspiration from his more recent real-life experiences, as he had earlier expressed it, "as an actor and a writer and a husband and a father." Naturally, for this new and far more encompassing work, Reiner would need an all-new protagonist. And so it was, in the summer of 1958, that Carl Reiner bid a fond farewell to David Kokolovitz and welcomed the arrival of the character who would serve as the writer's fictional alter ego for the next eight years.

That character's name was Robert Petrie.

CHAPTER 2

Sifting Through Sand

WHEN SID CAESAR'S THIRD VARIETY SERIES OF THE 1950s was canceled in May of 1958, Carl Reiner suddenly found himself out of work for the first time in nine years. And yet, despite the fact that he was facing his first major bout of unemployment since the end of World War II, Carl Reiner seemed to be taking it exceedingly well. And why shouldn't he? After all, with his first novel due to hit the bookstores later that year, the optimistic performer figured he could always devote his energies to writing. Indeed, if nothing better came along, Carl Reiner was fully prepared to spend his summer on Fire Island writing a follow-up novel to *Enter Laughing*. And had it not been for the timely intervention of his agent from the William Morris office, that's probably exactly what Carl Reiner would have done.

But Harry Kalcheim had other ideas.

Writing books might make a wonderful summer pastime, the agent insisted, but it would never put food on the table the way performing did. No, Kalcheim explained, writing books was not the answer. Instead, the agent had consulted his crystal ball, and what he saw suggested only one possible direction for Carl Reiner in 1958. And that was to star in a situation comedy.

Carl Reiner immediately recognized that Kalcheim had a point. "Variety shows were almost extinct," says Reiner today, "so I knew I had to find something else." Of course, the former Broadway star might have considered returning to the stage. And, in fact, it was around this time that the actor's old friend Neil Simon offered Reiner a leading role in the comedy that was set to be the playwright's first Broadway show, *Come Blow Your Horn*. But despite Carl Reiner's abiding respect for his old crony from *Your Show of Shows*, he had little interest in making a return

Sid Caesar and second banana Carl Reiner in *Your Show of Shows*.

trip to the Great White Way. "I'd been on Broadway," says Reiner, "and I didn't want to go back. Once you're in television, there's an everyday excitement to the work that's not there on Broadway, where you have to do the same thing three hundred and sixty-five days a year."

Of course, the greatest advantage to acting in a situation comedy, as Harry Kalcheim was only too pleased to point out, was that it was a field in which a seasoned performer like Carl Reiner stood to make a killing. To prove his point, the agent had only to point to the careers of Jackie Gleason, Lucille Ball, and Danny Thomas, three situation-comedy head-liners who, like Reiner, had each been long-established variety perform-ers before they made the switch to situation comedy, and all of whom ended up getting very, very rich in the process. There was certainly no reason why, at the age of thirty-six, Carl Reiner couldn't make an equal-ly successful transition to the half-hour form. All Reiner had to do, sug-gested Kalcheim, was find a situation comedy vehicle that seemed reasonably well suited to his particular talents. "Is that all?" Reiner remarked. "Well, how hard could that be?"

The answer to that query would become painfully obvious almost as soon as Reiner opened the first in the small pile of proposed situation-comedy scripts his agent sent around for his approval. To the actor's dis-may, what he read in that first script gave him pause. "It really wasn't very good," recalls Reiner. Nor did he find much to hold his interest in any of the subsequent half-dozen scripts that his agent submitted to him over the course of the next few days. "None of them were any good," he says. "Or, if they were good, they weren't for me." Finally, just as the actor had begun to wonder if he'd ever find an appropriate vehicle to propel him to the next stage of his career, the answer came to him from a wholly unex-pected source—his wife.

After a few days of listening to her husband's not-so-hushed complaints about the quality of material he'd been reading, Estelle Reiner finally picked up one of the scripts and began reading it herself. A few minutes later, she set it down, satisfied that her husband's appraisals had not been far off the mark. "You're right, these aren't very good," she volunteered, adding, quite matter-of-factly, "I'll bet *you* could write a better script than any one of those yourself."

It was intended as a casual observation, a statement so obvious that it hardly needed to be voiced at all. And yet, after more than thirty-five years, Carl Reiner is still struck by the lasting impact of that single utter-ance. "My wife, in her infinite wisdom, said I could write better than that," Reiner has observed. "Of course, I'd never written a sitcom. But when your wife thinks you can—you can."[11]

And so, with no greater preparation than his wife's encouragement, Carl Reiner resolved to spend the summer of 1958 on Fire Island, where he would take a few weeks off to create his very own situation comedy. If he was the least bit daunted by the challenge of the undertaking, he doesn't reveal it in his recollection of those heady days. "I'd written *Enter Laughing* the summer before," Reiner says, displaying a characteristic modesty, "so at least I knew I could type fairly well."

Once he'd made up his mind to create a situation comedy for himself, Reiner's first order of business was to decide exactly what it was that he wanted to write about. And, as he recalls it, the writer's search for a comic premise didn't take him very far from home. "You always have to write about what you know," he suggests. "So I just asked myself the question, On what piece of ground do I stand that no one else occupies?" Curiously, the answer to Reiner's self-imposed query finally came to him a few days later as he was driving into Manhattan one morning from his home in suburban New Rochelle.

"I can tell you exactly where I was the moment it came to me," Reiner boasts. "I was on the East Side Highway, driving downtown, near Ninety-sixth Street." It was there, as he maneuvered his car into the city through rush hour traffic, that it suddenly struck Carl Reiner that his own life, with only minimal embellishment, would provide the ideal fodder for a compelling weekly comedy. It was an idea whose brilliance lay in its simplicity—what could be easier for a New York comedy writer from New Rochelle to write than a series about a New York comedy writer from New Rochelle? "I knew that scene," recalls Reiner, "living in New Rochelle, coming home at seven o'clock, talking about what happened at the office. And then going back to the office the next day and talking about what happened at home. That's what I knew about, so that's what I wrote about."

Once he put his mind to it, Reiner had little trouble populating his proposed series with a colorful cast of characters drawn largely from people in his own life. The show would revolve around Robert Petrie, a TV writer who lives in New Rochelle with his wife, Laura, and their six-year-old son, Ritchie, much as Reiner had lived in that Westchester County suburb during his years as a writer and performer on *Your Show of Shows*, with his own wife and real-life son, who—like Reiner's firstborn TV creation—was also named Robert. In the original script for his proposed series, Reiner's alter ego works for a self-centered variety show star named Alan Sturdy, a character that many of the writer's friends recognized as a comic exaggeration of Reiner's own longtime TV boss, Sid Caesar. Robert Petrie's co-writers, Buddy Sorrell and Sally Rogers, also had real-life coun-

Carl Reiner improvises a 2000-Year-Old-Man routine in an early sixties television appearance with Mel Brooks, the comic wunderkind who provided the real-life inspiration for the Van Dyke show's Buddy Sorrell.

terparts. "Sally was a combination of Lucille Kallen and Selma Diamond," Carl Reiner has said, "and Buddy was Mel Brooks."[12]

Although Carl Reiner hewed pretty close to reality in his fictionalized recreation of the writers' room on *Your Show of Shows*, it's interesting to note that he chose to depart from the actuality of his own experience in one small, if telling, detail. While Reiner himself had been no more than an uncredited "writer without portfolio" on *Your Show of Shows*, the writer's fictionalized alter ego would suffer no such indignity. And so, from Reiner's very first sample script, Robert Petrie would enjoy the lofty status of head writer on his show's writing staff. Reiner's elevation of his fictional character's status represented an understandable bit of wish fulfillment on his part. If nothing else, Robert Petrie would never be shut out of a comic debate with the dismissive challenge, "What do you know? You're only an actor!"

With his cast of characters firmly in place, Reiner sat down at the typewriter, where he found that he had little difficulty filtering his own real-life experience through the comic prism of situation comedy. "I was with the family on Fire Island," Reiner remembers, "and the first script flies out of me in three or four days!" Then, buoyed on the wings of his agreeable muse, Reiner sat right back down at the typewriter and started work on a second script. And, after polishing off that one within a week, he set to work on a third. And then a fourth. And, in a remarkable burst of creative energy, Carl Reiner didn't stop writing until he'd completed a full thirteen episodes of *Head of the Family*, as he'd decided to call his new series.

The idea that a relatively inexperienced writer like Reiner would actually sit down to write a baker's dozen half-hour comedy scripts in as many weeks struck many of the more established television writers in Reiner's circle as little short of astonishing. But at the time, Carl Reiner had little notion of the magnitude of his achievement; in his mind, he merely attributed his prodigious productivity to an extremely disciplined work routine that rarely varied throughout the summer of 1958.

Each morning, Reiner would rise, shower, shave, and have breakfast with his family. Then, by nine o'clock, he'd be seated at his typewriter in the den of his family's beachfront house, typing. Reiner's approach to his actual writing chores was no less straightforward: he'd begin his labors each day by simply typing the first words that happened to pop into his head. "I'd sit down without a thought," he recalls, "and I'd write a first line. It didn't matter what the line was. Then I would build from that."

Because most of his storylines were drawn from the rich fabric of his own life, the writer reasoned that he was immune to the problem of writer's block. Whenever he felt his creativity beginning to falter, Reiner had only to glance up from his desk for inspiration. The writer's decidedly personal connection to his material probably goes a long way toward explaining some of the more off-kilter premises that eventually found their way into the scripts for what would become *The Dick Van Dyke Show*, including one show that Reiner says, only half-joking, he wrote to appease the family dog.

"One morning," he elaborates, "it's like the third or fourth show. And I had nothing." Suddenly, Reiner looked up and noticed the family pet sitting in a corner of the room, staring at him. "I had a big German shepherd, Rinny, who just sat there looking at me. So I said, 'Okay, Rinny, I'll write you a show.' Then I wrote the show where Rob brings Buddy's dog home." Three years later, that very script would be filmed—with minor revisions—as *The Dick Van Dyke Show*'s seventh episode, "The Unwelcome Houseguest."

By two each afternoon, his day's work finished, Reiner would stack his fresh pages into a neat pile and quit for the day. Then he would make a dash for the beach, where he would try to spend at least a few of the remaining daylight hours playing with his two kids. Considering the enormous bulk of material that he would finally create over the course of that summer on Fire Island, the writer's daily routine was actually quite relaxed. But, explains Reiner, it's surprising what a writer can accomplish in little more than a half-day at the typewriter, so long as he remains focused. "And," he adds , "I'd never been that concentrated in my life."

Of course, Reiner's sudden dedication to the lonely life of the writer represented a marked departure for someone who had until then been viewed by most of his friends as a gregarious performer. And Reiner admits that his transition from prime-time clown to man of letters was greeted with particularly keen skepticism by acquaintances who'd known him only as a second banana on Sid Caesar's shows.

This was especially true of Reiner's neighbors from Fire Island's literary community, many of whom viewed the comedian's arrival into their ranks with a bemused resistance that bordered on disbelief. In fact, Reiner recalls that at least one of his Fire Island neighbors—the noted screen and television writer Reginald Rose—took an uncommon delight in teasing the novice writer's literary intentions by trying to distract Reiner from his work at every possible opportunity. "Reggie Rose used to throw pebbles up at my window!" says Reiner, who recalls that his neighbor's playful efforts to keep him from his labors were rarely successful. Whenever Reiner heard the distinctive clicking of tiny rocks skipping off his window, he'd stop typing only long enough to part the curtains and wave his would-be tormentor on his way, at which point Rose—the eminent author of *Twelve Angry Men* and a few dozen of the most distinguished teleplays of TV's Golden Age—would drop his handful of pebbles and walk on down the beach, grinning broadly at his mischief.

Comedy writer Frank Tarloff is another old friend of Reiner's who confesses that he was openly skeptical when he first discovered the fledgling writer's plan to finish off a half-season's worth of scripts over the course of a single summer. "I thought he was nuts!" says Tarloff, who ran into Reiner during a visit to Fire Island that summer. "I said, 'Carl, nobody ever starts out with thirteen finished episodes! It just doesn't work that way.'"

But despite the doubts of his more seasoned colleagues, Reiner's rationale for creating a thirteen-episode backlog for his new series was actually quite sound. "I knew I didn't want to do a show unless I could act in it," he explains. And, since Reiner anticipated that his chores as the show's star would keep him quite busy in front of the cameras, he thought it made sense to have at least a half season's scripts ready in advance, if only to make life easier on the show's eventual scriptwriters, who would then have thirteen rock-solid examples of the show's style, rhythms, and character to serve as a guide. "I knew that if I wrote thirteen up front," says Reiner, "the writers would have a pretty good idea of how to take it from there. That was the idea."

Reiner maintained his remarkable pace throughout the summer, completing a new script, he says, "every three or four days," until, he recalls, "in six or seven weeks, I had thirteen shows all written." Finally, late in the summer of 1958, the writer bundled his package of scripts together and dropped them off with Harry Kalcheim, whose task it would be to find a backer willing to turn them into a full-fledged television series.

While Carl Reiner waited for his agent to work his magic with *Head of the Family*, he came to the sobering realization that he still had a wife, two kids, and a German shepherd to feed. And so, in September of 1958, Reiner signed on as the host of *Keep Talking*, a lively game show that spotlighted talkative celebrity panelists expounding at length on various humorous topics. Among the frequent panelists on the weekly show were Peggy Cass, Joey Bishop, Pat Carroll, and a popular New York nightclub comic and TV personality named Morey Amsterdam.

Although Reiner seemed perfectly happy with the light duties demanded of him as a game show host, he maintained few illusions about the job. "It was an easy way to make a good living," he later explained. "I wasn't really working at anything, creating anything. I just grabbed the money and ran."[13] For Reiner, *Keep Talking* represented little more than a temporary stopgap, something to tide him over while he waited for that lucky day when Harry Kalcheim would call to report that the writer's ship had finally come in.

CHAPTER 3

Head of the Family

CARL REINER'S LUCKY DAY ARRIVED SOONER THAN HE expected. In its September 20, 1958, issue, *TV Guide* carried the first public announcement of the series that would eventually evolve into *The Dick Van Dyke Show*. "Carl Reiner has written eight of the first thirteen chapters in a new series,"[14] read the short newsbrief, "tentatively titled *Head of the Family*, in which he will star. Peter Lawford put up the money for the test film, which will be shot in October in New York."*

Although the news blurb turned out to be somewhat optimistic in its projection that the pilot was set to roll in October—*Head of the Family* would not actually be filmed until two months later, in December of

---

*It's interesting to note that *TV Guide* attributes the writer with having completed only eight scripts prior to the start of production on *Head of the Family*, while Reiner staunchly maintains that he'd finished thirteen complete scripts during his summer on Fire Island. "I know it was definitely thirteen," he says today. "That's what I had!" To add to the confusion, in the May 14, 1960, issue of *TV Guide* —which appeared a full year and a half after the magazine's initial blurb— Reiner told writer Dan Jenkins that he'd "knocked out 14 scripts" for *Head of the Family* before it ever went into production. Fourteen is also the number recently cited by Reiner's friend and longtime manager, George Shapiro, who also happens to be Estelle Reiner's nephew, and was thus a frequent visitor to the Reiners' Fire Island home when the scripts in question were first composed. Of course, whatever the exact number of scripts—whether eight, a dozen, thirteen, or fourteen scripts—no one disputes the essential fact that the enthusiastic writer generated far more material in preparation for his proposed TV series than was dictated by accepted industry practice.

1958—the release correctly identifies film star Peter Lawford as the primary benefactor of Carl Reiner's pilot.

Peter Lawford's involvement came about after Harry Kalcheim discovered that the former matinee idol—who himself had recently signed to star in NBC's *Thin Man* series—was actively looking to get a toehold in the extremely lucrative production end of the business. Since Kalcheim was well aware of Lawford's strong ties to the Kennedy family—the movie star was at that time married to Patricia Kennedy, a scion of the powerful Boston political clan—the agent had good reason to believe that Lawford could, in fact, put his hands on sufficient capital to make a pilot film of Reiner's series. And so Kalcheim submitted the first of Reiner's thirteen scripts to Lawford, who liked what he saw well enough to request a meeting with the gifted actor/writer.

Carl Reiner's first and only meeting with Peter Lawford took place one morning in early September 1958, in Lawford's suite in New York's swank Pierre Hotel. "It was the kind of meeting you have with a producer who's not going to do much except put up the money," Reiner says. "But I'll never forget it." As Reiner recalls, it was already past 11:00 A.M. when he and his agent arrived at Lawford's suite; even so, the suave actor answered the door dressed in nothing but a thick, plush bathrobe and a pair of matching velvet slippers. In his palm, Lawford cradled an oversized snifter of what Reiner describes as "one of those giant red drinks—something and grenadine on the rocks. At eleven in the morning!" As it turned out, the meeting didn't last long. "Lawford agreed to put up the money to do the original pilot," recalls Reiner. There was, however, one slight condition. "They said I had to send a script down to Joseph P. Kennedy in Florida!"

Although Harry Kalcheim had correctly surmised that Lawford's financial backing would come from the Kennedy family coffers, the agent never dreamed that Lawford's financial arrangement would be dependent on script approval from the Kennedy family patriarch himself. But, apparently, that was the case. "Joe Kennedy had to read it," explains Reiner, "before any of his family's money went into the product." And so, a few days later, the script was dutifully submitted to Joseph P. Kennedy in Palm Beach, Florida. The elder Kennedy was apparently impressed—or so Reiner has always assumed, since he got the official go-ahead to start casting his pilot within a few days of the Florida submission.

Assembling a cast for *Head of the Family* posed little challenge for Carl Reiner, who already carried an indelible image of each of the show's characters in his head. As planned, the writer cast himself as Robert Petrie, and child actor Gary Morgan was signed to play young Ritchie. For his man-hungry woman writer, Reiner tagged future Oscar nominee Sylvia

Miles, who was then best known for her work as a comic sketch performer on *The Steve Allen Show*. The part of comedy writer Buddy Sorrell—described in Reiner's original script as a twenty-three-year-old hypochondriac—went to New York comic Morty Gunty. And, with the addition of Milt Kamen—a character actor who had worked with Reiner on *Sid Caesar Invites You*—in the role of the Snappy Service deli man, Reiner had every part on the show cast. Except one. He still hadn't found his Laura.

And casting the all-important role of Mrs. Petrie was proving a far more difficult task than Carl Reiner had anticipated. "I looked at about twenty girls," says Reiner, who was convinced he'd finally struck gold after he met Joanna Moore, an attractive blonde who possessed the exact combination of sexiness and maternal charm that Reiner had envisioned when he wrote the part. "She was the one that I really wanted," he recalls. But,

Barbara Britton, Gary Morgan, and Carl Reiner were the original Laura, Ritchie, and Robert Petrie in Reiner's 1958 *Dick Van Dyke Show* prototype, *Head of the Family*.

unfortunately, Moore was unavailable during the time *Head of the Family* was scheduled to shoot in New York, having already committed to star in an episode of *Alfred Hitchcock Presents* that was to be filmed in California that same week.

Jenifer Lea was another actress who came close to nabbing the part of Laura Petrie—so close, in fact, that a news blurb in the November 22, 1958, issue of *TV Guide* claimed that the actress had already been signed to play the role. It was an announcement that would prove somewhat premature. When the pilot for *Head of the Family* was shot a few weeks later, the role of Laura Petrie was played by Barbara Britton, an attractive blond actress whose previous TV credits included numerous dramatic and light comic roles on *Robert Montgomery Presents* and a number of other anthology shows of the fifties. A few years earlier, the actress had also starred as Pamela North on *Mr. and Mrs. North*, a lighthearted mystery series that had brief runs on both CBS and NBC in the early fifties.

Carl Reiner's pilot for *Head of the Family* finally went before the cameras at New York's Gold Medal Studios a few weeks before Christmas 1958. Produced by Stuart Rosenberg and Martin Poll, the half-hour telefilm was directed by Don Weis, a veteran feature director whose credits included the Debbie Reynolds musical *I Love Melvin*, as well as the original feature version of Max Schulman's *The Affairs of Dobie Gillis*.

Watched out of context, Reiner's original *Head of the Family* pilot film—a copy of which today holds a place of honor in the permanent collection of New York's Museum of Television and Radio—appears to be little more than a mildly engaging example of the kind of family-oriented situation comedies that were popular in the late fifties. And, as such, the show is certainly not without its charms. However, when viewed as a dry run for the series that would be reborn as *The Dick Van Dyke Show* just over two years later, the pilot affords a fascinating documentary glimpse of the first faltering steps of a genuine TV classic.

The show opens, as would so many later episodes of *The Dick Van Dyke Show*, in the kitchen of Robert and Laura Petrie—here pronounced PEE-tree—where Laura is busy preparing a meat loaf for the family dinner. Before long, she's interrupted by Mrs. Harley, a neighbor who arrives hoping to retrieve a school bulletin that Laura's husband—big-time TV writer Robert Petrie—has promised to compose as a favor to the promoters of the local PTA bazaar. When it becomes apparent that her husband has failed to make good on his commitment, Laura stammers out a halting apology, which causes her guest to turn toward the door in a huff. "It'll be in the mail!" Laura calls after her. "We'll see!" snaps the skeptical neighbor.

Returning to her domestic duties, Laura is surprised to discover that her six-year-old son, Ritchie, has sequestered himself in a kitchen cabinet. "How long are you going to stay in there?" she asks. "'Til I'm older than Roy and Freddy," he vows. Apparently, the boy is upset because a few of his school chums have been teasing him about his dad's unorthodox occupation as a TV writer. "Why can't daddy get a real job?" the boy demands, mortified that his father would waste his time typing all day, while all the other fathers in his neighborhood manage to find time to accompany their sons to little league games. Laura does her best to placate the distraught lad, with little success. With his frustration mounting, Ritchie is finally moved to declare, "I don't like my Daddy!"

When Robert Petrie arrives home from a hard day at the office a few minutes later, he's naturally dismayed to discover that his son has suddenly turned against him. "I'm universally well liked," Petrie protests. "Everybody likes me! You like me, don't you?" he inquires of Laura. "See!" he declares as she signals assent. "And you got great taste." Laura finally suggests that her husband might be able to restore some measure of the boy's lapsed faith by taking Ritchie down to the office, where the lad will at least have the opportunity to see his dad in action. Though skeptical, Robert reluctantly agrees to give Laura's plan a shot—if only to prove her wrong. "Ninety-five percent of the time you're right," he coos. "Love to lower your average just a little."

The next morning, with Ritchie in tow, Robert arrives at the Manhattan town house office where TV's *Alan Sturdy Show* is written and produced. In the moments before their arrival, we watch the show's gal writer, Sally Rogers, water her pet philodendron and exchange barbs with fellow writer Buddy Sorrell, a fastidious hypochondriac who insists on gulping five sugars in his morning coffee. "I need a lot of sugar," he whines. "I have a fluctuating metabolism and a hyperactive thyroid!" "How did you manage to get so unhealthy in twenty-three years?" Sally wonders aloud. "I go to nightclubs," is Buddy's grumbled response.

A moment later, Robert Petrie enters and introduces Ritchie, explaining that he has brought his son to work because the boy "has no idea how his father earns a living." "And you want him to find out?" quips Sally. Naturally, the child is singularly unimpressed by his father's job. "Do you need *them* to help you, Daddy?" Ritchie asks, eyeing his father's two writing partners with suspicion. "Well," Petrie stammers, withering under his co-workers' steely gaze, "Yes. I need them. But," he volunteers, in a futile attempt to recover lost ground, "I'm the main one—*I'm* in charge. I'm like Casey Stengel!"

Ritchie is unconvinced. And the boy's flagging enthusiasm droops even lower when the Snappy Service office coffee man arrives and launches a particularly scathing critique of the previous week's *Alan Sturdy Show*. Finally, just when it appears that Ritchie's opinion of his father's worth could sink no further, Dad is summoned to Alan Sturdy's office. There the boy is forced to watch as his father kowtows to the boorish employer, a pitiless egomaniac who appears to take pleasure in browbeating his helpless head writer without mercy. After witnessing a few minutes of this demoralizing spectacle, Ritchie is finally reduced to tears, prompting his father to groan, "I wonder if I'm too old to start dental school?"

At breakfast the next morning, Ritchie offers a cold shoulder to his father's affections, refusing to muster even a simple goodbye kiss for the old man before he heads off to school. But just when it looks as though Dad might never regain his stature in the young boy's eyes, things take an unexpected turn. When Ritchie arrives at school, he notices a throng of his classmates chuckling appreciatively at a clever PTA announcement that's been posted on the school bulletin board. As it turns out, the announcement, which has been composed in the form of a funny little poem, is the handiwork of one Robert Petrie, a fact that inspires admiration among Ritchie's envious classmates. "Your father's a pretty good poem writer!" one of the kids declares, as Ritchie beams with pride.

It's a far different boy that greets Robert Petrie when he returns home from work that evening. Grinning like the Cheshire cat from atop the hat shelf in the family closet, the boy exclaims, "I like my daddy!" to his father's obvious delight. In the show's closing moments, Ritchie challenges his dad to compose a funny poem on the spot—a request to which the happy father cheerfully complies as the episode fades out.

While the tryout film for *Head of the Family* naturally suffers in comparison to the fine-tooled brilliance that the same basic material would yield in its later incarnation as *The Dick Van Dyke Show*, what's surprising is just how many of the elements that would make Reiner's later show such a groundbreaker were already in place in this first, embryonic draft.

Chief among those breakthroughs is the show's realistic depiction of Robert Petrie's workplace. Carl Reiner wasn't the first TV creator to show his leading character at work—audiences had previously seen Ralph Kramden in the Brooklyn bus depot where he labored on *The Honeymooners*; and from time to time viewers had caught glimpses of Ricky Ricardo leading the orchestra that provided *I Love Lucy*'s Cuban bandleader with the income to finance his wife's madcap schemes. But as stylized as they were, even those depictions of the workplace were exceptions to the norm for domestic situation comedies of the 1950s, where the breadwinner almost invariably disappeared each morning at nine, only to return eight hours later to issue the mating cry that has become one of television's most enduring clichés: "Honey, I'm home!"

Not so on *Head of the Family*—and, of course, the later Van Dyke show—where you not only knew exactly how Rob Petrie earned a living, you actually watched him doing it. A stickler for realism from the very start, Carl Reiner was not content to shy away from all the routine details of his leading man's everyday life—and so he made them a virtue. In the world that Reiner created for Rob Petrie, the details that were all but ignored on most TV shows provided the writer with the very fabric of his show's rich comic tapestry. By choosing to explore this previously untapped vein of comedy, Reiner was able to invest his series with a dimension that TV audiences hadn't seen before. As the writer himself would later observe, "This was the first situation comedy where, when the guy came home and said, 'Honey, I'm home,' you knew where he'd come home from."[15] *The Dick Van Dyke Show*'s twin emphasis on its leading character's home and work environments would prove to be one of the show's most potent legacies, providing a durable format that would inspire dozens of subsequent half-hour comedies, including *The Mary Tyler Moore Show* and *The Bob Newhart Show*, to name two of the more outstanding examples.

Judging by the evidence on screen in *Head of the Family,* Carl Reiner's penchant for mining rich comic atmosphere from the finely observed details of ordinary life was already in full flower when he shot the historic pilot film. In one early scene, the otherwise routine staging of a husband-and-wife discussion is suddenly enlivened when Robert grabs a bunch of celery and begins stripping the stalks into the kitchen sink. It's a small detail—and yet, Robert Petrie's unbidden effort to pitch in and help out with the domestic chores provides a fascinating and highly economical subtext to the marital conversation, even as it serves to ground the scene in a believable and very specific reality.

One area where Reiner's pilot differs markedly from the later *Dick Van Dyke Show* is in the technique used to film it. While *The Dick Van Dyke Show* was filmed before a live audience, using the so-called three-camera method first popularized by *I Love Lucy* in the early fifties, *Head of the Family* was shot "one-camera," with a single camera recording the action in separate scenes filmed piecemeal over the course of a few days, much as a feature film is made.* Unlike the stagebound three-camera system, the

---

*Although *Head of the Family* was filmed without a studio audience in attendance, the laughter heard on the show's soundtrack was recorded live at a special

one-camera method was particularly well suited for outdoor and location shooting, which made it the system of choice for the producers of the more naturalistic-looking domestic comedies of the era, shows like *Father Knows Best* and *Leave It to Beaver*. It was a consideration that was not lost on Carl Reiner, who freely admits his debt to *Father Knows Best* and the other one-camera family comedies that were popular in the late fifties.

"I was influenced by the flavor of *Father Knows Best*," explains Reiner, "and by the fact that I could comfortably watch it." But, says Reiner, the show that probably provided the greatest influence on the series that would become known as *The Dick Van Dyke Show* was *Leave It to Beaver*, the classic late-fifties comedy that depicted small-town life through the eyes of eight-year-old Theodore "Beaver" Cleaver and his brother Wally. That series, which debuted on CBS in October of 1957, was the brainchild of Joe Connelly and Bob Mosher, two unsung masters of the situation comedy form who, like Carl Reiner, divined their greatest comic moments from simple observations of the world around them. "I remember laughing," says Reiner, recalling an exemplary *Leave It to Beaver* moment, "when two kids were arguing and one of them said, 'Aw, your sister drinks gutter water!' I said, 'That's so sweet! Your sister drinks gutter water!' That show had a sweetness to it, and a reality that I liked."

There was no question that Harry Kalcheim loved Carl Reiner's pilot. The agent laughed out loud when he first screened a copy of the finished work print in early 1959. In fact, the film had barely ended before Kalcheim made the optimistic prediction that he would have no trouble at all convincing any one of a dozen sponsors to back the pilot as a new series for the fall 1959 season.

Unfortunately, he was wrong.

During the first few months of the new year, Kalcheim and his colleagues in the TV department of the William Morris agency showed Reiner's *Head of the Family* pilot to the top media buyers at some of the biggest ad agencies in New York, as well as to the high-ranking program executives at all three networks. But, despite the best efforts of Harry Kalcheim and his colleagues, *Head of the Family* earned little more than a few curious nibbles, and in the end the show was not picked up for the 1959 television season.

"We got very nice mentions," insists Carl Reiner, who has long main-

---

screening of the pilot that Reiner arranged for the express purpose of capturing an authentic response for the show's laughtrack.

tained that his first pilot failed chiefly because the networks simply weren't looking to buy situation comedies in 1959, a year when westerns and detective shows were all the rage in prime time. "They were looking for elaborate adventure series," says Reiner, "and horses and guns." But, while the fall 1959 prime-time schedule did contain an inordinately high percentage of horse operas and shoot-'em-up series, situation comedies had by no means become extinct. In fact, that season saw the debut of more than a half dozen new half-hour comedies, including a pair of hardy perennials in *Dennis the Menace* and *The Many Loves of Dobie Gillis*. And, although it's certainly possible, as Reiner maintains, that *Head of the Family* got lost in the shuffle of an extremely tight market, it's equally likely that Carl Reiner's pilot film was overlooked because it simply left the sponsors, programmers, and network executives cold.

One theory that's been bandied about in recent years is that advertisers and network executives of the era may have been concerned that *Head of the Family*'s leading man, as portrayed by Carl Reiner, might have seemed a little too Jewish for mainstream tastes of the late fifties. It's an intriguing notion—but completely unfounded, according to Carl Reiner, who dismisses outright any charges that anti-Semitism played a significant role in the demise of his first pilot. "I never had Jewish rhythms in these shows," he insists. "I mean, even in the very first pilot I did with Barbara Britton, it was a very gentile show. I would never *not* admit that I was a Jew—but I wasn't going to do a show about Jewishness. I knew that the country was not looking for a Jewish ethnic show. Not yet."

Longtime William Morris agent Sol Leon offers the following firsthand anecdote, which seems to shed some light on the resistance that he and his colleagues faced when they pitched Reiner's pilot to potential buyers in the winter of 1959. "I almost had it sold to CBS," recalls the agent, who remembers screening the film for a high-ranking CBS program executive named Harry Ommerle in early 1959. According to Leon, Ommerle watched the pilot with a reasonably keen interest. But when the film ended, he scratched his ear and remained silent for a very long moment before he eventually spoke up. "It's good," the network honcho finally volunteered. "But," he continued, searching for the right words to express his vague sense of dissatisfaction. "It's just...lacking something."

And, of course, he was right. Something *was* lacking in the series that was then known as *Head of the Family*. But, in the early days of 1959, it would still be more than a full year before someone would finally identify that the element lacking in the pilot for the series that would eventually become *The Dick Van Dyke Show* was, in fact...Dick Van Dyke.

CHAPTER 4

A Basket Full of Scripts

BY SEPTEMBER OF 1959, CARL REINER FIGURED IT WAS ALL over. Robert Petrie was dead. Gone. In less than a year, the pilot that he'd poured his entire life into—quite literally, as it turned out—was now just another unsold reel of film gathering dust on a shelf at the William Morris office. "It was inventory," says Sol Leon. For his part, Carl Reiner maintains an even more jaundiced view of those dark days in the protracted gestation of what would finally become *The Dick Van Dyke Show*. "After *Head of the Family* failed to sell," sighs Reiner, "it laid foul."

Even so, Carl Reiner wasn't about to let one minor setback impede the trajectory of a career that was in all other areas very much on the rise. In the wake of his pilot's untimely failure, the writer wasted little time relocating to California, where he'd managed to secure steady employment as a staff writer and sometime performer on *The Dinah Shore Show,* beginning in fall of 1959. In the two productive years that fell between *Head of the Family*'s demise and the Van Dyke show's startup in 1961, the ambitious writer/performer also found time to act in three feature films—*Happy Anniversary, The Gazebo,* and *Gidget Goes Hawaiian*—and to write the script for a fourth, *The Thrill of It All.* During that period, Reiner also contributed sketches and specialty material for a 1960 Debbie Reynolds TV spectacular, and managed to record the first of four *2000 Year Old Man* comedy albums with Mel Brooks. And, on top of his many professional obligations, in August of 1960, Carl Reiner became a father for the third time when his wife Estelle gave birth to Lucas Reiner, who would eventually grow up to follow his father and elder brother into a career as a film director.

Carl Reiner and Dinah Shore. In the months following *Head of the Family*'s untimely demise, Reiner found steady employment as an actor and writer on the singer's late fifties variety hour, *The Dinah Shore Show*.

But despite the impressive list of creative triumphs that Carl Reiner chalked up in the months immediately following the dispiriting failure of his first pilot, Harry Kalcheim refused to abandon hope that his client might yet be able to retool and revamp *Head of the Family* into a viable series— and, to hear Reiner tell it, the agent spent the better part of 1959 and 1960 trying to persuade his client to do just that. "Harry Kalcheim bugged me for a year," muses Reiner, who recalls that the agent practically begged him to sit down and start work on a new, revised pilot script, despite the writer's understandable reluctance to climb back on the horse that had so decisively thrown him just a season before. "I told him, 'Screw 'em!'" says Reiner. "'That was my best shot. I'm never gonna write a better show than that. If they don't want it, that's fine. I'm happy not to do a TV show. I'll write movies.'"

But Harry Kalcheim would hear none of that. Having been with the William Morris Agency's TV department since its inception in the late forties, the agent knew as well as anyone the nearly stratospheric rewards that Carl Reiner stood to reap as the creator/writer of a successful situation comedy—profits that would almost certainly dwarf anything that Reiner could hope to earn in an entire career as a performer and writer for hire. But even after listening to his agent's most impassioned arguments, Carl Reiner remained squarely on the fence on the matter of whether to revive his series or not. And there he may very well have stayed had Harry Kalcheim not decided to call on one of his other clients to give the writer a gentle nudge in the right direction. As fate would have it, the nudger that Harry Kalcheim recruited for the task turned out to be Sheldon Leonard, the talented actor/writer/ producer and Hollywood legend who would eventually prove to be one of the most crucial players in *The Dick Van Dyke Show* saga.

Born in New York City on February 22, 1907, the former Sheldon Leonard Bershad grew up on the mean streets of the east Bronx, where he naturally came by the scrappy demeanor and thick Bronx accent that would become his Hollywood trademark throughout the 1930s. Though the incongruously erudite performer had earned an honors degree in sociology from Syracuse University in 1929, Leonard's pugnacious profile and imposing physical stature—combined with the unforgettable lilt of his Damon Runyonesque vocal inflections—soon won the handsome character actor steady work as one of the preeminent tough guys of the Hollywood studio era. Leonard would polish the role of the smooth-talking,

The Dick Van Dyke Show's founding fathers, Sheldon Leonard and Carl Reiner, pictured with William Morris agent Harry Kalcheim, the matchmaker who first brought them together.

multisyllabic gangster to perfection in a seemingly endless succession of strong-arm parts in stage shows, radio plays, and feature films of the thirties, forties, and fifties, including *Another Thin Man, To Have and Have Not,* and both the stage and film versions of *Guys and Dolls*, to name only a few. But though Leonard would also play a handful of leading roles in a few long-forgotten programmers of the forties, the actor will probably be best remembered by future generations for his relatively small supporting role as Nick, the cold-hearted bartender who turns Jimmy Stewart's George Bailey and his guardian angel out into the snow in Frank Capra's 1946 film *It's a Wonderful Life.*

Although Leonard would continue to accept the occasional acting assignment until well into his retirement years, he had already begun to focus his creative energies behind the scenes by the early fifties, when he signed on as house director—and, later, producer—of the long-running *Danny Thomas Show,* one of the first situation comedies to be filmed on Hollywood's Desilu Cahuenga lot. Leonard soon proved himself as adept behind the cameras as he'd been in front of them, and in no time at all he had parlayed his success on the Thomas show into a burgeoning career as one of the most prolific TV directors of the 1950s. In early 1960, the already successful producer/director upped the ante a notch further when he introduced a popular humorist named Andy Griffith in the role of small-town sheriff Andy Taylor on an episode of *The Danny Thomas Show*. Eight months later—using the Thomas episode as a "backdoor pilot"—Leonard launched *The Andy Griffith Show* on the CBS network's Monday night lineup, where the series quickly established itself as one of the biggest hits of its era and, eventually, as one of the most beloved TV shows of all time. But Leonard was by no means content to stop there. And so, by the end of 1960, with the top-rated Griffith and Thomas shows as anchors, the producer—in partnership with Danny Thomas—stood poised and ready to expand his production base on the Desilu Cahuenga lot into one of the most formidable comedy factories in television.

Enter Carl Reiner.

"Harry Kalcheim came to me and said that Carl Reiner wanted to break into the field of situation comedy," recalls Leonard. Would Leonard, the agent inquired, be willing to show Reiner the ropes? "Of course, Carl is welcome," replied the well-established producer/director, who was already familiar with Reiner's work from the actor's tenure on *Your Show of Shows*. "He is more than welcome. Send him in," Leonard recalls telling the agent, "I'll be very happy to give him free access to anything we are doing."

But before he would arrange this meeting of the minds, Harry

An early publicity shot of Sheldon Leonard, the Syracuse University sociology major whose pugnacious profile and Bronx accent ensured that he would find no shortage of work as one of Hollywood's preeminent tough guys.

Kalcheim insisted that Leonard take a look at Carl Reiner's *Head of the Family* pilot—a condition to which the producer readily acceded. And so, a few days later, Leonard spent the better part of a lunch hour watching Carl Reiner's all but forgotten pilot in a screening room on the Desilu lot. Joining the producer at the screening was Danny Thomas's nephew, Ronald Jacobs, who was at that time one of Leonard's most trusted assistants. According to Jacobs, Sheldon Leonard's enthusiasm for the pilot was immediate and unrestrained—with but a single reservation.

"We loved the idea of the show," recalls Jacobs, who would later serve as associate producer of *The Dick Van Dyke Show*. But despite their shared enthusiasm for the film, notes Jacobs, both he and Leonard agreed that Carl Reiner's pilot suffered from one fatal flaw: The writer had completely miscast himself in the role of Robert Petrie. "I thought the reason the pilot had failed was principally because of the casting," says Leonard, who insists that Carl Reiner was not the show's only casting miscalculation. "Barbara Britton was a very lovely lady," acknowledges Leonard. "A beautiful lady." But, in his view, Britton's cover-girl looks made her appear too glamorous to be believable in a down-to-earth role like Laura Petrie. "She was too far too beautiful for the girl-next-door kind of characterization that you need in television." Leonard was also unimpressed with Reiner's casting of Morty Gunty and Sylvia Miles as Robert Petrie's co-workers. "I thought they added nothing whatever to it," he says. "They were there. They performed a function—but they brought nothing positive to it." But, finally, the producer reserved his harshest criticism for Carl Reiner's performance in the show's central role. "Carl brought with him the aura of sketch comedy, of which he had been born, or more or less bred," says Leonard. "And that sketch comedy approach didn't work for him in the situation comedy environment."

And yet, despite Leonard's reservations about the execution of Reiner's pilot film, the producer had nothing but praise for the show's underlying source material—the thirteen scripts Carl Reiner had labored over during his summer on Fire Island. "I thought that basketful of scripts was the best body of material it had been my good luck to find," Leonard would later observe.[16] "I thought the quality of the writing was very good indeed—first class," he says today, "and I realized that this was a body of material that deserved a second chance."

Comedy czar Sheldon Leonard on one of his sets at Desilu Cahuenga, where he presided over one of the most formidable comedy factories in television history throughout the late fifties and early sixties.

But before Leonard could even begin to give serious thought to reviving Reiner's moribund series, he knew that he would first have to resolve the casting issue. In his mind, there was simply no way the show was going to fly with Carl Reiner in the lead—and the sooner Reiner understood that, the better. "The feeling was," says Jacobs, "it's a good script. Now, let's find someone who can really do it." Of course, as an actor himself, Sheldon Leonard recognized that breaking this news to Carl Reiner would almost certainly require a considerable amount of delicacy. "How do you tell an actor he's just not the type to play himself?" the producer wondered.[17]

He would find out a few days

later, when Carl Reiner arrived at Desilu for his initial meeting with Leonard, which most likely took place sometime during the first few months of 1960. "Carl came to my office," recounts Leonard, "and we found ourselves to be compatible. He was very self-assured. And very lively." He was also, according to Leonard, quite intrigued by the veteran producer's sudden interest in a pilot that Reiner himself had all but written off. "Carl considered the thirteen scripts that he had written at Fire Island a dead issue," insists Leonard. "He'd done them and they hadn't paid off—too bad, and that's that." But, of course, Sheldon Leonard had other ideas, and he was only too happy to share his vision for the series with the attentive writer. "I asked Carl if he would be willing to let me try it again," recalls Leonard. "If he would let me reassemble the show in a manner that I thought would work."

Leonard's offer was tempting, though Carl Reiner admits he greeted it with mixed emotions. "I told Sheldon, 'I don't want to fail twice with the same thing,'" recalls Reiner.

"You won't," Leonard shot back, "because you're not going to act in the show. You're going to produce it."

"Produce it?" Reiner gasped. "But I don't know how to be a producer."

"Sure you do," insisted Leonard, who decided to demonstrate his point by plucking one of the *Head of the Family* scripts from a box that sat on the floor next to his desk. "Look," Leonard exclaimed, opening the script at random and indicating one particularly dense section of type that he found there. "It's all right here!"

Reiner leaned forward and read a few words of the text that the producer had highlighted with a quick sweep of his forefinger—a passage in which Reiner had described the setup and execution of a sight gag in painstaking detail, including a complete inventory of all the props, costumes, and set pieces that would be required to pull it off. "Look at the way you describe every character's reaction," Leonard explained. "Everything you need on the set is accounted for. The man who wrote this script was thinking like a producer."

"Yeah," Reiner interrupted, slightly confused. "But the reason I wrote all that stuff down like that is because I knew I *wasn't* going to be the producer—and I didn't want to leave anything to chance."

"That's the point," Leonard declared. "You don't leave anything to chance. You write like a producer. And you think like a producer. Therefore," the producer concluded with a flourish that signaled the end of the debate, "I must assume that you can produce."

According to a colorful account of that fateful meeting that Reiner

"While I was sitting there," says Carl Reiner, "Sheldon Leonard hyphenated me. I became a creator-writer-producer." Pictured, from left, Ron Jacobs, Sheldon Leonard, and Carl Reiner.

related to a reporter some years after the fact, Sheldon Leonard's most persuasive argument in favor of the producer's life came when the former character actor launched into an informal inventory of all the lavish adjustments he'd made in his own lifestyle since he'd largely abandoned the actor's trade for the producer's suite a few years earlier. "He showed me the expensive shoes he was wearing," recalled Reiner, "pointed to his extensive waistline, told me of the homes he had bought, and asked me if my two Emmys were supporting me."[18] His point well made, Leonard then added, almost rhetorically, "Where are you going as an actor?"[19] It was a question that gave Reiner a moment's pause. "While I was sitting there, thinking of an answer," Reiner recalled, "Sheldon hyphenated me. I became a creator-writer-producer."[20]

In later years, Sheldon Leonard would admit that he'd been surprised at how easy it had been to convince Carl Reiner to step out of the limelight on his own series. "I never saw anybody take that kind of blow to his ego and roll with the punch so gracefully."[21] But according to actress Doris Singleton, Carl Reiner didn't abandon his dream of playing Robert Petrie without some regret. "He was depressed about it," recalls Singleton, whose husband, Charlie Issacs, was then Reiner's writing partner on

The Dinah Shore Show. "He thought it would've been great to star in the series that he created." Fortunately, adds Singleton, Reiner's blue mood was extremely short-lived. Today, Carl Reiner freely acknowledges that Sheldon Leonard's suggestion that he find someone else to step into Robert Petrie's shoes may have been the best piece of advice he's ever been given. "I'll always be grateful to Sheldon Leonard," he has said, "for telling me I was a producer, when I thought I was an actor."[22]

With Carl Reiner now installed as the show's producer, and Sheldon Leonard taking on the responsibilities of executive producer, the pair began the arduous process of transforming a failed pilot into an entirely new and viable television series. The first item on the agenda would be to come up with a fresh title for the series, as they both agreed that the name *Head of the Family* carried too much baggage from the earlier series. Besides, the producers reasoned, if they were going to create a brand-new show from the ground up, it was only fitting that they start out with a brand-new title. And so, by the spring of 1960, the producers had dubbed their new series *The Full House*, which was but the first in a long succession of titles that would be attached to Carl Reiner's failed pilot in the months before it finally resurfaced in almost wholly unrecognizable form the following January, by then sporting the elegant, if simple, moniker by which it would become known by all posterity: *The Dick Van Dyke Show.*

CHAPTER 5
Fall Guy

ONE OF SHELDON LEONARD'S EARLIEST AND MOST significant contributions to the evolution of *The Dick Van Dyke Show* was his decision to put the show in front of a live audience. After watching Reiner's original pilot—which had been filmed in the one-camera method in the sterile confines of a movie studio—Leonard was convinced that the material would be far better served by the more theatrical three-camera approach, where the scenes could be played straight through on a stage, like a play, while three cameras quietly captured the action as it happened. Leonard had nothing against the one-camera method; in fact, he would employ that technique quite effectively to film eight years of Andy Griffith shows throughout the sixties. Even so, for the new Carl Reiner series, the executive producer had a strong hunch that the faster pace imposed by the three-camera approach would result in a livelier, more theatrical show. And, as would soon become quite obvious, Sheldon Leonard's hunch was right on the money.

The challenge of reworking Carl Reiner's thirteen Fire Island scripts to suit the very different production demands of a three-camera show fell to Reiner himself, who admits that his only preparation for the task was a single half-hour crash course in three-camera technique with his executive producer. "Sheldon showed me in one sitting how to do that," Reiner recalls. "I sat with him one day and he took a couple scripts and said, 'Look. Forget this exterior. Move this scene here. Then, take these lines and move them to the interior.' He showed me how one-camera shows have more scenes, but they're shorter. So, for a three-camera show, I needed fewer scenes, but I had to extend each one a little further. I learned that pretty quickly. Writing a three-camera show was more like playwriting. So I had to become more of a playwright than a one-camera film writer." Reiner turned out to be a quick study—in May of 1960, the writer filed an optimistic appraisal of his recent efforts in the pages of *TV Guide*. "I've reworked all the scripts to fit a new series," Reiner told reporter Dan Jenkins, "'The Full House.'"[23]

On July 19, 1960, a few months after Carl Reiner began reworking his Fire Island scripts to suit the new series, his original pilot received its first and only network broadcast. Aired with little fanfare, *Head of the Family* finally surfaced as an episode of *The Comedy Spot*, a CBS anthology series that served as the final dumping ground for most of the network's more ambitious unsold pilots. "They got burned off in the summertime," notes William Morris agent Sol Leon, "and then they were forgotten about."

The producers briefly considered casting Johnny Carson as Rob Petrie, until Sheldon Leonard suggested they consider a lanky New York stage actor named Dick Van Dyke for the part. "It was like a great marriage of actor and role," notes Carl Reiner.

But if Carl Reiner had any misgivings about the decidedly humble final disposition of the pilot episode of his first-born series, he wasn't about to lose sleep over it. By the time his agents made the deal to "burn off" the *Head of the Family* pilot, Reiner was already busy searching for an actor to star in his new, improved version of the same series. Of course, before Carl Reiner and Sheldon Leonard could begin their quest for a new Robert Petrie in earnest, the producers first had to decide what it was they were looking for. "I knew it had to be somebody who didn't seem like a performer," recalls Reiner. "Writers are—most of them—retiring characters. These guys are as funny as comedians, only they're *not* comedians—except maybe when you get them in a room. So we said, we need somebody like that. And then we started throwing names around."

One of the first names to surface in their discussions was Johnny Carson, who was at that time still best known as the host of the popular daytime quiz show *Who Do You Trust?** "But," admits Reiner, "that was just a passing idea." Far more compelling was a suggestion that Sheldon Leonard made, seemingly out of the blue. "There's a guy in New York," the executive producer announced. "He's doing *Bye Bye Birdie* on Broadway. His name is Dick Van Dyke."

Although Dick Van Dyke was then still largely unknown outside of New York show business circles, his talent was no secret to Sheldon Leonard. The producer had been a fan of the lanky comedian since the previous November, when he first spotted Dick Van Dyke in the supporting cast of *The Girls Against the Boys*, a musical revue headlined by Bert Lahr and Nancy Walker that had a short run at Broadway's Alvin Theatre in 1959. Leonard attended the revue on the advice of Harry Kalcheim, who had been singing Dick Van Dyke's praises ever since he'd caught the show earlier that same week.** And, as Leonard would later

---

*Ironically, Johnny Carson would make a wholly independent bid for situation comedy stardom that same season when he filmed the pilot for an ill-fated vehicle called *Johnny Come Lately*. Unfortunately, Carson's pilot fared no better than did Reiner's *Head of the Family*—in fact, by an odd coincidence, Carson's unsold pilot would be "burned off" on the CBS network's *New Comedy Showcase* on August 8, 1960, just three weeks after the same network gave *Head of the Family* its single airing. Stranger yet, on August 22, 1960—exactly two weeks to the day after CBS aired Carson's forlorn pilot—the network ran yet another unsold pilot, *The Trouble with Richard*, a half-hour comedy that had been designed to showcase the talents of a would-be star named Dick Van Dyke.

**Although Sheldon Leonard gives full credit to the late Harry Kalcheim for being the first to bring Dick Van Dyke to his attention, Van Dyke himself insists that he can list at least a dozen other show business acquaintances he's met over the years who've claimed the distinction of making that fateful introduction. "It tickles me to death," says the star, "how many people take credit for having been the very first to mention me to Sheldon Leonard."

tell *TV Guide*, his own first exposure to Dick Van Dyke left an equally lasting impression. "He did a bit that fractured me," Leonard recalled, "the fella who comes home loaded from a night with the boys, but every time his wife comes in snaps to attention."[24] Before the final curtain rang down that evening, Sheldon Leonard had made a mental note to keep his eye out for a TV project that might exploit the singular talent that he'd just discovered. "Sooner or later," says Leonard, "I was pretty sure I'd find something for him."

Leonard says that he initially hoped to cast Dick Van Dyke as Danny Williams's son-in-law on *The Danny Thomas Show*, though he admits that he never acted on that impulse, fearing that Van Dyke would appear too old for the role, which eventually went to Pat Harrington. But now, with the role of comedy writer Robert Petrie, Leonard was convinced that he'd finally found a part worthy of Van Dyke's protean abilities. And just to be sure, in the late summer of 1960 Sheldon Leonard made a second trip to Broadway, where Dick Van Dyke was starring in *Bye Bye Birdie*, which had been playing to capacity crowds at The Martin Beck Theatre since April 14. After seeing the way Van Dyke dazzled audiences in the role of Albert Petersen, Leonard had little doubt that he'd found the man to replace Carl Reiner as Rob Petrie.

"After Sheldon saw Dick in *Bye Bye Birdie*," recalls Grant Tinker, who was then a creative executive at New York's Benton and Bowles advertising agency, "he walked into my office with a huge smile on his face and said, 'I've found Rob Petrie!'" Before the day was out, Leonard called Carl Reiner in Los Angeles and insisted that the writer hop the next plane to New York. And when Reiner finally caught *Bye Bye Birdie* himself a few days later, he left the show in absolute accord with his executive producer. "I thought, 'Geez, he's perfect!'" recalls Reiner. "It was like a great marriage of actor and role that seemed completely accidental. But that was Sheldon. He was the great matchmaker."

But despite the actor's uncanny fitness for the role of Rob Petrie, Carl Reiner admits that hiring Dick Van Dyke to anchor their brand-new series was by no means a safe choice. "It wasn't a good odds bet," says Reiner. For one thing, both Leonard and Reiner were only too aware that their new series would not be Dick Van Dyke's first exposure on national television. Far from it. As Reiner recalls, "Dick had done, like, twelve pilots in a row that had failed."

Though Reiner exaggerates the number of Van Dyke's previous times at bat, there can be little doubt that the Broadway star's television career had not exactly been charmed up to that point. In fact, long before he even met Carl Reiner, Dick Van Dyke had already filmed a pilot for something called *The Dick Van Dyke Show*, though that series was a failed variety show that bore little resemblance to the star's later situation comedy. "I did a monologue and sketches and fell down a lot,"[25] is how Van Dyke later described the unsold pilot for his first *Dick Van Dyke Show*, which was created and produced by Aaron Ruben, a veteran TV writer who had worked with Van Dyke on the comedy sketches in *The Girls Against the Boys*. After their variety show failed to attract a buyer, Ruben and Van Dyke teamed up for yet another pilot, *Poor Richard*, a situation comedy, "in which," Van Dyke would later recall, "I fell a lot, too."[26] The unsold pilot for *Poor Richard* was aired—under the title *The Trouble with Richard*—on August 22, 1960, ironically, just a few weeks after *Head of the Family* received its first and only network airing on CBS.*

But the star's most tantalizing early project may well have been a TV series that never even made it to the pilot stage. According to Van Dyke, a few months before Carl Reiner signed him to play Rob Petrie, the star had been having discussions with another producer, whose name Van Dyke has long since forgotten, who approached him with a very intriguing proposal. "Someone had an idea for a series based on the Jacques Tati character, Monsieur Hulot," recalls Van Dyke, who was flattered to be compared to the popular French director and star of the landmark comedy, *Monsieur Hulot's Holiday*. "There would have been a lot of mime and visual humor," says Van Dyke, recalling the premise of the proposed series. "I would've played an assistant professor from a small middle western college who was on a sabbatical, saddling around in Europe on a Vespa motor scooter with a typewriter on the back." But, alas, as fascinating as it sounded, Van Dyke admits that the project never got past the discussion stage. "There was no script or anything. We had simply talked about it in conceptual terms."

But even after the Tati series finally sputtered and died, Dick Van Dyke refused to get too upset. Over the course of a career that had been marked by many more failures than successes, Dick Van Dyke had developed an almost limitless capacity for patience. After all, by the time he met Carl Reiner in 1960, the fledgling star had already spent almost five years as one of television's most promising newcomers.

Born on December 13, 1925, in West Plains, Missouri, Dick Van Dyke

---

*After their second TV pilot failed to sell, Aaron Ruben finally gave up on trying to find a vehicle for Dick Van Dyke's TV debut and moved to the West Coast, where he ended up producing *The Andy Griffith Show,* which was filmed just a few stages away from *The Van Dyke Show* on the Desilu lot.

By 1960, with two failed pilots behind him, Dick Van Dyke had been television's most promising newcomer for more years than he cared to remember.

was raised in Danville, Illinois, a small midwestern town where his father worked as a freight agent. As a boy, Van Dyke recalls spending countless Saturday afternoons haunting the local movie palaces. It was there that the future comedy star developed his lasting passion for the expressive comedians of the late silent and early sound era, including Buster Keaton, Harold Lloyd, Charlie Chaplin and, especially, Stan Laurel. When Van Dyke finally began performing his own self-styled pantomimes in local Danville variety and talent shows, it was Stan Laurel who provided the star-struck midwesterner with his greatest inspiration, not to mention his best material, most of which, Van Dyke would later confess, he lifted directly from the vast Laurel and Hardy repertoire.

With the outbreak of World War II, Van Dyke enlisted in the air force, where his inspired clowning invariably drew the loudest response from his fellow servicemen in cadet variety shows. "He had a natural stage presence," Van Dyke's old air force chum Byron Paul would later recall. "He did a little thing—a man walking a dog in a high wind. But he was not fumble-footed."[27] Paul, who would eventually become Van Dyke's manager and close friend, was so impressed by the young cadet's extraordinary performance that he was moved to predict that Dick Van Dyke would one day be among the biggest comedy stars in the business. It was a prediction that neither of them would soon forget.

But Dick Van Dyke's day in the sun was still a good way off in 1946, the year that the future star finally received his air force discharge papers. After the war, Van Dyke returned to Danville, where he dabbled briefly in advertising before deciding to renew his commitment to a life in show business. For the next few years, Van Dyke toured the country as one of the Merry Mutes, a musical pantomime act that he formed with an old friend named Phil Erikson. Although the pair finally achieved minor notoriety on the nightclub circuit of the late forties, they were certainly not above playing third-rate supper clubs and recreation halls for twenty-five dollars a night.

By 1948, times were so tough that when Van Dyke proposed to his hometown sweetheart, the former Marjorie Willett, he and his intended had to get married under the auspices of *The Bride and Groom Show*, a then popular radio—and, later, television—show that offered to pay for the couple's wedding ceremony and honeymoon in exchange for a few minutes of on-air chatter with the nervous newlyweds after the vows. "They bought us the ring and the license," Van Dyke later recalled, "and they gave us furniture and appliances and sent us up to Mount Hood, Oregon, for a week's honeymoon. That's the only way I could afford to get married."[28]

Now a married man with children on the way—sons Christian and Barry were born in 1950 and 1951, respectively; daughter Stacy came along in 1955, and the youngest, Carrie Beth, was born in 1961—Van Dyke decided to settle down in Atlanta, Georgia, where he'd landed a job as a morning disk jockey and radio talk show host. It wasn't long before the personable star made the leap to television, and by 1953, Van Dyke was hosting his own daily kid's show on a local Atlanta station. Though the program was ostensibly aimed at the after-school set, Van Dyke's smart combination of comedy, pantomime, and clever small talk soon earned the star a sizable following among Atlanta's adult demographic group as well. He was also having the time of his life. "I had finally achieved what I figured was my ultimate success," the actor would later recall. "I had very high ratings, and that was it for me, I was going to stay there."[29]

Dick Van Dyke recalls that his decision to leave the cast of a successful Broadway show to play *The Dick Van Dyke Show*'s Rob Petrie was not a hard choice to make. "Once I saw the quality of Carl's writing," recalls the star, "well, that just sealed it."

And there he might have stayed, had not fate stepped in, in the guise of an old air force buddy. Though Byron Paul had gone on to become a successful television director for CBS in New York, he had never forgotten Dick Van Dyke. And as soon as he was in a position to do so, Paul volunteered to set his old pal up with an audition for the CBS brass in New York. It was a tempting offer, and one that Van Dyke ultimately found impossible to resist, despite his own slightly mixed feelings about making the leap to the big leagues. "Byron Paul brought me to New York in 1955," the reluctant star later recounted, "but he had to drag me up, because I figured I didn't want any of that."[30]

As it turned out, Van Dyke's initial instincts may have been on target. After a promising start—CBS signed him to a five-year contract soon after he arrived in New York—Dick Van Dyke ended up spending the better part of television's golden age laboring in a long string of thankless assignments, beginning with an ill-fated appointment to the anchor chair of the network's *Morning Show*. By 1955, CBS's troubled morning news and chat show had already resisted the best efforts of three previous anchormen, an illustrious group that included Jack Paar, John Henry Faulk, and Walter Cronkite. When Dick Van Dyke proved similarly unable to bolster the show's ailing format, his own stock at the network plummeted precipitously. Within a year's time he'd been assigned to host *The CBS Cartoon Theatre*, where the once promising newcomer was reduced to playing second banana to Gandy Goose, Dinky Duck, and Heckle and Jeckle. Two years later, in 1958, Van Dyke's contract with the network was dissolved by mutual consent.

Dick Van Dyke spent the next few years marching through a seemingly endless parade of guest appearances on shows as varied as *The Armstrong Circle Theatre* and *The Phil Silvers Show*. But despite his near constant exposure on television throughout the late fifties, Van Dyke's career seemed hopelessly stalled in the frustrating category of minor celebrity. By 1960, after nearly fifteen years in show business, the thirty-five-year-old star was still waiting for his big break.

Ironically, when that breakthrough finally arrived, it was not on television at all, but on the Broadway stage. And, as the noted theater director and choreographer Gower Champion might have proclaimed, television's loss was Broadway's gain. For it was Champion who finally took a chance on the young star when he cast Van Dyke as the romantic lead in the musical *Bye Bye Birdie*—despite the fact that Van Dyke readily confessed that he didn't know the first thing about dancing! Fortunately, the actor proved a quick study, and the day after *Bye Bye Birdie* opened, Dick Van Dyke awoke to discover that he'd suddenly become an overnight success.

But despite the acclaim that greeted his Broadway debut, the practical performer never lost sight of his long-range goal: to find regular work in television. "By that time I had three kids and I was looking for steady work," he explains. "I just couldn't take a chance on hanging around the theater and hoping to get another hit. And so a series was the best answer for me."

And so it was with more than casual interest that Dick Van Dyke agreed to meet with Sheldon Leonard a few weeks after the producer finally caught the actor's head-turning performance in *Bye Bye Birdie*. According to agent Sol Leon, who remembers being present at the first meeting between Dick Van Dyke and Sheldon Leonard, the pair met for an informal chat one Friday evening, a few minutes before Van Dyke was due to report to the Martin Beck for his evening performance. "Dick met us at six o'clock," recalls Leon. "And Sheldon said, 'I've got three scripts that I would like you to read.' Then Dick said, 'I'll read them over the weekend.'" Three days later, Van Dyke was in. "I called Dick on Monday," says Leon, "and he said, 'I've been offered a lot of scripts. But nothing like these.'"

"Once I saw the quality of Carl's writing," the actor concurs. "Well, that just sealed it."

A deal to secure Van Dyke's services was quickly struck with Byron Paul, who was by that time acting as Van Dyke's manager. Under the terms of his initial contract for the series, the star was to be paid a relatively modest starting salary of $1,500 per episode, with standard raises built in for subsequent years in the event that the show went beyond a single season. In addition, Van Dyke would also receive ownership shares in the proposed series, a deal point that the actor would later credit to Byron Paul's business acumen. And a savvy move it was.

In the years since *The Dick Van Dyke Show* left the air, the star's financial stake in the series has generated far greater revenues than he ever earned as a performer on the show. Van Dyke's ownership status also ensures that the actor will continue to derive income from the show's perpetually remunerative reruns, which makes him the only member of the show's original cast to so profit, the other actors having long since exhausted the skimpy residual payment plans that were standard in the early sixties.*

With Van Dyke now installed as an official partner and co-owner of the new series, he and the show's other owners promptly formed a legal partnership that they christened Calvada Productions, based on an acronym that incorporated the first letters in each of the primary partner's names—*CA* for Carl Reiner, *L* for Leonard, *VA* for Van Dyke, and *DA* for Sheldon Leonard's deep-pocketed business partner Danny Thomas, who would earn a substantial stake in the company by providing the operating capital to film the pilot and subsequent episodes of *The Dick Van Dyke Show*. As things turned out, it would prove to be one of the best investments Danny Thomas ever made.

---

*In the show's later years, *Dick Van Dyke Show* co-owner Danny Thomas finally did offer Mary Tyler Moore a tiny percentage of the series in lieu of a salary increase during one of the show's final seasons. But though she may well have been tempted by the—as it would turn out—generous offer, the actress finally chose to forgo a minority stake in the series in favor of a higher upfront salary.

CHAPTER 6
Casting Calls

WITH DICK VAN DYKE SIGNED TO PLAY THEIR LEAD, CARL
Reiner and Sheldon Leonard were ready to begin the critical task of casting the show's supporting ensemble. And when it came to the business of
casting, Sheldon Leonard was in his element. As executive producer of
The Andy Griffith Show, the producer had already assembled one of the
strongest acting companies on television. "I'd learned very quickly on the
Griffith show how important it was to surround your lead with a rich,
amusing, supporting cast," says Leonard, who was anxious to apply the
lessons he'd learned on that series to the task at hand.

The first role cast—after Van Dyke himself—was also the easiest.
"There's only one person to play Sally Rogers," Sheldon Leonard told
Reiner, "and that is Rose Marie."*

And he was right, of course. Not that it required any great powers of

---

*Curiously, Sylvia Miles insists that she was offered the opportunity to reprise
her pilot role in the Van Dyke series but turned it down to pursue a thriving stage
career in New York. "William Morris wanted to sign me to a five-year deal," says
Miles, "and they were very angry with me when I turned that down." But, while
it's entirely possible that an agent at the William Morris Agency may have
approached the actress, it's extremely doubtful that anyone directly connected
with the series itself made any serious overtures to Sylvia Miles, if for no other
reason than Carl Reiner's determination to distance the new series from the pilot
he'd filmed in New York. "Now that we were in California," notes Reiner, "we
wanted to start over again. That way, no one at the network could say, 'Oh, we
saw that show,' and turn us down a second time."

"There's only one person to play Sally Rogers," Sheldon Leonard told Carl Reiner, "and that is Rose Marie."

perspicacity to envision Rose Marie playing a brash, funny lady who sings and tells jokes—it was a role she'd already been playing for a lifetime. Born in New York City on August 15, 1923, Rose Marie Mazetta was all of three years old when she made her professional radio debut as Baby Rose Marie, a three-foot-tall singing and dancing dynamo. Over the next decade, Baby Rose Marie would log hundreds of appearances on stage, screen, and radio, until, by the early forties, the former child star—her name now shortened to Rose Marie—had flowered into one of America's best-known radio and nightclub entertainers. The singer would continue her tireless schedule of personal appearances throughout the decade, culminating in an extended engagement in support of Phil Silvers in *Top Banana*, a popular musical revue that opened at Broadway's Winter Garden Theatre on November 1, 1951.

By the late fifties, television had discovered the versatile Rose Marie, whose range as a singer and actress made her equally at home in variety show or situation comedy settings. Before the decade ended, Rose Marie had racked up an impressive list of credits on shows as varied as *The Jackie Gleason Show*, *M Squad*, *The Many Loves of Dobie Gillis*, and *Gunsmoke*. For a short spell in 1960, the actress also had a recurring role on *My Sister Eileen*, a short-lived situation comedy that was canceled, fortuitously, just before the Van Dyke show went into production in 1961. Considering the bounty of work that had already come her way by the time Sheldon Leonard called her in to interview for a part on his new

When Sheldon Leonard finally called Rose Marie in to interview for the part of Sally Rogers on his new series, the actress recalls that the first words out of her mouth were, "Sheldon! What took you so long?"

series, it seems ironic that her first response was, "Sheldon! What took you so long?"

"I'd known Sheldon Leonard for years," she explains, recalling personal and professional ties that went all the way back to radio, where Rose Marie had played Leonard's sister on *The Phil Harris Show*. In the years since, Leonard had proved himself one of the entertainer's most loyal and vocal supporters. Whenever Rose Marie played a nightclub engagement in southern California or Las Vegas, she recalls that she could usually count on seeing Leonard sitting ringside, often alongside Danny Thomas, another of the singer's long-standing friends. And yet, for all the attention they lavished on her, Rose Marie found it puzzling that neither Sheldon Leonard nor Danny Thomas had ever called on her to make an appearance on *The Danny Thomas Show*. "I used to ask Sheldon," she recalls, "'When am I gonna do a guest shot on Danny's show?'"

And, according to the actress, his response was always the same. "Don't worry, Rosie," he would promise. "Your time will come. Your time will come." Finally, Rose Marie had heard that refrain so often that by the time she actually did get a call from Sheldon Leonard's in-house casting agent in the final weeks of 1960, the actress seemed genuinely surprised. "Oh, God!" she exclaimed to casting agent Ruth Burch. "Does this mean I'm finally gonna be on Danny's show?"

"Oh, no, no," explained Burch. "This is for *The Dick Van Dyke Show*."

"Oh?" the actress recalls asking. "What's a Dick Van Dyke?"

No sooner had the casting agent finished answering that query than Rose Marie was out the door and on her way to the studio. "I was the second one cast on the show," she says, "after Dick." According to Carl Reiner, it became obvious that Rose Marie's casting interview would be little more than a formality a few moments after the actress walked into his office. "As soon as I met her," he insists, "I said, 'Absolutely!'" So certain were they that they'd found their Sally Rogers, the producers never even bothered to give Rose Marie a copy of the script at the audition. Instead, they launched directly into a detailed description of the show's premise and her role in the series. "When they told me that I would play a television writer," recalls Rose Marie, "I said, 'Oh, my God! You're

Former child star Rose Marie as Sally Rogers, the role
she'd been born to play.

gonna let the public know that comics are not so funny on their own? That they have writers?'"

For her services, the actress was offered a generous, if not extravagant, salary of $1,000 per episode. "It was one of those things where they said, 'Well, we're paying this kind of money,'" the actress recalls. Reasoning that the figure mentioned seemed fair enough, the actress accepted the job on the spot. "I thought I'd made the greatest deal in the world," she remembers, "because they gave me everything I wanted. But then, as I walked down the steps, I said, 'Damn it, I should have asked for more money!'"

Before her matter-of-fact interview drew to a close, Rose Marie made one additional, and, as it would turn out, very significant suggestion to her new producers. "Have you got anyone in mind for the third writer?" she asked.

"No," Reiner replied, "we haven't picked him yet."

"Good," she declared, "because Morey Amsterdam would be just great for this." Carl Reiner paused to consider the suggestion while Rose Marie elaborated. "He used to be a writer for Fanny Brice and Milton Berle and Fred Allen. And he's also a comic."

The actress continued her pitch, but Reiner, who during his tenure as host of *Keep Talking* had already witnessed Morey Amsterdam's comic inventiveness as a celebrity panelist, didn't need much convincing. True, at forty-eight, Morey Amsterdam was a good deal older than the character Reiner had originally envisioned as a twenty-three-year-old hypochondriac wunderkind in his early *Head of the Family* scripts. But it didn't take Reiner long to recognize that there were distinct possibilities in the notion of reconceiving Buddy Sorrell as a veteran comedy writer steeped in the shticks and traditions of the old school. And if anyone in show business fit this new concept for the role better than Morey Amsterdam—the self-proclaimed "Human Joke Machine"—Carl Reiner certainly didn't know him. "Do you know where Morey is?" Reiner finally asked Rose Marie.

"Are you *kiddin'*?" she shot back, still flush with enthusiasm. "I'm his daughter's godmother! I've known Morey since I was eleven years old—when we did *The Al Pierce Show*—"

"Okay, Rosie," Reiner interrupted. "You win. Now, where do we find him?"

"In Yonkers," she replied. "I'll give you his number."

Carl Reiner placed the call that same afternoon, and it was a conversation that Morey Amsterdam says he'll never forget. "When the phone rang," he recalls, "I was out in the backyard, shoveling snow out of the driveway." After the comedian's wife called him in from the snow,

Amsterdam remembers that he and Reiner exchanged no more than a few seconds of pleasantries before the producer introduced the real purpose of his call. "Carl said, 'Morey, we're doing a show. I made a pilot on it with me playing the lead, but we're doing it again with a guy named Dick Van Dyke.' And he says, 'We want to know if you're interested. Can you get out here by day after tomorrow?' I says, 'I can leave here in fifteen minutes! I want to get out of this goddamned snow.' And that was it."

Amsterdam did fly to Los Angeles a few days later, and Reiner insists that any lingering reservations he may have harbored about having to rework his original conception of Buddy Sorrell evaporated the instant Morey Amsterdam arrived. "When Morey came in," Reiner recalls, "I said, 'My God, is that right!' He epitomized every hack comedy writer in the business." In Reiner's eyes, Amsterdam *was* Buddy Sorrell—which is an observation that the actor himself would be the last to dispute. "I just played myself," Amsterdam cheerfully admits.

Naturally, the actor's instinctive decision to draw on his own background in the creation of his on-screen persona received a hearty endorsement from the show's creator, who would himself draw liberally from Amsterdam's lengthy personal resume in his fictional construction of the character. In fact, Amsterdam's personal biography bore so many parallels to his fictional character's dossier that it was often difficult to divine exactly where Morey left off and Buddy began.

The real-life Morey Amsterdam was born on December 14, 1908, in Chicago, Illinois, though he spent his formative years in San Francisco, where his father was for many years concert master of the San Francisco Symphony Orchestra. "I was raised to be a concert cellist," says the comedian, who recalls that his father would have been delighted to watch his son follow in his footsteps. But by his early teens, the younger Amsterdam had discovered that he found Borscht more compelling than Bartok, and by the late 1920s, the would be comedian had abandoned the symphonic stage for the garish prosceniums of vaudeville. But, perhaps in deference to his father's wishes, Morey Amsterdam kept the cello in his act, where it would become the comedian's most distinctive trademark.

By the early thirties, the cello-playing comic had moved his act to radio, where Amsterdam soon discovered that he had a prodigious facility for creating and cataloging jokes and one-liners, a skill that he would eventually parlay into a substantial second income as a joke doctor for some of the era's more notable stage and radio entertainers, including Will Rogers, Fanny Brice, Jimmy Durante, and Pearl Bailey, among hundreds of others. Throughout the thirties and forties, the comedian maintained a rigorous schedule of radio and personal appearances, and also found time to pen music or lyrics for a handful of popular novelty songs of the era, including the Andrews Sisters' wartime hit *Rum and Coca Cola*, which was coauthored by Paul Baron and Geri Sullivan. With the coming of television in the late forties, Amsterdam's ability to think on his feet practically assured the versatile performer of steady employment in the burgeoning medium of live TV. By 1948, he was hosting *The Morey Amsterdam Show* for CBS, an assignment that eventually led to the comic's appointment as one of the hosts of NBC's *Broadway Open House*, the pioneering 1950 late-night talk show that would serve as a prototype for the network's immensely popular *Tonight Show*.

In the years between *Broadway Open House* and the start of *The Dick Van Dyke Show* a little more than a decade later, Amsterdam logged hun-

"Have you got anyone in mind for the third writer?" Rose Marie asked Carl Reiner just before she made the inspired suggestion of casting Morey Amsterdam in the role.

"When Morey came in," recalls Carl Reiner, "I said, 'My God is that right!' He epitomized every hack comedy writer in the business."

dreds of additional appearances on a vast array of TV variety shows and celebrity panels, where the comedian frequently billed himself as the "Human Joke Machine," a boastful reference to his almost uncanny ability to cook up a joke on any topic put to him—a talent that would, incidentally, prove a most valuable asset to *The Dick Van Dyke Show.*

"We couldn't have had a show without Morey Amsterdam," acknowledges Carl Reiner, who cheerfully admits that he and his writers thought nothing of plundering the comic's vast repository of jokes and one-liners whenever they got stuck. "He literally was the Human Joke Machine," Reiner notes. "You'd give him a subject and he'd do five jokes on it." Adds longtime Van Dyke director John Rich, "They weren't always the best jokes. But if you weeded them out, you would get winners." And though Amsterdam would eventually provide punchlines for every character on the series, it was only natural that the comedian's vast joke library proved most valuable as a source of one-liners for the character closest to him. "When the script needed a Buddy joke," Reiner recalls, "he'd give us five." After a while, says Reiner, the actor grew so adept at providing his own one-liners that it became a point of pride among the show's writers whenever one of them managed to think up a wisecrack that the comedian hadn't already heard. "Once in while, we'd come up with a Buddy joke for Morey," says Reiner, "and he'd be very thankful."

"We couldn't have had a show without Morey Amsterdam," says Carl Reiner. "He literally was the Human Joke Machine."

Carl Reiner's decision to hire the bald and bespectacled character actor Richard Deacon to round out the Van Dyke show's office ensemble was a choice as inspired as it was obvious. By the time Richard Deacon was hired to play *The Dick Van Dyke Show*'s fastidious and high-strung Mel Cooley, the popular character actor had already burnished his reputation with dozens of similar characterizations in countless films and situation comedies of the fifties, including recurring roles on *A Date with the Angels* and *The Charlie Farrell Show*, as well as a lengthy stint as the long-suffering Fred Rutherford on *Leave It to Beaver*. In fact, it was Deacon's letter-perfect portrayal of *Beaver*'s easily flustered Fred Rutherford that convinced Carl Reiner to bring the actor in for the part of Mel Cooley in the first place. "He just looked so right," says Carl Reiner. "He was angry and fussy. Just wonderful for that part."

"He just looked so right," says Carl Reiner, recalling his first meeting with Richard Deacon. "Just wonderful for that part."

Like most of the characters who would come to populate the Van Dyke show, the *Alan Brady Show*'s much put-upon producer had a real life precedent—or, in his case, a pair of them. "Mel was based on a couple of producers we had on the *Show of Shows*," remembers Carl Reiner. "They were good guys—nice, family guys. But they were also the kind of guys who took shit from everybody, because they were always the ones bringing us bad news. And since you couldn't go up to the vice president of NBC and yell at *him*, you'd yell at these guys." Naturally, Reiner recalls, it wasn't long before all of this verbal abuse began to take its toll. "One of the guys used to chew pencils," remarks Reiner, "right down to the lead. And then he'd swallow it! He always looked like he had licorice on his mouth." Fortunately for Richard Deacon, his character was spared that particular indignity—though Carl Reiner may have saddled his fictional producer with an even greater cross to bear when he made Mel Cooley the star's brother-in-law. "I just invented that," says Reiner, acknowledging the fertile range of joke opportunities that Alan Brady's nepotism opened up for the show's writers. "It just made it more fun."

Of course, Mel Cooley's most striking feature could be found at the very top of his head—a noticeably hairless expanse that inspired the relentless stream of barbed one-liners that would come to define the producer's tempestuous relationship with his chief nemesis, comedy writer Buddy Sorrell. According to Morey Amsterdam, Buddy's habit of zinging Mel with bald jokes at every possible opportunity was not an element in Carl Reiner's original conception of the show, but sprang from a few on-set quips that the real-life actors exchanged during early rehearsals. "I was always kidding Richard Deacon about his bald head," recalls Amsterdam. "One day we're kidding around, and Deac said something innocuous. And I said, 'Deac, that makes no sense at all. Sometimes I think your hair didn't fall *out*—it fell *in* and clouded your brain.' It broke up everybody on the set, and Carl came running out and said, 'Let's keep that in.' And that was the start of that relationship between me and Mel."

And, just so the Buddy versus Mel Cooley debates wouldn't seem too one-sided, the show's producers occasionally allowed Mel the opportunity for a comeback, the most famous of which was inaugurated in the show's third episode, "Jealousy." Legend has it that during rehearsals for that episode, Carl Reiner and director John Rich were searching for a suitable comeback for the character to parry in response to Buddy's latest broadside. Finally, at his wit's end, Reiner turned to Richard Deacon and asked the actor how he would react to a tormentor like Buddy Sorrell in real life. Without a pause, Deacon uttered, "Yeecchh!" And without further discussion, the actor's monosyllabic response was duly incorporated into the script of that and many subsequent episodes.

If Richard Deacon shared certain characteristics with his on-screen alter ego, Mel Cooley's humorlessness was certainly not one of them. "Richard Deacon was the funniest human being on the face of the earth," states the show's film editor, Bud Molin, who submits as evidence the surreal spectacle of the rotund actor performing an impromptu striptease for the cast and crew—an event that Molin swears actually took place during one of the show's Christmas parties. "All of a sudden Deacon decides he's gonna do a striptease," says Molin. "And so he got up and started to strip—to music—for twenty minutes! He never stopped working, but at the end of that twenty minutes, all he'd taken off were his cuff links. That was it! He was just a funny, funny guy."

Another significant difference between Richard Deacon and the character he played on the show is that, unlike Mel Cooley, the real-life Richard Deacon was almost universally loved by everyone on the set. "He was a joy to have around," says Carl Reiner, who remained on friendly terms with Deacon until the character actor's untimely death in 1984.

"Morey and Rosie loved Deacon," notes Reiner. "Everybody did. He was a dear man."

Having assembled a first-rate ensemble of character actors to populate Rob Petrie's office family, the show's producers moved on to the more exacting task of casting Rob Petrie's other clan: his wife, Laura, and their son, Ritchie. As casting agent Ruth Burch recalls it, the task of finding an actor to play the Petries' six-year-old son was accomplished with a minimum of fuss. "We had interviews of children that were five and six years old," Burch recalls. Based on these introductory interviews, Carl Reiner quickly narrowed the field down to four or five final contenders, each of whom was then called on to demonstrate their acting skill by performing one of the most rudimentary exercises of all. "Carl asked me to pretend like I was sick," recalls Larry Mathews, who would finally win the role. "I was supposed to be ill in the pilot, so he wanted to make sure I could do that well."

According to Ruth Burch, Mathews had the part sewn up after that single audition. "They just zeroed in on him," she recalls. "He was a cute little guy. Not at all as supercilious as kids are nowadays." As far as Carl Reiner was concerned, Larry Mathews's utter lack of precocity put him at a distinct advantage in the running for the role. As Morey Amsterdam recalls, "Carl said, 'I want a kid who hasn't done anything and who hasn't been in anything.'" In other words, what Reiner wanted was a real, live, all-American boy. And, as the producer would be delighted to discover, in Larry Mathews, he had found just that.

Born Larry Mazzeo, on August 15, 1955, in Burbank, California, Larry Mathews had never even acted professionally before his audition for the Van Dyke show in early January of 1961. A tow-headed five-year-old from the San Fernando Valley, Mathews had taken his first acting lesson only a few months earlier, when his parents, acting on a whim, enrolled him in a children's drama workshop. There, the outgoing five-year-old attracted the attention of a children's talent agent, who offered to recommend the young actor to Carl Reiner, who was then looking for a real kid to join the cast of his new series. And, within a few days of that audition, the producer signed young Larry Mazzeo—who had by that time adopted Larry Mathews as his stage name—to play Ritchie Petrie on the Van Dyke show.

By the second week of January 1961, Carl Reiner had cast all the principal roles on *The Dick Van Dyke Show*, save one. But with rehearsals for the show's pilot episode scheduled to start in less than a week, the producer was growing understandably nervous that he still hadn't found an actress to play Laura Petrie—though it certainly wasn't for lack of trying.

Morey Amsterdam and Phil Leeds—as Buddy's wayward brother, Blackie Sorrell—explore Richard Deacon's most striking feature, in a publicity shot from episode 35, "Hustling the Hustler."

"He was a cute little guy," says casting agent Ruth Burch, recalling child actor Larry Mathews, "not at all as supercilious as kids are nowadays."

"I must have looked at every young actress in town," he sighs. "I saw about sixty girls for Laura. Literally—sixty!" And, as if the novice producer didn't have enough troubles, he knew that he would have to go this one alone. By that point in the show's casting process, Sheldon Leonard had long since refocused his own attentions on his many other duties on the lot, leaving Carl Reiner to sort though the seemingly endless parade of potential Laura Petries on his own. "He left me sitting alone in a room," explains Reiner, "reading sixty actresses!"

And there Reiner would stay, for days on end, meeting, reading, and ultimately rejecting scores of hopeful ingenues who, for one reason or another, failed to live up to Reiner's image of Robert Petrie's wife. "I just couldn't find the right type," he explains. After he'd interviewed at least three dozen actresses, Carl Reiner recalls that he finally turned to Sheldon Leonard and said, "Gee, I don't know what I'm looking for!" But Leonard, who'd been in Reiner's spot himself, knew that there was little he could do to alleviate his younger partner's frustration. "You'll know what you're looking for," Leonard counseled, "when you find it."

CHAPTER 7

The Girl with Three Names

THE FIRST BRIGHT MOMENT IN CARL REINER'S MARATHON auditions to find Laura Petrie arrived when he heard about the availability of a young actress named Eileen Brennan. In early 1961, the future Oscar nominee was then a newcomer who was just starting to attract attention for her work in *Little Mary Sunshine*, an off-Broadway musical spoof that had been running for more than a year. "Somebody said, 'You really ought to fly her out here. She's sensational!'" recalls Reiner. But despite the glowing notices, the producer was hesitant to fly Eileen Brennan all the way across the country for a single audition, if only because he couldn't see how he could possibly justify the expense of the airfare to Danny Thomas, who had by that time agreed to foot the expenses for the Van Dyke pilot. "We never flew anybody out in those days," says Reiner. Even so, the producer finally decided that, with his shooting date looming less than two weeks off, he didn't have much choice. And so, inching out on what he felt was a precarious financial limb, Reiner authorized the purchase of a round-trip airline ticket to fly Eileen Brennan out to Los Angeles for the interview. "I still remember the amount," he recalls. "It was five hundred dollars."

"She's wonderful," is how Carl Reiner describes Eileen Brennan today. But despite his obvious regard for her talent—both then and now—Carl Reiner's spirits began to sink the moment the actress picked up her script and began reading. "She was a brilliant actress," he insists, "but it just wasn't working." To her credit, notes Reiner, Brennan's interpretation of Laura Petrie was remarkably assured. But, ironically, the actress's vigor-

"I must have looked at every young actress in town," remembers Carl Reiner, who interviewed more than sixty candidates for the role of Laura Petrie before he finally struck gold with a twenty-four-year-old charmer named Mary Tyler Moore.

ous reading of the role may actually have worked against her. As Carl Reiner would later assess it, "We knew she would be too strong for Dick."[31]

In the end, Reiner was finally forced to send Eileen Brennan back to New York empty-handed. It was a decision which made the producer feel worse than ever—now, not only had he rejected the most promising actress he'd yet seen for the role of Laura Petrie, but he'd spent five hundred dollars of his backer's money to do it! Reiner finally decided that a visit to Danny Thomas himself might be in order, if only to apprise his benefactor of the dead end that he'd run up against in casting their pilot. "I figured Danny had a right to know how we were spending his money," notes Reiner. And so, with the start date for their pilot hovering just days away, Sheldon Leonard and Carl Reiner resolved to break the news to Danny Thomas that they still hadn't found a leading lady for their show.

When they finally caught up with him, the pair found Danny Thomas reclining in a barber's chair in his dressing room, reading a script while the studio's barber applyed a quick touchup to the star's prematurely graying hair. "They were coloring in the part," remembers Reiner, who recalls being surprised that Thomas's hair was actually quite white where the makeup man had yet to apply his brush. After a few moments of small talk, Reiner finally summoned the courage to broach the subject that had brought him there. "Danny," he confessed, "we just spent five hundred dollars of your money to fly Eileen Brennan out here from New York, and it didn't work out. And now we still haven't found a girl to play the wife on the show."

"Oh," the star replied, unfazed. As the makeup man continued his diligent labors, Danny Thomas fell silent for a few very agonizing seconds, lost in thought. Finally, just as Leonard and Reiner were about to turn for the door, Thomas sat up with a start. "You know," he announced, "there *was* a girl who auditioned for me a couple months ago—she read for the daughter on my show. I didn't use her, and I don't remember her name. But, boy, did she read terrific!"

His curiosity piqued, Carl Reiner listened with growing interest as Sheldon Leonard joined Danny Thomas in trying to remember the name of the mystery actress who had just become a front-runner in the Laura Petrie sweepstakes.

"I just remembered something else," declared Thomas. "The girl we're looking for had three names!"

"Wait a minute," said Sheldon Leonard, suddenly recalling a clue of his own. "Wasn't she the one with the legs?"

"Yes!" exclaimed Danny Thomas, "that was her!" And then, noticing the slightly confused look on Carl Reiner's face, Thomas quickly explained this latest clue in their little mystery. A few months before she came in to read for them, Thomas recalled, the girl they were now seeking had created quite a stir in the role of Sam, the curvaceous receptionist whose legs were the most outstanding feature of the old *Richard Diamond, Private Detective* show. "So now we knew that she had great legs," says Carl Reiner. "And three names. But that was all we had to go by."

Apparently, it was enough. With the help of casting director Ruth Burch, it took the eager producers no more than a few hours to track down the elusive actress with the three names and great legs. And before the end of that afternoon, Carl Reiner had arranged an appointment to meet Mary Tyler Moore in his office the very next day.

"Mary was practically out of the business when we brought her into the show," notes Sheldon Leonard, intoning one of the more durable *Dick Van Dyke Show* legends. "She had given up on the idea of a career in acting. She was that disheartened about her career." It's a colorful story, and one that's been repeated more than once over the past thirty years. But despite the irresistible irony implicit in Leonard's depiction of the young Mary Tyler Moore as a struggling outsider in the days before she was hired to costar in *The Dick Van Dyke Show*, that interpretation doesn't really do justice to the actress who arrived at Carl Reiner's office for an eleventh-hour audition for the role of Laura Petrie in January of 1961. The fact

An early publicity still of Mary Tyler Moore, the former dancer who passed up college to become a star, and then achieved that goal before her twenty-fifth birthday.

is, Mary Tyler Moore came to that reading armed with an impressive array of TV credits and an almost intimidating desire to succeed in her chosen field. While it's undeniable that *The Dick Van Dyke Show* contributed immeasurably to making Mary Tyler Moore a household name, it's equally significant that the young actress had been determined to see her name up in lights long before she ever met Sheldon Leonard, Carl Reiner, or Dick Van Dyke.

"I gave up college to learn to become a star," Mary Tyler Moore told a reporter early in her career. "I don't just hope for it. I work for it. I expect it."[32] In fact, Mary Tyler Moore's preparation for stardom began a good many years before she made the decision to forgo college. Born in Brooklyn, New York, on December 29, 1936, Mary Tyler Moore had already enrolled in her first ballet class while she was still in grammar school. After her family moved to Los Angeles in the late forties, the would-be performer continued to pursue dance and drama lessons with equal passion throughout her elementary and high school years. That unwavering dedication began to pay off within days of her high school graduation, when Mary Tyler Moore landed her first professional engagement as a commercial mascot for the Hotpoint Appliance Company at the ripe old age of eighteen. Clad in pointy ears and a form-fitting leotard, the young dancer/actress portrayed Happy Hotpoint, the tiny sprite who danced her way through a series of Hotpoint commercials that aired on *The Ozzie and Harriet Show* throughout 1955.

By the end of that year, the actress—who had by then married her first husband, a salesman seven years her senior, named Richard Meeker—was forced to trade Happy Hotpoint's ears and leotard for a maternity wardrobe after she discovered she was pregnant with Richard, Jr., who was born in July of 1956. The actress devoted the next two years to motherhood, but by 1958, she was back on television, paying her dues as a dancer in the chorus lines of a half-dozen variety shows of the era. In early 1959, Mary Tyler Moore landed her first significant network role as Sam, the secretary on David Janssen's series, *Richard Diamond, Private Detective*. Unfortunately, the exposure that Mary Tyler Moore received on the *Richard Diamond* series was not exactly what the ambitious young performer had in mind. For it was one of the show's playful conceits that viewers never actually saw Sam—only her legs were ever shown on camera! And though Mary Tyler Moore's shapely gams certainly drew considerable attention to the series, the actress herself received very little notice in the uncredited role. To make matters worse, she was hardly well paid for her efforts. "I was getting scale," the actress would later recall, "Eighty dollars a week."[33]

Mary Tyler Moore finally walked away from the unrewarding role after her thirteen-week contract expired, though not before she went public with her true identity—a canny move that was calculated to milk as much publicity as possible from the otherwise thankless assignment. It was a brilliant ploy. Newspaper and magazine editors loved the idea that they now had a face to go with the most famous legs on television, and they happily obliged the actress with a small gusher of favorable press coverage, including a particularly eye-catching photo layout in the pages of *TV Guide*. In the wake of this publicity blitz, Mary Tyler Moore soon found that casting agents all over town were clamoring for her services. "Other shows seemed to want to use the girl who played Sam,"[34] the actress would later observe. In the two years that fell between her departure from *Richard Diamond* in 1959 and the start of rehearsals for the Van Dyke show pilot in early 1961, Mary Tyler Moore logged a bounty of guest-starring roles on a wide variety of weekly TV shows, including episodes of *The Millionaire, Bourbon Street Beat, Surfside Six, The Deputy, 77 Sunset Strip, Bachelor Father, Thriller*, and *Hawaiian Eye*, to name just a few.

But Mary Tyler Moore's most significant engagement in the months before she was signed to the cast of *The Dick Van Dyke Show* may well have been her audition for *The Danny Thomas Show* in the summer of 1959. She'd been called in to read for the part of Danny's daughter, Terry, a role that was originally played by Sherry Jackson, who had departed the series a few months earlier. Although Mary Tyler Moore would eventually lose the part to Penney Parker, Danny Thomas was so impressed by the actress's audition that he finally called her back three times before he told her that she'd lost the part—quite literally—by a nose. "She had the wrong nose," as Thomas would later explain it to Carl Reiner. "She had a cute little turned-up nose."[35] But as much as he admired her talent, Thomas was convinced that Mary Tyler Moore's button nose was enough to disqualify her from playing his daughter, given the size of his own prominent snoot. "Honey," Thomas reportedly told her, "people just won't be able to believe you could belong to me."[36]

According to an account of that fateful audition that later appeared in the pages of *TV Guide*, when she was informed of Danny Thomas's decision, Mary Tyler Moore offered, only half jokingly, to have her nose surgically altered to match the star's own. "I'll have it fixed," she supposedly volunteered, "to put a bump in it."[37] Although Thomas wisely decided not to take her up on that offer, he would not soon forget his meeting with the spirited actress. Nor would Carl Reiner, who finally met Mary Tyler Moore—at Danny Thomas's suggestion—during the second week of January 1961.

According to another of the show's oft-told legends, on the day of her audition for *The Dick Van Dyke Show*, Mary Tyler Moore very nearly decided to stay home. "She'd already been on three or four auditions that week, and they hadn't gone well," remembers Carl Reiner. "And we call, and she's decided not to go on another one. 'That's it!' she says. 'I'm outta this. I quit. I'm never going on another audition!' But then, at the last minute, she decided to go."

"I was so nervous when I went in to read for him," recalls Mary Tyler Moore, remembering that fateful meeting. According to the actress, she wasn't even aware that she would be reading for Carl Reiner himself until after she'd arrived for the audition. "I almost blew it," she says, "because of my awe of him as a performer. He was my hero—not only as a writer, but as a performer on *Your Show of Shows*." But if Mary Tyler Moore was the least bit overwrought during her audition, Carl Reiner insists that it certainly didn't come through in her reading, which he recalls as one of the most natural he'd ever witnessed. "I remember it as if it were yesterday," says Reiner. "She walked into the office, and she sat down. She read three lines. And they were a simple three lines—the first three lines of the

"I was so nervous
when I went in to
read for him," says Mary
Tyler Moore, recalling her
initial
audition for
Carl Reiner,
"I almost blew it."

opening of the pilot, 'The Sick Boy and the Sitter.'* That's all it took—three lines. And I heard the sound. And I thought, Oh, Jesus! She said hello like a real person!"

Carl Reiner insists that he leapt to his feet like a man possessed the instant he heard Mary Tyler Moore's perfectly natural, unassuming line readings. "I started walking toward her," he says. "And there was only the two of us in the room—so she got scared for a moment. Then I grabbed the top of her head, and I never let go." Speechless, the startled actress rose to her feet as Reiner led her toward the door. "'Come with me!' I told her. 'Just come with me.'"

Then, still grasping the frightened actress by the crown of her head, the delighted producer led her right out of his office, past a completely unfazed secretary, and across the narrow balcony that connected his office with Sheldon Leonard's private suite next door. And Carl Reiner didn't stop until he and his slightly confused charge arrived at Leonard's inner sanctum, where they found the executive producer seated calmly behind his desk. "I meant to let go, but I couldn't take my hand off the top of her head," confesses Reiner. "And when I got Mary to Sheldon's office I said, 'This is the girl, Sheldon. This is her! She said hello just like a real person!'"

The imperturbable executive producer glanced up from his paperwork, took a quick look at the dumbstruck actress, and shrugged his shoulders in assent. "Fine," he muttered, turning right back to his work.

"She was just right for what we wanted at the time," explains Sheldon Leonard, who insists that neither he nor Carl Reiner had the slightest qualms about hiring the largely unknown actress on little more than a shared gut instinct. "She looked like a nice, attractive Westchester housewife with good legs," says Leonard. "And she had good timing." It was only later, explains Leonard, that he and his partner came to recognize that their latest discovery was in fact an accomplished dancer, a gifted singer, and a trained actress of unerring comic instinct. "We discovered all that bit by bit," says Leonard. "But, when you find it, you exploit it."

And exploit it they did. Within a few days of her initial audition, Sheldon Leonard and Carl Reiner had signed Mary Tyler Moore to a five-year contract to star as *The Dick Van Dyke Show*'s Laura Petrie. And, according to Sheldon Leonard, owing largely to her relative obscurity, he was

---

*For the record, Laura's first three lines in the filmed pilot, spoken over the phone to her neighbor, Dottie, are: "Hello." "Why are you sending him home?" and, "Does Ellen have a temperature?"

able to secure Mary Tyler Moore's services at bargain basement rates. "Mary," boasts the former executive producer, "was signed up for nickels and dimes!"

Not that anyone heard any complaints from the actress. Even today, Mary Tyler Moore still recalls the joy she felt at the prospect of working with Carl Reiner on a weekly basis. "For me," the actress explains, "Carl was every man in a young girl's life. He was my mentor, my father confessor, my teacher. I just loved that man. And still do." And it didn't take long for the actress to inspire an equally passionate devotion in her mentor. "If I were a dirty old man," Reiner would later gush, "Mary Tyler Moore would be my girlfriend. But I'm not, so she's sort of my daughter. I'm just crazy about that girl."[38]

CHAPTER 8

Nervous Wrecks

"THE TOTAL COST OF *THE DICK VAN DYKE SHOW* PILOT WAS forty thousand dollars from start to finish," boasts Sheldon Leonard, with justifiable pride. And though Carl Reiner remembers a slightly higher figure—in his recollection, the total was closer to $47,000—at either amount the figure seems incredibly modest by today's standards, when that kind of cash barely covers a week's pretzels and petty cash on the average Hollywood set.

Most of the credit for the Van Dyke show's cost efficiency must go to executive producer Sheldon Leonard, whose genius for maximizing *The Dick Van Dyke Show*'s relatively limited resources began with the show's very first episode. "By that time I had already learned the technique of making cheap pilots," says Leonard, who had caused industry observers to sit up and take notice the year before, when he managed to sell *The Andy Griffith Show* to CBS without making a pilot film at all. Instead, the canny producer had contrived to introduce Andy Griffith's Sheriff Andy Taylor character—along with rest of Mayberry's more notable citizens—on an episode of *The Danny Thomas Show*. Then, using that Thomas show as a working sample of his proposed Griffith series, the producer was able to convince CBS and General Foods to add *The Andy Griffith Show* to the network's fall 1960 schedule—all without having invested a cent to make an actual pilot episode of the series. Of course, it didn't escape the notice of Leonard's peers that in creating this "backdoor pilot" for the Griffith show, the producer had also pioneered what would come to be known as the television spin-off, a cheap and highly effective means of generating prime-time programming that is, for better or worse, still quite popular among TV programmers and producers to this day.

But despite the success he'd experienced in selling the Griffith Show without a pilot in 1960, Leonard quickly recognized that he would have to develop an entirely different strategy when it came time to pitch the Van Dyke show to potential networks and sponsors a season later. Owing to a complex list of legal and creative restrictions, Leonard was forced to rule out the possibility of simply introducing the Van Dyke show's cast and characters on an episode of *The Danny Thomas Show*. Instead, he did the next best thing when he arranged to shoot his Van Dyke pilot on *The Danny Thomas Show*'s stage during a temporary layoff in that show's weekly production schedule—an ingenious scheme that allowed the thrifty producer access to the Thomas show's fully staffed and equipped studio, without having to spend a dime on the additional overhead charges and costly start-up expenses that are usually incurred when shooting a pilot. And because his above-the-line talent expenses on *The Dick Van Dyke Show* were relatively modest, Sheldon Leonard was actually able to bring in the show's pilot episode for even less money that he spent on the average episode of *The Danny Thomas Show*. All of which must have come as good news to Danny Thomas himself, whose financial commitment to *The Dick Van Dyke Show* would extend well beyond the show's pilot episode.

Under the terms of the financial arrangement he'd worked out with Sheldon Leonard, Danny Thomas agreed to pick up the show's production tab per episode even after the Van Dyke show went to series, which was no small proposition. With estimated expenses of around $40,000 per episode, the investment required to capitalize the show's first season alone was projected to fall somewhere between 1.25 and 1.5 million dollars.*

Naturally, that kind of support didn't come cheap. As Sheldon Leonard observes, "You have to give up something for that kind of financing." In the case of *The Dick Van Dyke Show*, what the producer had to give up was nothing less than a substantial ownership stake in the series. In exchange for fronting the show's initial start-up budget and production

---

*Of course, that 1.5-million-dollar figure actually looks downright paltry when viewed from the perspective of today's TV marketplace, where the cost to film a single episode of a filmed situation comedy can easily approach or even exceed that amount. In fact, when NBC's long-running *Cheers* left the air after eleven years in 1993, its production costs were said to exceed $2 million per episode, an amount approximately equivalent to what it cost Danny Thomas, in 1961 dollars, to finance the first *forty* half hours of *The Dick Van Dyke Show*!

Carl Reiner and Sheldon Leonard flank Danny Thomas, the
deep-pocketed star who agreed to foot the bill for
The Dick Van Dyke Show pilot in exchange for a hefty
ownership stake in the series.

costs, it was agreed that Danny Thomas would be entitled to a sizable-share of the enormous profits the show stood to earn in syndicated reruns. For Danny Thomas, the arrangement turned out to be a very good investment, indeed. In fact, after more than three decades, the *The Dick Van Dyke Show* continues to generate significant revenues for the late star's heirs, even as it continues to enrich the bank accounts of the surviving members of the show's original partnership to this day.

The *Dick Van Dyke Show* pilot finally went into production on stage 5 of the Desilu Cahuenga Studios during the week of January 16-20, 1961, a week that would prove to be a relatively quiet one for the normally bustling lot. With *The Danny Thomas Show* on hiatus, only four shows—including the Van Dyke pilot—were in production on the facility's nine soundstages during that week. On stages 1 and 2, Andy Griffith and his cast were hard at work on the twenty-third episode of *The Andy Griffith Show*, an episode titled "Andy and Opie, Housekeepers." According to the studio's official production roster for that week, the other two shows in production on the lot that week were a pair of now long-forgotten situation comedies: *One Happy Family*, a domestic comedy that starred Dick Sargent and Jody Warner as newlyweds, and *Angel*, another domestic situation comedy, this one starring Marshall Thompson and Annie Farge. Curiously, that same Desilu studio production manifest lists *The Dick Van Dyke Show* pilot, somewhat cryptically, as "Carl Reiner Show; #800, All in a Day's Work—Pilot."

According to Dick Van Dyke, the week he shot his show's pilot also happened to fall at the very height of the Broadway theater season, a fact that was not lost on the producers of *Bye Bye Birdie*, who were naturally not anxious to see their leading man vanish for a week to film a TV pilot

NO.	SHOW	NO. & TITLE	UNIT	PROD.MGR. & ASST.DIR.	LOCATION
		PRODUCTION SCHEDULE FOR WEEK OF JAN. 16 Thru JAN. 21, 1961		PAGE 2	
DESILU CAHUENGA					
6203	ANDY GRIFFITH SHOW	#23 ANDY & OPIE HOUSEKEEPERS #24 THE NEW DOCTOR		MYERS-- BILSON	STAGE 1-2 1/16,17,18 STAGE 1-2 Reh. 1/19,20
6230	DANNY THOMAS SHOW	LAYOFF (1/16 thru 1/20/61)		MYERS-- SANDRICH	LAYOFF
6230	CARL REINER SHOW	#800 ALL IN A DAYS WORK-Pilot		MYERS-- SANDRICH	STAGE 5 Prepare 1/16 STAGE 5 Reh. 1/17,18 (AUD.PREV.) Bl. 1/19 Sh. 1/20
6275	ANGEL	#26 FRENCH LESSON #27 PHONE FUN		ALLWORTH	STAGE 4 Reh. 1/16 Bl. 1/17, Sh. 1/18 STAGE 4 Prep. 1/19 STAGE 4 Reh. 1/20
6269	ONE HAPPY FAMILY	#8 CHARLIE, EXECUTIVE AT LARGE #9 RAINY AFTERNOON		J.McEVEETY	STAGE 3 Bl. 1/16, Sh. 1/17 STAGE 3 Prep. 1/18 STAGE 3 Reh. 1/19,20
DESILU CULVER					
6118	THE UNTOUCHABLES	#49 THE LILY DALLAS STORY #47 THE NICK MOSES STORY (Pickup on #47) #50 MAN UNDER GLASS		STUART-- PETSCHNIKOFF STUART-- V.McEVEETY	STAGE 4,2,3 1/16 STAGE 2,3(PROCESS)&4OA 1/17 STAGE 3,4 1/16 STAGE 3 (6118-49) & CULVER LOT (6118-47) 1/19 STAGE 3,4,RAMP ? 1/20
6130	GUESTWARD HO	#21 BILL, THE CANDIDATE #23 HAWKEYE, THE MOTHER (Reh. & Rehʼl only)½8 #22 BABS, THE GUEST (Reh.1/17,20)		SCHILZ	4OA COMPOUND, GUEST, RANCH & STAGE 11 1/16 STAGE 11 1/17 STAGE 11 Road & Rch. 1/18 STAGE 11 Reh. 1/19 STAGE 11,4OA GUEST, RANCH Reh. 1/20
6233	THE REAL MC COYS	#129 THE HORSE EXPERT #130 (TO BE DETERMINED)		DONAHOE-- EVANS	4OA McCOY FARM 1/16 4OA W.ST.BARN 1/17 STAGE 14 1/18 STAGE 14 Rch. 1/19 4OA MC COY FARM 1/20
6267	MIAMI UNDERCOVER	#400 AUTO MOTIVE ROOM 9		POLVER-- WHELAN JIM PAISLEY	CULVER CITY HIGHWAY & STS.1/19 (SEE GOWER SCHEDULE)

The pilot for what would soon be christened *The Dick Van Dyke Show* was identified only as "Carl Reiner pilot: All in a Day's Work" in the original Desilu Studios production roster for the week ending January 21, 1961.

Although future star Dick Van Dyke seems to exude self-confidence in this publicity still taken shortly after his arrival in California in 1961, the star later confessed that he'd been a nervous wreck the week he filmed his show's pilot episode.

in California. Under the circumstances, Van Dyke was released from his *Birdie* contract with the strict proviso that he take off *one* week and *one* week only—the star was to be back on stage at the Martin Beck for the following Tuesday night's performance. And so, for a single week in January of 1961, it was arranged that understudy Charles Nelson Reilly would step into Dick Van Dyke's shoes in the cast of *Bye Bye Birdie*, while the musical's nominal star traveled 3,000 miles west for what he would later come to regard as the five scariest days of his entire career.

"I was a nervous wreck," insists Dick Van Dyke, recalling his general state of mind during rehearsals for the Van Dyke show pilot. "I think I lost five pounds that week." According to Carl Reiner, Van Dyke's weight loss wasn't the only malady to plague him during that fretful week. "He developed a cold sore," recalls Reiner. "If you look at the pilot, you can see that Dick's got a cold sore on his lip." It's a memory that still makes the star wince. "I remember that they had to use a lot of makeup on me," says Van Dyke, "because I had about four fever blisters that had popped up just from pure nerves."

As Dick Van Dyke recalls it, he got his biggest shock when he finally met the youthful actress that Carl Reiner had cast to play his wife. "She was still in her early twenties, and I was thirty-five!" notes the actor, who remembers leaving the show's first rehearsal convinced that his producer had made a terrible casting blunder. In Van Dyke's opinion, there was simply no way that audiences were going to accept the mere sprig of a girl like Mary Tyler Moore as the wife of a man who was—in reality—eleven years her senior. "I just thought, 'God Almighty! This is never going to work,'" says Van Dyke. And, at the first opportunity, the star took his producer aside and told him so.

"Dick kept saying, 'Mary's too young for me!'" recalls Carl Reiner, who insisted that the show's audience would hardly notice the disparity in their ages. After all, as Reiner explained to his leading man, "No one ever says Cary Grant is too old for his costars."

"Yeah," Van Dyke retorted, still unconvinced, "but *I'm* not Cary Grant!"

Despite his leading man's initial—and short-lived—skepticism, Carl Reiner became convinced that he'd made the right choice in casting Mary Tyler Moore as soon as he saw the sparks that she and Dick Van Dyke generated on stage. It was a rare example of pure chemistry between two actors, and it was a quality that the producer jokingly encouraged at every opportunity. "Carl told us, 'I want you both to go away and spend the weekend together,'" recalls Dick Van Dyke, who hastens to add, "Which we didn't! But he was making a point—that if you don't really like each other, no amount of good acting or writing is gonna make people believe you do."

Ironically, even as Reiner and his actors began to explore the rapport that would provide the foundation for Rob and Laura's on-screen attachment, the seeds of an offstage romance were planted when Sheldon Leonard introduced Mary Tyler Moore to a handsome young advertising executive named Grant Tinker after one of the show's first run-throughs. Although Tinker wouldn't actually ask Mary Tyler Moore out on a date until after the actress had separated from her first husband a few months later, at least one eyewitness to the couple's protracted courtship suggests that the pair's romantic paths were on a collision course well before they ever started dating.

According to an anecdote that Ron Jacobs delights in retelling, he got his first hint that Mary Tyler Moore and her future husband were fated to come together one evening early in the show's run, after Grant Tinker joined the entire Van Dyke company for an informal postshow dinner at a small restaurant near the studio. As the festivities drew to a close, recalls the former associate producer, the party moved out to the sidewalk in front of the restaurant, where most of the cast milled about while they waited for the parking attendants to retrieve their cars. Finally, the valet drove up in Mary Tyler Moore's car. "Mary said goodbye and jumped in her car," recounts Jacobs. Then Grant Tinker's car arrived, and he waved and drove off in the same direction the actress had taken a few seconds earlier. That was just before they heard the crash.

Jacobs and the rest of the company were still standing at the curb when they heard the thud of metal hitting metal, a sound that seemed to emanate from down the street. "We all laughed," notes Jacobs, "and said, 'Ha! Grant must've run into Mary!'" Jacobs insists that he was only joking at the time, which is why he was so surprised when he finally poked his head out into traffic and saw that his jest had not been far from the mark. "Mary had stopped suddenly," says Jacobs, "and Grant plowed right into the back of her car!"

Fender-benders notwithstanding, Grant Tinker maintains that he and his wife-to-be didn't finally get together until much later that year, after the actress traveled to New York on a promotional tour for the show—which would have put the date somewhere in the early part of October 1961. The morning after the couple's first date, the New York columnists dutifully reported that the pair had taken in the Broadway show *Mary, Mary* before they wound up the evening dancing at New York's then trendy Peppermint Lounge. But though it was only the couple's first date, it would certainly not be their last. As Mary Tyler Moore would later confess in the pages of *TV Guide*, "I woke up the next morning and knew I was in love."[39]

As a creative executive at an ad agency with strong ties to Sheldon Leonard, Tinker was a frequent visitor to the Van Dyke set even before his friendship with the show's female star began to blossom during the latter part of the show's first season. Even so, as more than one observer would note with bemused curiosity, the frequency of the ad man's visits seemed to increase significantly in the months that followed Mary Tyler Moore's trip to New York in the autumn of that year.

"Grant would come and pick Mary up after rehearsals during the day," notes Van Dyke show costumer Harald Johnson, who insists that despite such occasional giveaways, the couple maintained a remarkably low profile throughout the early days of their courtship. In fact, so discreet were Tinker and Mary Tyler Moore that when the pair finally wed on June 1, 1962, more than a few of her co-workers expressed surprise on hearing that the couple had paired up in the first place. Even so, the union was greeted by near unanimous enthusiasm by their friends on the set, most of whom agreed that the two were an ideal match.

"Everyone liked Grant when they met him," Harald Johnson remembers. "He had a lot of class and a sophisticated look about him." Adds actor Bill Idelson, who played Herman Glimsher on the show, "Grant was like the perfect goy—a white bread goy from beginning to end, and perfect for Mary Tyler Moore. The ultimate shiksa and the ultimate goy. They made a perfect pair."

BY the middle of January 1961, with their cast poised to begin rehearsals for the pilot episode of their brand-new series, Sheldon Leonard and Carl Reiner decided that the time had arrived to settle on a permanent title for the show. The producers had discarded the show's first working title, *The Full House*, almost as soon as they'd come up with it the previous spring. In the intervening months they'd tried at least a half-dozen different monikers on for size, though none of them seemed to last more than a few days, or, in some cases, hours. *Double Trouble*, a title that was intended to reflect the show's twin-arena setting, was an early favorite, though it would finally be rejected as too obscure; *All in a Day's Work* was also popular,

until the producers decided that it was too prosaic a title for a situation comedy. But finally, with the pilot's start date looming and the show still officially without a title, Reiner and his creative partners had to admit they were stymied. "We just couldn't come up with a name," recalls Dick Van Dyke.

Though Dick Van Dyke and Mary Tyler Moore eventually shared an on-screen chemistry unmatched in television, Van Dyke was initially skeptical that audiences would accept the youthful actress in the role of his wife. "She was still in her early twenties and I was thirty-five" he says, "I just thought, God almighty, this is never going to work!"

Finally, it was Carl Reiner who broke the deadlock by suggesting that the new series be called *The Dick Van Dyke Show*, following the pattern already established by the Andy Griffith and Danny Thomas shows, both of which had been self-titled to capitalize on the name value of their respective stars. Of course, the only problem with titling their new series to capitalize on Dick Van Dyke's star power was that he didn't really have any. As Dick Van Dyke himself was gracious enough to insist as soon as he heard his producer's inspiration for the show's title, his was not exactly a household name in the homes of America in 1961. "At that time," Van Dyke admits, "nobody knew who I was!"

No matter—as far as Carl Reiner was concerned, his leading man's obscurity was about to become a thing of the past anyway. "In my mind, Dick Van Dyke *was* a star," recalls the producer. "And I said, 'If the rest of the world doesn't know it yet, let's tell them.'"

"Dick was a relative unknown at the time," concedes Sheldon Leonard, who maintains that he too viewed Dick Van Dyke's relative anonymity as a transitory proposition. "I thought that part of our job," says Leonard, "to make the show popular, was to make Dick popular." And so, in a bit of circular logic that speaks to the underlying optimism of its two producers, the show was named after its star, at least partially in an effort to make him famous enough to have a situation comedy named after him.

Although *The Dick Van Dyke Show* was not officially christened until quite late in its gestation, the series had already found its indelible signature in the snappy theme song that had been composed for the series by Earle Hagen, the resident musical genius on the Desilu Cahuenga lot. As Sheldon Leonard's house composer, the former big band trombonist had long been responsible for scoring, orchestrating, and often conducting most of the music that found its way into the shows in the producer's ever-expanding stable. But Hagen's most lasting claim to fame will almost certainly rest on the distinguished catalog of TV themes he created for some of the most enduring shows of his era, including the melodies that kicked off each episode of *The Andy Griffith Show*, *That Girl*, *I Spy*, *The Danny Thomas Show*, and *Gomer Pyle, USMC*, to name just a few of this prolific composer's better-known works.

But, in Carl Reiner's opinion, Hagen's masterpiece was the unforgettable tune the composer crafted to serve as *The Dick Van Dyke Show*'s theme song. "That was a wonderful theme he wrote for our show," acknowledges Reiner, who still recalls the thrill he felt when Hagen arrived at his office with a demo tape of the freshly composed tune. "He played it," recalls Reiner, "and as soon as I heard, 'Tah-dah da-da-da-da-da-da,' I said, 'That's it! That's Dick!' It sounded like him!"

Today, after being heard in countless repetitions on *Dick Van Dyke Show* reruns that continue to play every day in virtually every corner of the globe, the show's theme surely must rank as one of the most instantly identifiable melodies on the planet. And yet, according to its composer, the durable theme song was hardly composed with posterity in mind. In fact, notes Hagen, he wrote the Van Dyke theme quite quickly—after only a cursory reading of Carl Reiner's pilot script—and then arranged and recorded the song a few days later in a single take. "You hear the orchestra in your head," the composer explains, struggling for words to define a creative act that he has always perceived as being almost purely instinctual. "And then you put it down on paper. For the Van Dyke song I was just trying to find something in that particular show that was contemporaneous for the time."

Hagen finally recorded the song one afternoon on a whim, he says, after

he realized he had a little time left on an orchestral session that he'd called to record incidental music for a *Danny Thomas Show* episode. With the musicians already in place, the composer decided he might as well use the remaining time productively, and so, a few minutes later, the composer produced and distributed copies of his latest composition to the waiting band members. "I had already

Though Dick Van Dyke was hardly a household name when the actor won the part of Rob Petrie, the show's producers were so determined to make him a star that they named their show after him anyway.

made the arrangement of the Dick Van Dyke theme," recalls Hagen, "so, when that session was over, I just ran it down and recorded it."

As die-hard fans of the series are almost certainly aware, a slightly less familiar arrangement of Hagen's well-known Dick Van Dyke theme song was played under the opening credits of the show's first fourteen episodes. This alternate version of the show's familiar theme—which is easily distinguished by its brassier fanfare arrangement and a prominent, if slightly incongruous, conga line backbeat—would be retired in the middle of the show's first year, one of the first casualties in the midyear facelift that would accompany the show's midseason move to Wednesday nights. It was only then that the more familiar version of the show's theme—which until that time had been used as the show's closing theme, appearing exclusively under the end credits on the show's first fourteen installments—was moved to the top of the show, where it would remain firmly in place for each of the show's final 144 episodes.

Curiously, despite its prominent placement at the start of each of the show's first fourteen episodes—where it can still be heard today after more than thirty years of reruns—the song's composer claims no memory of having written, recorded, or conducted this variant arrangement of the show's signature tune. In fact, when Hagen heard this alternate version of the Van Dyke show theme not long ago for the first time in many years, he expressed his disdain for the arrangement in no uncertain terms. "I must've made it," he admits, "but I'll be damned if I remember doing it. And, as a matter of fact, it shocks me to hear bongos on there, because I hate them!"

CHAPTER 9
Casting Off Pearls

AT A FEW MINUTES PAST 10:00 A.M. ON THE MORNING OF January 16, 1961, Carl Reiner and Sheldon Leonard assembled their newly hired acting company around a pair of folding tables on an otherwise vacant stage on the Desilu Cahuenga lot and called to order the first official rehearsal for the pilot episode of *The Dick Van Dyke Show*. Because the studio's carpentry crew was still hard at work constructing the show's standing sets on the lot's soundstage 5, the company would be forced to spend their first day of rehearsal on a different stage than the one on which they intended to film their pilot. Of course, where they met for their initial rehearsal didn't really matter, since the company would remain seated throughout most of that first day, which was to be devoted to a painstaking read-through of the script of the episode that had been chosen as the series' maiden effort, "The Sick Boy and the Sitter."

Once his cast was seated, Carl Reiner picked up his copy of the script and, clearly savoring the moment, announced, "Page one!" Then, inaugurating a ritual that would be repeated at the first reading of each of the following 157 episodes, the company opened their scripts to the first page and began reading aloud. Over the next two or three hours, the actors and their producers would scrutinize every line in the script, laughing out loud at all the jokes that worked, and tossing out all the ones that didn't. Whenever they ran into a major stumbling block, they would halt their reading until the problem was fixed. And once they'd stopped, it was fully understood that the floor was open to anyone at the table who wanted to kibbitz, complain, or simply offer helpful suggestions on how the show might be made better.

And from the very start, it was obvious that no one in the Van Dyke company would be shy about tendering their suggestions. One proposal that was adopted without debate at that very first reading was Dick Van Dyke's suggestion that they alter the pronunciation of his character's name, which Carl Reiner had pronounced PEE-tree when he played the role in the *Head of the Family* pilot. "Dick asked if it wouldn't be PEH-tree," says Reiner. "And I said, 'Sure!'"

Coincidentally, the name of Rob Petrie's employer would also be changed after it, too, came under scrutiny during that same script conference. In Reiner's *Head of the Family* pilot, Rob's boss had been named Alan Sturdy—an appellation that the writer hastened to revise after Morey Amsterdam identified a peculiar tendency in the pronunciation of the name as written. "I told Carl that if you said 'Alan Sturdy' fast," explains Amsterdam, "it sounded like you were saying 'Alan's dirty!'" The producer conceded the point immediately and promptly rechristened the character Alan Brady—a name that Amsterdam insists was borrowed from a hapless delivery boy who happened to pass through the rehearsal hall in the midst of the debate. "We were trying to come up with a name when this guy walks in delivering coffee," Amsterdam says. "Carl says to him, 'Excuse me, what's your last name?' The guy says, 'Brady.' And Carl says, 'That's perfect. We'll call our guy Alan Brady.'"

The script that Carl Reiner and Sheldon Leonard picked to launch their new series, "The Sick Boy and the Sitter," was not an arbitrary choice, but was carefully selected from among the thirteen scripts that Reiner had written more than two years earlier during his summer on Fire Island. Nor was the script chosen because it was the best of the bunch. Far from it. In the episode's storyline, Rob convinces Laura to attend a dinner party at Alan Brady's penthouse, despite the fact that her maternal instincts seem to be telling her to stay home and tend to their ailing six-year-old son, who has come down with a slight fever. It was not a terribly compelling premise, as Carl Reiner himself is the first to concede. "It wasn't our strongest one," he sighs.

But while the episode might've lacked the comic bite that would invigorate many of the writer's later efforts, Carl Reiner insists that his script for "The Sick Boy and the Sitter" possessed a quality that was vital for the inaugural episode of a brand-new series—it had heart. In his opinion, the domestic conflict of a husband who's torn between twin loyalties to his boss and his six-year-old son offered a far more compelling introduction to the show and its characters than the slapstick situations that propelled many of his more comical efforts. "We picked *that* show," notes Reiner, "because it was the one that best explained the characters."

Sheldon Leonard was equally keen to inaugurate the series with "The Sick Boy and the Sitter," though for somewhat different reasons. While Leonard undoubtedly appreciated the gentle domestic interplay that Reiner felt did so much to define the show's characters and setting, the executive producer was even more excited by the inherent potential of the party sequence that dominates the episode's second act, where Buddy, Sally, and Rob find themselves drafted into performing an impromptu variety show for the guests at Alan Brady's penthouse. In Leonard's view, the sequence provided nothing less than a perfect showcase for the talented trio of Amsterdam, Van Dyke, and Rose Marie, each of whom could be reasonably expected to shine in the self-contained musical variety block that the producer was convinced would anchor the pilot with at least one ten-minute sequence of sure-fire, proven entertainment.

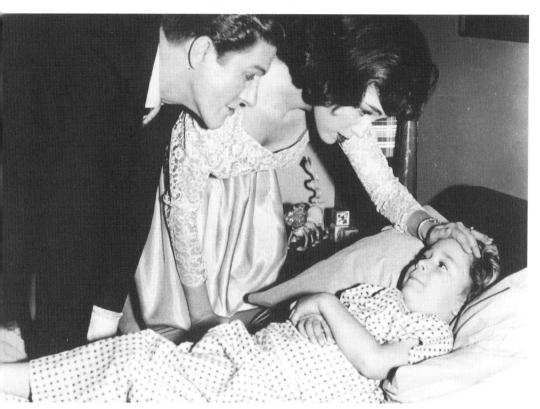

Dick Van Dyke and Mary Tyler Moore comfort Larry Mathews in "The Sick Boy and the Sitter," a script that Carl Reiner chose to film as his show's pilot episode because it was the one that best explained the characters.

"I thought it was brilliant that they came up with that party scene," says Dick Van Dyke, who was only too happy to borrow from his own personal repertoire of specialty material to ensure the success of the sequence. In this case, Van Dyke's contribution was a short pantomime in which he plays a drunk husband trying to sneak into the house after a bender. It was, of course, very similar to the piece that the star had performed to such acclaim in *The Girls Against the Boys*, the 1958 revue that brought him to Sheldon Leonard's attention in the first place. Not surprisingly, Van Dyke's cheerful plundering of his own comic backlog was an act of creative larceny that was undertaken with Sheldon Leonard's unquestioned endorsement. "Dick's personal repertoire of bits and shtick were an asset," admits the executive producer, "and we simply exploited them until we'd used them up."

Once his cast concluded their first table reading of his pilot script, Carl Reiner grabbed his notes from the session and beat a hasty retreat to his office on the second floor of the studio's Building A, where the writer labored well into the night to remove all the bugs that had suddenly become evident during the script's first read-through. The next morning, after the carpenters had finally finished their own labors on stage 5, director Sheldon Leonard and the cast moved down to the set, where they would spend most of their second rehearsal day putting Reiner's newly revised script on its feet. By the end of day three, Leonard and the cast had finished working out the show's preliminary camera blocking, and the company was ready to face their first moment of truth: the first-ever run-through of the entire show, from start to finish.

Although this initial run-through was supposed to be no more than a technical exercise—a dry run performed mainly for the benefit of the show's camera, lighting, and technical crews—associate producer Ron Jacobs recalls that the cast, who could hardly be expected to rein themselves in, would invariably play the first run-though with all the stops out. "They were trying to test the material out," says Jacobs.

But, as Jacobs admits, trying to get a rise out of a room full of distracted stagehands, dolly grips, and other jaded Hollywood professionals could be a daunting prospect. "They were a tough crowd," acknowledges Jacobs. "These guys had seen it all." And yet, in one of their earliest professional triumphs, Dick Van Dyke and his fellow players transformed every focus puller, key grip, and gaffer in that studio into a fan well before the end of their first Wednesday afternoon run-through. "The crew was supposed to be watching it very technically," notes Jacobs, "but they ended up laughing. A lot. They really enjoyed themselves."

"I never will forget watching Dick Van Dyke," concurs camera coordinator Jim Niver, who was among those present at that first Van Dyke show run-through. "I remember the bit where Dick flows down off that chair," he recalls, referring to the moment in the comedian's tour de force drunk act where his inebriated character seems to slide off of his chair and into oblivion. "I'd never seen anyone do anything like that," adds Niver. "He was like a human waterfall." But of all those on the set that day, few would be more impressed by the star's pantomimic artistry than Carl Reiner himself. "Dick's ability to move amazed me," notes the producer. "He could do things that nobody in the world could've done like him. He had the kind of body that would not quit."

On the evening of Thursday, January 19, 1961—a scant twenty-four hours before *The Dick Van Dyke Show* pilot was scheduled to go before the cameras—the company presented a final onstage dress rehearsal for an invited audience of friends, family, and other assorted well-wishers who had wandered over from some of the other stages on the lot. Also included in the crowd that night was a small clutch of agents from the Morris office, who had arrived to check on the status of a show whose progress many of them had already been following for more than two years. And if the show's cast and producers had been gratified by the response they'd earned at the Wednesday afternoon run-through, they were positively flabbergasted by the uproarious laughter and applause that greeted their first run-through before a live studio audience, most of whom seemed genuinely taken with the evening's performance.

Most. But not all.

According to Sheldon Leonard, one particular attendee at the Van Dyke show's final dress rehearsal held an opinion of the show that was markedly at odds with the majority of the crowd—an opinion he wasted little time in sharing with the executive producer. "Some people from the William Morris Agency came to see the final dress rehearsal," Leonard explains. "And one of the men from the agency—who will be nameless, but who considered himself the guardian of my career—was greatly disturbed."

"That was fun," Leonard recalls the agent telling him a few minutes after the actors had taken their final bows. "And it's a very nice show. But—" At that point, says Leonard, the agent suddenly lowered his voice to a whisper before continuing in an almost conspiratorial tone. "You've got to back out of this," he insisted. "I cannot allow you to do this show."

"What?" Leonard responded.

"It's a loser," Leonartd remembers the agent explaining. "A sure loser." And then, according to Leonard, the agent proceeded to identify a few of

Dick Van Dyke's amazing physical capabilities were a source of constant amazement on the set. As one crew member describes it, "He was like a human waterfall."

what he imagined to be the show's most insurmountable stumbling blocks. "You've got material that's already failed once," he explained. "A star who's made a number of pilots before—none of which have sold. And," the agent concluded, "you've got Morey Amsterdam and Rose Marie—two stars from radio! This show cannot make it. And I cannot let you do it."

In Leonard's recollection, his conviction was hardly shaken by the agent's well-meaning advice. "I told him to sit down and take a Valium," recalls Leonard. "He was only trying to protect my career. But I rejected his excellent advice nonetheless. You gotta respect your own opinion."

The pilot episode of *The Dick Van Dyke Show* that was filmed the following evening, on Friday, January 20, 1961, was a triumph by any measure. Under the painstaking supervision of producers Leonard and Reiner, the show's writing, direction, and production values were conspicuously assured. But an equally noteworthy factor in the pilot's success—and, significantly, the key element that had been missing in Reiner's first pass at the material in *Head of the Family*—was the tangible sense of ensemble that the producers had somehow managed to instill in their diverse company of players after a scant five days of rehearsal. In Dick Van Dyke's view, the company's ineffable chemistry was the result of chance—pure and simple. "It was just luck in casting that it worked that well," observes the star. "It was pure serendipity. From the very beginning, the chemistry between us all was so good. Everyone in that cast had the right rhythm and the right character from the very first day."

And nowhere was the show's fabled chemistry in greater evidence than in Van Dyke and Mary Tyler Moore's depiction of Rob and Laura Petrie, who emerge as a completely convincing married couple from their very first few minutes on-screen. The extended sequence in the show's pilot episode where Rob bargains to convince Laura to attend a dinner party that she'd just as soon skip offers a prime example of the acting team's camaraderie at work. Where the typical situation comedy might show us a bickering couple locked in pitched battle over a forgotten anniversary or a burnt pot roast, Reiner and his actors offer a knowing depiction of real-life marital compromise that is instantly familiar—and thus terribly funny—to anyone who has ever conducted petty negotiations with a loved one of his or her own. "I'll tell you what I'll do for you if you come with me," Rob barters. "I'll go to *two* decorator shows and *three* PTA meetings."

"*Five* PTA meetings," Laura counters.

"You'll go?" asks Rob, his mood brightened by the apparent ease of his unexpected victory.

"Well, all right," Laura replies. "But," she adds, raising the stakes with one final emotional gambit, "I refuse to enjoy myself!"

It's a funny exchange—and a remarkably assured piece of comic writing. For in this deceptively simple patch of dialogue, the writer succeeds in moving his storyline forward, even as he offers a surprisingly perceptive glimpse at the subtle emotional stakes that come into play in any modern marriage. If nothing else, Reiner's take on Rob and Laura's marital debate offered a view of domestic discord that served as the perfect antidote to the slapstick hijinks that had come to define married life on prime-time television up until then. And that was no accident. Carl Reiner has long maintained that he created Rob and Laura Petrie at least partially as a response to the retrograde approach to domestic reality he'd observed on *I Love Lucy* and at least a dozen other situation comedies from the era that immediately preceded his own series. "The battle of the sexes was the big plot device," he explains. "It's the easiest one to write—you scream at me, I'll scream at you. And a lot of people identified with that. More people lived like that than lived like Rob and Laura."

As for the immensely popular *I Love Lucy*, Carl Reiner confesses that the brand of sexual politics routinely practiced by Lucy and Ricky Ricardo usually left him cold. "I didn't like their premise," the writer says. "They were hilarious—no doubt about it—but it was always Lucy fooling Ricky. Lucy and Desi made you wonder why they stayed together. You'd say, 'How could they love each other? He never caters to her, he always calls her a dope!'" And so, when it came time to create his own series, Carl Reiner was determined to shoot for a different sort of truth— one that was firmly rooted in a reality that he knew.

"My show was based on a mutually respecting husband and wife," says Reiner. "It was two against the world. And even when it was one-against-one, it was the kind of one-against-one you have in a family that loves each other." And, as the writer freely admits, he discovered the perfect model for Rob and Laura's emotional truth in his own extremely durable marriage. "I was trying to pattern it off a life that I knew."

It's also noteworthy, in light of Rob and Laura's obvious affection for each other, that Carl Reiner only rarely felt compelled to cause his on-screen couple to utter the words "I love you"—if only, he says, because he simply didn't feel it was necessary. "I always objected to that kind of schmaltziness," asserts Reiner, who says that he saw little point in trying to telegraph his leading couple's devotion in mere words, especially when there were so many more interesting ways to communicate their obvious attraction to one another.

And, as no one who's watched more than a few episodes of *The Dick Van Dyke Show* is likely to debate, it was evident from the start that Rob and Laura's feelings for each other were far from strictly spiritual. That there was a strong physical aspect to the couple's relationship is a fact that Sheldon Leonard readily acknowledges. "This was the first show to star an attractive young couple," he explains. "And a certain element of romance was inherent in these two attractive young people." And though it was rarely addressed directly in the show's scripts, Leonard admits that the series probably owed much of its appeal to the fact that its leading characters shared a bond that was physical as well as emotional. "With Van Dyke and Mary," states Leonard, "it was implicit that those characters had a certain degree of a sex life, which was a novelty. So the show was very popular—*very popular*—with young people."

Viewers requiring further proof that Rob and Laura's union contained a healthy physical component need look no further than the show's pilot episode, which concludes with a sequence that seems to leave little doubt. In the playfully suggestive scene that is supposed to take place late at night in the couple's kitchen, Laura is attempting to explain the source of her

"It was implicit that those characters had a certain degree of a sex life," says Sheldon Leonard, recalling one of the more fortuitous by-products of Dick Van Dyke and Mary Tyler Moore's remarkable onstage chemistry.

uncanny intuition to her starry-eyed husband. "Darling," she purrs, pausing just long enough to tease him with the barest hint of a kiss, "I'm a *woman!*" And then, in a single seductively fluid motion, she reaches back and unhooks the clasp on her string of pearls, which begin to slip from her neck as she slinks off in the direction of their bedroom.

"Yeah!" Rob replies. And the lascivious glint in his eyes as he follows Laura off leaves little question about what's really going on. Interestingly, the multitextured sequence works on another level as well. In casting off the ubiquitous string of pearls that had symbolically condemned so many earlier prime-time wives to a life of sexless domesticity, Laura Petrie and her creators seem to be offering their own long overdue farewell to the era of June Cleaver and her perfectly matched jewelry, tasteful coiffures, and sensible pastel dresses. And though it's unlikely that any of them were aware of it at the time, by choosing to conclude their show's pilot episode on such an undeniable note of defiance—however symbolic—Mary Tyler Moore and her collaborators were sowing the seeds of a prime-time revolution from which there would be no turning back.

CHAPTER 10

Soft Soap

BY THE MIDDLE OF FEBRUARY 1961, WITH A FRESHLY developed 16mm print of *The Dick Van Dyke Show* pilot film under his arm, Sheldon Leonard was ready to begin the potentially arduous process of shopping his new show's sample film to potential sponsors—a task that, even for a producer with Sheldon Leonard's unblemished track record, could quickly turn into a demoralizing and time-consuming process. Fortunately, in the case of *The Dick Van Dyke Show*, it would turn out to be neither.

The first name on Sheldon Leonard's list of potential Van Dyke show suitors was a man named Lee Rich, who was then the senior vice president in charge of Media and Programming at New York's Benton and Bowles Agency. As the canny Leonard was well aware, one of Benton and Bowles's prize clients just happened to be a midwestern soap company named Procter & Gamble. And in the early months of 1961 the Procter & Gamble company had made it known that they were very interested in doing business with Sheldon Leonard.

Actually, to refer to the Procter & Gamble Company of Cincinnati, Ohio, as a soap company is an understatement. A sprawling multinational corporation, Procter & Gamble had long been established as one of the largest manufacturers and distributors of detergents and other household products in the free world. If you lived in the United States in 1961, chances were good that somewhere in your kitchen, pantry, or bathroom you had at least one product that was made or marketed by Procter & Gamble, be it a carton of Blue Cheer in the laundry room, a bottle of Joy Liquid in the kitchen, or a tube of Crest toothpaste in the medicine chest. Naturally, the advertising required to support that kind of market satu-

Executive producer Sheldon Leonard at work in his office at Desilu Cahuenga in the early sixties.

ration didn't come cheap, and even in those preinflationary days, Procter & Gamble's monthly expenditures for television advertising alone ran into the multimillions. Of course, much of that was devoted to daytime programming, where the presence of Procter & Gamble and other household-products manufacturers was so pervasive that the broadcast industry had come to think of the afternoon serials that were the detergent makers' mainstay as "soap" operas.

But, by the late 1950s, having established itself as a formidable presence in daytime, Procter & Gamble was growing anxious to increase its nighttime visibility as well. So it was perhaps only natural that its aggressive efforts to gain a greater foothold in prime-time advertising would eventually lead it to Sheldon Leonard, who was at that time the prime mover behind a handful of the most popular half-hour comedies on television. And it probably hadn't slipped past the soap company's notice that Leonard's Andy Griffith and Danny Thomas shows were selling an awful lot of Maxwell House Coffee for Procter & Gamble's rivals at General Foods. Recognizing that it was already too late to buy into any of the producer's existing hits—most of which were already locked into long-term sponsorship commitments to General Foods—Procter & Gamble decided that the next best thing would be to get in on the ground floor of Sheldon Leonard's next series, whatever that might be.

"Procter & Gamble were prepared to finance anything I wanted to do," recalls Leonard. "*Any* subject. *Any* project. And, at the time, what I was about to come up with was *The Dick Van Dyke Show*."

Under the circumstances, the producer had little trouble convincing the soap manufacturer to snap up the sponsorship rights to *The Dick Van Dyke Show*. "They bought it right off the first look at it," says Leonard, who recalls that Procter & Gamble pledged a full year's sponsorship commitment for the series based on a single viewing of the show's pilot film.

Once they'd signed on as sponsors of the new series, Procter & Gamble authorized Lee Rich to offer the series to CBS, where—in light of Leonard's track record and Procter & Gamble's own well-established clout—obtaining a berth for the show on the broadcaster's upcoming fall schedule should have been a foregone conclusion. Still, Sheldon Leonard allowed himself only guarded optimism. Despite the insurance policy that Procter & Gamble's full season sponsorship guarantee afforded the series, Leonard remained skeptical about the show's odds of actually getting picked up by CBS. For one thing, Leonard knew that before the Van Dyke show could earn a slot on the network's fall schedule, it would have to pass the scrutiny of CBS President James T. Aubrey. And *that*, as Sheldon Leonard knew only too well, could be a problem.

In a line of work that's never been particularly dependent on personal congeniality, network boss Jim Aubrey had earned a reputation for performing his executive duties with such cold-hearted dispatch that even his colleagues routinely referred to him as the Smiling Cobra—though never, of course, to his face. And, as someone who'd locked horns with the formidable executive on more than one occasion, Sheldon Leonard was already familiar with Aubrey's steely demeanor. "I had a very hard relationship with Aubrey," says Leonard. "I didn't dislike him—but we didn't think the same way."

As the producer recalls, one of the principal areas where he and the executive failed to see eye to eye was in the field of situation comedy. "I had a chip on my shoulder about him because he had expressed his dislike for *The Danny Thomas Show* in too many places," Leonard admits. And, as the producer would discover shortly after the network president finally got a chance to screen the Van Dyke show pilot, Aubrey was not exactly enamored of the producer's latest effort, either. "It was his opinion that a series with a show business background would have no popular appeal," says Leonard, citing what he recalls as the network president's chief criticism of *The Dick Van Dyke Show*.

According to Leonard, Jim Aubrey was not particularly pleased that Carl Reiner had chosen to create a leading character who was a TV writer, an occupation that was, in the network executive's opinion, far too exotic for the average television viewer. "He told us to make him something that people can identify with," recalls Leonard, "like a real estate agent or an automobile salesman. But I wouldn't do that." And, as Leonard fully expected, his open antipathy to the network chief's creative suggestions for *The Dick Van Dyke Show* wound up costing him—and the series—no small amount of goodwill from the network. "Aubrey said, in effect, 'If you won't cooperate with me, I won't cooperate with you. The hell with you!'"

But, despite almost certain odds that he'd incur the executive's wrath by doing so, Sheldon Leonard stood his ground—though it must be conceded that, in this particular skirmish at least, Sheldon Leonard had good reason to believe he held the upper hand. "If I needed support," explains Leonard, "I could always go to Procter & Gamble and say, 'Look, the network is giving me trouble.' And Procter & Gamble would rear up over Jim Aubrey's head and say, 'What in the hell are you trying to do to my show?'"

Naturally loath to risk alienating one of his network's most powerful advertisers, Jim Aubrey finally set his own personal and creative reservations about the Van Dyke show aside and gave his programming chiefs the nod to slate *The Dick Van Dyke Show* onto the CBS fall lineup for 1961, where it premiered in the Tuesday 8:00 P.M. time slot on October 3, 1961.

Carl Reiner claims he can still remember the exact moment when he first discovered that *The Dick Van Dyke Show* had finally been given the green light. A few days before CBS issued their formal announcement, Reiner remembers he was back in New York, where he happened to run into a high-ranking executive from Procter & Gamble's ad agency on a Manhattan-bound commuter train. "He sat across the aisle from me, and didn't say a word," as Reiner would later recall. "But then I noticed that he made a little 'okay' sign with his hand. That was when I knew we were going to be okay."[40]

Once the series was officially announced, William Morris agent Sol Leon recalls being first to call Dick Van Dyke with the news. "I told Dick, 'You're on the air!' And he couldn't believe it," the agent remembers. "He moved out to California in—like—thirty seconds. He couldn't get out here fast enough."

With his series scheduled to go into production in June 1961, Dick Van Dyke dutifully notified the producers of *Bye Bye Birdie* that he would be leaving the show for good once his contract to star in the musical expired

"They said I was crazy to do television," recalls Dick Van Dyke, who says he had personal reasons for walking away from a potentially lucrative—if risky—career on the Broadway stage. "By that time I had three kids," he explains, "and I was looking for steady work."

in mid-April 1961. And although *Birdie*'s producers had little choice but to accept the star's resignation, they didn't hesitate to informVan Dyke that they thought he was making the worst mistake of his life. "They said I was crazy to do television," says Van Dyke, who acknowledges that his

Broadway producers weren't the only ones to take a dim view of his decision to abandon the Great White Way. "*Everybody*," says Van Dyke, "tried to talk me into staying in New York."

But, according to Van Dyke, the person most opposed to the actor's infatuation with television stardom was Gower Champion, the legendary Broadway impresario who had directed the star's breakout performance in *Bye Bye Birdie*. Says Van Dyke, "He told me, '*This* is where you belong! You're born to do theater!'" But in the end, not even Gower Champion could sway the determined actor. "I wasn't listening to any of them," he says, "because I knew you just couldn't work steadily in theater."

Dick Van Dyke finally left *Bye Bye Birdie* on April 15, 1961, exactly a year and a day after he'd opened the show. In his wake, the role of Albert Petersen was assumed by Gene Rayburn, a light comic actor who would eventually achieve a certain degree of celebrity as the perennial host of TV's long-running *Match Game*. According to Norm Liebmann, who later became a contributor to the Van Dyke show—and who was then writing scripts for *Flair*, a daily syndicated radio series that Van Dyke hosted during his final days in New York—the star-to-be was so anxious to begin shooting his situation comedy that he was literally counting the days that remained before his eventual departure for the West Coast. "Dick was anxious to be done with *Bye Bye Birdie*," says Liebmann, who recalls watching with amusement as the star gleefully ticked off each of the remaining performances in his *Birdie* contract. "Every time I'd see him," says Liebmann, "he'd go, 'Only nine—or eight or seven—more to go!'"

It wasn't that Dick Van Dyke had anything against starring in *Bye Bye Birdie*. On the contrary, the star has always spoken of the show as a turning point in his career. But, after a year of six-day weeks, the anxious actor had simply begun to grow weary of the drudgery of performing the same show every single night. "After six or eight months," the star would finally observe, "a Broadway show gets to be a grind. You've tried everything you can think of in the first half year, then you run out of fresh approach ideas."[41] Fortunately, that was a dilemma the star would not often face in his chosen medium. "With TV," he explained, "there's a new script each week, a new challenge, something fresh to concentrate on."[42]

But if it was a fresh challenge that Dick Van Dyke sought as he and his family packed their belongings and began to plot their cross-country trek from Broadway's Great White Way to Hollywood's Cahuenga Boulevard, he would certainly not be disappointed. Though the road maps would peg the distance between the two points at just a shade less than 3,000 miles, Dick Van Dyke was about to discover that, in reality, the two places were worlds apart.

CHAPTER 11
The Best of Times

THE LOT THAT WAS ONCE FAMILIARLY KNOWN AS THE
Desilu Cahuenga studio is still in operation at 846 Cahuenga Boulevard
in Hollywood, though these days the quaint little studio does business
under the decidedly less resonant moniker of Ren-Mar Studios. And yet,
in most other ways, the modest seven-acre facility has remained surprisingly unchanged since its heyday as Hollywood's sitcom mecca in the late
fifties and early sixties. The studio's nine soundstages have been engaged
in the manufacture of dreams for well over five decades now; and yet, like
most factories, the place isn't much to look at from the outside. From the
street, the place appears to be little more than an unassuming string of
industrial edifices, fronted by a nondescript entrance gate. Gleaming Hollywood tour buses streak past this treeless stretch of Cahuenga Boulevard
every single day—but rarely do the coaches pause to allow their cargoes
of curiosity seekers to stop and take a peek inside those walls, despite the
fact that some of our culture's most cherished collective memories were
born there.

It was there, on the lot's soundstage 9, that America watched Lucy's
Little Ricky grow up. Desilu Cahuenga also provided the setting for the
fictional hamlet of Mayberry, North Carolina, during the eight seasons
that *The Andy Griffith Show* was in residence on the studio's stages 1 and
2. And, of course, from 1961 through 1966, the lot also served as the
home base for five seasons of *The Dick Van Dyke Show*.

There were others, as well. Hundreds of them, from *Our Miss Brooks*
and *I Married Joan* in the fifties, through *That Girl*, *The Mothers-In-Law*
and *Gomer Pyle, USMC*, in the sixties, *Soap* in the seventies, and—in more

recent years—*The Golden Girls* and *Empty Nest*. In fact, the former Desilu Cahuenga studio has played host to so many countless hours of classic television comedy over the past four decades that it's almost impossible to comprehend the magnitude of human laughter that's been generated by comic material originally filmed on those nine soundstages. Still, it's probably a safe bet that no other parcel of real estate on earth can lay claim to inspiring more human mirth than the seven square acres that lie beyond the gates at 846 Cahuenga Boulevard.

But the history of Hollywood's liveliest little studio actually predates the boom years that began after *I Love Lucy* moved on the lot in 1953. The studio was founded in 1946 as the Motion Picture Center Studios, a B-movie lot that did a brisk business providing rental stages for the producers of the low-budget features and quota quickies that Hollywood

"It was the best of times," says writer Sam Denoff, recalling the extraordinary working conditions that prevailed on the Van Dyke set, "but the worst of times just were not there."

churned out during the postwar years of the late forties. With the arrival of television a few years later, the owners of the Motion Picture Center Studios, quick to react to changing times, had little trouble adapting their facility to suit the needs of TV's earliest producers—a transition made somewhat easier by the fact that many of those early TV pioneers were themselves former B-movie moguls who were only too happy to continue cranking out their formula westerns, detective melodramas, and domestic comedies for the hungry new medium.

In fact, it wouldn't be until 1953 that an enterprising television producer arrived on the lot with a revolutionary approach to the production of filmed television entertainment that was specifically geared to the exacting demands of the bold new medium. That producer's name was Desi Arnaz, and the technique that he brought to the Motion Picture Center Studios was the three-camera system. A groundbreaking approach to filming half-hour comedies, the three-camera system had been perfected during the early years of *I Love Lucy*, the immensely popular comedy that starred Arnaz and his real-life wife, Lucille Ball.

By 1953, after completing two phenomenally successful seasons of *Lucy*, the Arnazes were looking for a permanent home base for their ever-expanding Desilu empire, which had already generated a pair of *I Love Lucy* clones, *Our Miss Brooks* and *I Married Joan*, both of which debuted in 1952. It was Desi's dream to transform an entire studio into a state of the art television factory dedicated to the assembly-line production of half-hour comedies forged in the Desilu style. And to his mind, the modest facility at 846 Cahuenga seemed perfect.

By the summer of 1953, Lucy and Desi Arnaz had negotiated a long-term lease with the owners of the Motion Picture Center Studios, which would eventually come to be known as the Desilu Cahuenga studios. No sooner was the lease signed than the Arnazes initiated a multimillion-dollar facelift of the sleepy production facility.

Employing all the technical advances that he'd pioneered with *I Love Lucy* staffers Al Simon, Karl Freund, and Jess Oppenheimer, Arnaz retrofitted the lot's largest soundstages into so-called Desilu Playhouses: highly efficient, audience-friendly stages that would come equipped with stadium-style bleachers, as well as special, acoustically sealed doorways that would provide the lot's studio audiences direct access from street to studio, the better to accommodate the teeming crowds that were such a vital element in the three-camera Desilu process. At the same time, Arnaz also constructed plenty of new offices to house the influx of writers, producers, designers, and directors that he envisioned working side by side on the soon-to-be-thriving lot. And, in a final touch, Arnaz installed a suite of offices and dressing rooms adjacent to the studio's soundstage 9, where he and his wife would film more than 125 episodes of *I Love Lucy*, including the thirteen infrequently screened hour-long installments that would complete the show's run in the late fifties.

With *I Love Lucy* as an anchor, the newly refurbished studio quickly attracted the attention of TV producers all over town. And in no time at all, the tiny lot was bursting with activity, hosting production of scores of situation comedies and dramas, including *December Bride*, *The Ray Bolger Show*, *Love and Marriage*, *Desilu Playhouse*, and *Whirlybirds*, to name just a few. But, with the notable exception of Lucille Ball herself, the lot's most conspicuous tenant throughout the fifties was a song-and-dance man of Lebanese extraction named Danny Thomas, who would begin filming his own long-running series, *Make Room for Daddy*—later retitled *The Danny Thomas Show*—on the lot in 1953.

Like Lucy and Desi before him, Danny Thomas did quite well in weekly television. By the end of the decade, Thomas and producing partner Sheldon Leonard were able to parlay the success of *The Danny Thomas Show* into a thriving production dynasty that would eventually rival even Desilu's own interests on the lot. In fact, when the Arnazes finally departed the lot in 1960, Thomas and Leonard were poised to fill many of the studio's newly vacant soundstages with products from their own rapidly expanding production slate—a bountiful roster of programs that would eventually grow to include *The Danny Thomas Show*, *The Andy Griffith Show*, *The Bill Dana Show*, *The Joey Bishop Show*, *Gomer Pyle, USMC*, *Mayberry, RFD*, and, of course, the series that Danny Thomas would refer to as the Cadillac of his entire empire, *The Dick Van Dyke Show*.

By the time the Van Dyke show arrived on the lot, the Desilu Cahuenga studio's golden age was already in full flower. And, according to the first-hand recollections of many of those who worked on the lot during that halcyon period in the early- to mid-sixties, they were heady days indeed. "It was the best of times," insists Sam Denoff, who started out as a lowly freelancer on the lot before he finally worked his way up to producer of *The Dick Van Dyke Show*. "But," he adds, "to paraphrase Dickens, the worst of times just were not there"—a circumstance Denoff attributes to the enlightened management policies practiced by Thomas and Leonard. "The working conditions on that little lot were extraordinary. Sheldon and Danny set up a work ethic that was so positive and rewarding that no one ever felt afraid to say exactly what was on their mind—or to fight for it. Which is probably why most of those shows were so good."

"It was a wonderful, open atmosphere," agrees Jay Sandrich, who

It all started with *I Love Lucy*, but Lucille Ball and Desi Arnaz wouldn't rest until they'd completely transformed the former B-movie lot at 846 Cahuenga Boulevard into the busiest television factory in Hollywood.

recalls that the constant flurry of activity on the bustling lot seemed to promote a healthy cross-pollenization of creative ideas among the writers, directors, and actors who worked on the various shows that were in production. "Everybody would wander in and watch everybody's show and make suggestions. There was no jealousy."

"It wasn't cutthroat at all," adds Harvey Bullock, who co-wrote *The Dick Van Dyke Show*'s thirty-third episode, "Bank Book 6565696," and would also contribute many classic scripts to *The Andy Griffith Show*. "The writers all knew each other, so there was no bloodletting. If one guy got a job producing a show, he'd be sure and use all the other guys. There was a lot of communal thinking then. And a lot of good, good feelings."

"It was a very collegial atmosphere," adds Sandrich, who retains particularly fond memories of the studio's campus-style cafeteria, a lively little lunchroom that also served double duty as the hub of social activity on the lot each weekday afternoon. "It was like high school," observes Bullock. "You'd plop down at a table and you'd see all the people you knew. Danny Thomas would come by and we'd kid him. And then he'd kid us. It was very egalitarian."

Director Al Rafkin is another Desilu regular who nurtures warm memories of the studio commissary's convivial atmosphere, if not the food. "It was the worst cafeteria in the world!" he insists. But, says the director, even more questionable than the food was the commissary management's peculiar tradition of naming menu items after whoever happened to be a reigning celebrity on the lot at that time. "They would name sandwiches after the guys on the shows," says Rafkin, who observes that the honor was flattering, so long as a celebrity's star remained on the rise. But, for someone whose celebrity status happened to be on the wane, Rafkin points out, that same studio menu board could quickly change into an equally adroit indicator of their rapidly withering status. "Bill Dana had a sandwich named after him," notes Rafkin, "until his show got canceled." When that happened, recalls the director, the commissary management's response was both swift and sure. "They ripped his name right off the board!" says Rafkin. Before the day was out, the director insists, the Bill Dana sandwich had been swiftly retired. "It went right back to being just plain bacon, lettuce, and tomato."

But, according to Jay Sandrich, the Desilu commissary's management initiated an even stranger policy when the lot's eatery became the only private studio cafeteria in the history of Hollywood to encourage the general public to eat within its walls—a disastrous and short-lived open-door policy, says Sandrich, that the commissary actively promoted by installing a public entrance that opened directly onto the sidewalk on Cahuenga Boulevard! "It was called Hal's Eat with the Stars," says Sandrich, "and people could wander right in off the street to eat there." But, despite the fact that the gimmick had somehow earned the endorsement of studio honcho Danny Thomas, Sandrich recalls that few others on the lot were quite so enthusiastic about the prospect of sharing their lunch hour with a roomful of camera-toting tourists. "It was terrible," remembers Sandrich. "You're sitting there having lunch with Danny or somebody, and people would wander right in off the street and ask for autographs!"

In the weeks before the Van Dyke company was due to arrive for their first regularly scheduled rehearsal on June 14, 1961, art director Ken Reid was already hard at work designing and supervising construction of the four standing sets that were to be erected more or less permanently on the lot's stage 8, the studio that would serve as the show's home base for the next five years. For the show's pilot, Reid had already built prototype versions of The Alan Brady Show writers' room and the Petries' kitchen. For the show's second episode, "The Meershatz Pipe," the art director would introduce an early version of Rob and Laura's bedroom, which would end up as the setting for much of the show's domestic interplay through episode four, "Sally and the Lab Technician," when Reid would finally unveil his proudest achievement—the Petries' sprawling, split-level living room/dining room, a spacious and attractive setting that would serve as the show's center stage for the next five years.

Ken Reid would have good reason to be proud of his design for the Petrie living room, whose chief virtue—beside its remarkable versatility—was its verisimilitude. Here was a soundstage on which it was possible to imagine that people might actually live. Which is not surprising, since Reid insists that the entire house was carefully appointed with the specific details of Rob Petrie's lifestyle in mind, right down to the amount of money the character was likely to spend furnishing it. "I wanted to be sure that Van Dyke's character could afford anything I designed," observes Reid, "so I asked Sheldon and Carl what kind of money a guy like that would make. They gave me an estimate of thirty thousand dollars a year or something like that. So I knew I couldn't get ridiculous."

And, in a fascinating sidelight of Van Dyke show lore, Ken Reid admits that his efforts to instill a convincing lived-in look in the Petrie home may finally have been more successful than he had dreamed. Or so the art director would discover a few years later, when he got a phone call from an enterprising real estate developer who actually hoped to incorporate the floor plan for Rob and Laura's fictional TV house into his designs for a real-life housing development that he was building on the East Coast. "He asked me to send him the plans for the Dick Van Dyke house," says Reid, who was so flattered by the request that he forwarded the blueprints without a second thought. And though he admits he never heard from the builder again, the art director says he has no reason to believe that the blueprints weren't finally incorporated into the contractor's plans. "Somewhere out there," fancies Reid, "there's a whole bunch of Dick Van Dyke houses around."

CHAPTER 12

Moving the Furniture

ON JUNE 20, 1961, THE VAN DYKE COMPANY KICKED OFF their first regular production season with the filming of episode 2, "The Meershatz Pipe." But despite its primary position in the show's production order, the episode itself was no groundbreaker—a fact that was not lost on the show's producers, who would bury the show as their tenth episode when they finally got around to arranging the shows for broadcast. And, based on the evidence on screen, it's not hard to see why.

In the episode's lackluster storyline, Rob becomes consumed by jealousy after he discovers that Alan Brady has rewarded Buddy Sorrell with a rare Meershatz pipe from his own private collection, a conspicuous display of approbation that leaves head writer Rob feeling more than a little slighted. Rob's insecurities are aggravated a few days later when flu forces him to remain bedridden while his able colleagues polish off a perfectly brilliant script without his help. It's only after Alan Brady publicly acknowledges the vacuum created by the head writer's absence that Rob realizes that his fears were without merit—a conclusion that is driven home a few days later when Buddy finally confesses that he completely fabricated the story about the Meershatz pipe, which turns out to be a worthless trinket that Buddy picked up at the corner drugstore.

Based on a staple premise of late-fifties situation comedy—that of the jealous husband/wife/co-worker who finally comes to discover how truly indispensable they really are—it's probably safe to say that "The Meershatz Pipe" was not one of Carl Reiner's more inventive scripts for *The Dick Van Dyke Show*. But if the premise for the show's second installment seems a tad on the shopworn side, it should be borne in mind that—like most of the show's earliest efforts—"The Meershatz Pipe" had begun life

Sally appears to be a reluctant guest at her own birthday party in this still from the show's 26th episode, "Where You Been, Fassbinder?" which featured a rare appearance from Buddy's wife, Pickles, who was played by Barbara Perry in this episode.

as one of the thirteen scripts that Carl Reiner composed on Fire Island during the summer of 1958. Which meant that by the time it was finally shot in June of 1961, the script for "The Meershatz Pipe" was already practically three years old.

The episode that followed didn't offer much in the way of improvement. Episode 3, "Jealousy"—in which Laura goes a little crazy after she discovers that Rob will be working overtime with a gorgeous movie starlet—offers slight variation on the time-tested motif of the jealous sitcom wife. But while the episode's script might not have added any particular luster to the nascent *Dick Van Dyke Show*'s reputation, the third episode would nonetheless bear the distinction of introducing a pair of notable additions to the series' teeming cast of characters—Jerry and Millie Helper.

"Jerry and Millie were friends of ours," explains Carl Reiner, who maintains that he based his characterization of Rob and Laura's next-door neighbors on Jerry and Millie Schoenbaum, a real-life couple who'd been Carl and Estelle Reiner's best friends and neighbors during the years they lived in New Rochelle. In fact, notes Reiner, he and his wife first befriended the Schoenbaums in the early fifties, long before they moved to New Rochelle, when both couples still lived in The Bronx. So close were the couples that when the Reiners finally decided to pull up stakes and leave the old neighborhood for the tree-lined security of New Rochelle, the Schoenbaums weren't far behind. "We moved up to New Rochelle, and then they moved up to New Rochelle," says Reiner, describing a scenario that would serve as the springboard for the Van Dyke show's fourth season episode, "My Home Sweet Home Is Your Home Sweet Home," in which the Helpers and Petries go househunting together and wind up in New Rochelle. "They were funny people," says Reiner, recalling his longtime friends. "We laughed with them for a lot of years."

Despite the obvious parallels between Reiner's fictional next-door neighbors and their off-screen counterparts, the writer hastens to add that he employed a healthy dollop of dramatic license in his televisual rendering of his real-life best friends. And so, even though Reiner depicts the show's Jerry Helper as a boisterous dentist with a weakness for practical jokes and a penchant for lodging his foot squarely between his molars, the writer insists that those traits bore little resemblance to the character's real-life namesake. In fact, confesses Reiner, Jerry Helper bore a far greater resemblance to the actor who would play him for five years, Jerry Paris, a man who was—by most accounts—every bit as outspoken and high-spirited as his on-screen alter ego.

"Jerry Paris was a wild man," recalls Bill Idelson, who'd been a close friend of the late actor for many years before Paris's passing in 1986, "he took lithium to keep himself on an even keel." But the actor's most distinctive personality quirk, says Idelson, was an almost total inability to hold his tongue. "Jerry would just say whatever was on his mind."

"He had absolutely no editor in his brain," concurs Dick Van Dyke, who also counted himself among Jerry Paris's closest friends. "Whatever Jerry thought or felt fell right out of his mouth. He was that spontaneous. And very often he'd say something that was inappropriate and make people mad." And yet, notes Van Dyke, even though the actor's unchecked outbursts left some people ill-at-ease, Jerry. Paris's indefitigable exuberance was a quality that few could resist. "He just ate up life in great big bites," reminisces Van Dyke. "I tell you, I loved him dearly. He was a unique human being."

And, as a character actor of vast and varied experience, he was also an ideal choice for this key supporting role on *The Dick Van Dyke Show*. Born in San Francisco on July 25, 1925, Jerry Paris got his start as a bit player on the Broadway stage in the late forties. Like so many other stage-trained actors of his generation, Paris made an easy transition to the live television environment of the early fifties, where his list of credits would include dramatic roles on many of the era's top anthology shows, including appearances on *Playhouse 90, Studio One*, and *The Kraft Television Theater*. Paris's feature film roles include appearances in *The Wild One, The Naked and the Dead*, and *My Foolish Heart*, as well as notable bits in the big-screen adaptations of *Marty* and *The Caine Mutiny*, among others.

According to Ann Morgan Guilbert, who'd been friends with Jerry Paris for years before she signed on to play his wife on *The Dick Van Dyke Show*, the show's producers began scouting for actors to play the Petries' next-door neighbors shortly after the pilot was shot the previous January. "They had another couple in the pilot," Guilbert explains, referring to Michael Keith and Barbara Eiler, the actors whose appearance as neighbors Sam and Dottie in "The Sick Boy and the Sitter" consisted of little more than a walk-on. "But they weren't comedians. And Carl wanted comedians." By Guilbert's account, Jerry Paris had been Sheldon Leonard's first and only choice to play dentist Jerry Helper. "Jerry was a friend of Sheldon's," recalls Guilbert, "and they were at the track, and Sheldon said, 'Why don't you come and do the neighbor on this show.'"

The actor promptly took the producer up on his offer, says Guilbert, who insists that it was Jerry Paris who finally recommended her for a role on the show—after a little judicious prodding from Guilbert's then-husband, TV producer George Eckstein. "Jerry kept saying, 'Oh, Annie, they need a funny person. You should be doing my wife!,'" recalls Guilbert.

Jerry Paris and Ann Guilbert made their first appearance as Jerry and Millie Helper in the show's third episode; Carl Reiner named the on-screen couple after his real-life neighbors in New Rochelle, New York.

"Finally my ex-husband said, 'Why don't you quit *saying* it and just get her an interview?' So Jerry took me down, and I auditioned for Carl."

While Jerry Paris may well have been responsible for bringing Ann Morgan Guilbert to his producer's attention, Carl Reiner recalls that the actress was no stranger to him when she walked into her audition for the show in the early summer of 1961. At least two years earlier the producer had spied the comic actress in the cast of *The Billy Barnes Revue*, a musical-comedy romp that played repeat engagements in different versions on Broadway and in Hollywood throughout the late fifties and early sixties. A big fan of the revue in all of its incarnations, Carl Reiner was especially fond of Ann Guilbert's contributions. "She was a sketch performer," notes Reiner. "And funny! Really funny. She had a way about her, a sound in her voice that made me laugh."*

Like most of the auditions for *The Dick Van Dyke Show*, Ann Guilbert's reading for the part of Millie Helper was a simple affair—straightforward and mercifully short. "Carl had me read a scene from an upcoming show," the actress recalls. "I read it with Jerry. And that was it." The producer hired the actress on the spot—a decision that he would have little reason to regret. "Annie turned into a great actress," he says today.

In his paternal zeal to give *The Dick Van Dyke Show* its strongest possible send-off, Sheldon Leonard had insisted on directing the show's pilot and first two episodes himself. But it was not until the show's fourth episode went into production during the last days of June 1961 that the executive producer felt confident enough in the show's progress to surrender the directorial reins to John Rich, a consummate craftsman whose arrival would mark a significant addition to the show's crack creative staff.

But then it hardly took a producer of Sheldon Leonard's keen instincts to recognize that John Rich was ideally suited to direct *The Dick Van Dyke Show*. Born in Rockaway Beach, New York, on July 6, 1925, John Rich came to the Van Dyke show with a weighty resumé that dated all the way back to 1952, the year that Rich got his start in TV as a director of live variety shows for singers Dennis Day and Ezio Pinza. By the mid-fifties, Rich had moved into the three-camera arena, where he served as a house director at Desilu, eventually helming multiple episodes of *Our Miss Brooks* and *I Married Joan*. By the end of the decade, the versatile Rich had mastered the art of directing one-camera drama and adventure series

----

*Nor would Ann Guilbert be the only member of the Billy Barnes troupe to strike Reiner's fancy. Over the years, the Van Dyke show's guest cast would be studded with names drawn from *The Billy Barnes Revue*'s illustrious alumni list, including Ken Berry, Jackie Joseph, Patty Regan, Joyce Jamison, and Len Weinrib, among others.

as well—a skill he would demonstrate throughout the late fifties and early sixties as director of dozens of episodes of *Gunsmoke*, *Twilight Zone*, *Bonanza*, *Bat Masterson*, and *General Electric Theater*, among many others. "Getting John Rich was one of those lucky things," observes Carl Reiner. "He was a highly intelligent man. And he was a good, solid director."

But far more important than Rich's impressive credits—at least as far as the fledgling company of actors awaiting his direction on *The Dick Van Dyke Show* was concerned—was his rock solid reputation as an actor's director. Unlike many—if not most—TV directors of the era, John Rich had cultivated an unusual degree of respect for actors, and he prided himself on his ability to communicate with performers in a language they understood. "John was the best comedy director in the world," says Rose Marie, who claims that Rich's keen directorial instincts were in evidence from his very first week on the set. "He would always tell me, 'I gotta find the relationship between you and Dick. And Dick and Mary. And Dick and Buddy. I gotta find out what the relationships are, so I can tell the audience.' So John spent the first couple shows telling everybody in the cast who we were and what our relationships were with one and other. And it was brilliant."

But if John Rich favored the kid-glove approach with his actors during those early rehearsals, the show's cast and crew would quickly discover their new director could also be an extremely demanding perfectionist come shooting night. As Bud Molin, the show's film editor, recalls, "He would shoot all night—the same thing forty times, until he got it the way he wanted it. John was a 'let's do it again' type—and he sometimes kept the actors there to the point of people getting very uptight about it." And, as Carl Reiner would soon come to appreciate, Rich's penchant for perfectionism was by no means limited to the areas of staging and direction. "I would write a scene," recalls Reiner, "and John would say, 'This could be better.' But he never told you how! So I used to go back and rewrite. And rewrite. He'd force you to write more and better. Sometimes better...sometimes just more. He would carpet everything." But if John Rich could be accused of occasional bouts of overenthusiasm, Carl Reiner concedes that the director's criticisms were invariably intended to improve the show. "I think he was just insecure that the show should be the best it could be," recalls the producer. "But everybody had great faith in him."

"John Rich was the kind of guy you always got an answer out of," says Jim Niver, who served as the director's camera coordinator on the show. "Other people might say, 'It doesn't matter.' But with John you always got, 'You're right!' Or, 'No, it works much better this way.'" And if John Rich earned the respect of his crew, he was practically revered by the individuals in his acting company, most of whom remain fiercely loyal to the director to this day. "Johnny Rich was brilliant," raves Morey Amsterdam. "I learned so much from that guy."

"Everyone looked up to John," states Rose Marie, "because he *knew*. He just *knew*." And, adds the actress, the director took particular pleasure in sharing that knowledge. "He used to explain everything to me. John would say, 'I'm using a 70mm lens here, because this will cut you at this angle. Then I'm gonna cut to Dick with this.' He even let me go into the editing room, where he'd ask me, 'Where would you cut this scene? What camera would you cut to?' I'd say, 'The party scene's over—I think we should cut to the master shot.' And he'd say, 'You're right.' And he'd cut it that way. He taught me so much."

But despite the accolades that he would eventually earn as the director of *The Dick Van Dyke Show*—which would include an Emmy in 1963 for Outstanding Directorial Achievement in Comedy—John Rich insists that his first week on the job very nearly turned out to be his last. The problem—as Rich relays in an anecdote that seems to grow more colorful with each retelling—was that, after three years in the fast-paced world of one-camera TV, he'd all but forgotten how to direct a live three-camera situation comedy by the time he arrived on the Van Dyke set. "In a single-camera show like *Gunsmoke*," he explains, "you're always in a hurry. You rehearse a sequence—sometimes maybe as long as two or three pages—and then you commit it instantly to film." Which, the director emphasizes, is a far cry from the relatively relaxed pace of a three-camera situation comedy, where the director often has as many as five days to rehearse with his actors before a single frame of film is shot. It's an important distinction, says Rich, and one that had, unfortunately, temporarily eluded him by the time he started work on *The Dick Van Dyke Show* in the summer of 1961.

"On my first day," recalls the director, "I put everyone on their feet and said, 'Let's start to work.'" And work they did! Moving along at the same breakneck pace that the director had grown accustomed to on one-camera shows like *Gunsmoke* and *Bonanza*, the director practically flew through every single scene in the show. "They're very quick actors," he says, "and we got a momentum going that was terrific." By the end of that first frenetic day, the cast had completely rehearsed Carl Reiner's entire forty-five-page script. "The show was ready," insists the director. "It was up. It was terrific!"

In fact, it was nothing short of a miracle. In a single day's rehearsal, the

Dick Van Dyke and Mary Tyler Moore huddle with director John Rich, the man
Rose Marie has called "the best comedy director in the world."

director had whipped the entire show into shape, and it was now ready
to roll. The only problem was, the shooting date was still four working
days away—which left the overzealous director and his hard-working cast
with absolutely nothing to do for four full days of rehearsal! Driving home
from the studio that night, John Rich could already smell disaster. "I was
like the coach of a football team who's got his players all ready to go a full
week before the big game! I thought, 'What am I gonna do now?'" Finally, the director decided, there was only one solution.

He had to move the furniture.

It was a brilliant, if risky, idea. The next morning, Rich would arrive at
work early. Then, before any of the cast members arrived, he would simply rearrange every single stick of furniture on the set. He would put sofas
where there weren't sofas before. He'd drop end tables in where the sofas
were. And then, once he'd rendered the set so confusing that it was practically impossible to navigate without a compass, he would invite the
actors to resume their rehearsals, feigning innocence all the while. If

everything went according to plan, the actors would be so disoriented by the reconfigured set that they would spend the better part of the next day stumbling around as they tried to reblock their original stage movement from scratch. Then, having successfully burned off a full day of slack time in the week's rehearsal schedule, the director would simply replace all the furniture in its proper position, which would leave the actors just enough time to *re*-rehearse the show before the Tuesday night filming. It was a desperate ploy, and the director knew it. But, at that point, John Rich just didn't see any other way out of the corner into which he'd so neatly painted himself.

And so, when the actors arrived at the studio the next morning, they were puzzled to find their director seated in the middle of the set, where he had already moved every piece of furniture on the stage to a different place from where it had been the day before. "I've had a few second thoughts on the set," the director announced to his by now dumbstruck actors. "Indulge me."

"I turned the entire room around," admits Rich, who promptly resumed rehearsal on the haphazard new floor plan. And, just as he'd hoped, the actors did their best to recapture the magic of the first day's rehearsal—to no avail. With unfamiliar furniture blocking their every move, the actors did little more than bump into each other for most of the afternoon. And by the end of the day, the show was in a complete shambles—just as Rich had planned. "I just wouldn't let them rehearse effectively," recalls John Rich.

The next morning, after wasting an entire day of rehearsal, Rich ordered his stage crew to move every piece of furniture back into its original position on the set. And, just as he'd hoped, the company spent the rest of the week retracing their footing, until finally, by the time the show went before the cameras the following Tuesday evening, they were finally secure enough to film the episode without a hitch. Of course, it was only after the shooting was finished that Rich let the company in on his little secret. "After the show," says Rich, "I finally took them aside and told them what I'd done."

Curiously, as much as Rich delights in recounting the story, Carl Reiner insists that he didn't hear the director's harrowing account of his first week on the Van Dyke show until many years after the fact—which may have been just as well. "When I heard that story," says Reiner, "I told John, 'If I'd known you did that, I woulda' killed you!'"

CHAPTER 13
Courtship

THE SHOW'S SIXTH EPISODE, "OH HOW WE MET THE NIGHT That We Danced," filmed on July 18, 1961, was a true milestone in the annals of *The Dick Van Dyke Show*. The first episode to feature an extended flashback to the stormy early days of Rob and Laura's courtship, "Oh How We Met the Night That We Danced" also gave us our first peek at Rob Petrie's days at Camp Crowder, Missouri, where he'd been stationed in the army's special services unit. The lighthearted episode details Rob's frustrated attempts to date a striking young USO showgirl named Laura Meeker, who—as his pal Sol Pomeroy is only too eager to warn him—has a reputation around the base as "a real cold potato." And, as Sergeant Petrie discovers when the dancer rebuffs his every advance, the reputation is well earned. Undaunted, Rob conspires to join the young dancer on stage during her act, where the enterprising serviceman vows to tender a marriage proposal during an impromptu soft-shoe. But even this romantic gesture ends in disaster when the overeager staff sergeant accidentally steps on his reluctant partner's toe—and ends up sending her to the infirmary with a broken foot! Of course, as the flashback ends, Laura reveals that she eventually did revise her opinion of her clumsy suitor, to his obvious, and everlasting, delight.

Inspired by the success of "Oh How We Met the Night That We Danced," Carl Reiner would return to the continuing saga of Rob and Laura's courtship and early married life frequently over the next five years. In fact, today Carl Reiner ranks the Van Dyke show's army episodes among his very favorite shows. And it's not hard to see why. Taken as a group, this remarkable subset of Van Dyke show flashback episodes would trace the fitful progress of Rob and Laura's romance in an unfolding saga rich in comic detail and poignant romantic observation. And, as should surprise no one familiar with Carl Reiner's self-reflexive style, most of those observations were inspired, with only minor embellishment, by the writer's own experiences. "Those army shows were all based on real things," admits Reiner. "I just invented the details."*

And, as a quick glimpse at Carl Reiner's personal dossier reveals, the Van Dyke show's many army flashback episodes were indeed rife with autobiographical echoes of Reiner's own life and career. Like Rob Petrie, the writer/producer had also been stationed at Camp Crowder, Missouri—though Reiner's hitch began a bit earlier than Rob's, in 1943, not long after the writer had met his own real-life Laura, the former Estelle Lebost. "She wasn't in the USO," says Reiner. "But she did used to visit me at Camp Crowder."

Reiner would continue to explore the axiom that truth can be stranger—and often funnier—than fiction when he returned to the army setting for the show's second-season classic, "The Attempted Marriage." The highlight of that episode was the unforgettable sequence where Rob stutters his faltering marriage proposal to Laura in an open-air jeep—a scene, says Reiner, that was no more than a thinly veiled takeoff on his own quaking proposal to Estelle. "I proposed to my wife at home," says Reiner, who recalls that, like Rob, he was fighting off flu at the time. "I was shivering, just like he was. I was twenty-one years old, and I was so scared! And I remembered that emotion when I wrote the scene. So that's why I had Rob say, 'Do y-y-you want to get m-m-married?' It was all felt."

Carl Reiner's next army script, episode 47, "Will You Two Be My Wife?"—in which Sgt. Petrie bids farewell to the girl he left behind—was largely a fiction, though Reiner would be back on the autobiographical track by the show's eighty-fifth episode, "Honeymoons Are for the Lucky." That episode described how Rob and Laura's honeymoon was nearly ruined by army regulations and the postwar housing crunch—another plot torn directly from the Reiners' own wedding album. "I

---

*One significant detail in this episode that was *not* made up was Laura Petrie's maiden name. Early in the episode, Mary Tyler Moore's character is introduced as Laura Meeker—an in-joke of sorts, since Meeker was the surname of Mary Tyler Moore's first husband, to whom the actress was still married when that episode was shot. After Mary Tyler Moore and Richard Meeker were divorced a few months later, Laura's family name would be changed—without explanation—from Meeker to Meehan.

Dick Van Dyke and Mary Tyler Moore perform a soft-shoe number in "Oh How We Met the Night That We Danced," a flashback episode that would serve as the opening chapter in one of the show's richest ongoing subplots.

wouldn't give those shows to anybody to write," insists Reiner, "because even though they were invented, the feelings had to be right."

Ironically, the one scene in "Oh How We Met the Night That We Danced" that Reiner admits he fabricated from whole cloth was the climactic soft-shoe number—where Rob attempts to tender his flippant marriage proposal to Laura in between verses of "You, Wonderful

You"—which may well be the best sequence in the episode. As Carl Reiner observes, "That was pure Dick and Mary."

"I invented that because I wanted to see Dick and Mary dance together," says the writer, who admits that he'd been pleasantly surprised to discover a few weeks into rehearsals that his two leading players shared an uncanny knack for song and dance. "Mary and Dick were incredible," notes Reiner, "the way they did those complicated dance numbers." It was a feat, says Reiner, that was all the more impressive in light of the show's extremely tight rehearsal schedule. "They'd have three, maybe four days to learn the number, do it, and shoot it."*

And though Van Dyke and Mary Tyler Moore appear to pull off their soft-shoe number with a particularly fluid grace, Carl Reiner insists that the effortless quality of the performance was extremely hard earned. "They came to me," says Reiner, "and said, 'We can't do this! It's just too hard!'" Fortunately, the producer wisely refused to heed their protests. "We had choreographers," says Reiner, "and they pushed them. No one made it easy for Dick and Mary, because we knew they were both so good." And, notes the producer, the results of that extra effort are still paying dividends thirty years later. "I saw that number, 'You, Wonderful You,' on TV the other day. And—gee!—they were both right on the button."

Dick Van Dyke's musical comedy skills came as little surprise to Carl Reiner, who was well aware that the actor had dazzled Broadway audiences for more than a year in *Bye Bye Birdie*. But, he confesses, his discovery that Mary Tyler Moore was similarly gifted came as a very pleasant surprise. "I already had Dick Van Dyke when I found out Mary could sing and dance," Reiner remembers. "And that was serendipity, because we didn't know that when we hired her." But if the producer was pleased to witness Mary Tyler Moore's emergence as a musical comedy star in the show's sixth episode, he was still completely unprepared for the eye-opening performance that she would turn in three weeks later, when the talented young performer finally came into her own as a comic actress in the show's ninth episode, "My Blonde-Haired Brunette."

---

*It probably came as some small consolation to the busy performers that they wouldn't actually have to worry about singing their various musical numbers live at the show's Tuesday night filming, since it was a common practice on the Van Dyke show—as it was on almost every other audience show of that era—to have the actors lip-sync to their own prerecorded vocals during the live performance.

The episode that would provide Mary Tyler Moore with her first real breakthrough on the series opens in the Petrie bedroom, where Rob has rebuffed Laura's good-natured attempt to rouse him from sleep with a good-morning kiss. In the face of such startling romantic apathy, Laura comes to the conclusion that the spark has finally drifted out of their marriage. And her fears appear to be confirmed a few moments later, when Rob arrives at their breakfast table clad in a shabby sweater and jeans, which Laura insists on reading as further evidence of Rob's growing marital disinterest.

Faced with such incontrovertible evidence of the decline in her marriage, Laura soon works herself into a serious depression. And it's in this vulnerable state that she allows Millie to talk her into bleaching her hair blond in a last ditch effort to recapture her husband's waning attentions. Naturally, Millie's harebrained scheme goes awry, and Laura ends up with a hideous two-tone dye job that leaves half of her hair blond and the other half brunette. And that's how she appears when she's finally forced to confront her by now thoroughly confused husband. When Rob makes the mistake of asking for an explanation, Laura barrages her hapless husband with a tearful monologue that is a masterpiece of confused, if heartfelt, emotional logic.

"Why?" Laura finally sobs, struggling for the words that might sum up the depth of her unwittingly self-inflicted malaise. "Well..." she sniffs, "yesterday morning..." And then, before she can even stammer out the rest of the sentence, she has shifted gears completely. "And I kissed you, and you said 'Don't do that!' And you came down to breakfast in your *yecchy* shirt!" And on and on she goes, sobbing in utter exasperation all the while, until her monologue has finally dissolved into a long string of barely comprehensible—though heartwrenchingly funny—non sequiturs. Finally, at her wit's end, Laura sobs, "and...the...general *yuck-i-ness...*" Finally, with no better way to communicate her desperate need for comforting—she collapses into Rob's waiting arms. "I understand, honey," he coos soothingly. "I understand." And, through some miraculous combination of acting, writing, and direction—we're convinced that he just might.

It's a remarkably written scene—unsettling, poignant, and wildly funny all at the same time. And Mary Tyler Moore's reading of the monologue is nothing short of a revelation—a performance of such unerring emotional truth that we finally find ourselves chuckling reluctantly at the sweet despair of the insecure young wife's poignant folly.

The monologue is also notable in that it marks the inaugural appearance of what would come to be one of the Van Dyke show's most durable trademarks—Laura Petrie's extended comical crying jags. In fact, boasts Carl Reiner, it was under his personal tutelage during rehearsals for this episode that Mary Tyler Moore actually perfected her trademark technique of sobbing her way through entire paragraphs of comical exposition. As Reiner recounts it, "Mary always said I taught her how to cry and make it funny.

"Mary always had a question of being real or being funny," explains the producer, who recalls that the actress had experimented with a number of more down-to-earth readings of the episode's hilarious closing monologue before he finally stepped in to correct her. "If you cry for real," he cautioned the actress, "it's not going to be funny." As Reiner explains it today, "There's a way to do a scene like that where you make people feel sorry for you—but you still get your laugh. And it's one of the things I can do." Which is essentially what Carl Reiner told Mary Tyler Moore at that early rehearsal for "My Blonde-Haired Brunette" more than thirty years ago. Naturally, as soon as the actress heard Reiner's boast that he'd mastered the art of stage crying, she promptly demanded a demonstration. "When I told her that was something I could do," recalls Reiner, "she said, 'Do it!' So I did it."

Without any further prompting, Carl Reiner proceeded to act out the entire monologue—tears, hysterics, and all—to Mary Tyler Moore's obvious delight. And once the actress had recovered from the extended bout of giggles that Reiner's rendition of the role had inspired, she reworked the piece until she'd figured out how to make it unmistakably hers. "That was a tour de force for Mary," says Dick Van Dyke, recalling her show-stopping performance in "My Blonde-Haired Brunette." "She was brilliant."

And Dick Van Dyke certainly wasn't the only one to notice the attention that Mary Tyler Moore had begun to attract by the show's ninth episode. Director John Rich suggests that Mary Tyler Moore's breakout performance in "My Blonde-Haired Brunette" was so outstanding that it finally forced the show's producers to rethink their conception of her character, which the director maintains had been up until that time far more limited. "When Mary came to the show," Rich elaborates, "she was supposed to be what we call an 'ear' for Dick Van Dyke—an ear being somebody to whom you turn at night and say, 'This is what happened at the office today, and this is what my problem is.'" But, notes the director, that limited approach to the character became outmoded the instant Mary Tyler Moore stepped into the role. "It soon became apparent," says Rich, "that Mary was a whole lot more than just an ear."

And just as the show's producers would come to recognize that they

"I had no experience in comedy," admits Mary Tyler Moore, whose comedic skills nonetheless flowered rapidly after her arrival on the Van Dyke show set. "Before you knew it," recalls Dick Van Dyke, "she could hold her own with no trouble at all. That's how bright she was."

got more than they bargained for when they signed Mary Tyler Moore, so, too, would the actress come to appreciate the exceptional opportunity the show afforded her. "Producers all over town had let me wear the same bangs and the same pants on their shows that I wear on this one, but nothing great ever happened," the actress later explained. "I think Laura came off because of a combination—what rubbed off on me before I came to the show, and the effect Carl and his cast had on it." [43] And, as the actress would freely acknowledge, she was not about to take this opportunity lightly. "With Dick and Rose Marie and Morey Amsterdam to play to, I think I also felt I'd better make something out of Laura, or *The Dick Van Dyke Show* would be the last of Mary Tyler Moore." [44]

Although Mary Tyler Moore thrived in the creative atmosphere fostered by Carl Reiner and her fellow players, the actress could not fail to notice the pressures that came with being the junior member of such a highly experienced ensemble. Three decades later, the actress still recalls the insecurity that dogged her in those early days. "I had no experience in comedy," she admits. "I was a dramatic actress. I started out as a dancer and went from that straight into working as an actress on a lot of episodic dramatic shows." The actress admits that with her slim comic resumé, stepping into a company of established pros—some of whom had roots dating all the way back to vaudeville—was not easy. "It was very intimidating, because they all had this comedy knowledge and background." And yet, to hear Dick Van Dyke tell it, Mary Tyler Moore took to situation comedy like she'd been born to the calling. "She was a serious actress when she came on the show," the star observes, "but she kind of picked up the rhythms from everybody else. And then, before you knew it, she could hold her own with no trouble at all. That's just how bright she was."

Ironically, Mary Tyler Moore's complete lack of comedic training might actually have been an asset. Without a polished comedienne's bag of tricks to fall back on, she was forced to build a character based entirely on her own instincts—which, as it turned out, wasn't such a bad idea. "I was a housewife and mother myself," she acknowledges. "So I thought, 'Well, I can bring to this something from my own background—and that's honesty.'" And she certainly got no argument from Carl Reiner, who encouraged his cast to draw on the raw material of their own lives at every opportunity.

"I think Carl would back me up when I say that I kept him honest," volunteers Mary Tyler Moore, who admits that she rarely hesitated to venture an opinion whenever she felt that her character's integrity might be at stake. "I would go to Carl and say, 'We can't do this joke, because last week we said thus and such about Laura, and this would be contradictory.'" And though Reiner certainly didn't accept all of her suggestions, the actress recalls that both he and Sheldon Leonard always found time to hear her out. "I generally made a pain in the ass of myself," she confesses, "but they took it with fond, fond acceptance."

But if only to shed light on a fascinating corner of the colorful history of *The Dick Van Dyke Show*, it's worth noting that the actress did in fact lock horns with her executive producer over at least one suggestion that she offered in the show's first year. In fact, as difficult as it may be to believe today, one of the show's earliest tempests stemmed from Mary Tyler Moore's seemingly innocent request that she be allowed to wear capri pants on the show. And yet, innocent or not, that simple request would set off a chain of events that would finally have a lasting impact not only on *The Dick Van Dyke Show*, but on practically every other domestic situation comedy to follow in its wake.

CHAPTER 14

Capri Pants

IT MAY NOT SEEM LIKE A PARTICULARLY RADICAL CHOICE today, but Mary Tyler Moore's insistence on wearing her own form-fitting slacks on television was little short of revolutionary in 1961. In the days before *The Dick Van Dyke Show* rewrote the prime-time dress code, the costume of choice for women in situation comedies was still a freshly pressed full-skirted dress worn with a single, tasteful string of pearls. "Little frocks," as Mary Tyler Moore describes them, "that were sweet and cute but didn't bear any resemblance to reality." And, as costumer Harald Johnson attests, there was no way that Mary Tyler Moore was about to let Laura Petrie be straitjacketed into a sweet little frock for five years.

"Mary liked to wear tight-fitting slacks," says Johnson, the man who would be responsible for dressing the cast of the Van Dyke show throughout the life of the series. "And a lot of Mary's own personality was in the character that she played, so those capri pants were one of the things she pushed for." And, adds Johnson, it was a decision that he supported wholeheartedly. "We wanted a more natural look, and we knew that ladies didn't sit around at home wearing pearls."

But neither did they lounge around the rec room wearing the extremely tight-fitting wool jersey slacks that the actress favored. Or so went the argument of Sheldon Leonard, who wondered if the dancer's form-fitting slacks might be a tad too revealing for a character on a family show—especially when that character was as naturally curvaceous as Mary Tyler Moore.

Nonsense! responded the actress, who argued that the capri pants Laura wore on screen were the same slacks that she herself wore to shop and run errands every day of her life—and she'd yet to hear anyone in the supermarket line accuse her of undermining their moral fiber.

Despite his reservations about Mary Tyler Moore's choice of wardrobe, Sheldon Leonard stopped short of ever actually forbidding his leading lady from wearing slacks on the air. But the capri pants controversy continued to rage throughout rehearsals for the show's early episodes, when it would invariably resurface as a hot topic whenever the actress showed up on the set clad in slacks. "We'd have three-way conversations about it," recalls Johnson, "right on the set, in front of everybody. Sheldon's argument was that the sponsors wouldn't like it—that they had certain ideas about what was protocol for shows of this type. There was a type of unwritten censorship in those days—and he wanted her to wear dresses."

"It wasn't Sheldon so much who was nervous," explains director John Rich, who holds the opinion that Leonard's stand on the capri pants controversy had nothing whatsoever to do with the executive producer's personal feelings, but was motivated almost entirely by a sense of responsibility to the show's sponsors. "Sheldon was just transmitting a feeling that had been expressed to him by Procter & Gamble.

Mary Tyler Moore models her trademark capri pants—a wardrobe preference that would eventually spark one of the most protracted behind-the-scenes controversies of the entire series.

They were afraid that the housewives around America would get nervous because Mary was wearing pants."

"The sponsors were upset," concurs Mary Tyler Moore, "because they started getting letters from housewives—probably older housewives—who were a little upset at the *clingy* aspects of those capri pants." And, according to Harald Johnson, the sponsors continued to apply pressure—via the show's executive producer—until late in the first season, when Mary Tyler Moore and Sheldon Leonard finally reached a truce. "They finally compromised and let her wear the pants every now and then," recalls Johnson, "just so long as they seemed natural for the scene." But, in Mary Tyler Moore's recollection, she was actually held to a far more exacting quota. "They restricted me to wearing them in only one scene per show," she recalls.

Whatever the precise terms of Mary Tyler Moore's capri-pants embargo, any restrictions that might have been placed on the actress were quickly forgotten once the show landed in the top twenty a year or so later. In the meantime, suggests John Rich, Mary Tyler Moore's tenacity may have had a more far-reaching impact than anyone on the Van Dyke set could possibly have imagined. "What she did," postulates the director, "was set a style trend. Partially as a result of Mary, women started to wear pants." And, as Rich is quick to point out, the fabric of our society hardly suffered at all as a result. "It didn't destroy the American family."

Harald Johnson's role as Mary Tyler Moore's chief advocate in the capri-pants debate was hardly the costumer's greatest concern in the show's earliest days. A far more urgent quandary—for him, anyway—was the question of how he was supposed to clothe an entire company of actors on a wardrobe budget that he describes today as paltry beyond belief. "Sheldon was a wonderful producer," Johnson acknowledges, "but he didn't loosen his purse strings in my department. And because we were on a low budget, I was always encouraged to save." One of the costumer's most effective cost-cutting measures was simply to require many of the show's performers to appear on the air in their own clothing. "Most of the men who appeared as guests on the show would be encouraged to wear their own clothes," says Johnson. "And Morey always brought in his own stuff. So did Richard Deacon."

Ann Guilbert was another Van Dyke regular who was obliged to wear her own clothes on the air. "If I needed something very special for a show," she observes, "like an evening dress, they would get it for me. But they didn't have a big clothes budget, so I almost always used my own clothing." Even Mary Tyler Moore was encouraged to do her bit to help the show's wardrobe austerity program after her capri slacks fell under the scrutiny of the show's budget-conscious wardrobe director. "Those pants were very expensive," says Johnson. "So Mary would wear her own slacks on the show all the time."

Dressing Dick Van Dyke presented its own unique set of challenges for the busy costume supervisor. For one thing, the star required an above-average supply of clean shirts on shooting day, or so reported *TV Guide* in a 1962 profile that described the star as a "highly strung worrier" who "still perspires through six shirts on the day of the performance."[45] And then there was the problem of the star's physique, which was so slender that Johnson found it almost impossible to find an off-the-rack suit that would fit Van Dyke's 6' 1", 147-pound frame. As a result, almost every-thing the lanky star wore on the show had to be custom-tailored. "Dick was very, very particular about his clothes," says Johnson. "He never wore off-the-rack suits. The only things he ever wore that were not cus-

Carl Reiner recalls that Morey Amsterdam and Rose Marie frequently lobbied him to include more scenes set in the writers' room, despite the producer's insistence that the show wasn't really about writers at all. "In my head," says Reiner, "it was a show about a husband and father who happened to be a comedy writer."

tom-made were sportswear items. I might buy him sweaters or sports shirts. But even his casual slacks were usually custom-made."

Naturally, all that custom-tailoring cost money. But, owing to an ingenious promotional arrangement that Sheldon Leonard worked out with the Botany 500 line of men's wear, Dick Van Dyke's wardrobe finally ended up costing the show's producers not a single penny. Under Leonard's deal, Botany 500 agreed to supply the star's wardrobe free of charge, in exchange for a promotional acknowledgment in the show's closing credits, that stated, "Mr. Van Dyke's wardrobe furnished by Botany 500."

It was an ironic credit, and more than a little misleading, considering that a clotheshorse like Dick Van Dyke would not have been caught dead in department store ready-to-wear. In fact, according to Johnson, Botany 500 didn't actually manufacture any of the suits that the star wore on camera, which were all custom-tailored by a prominent Beverly Hills tailor—at Botany 500's expense. "They were all custom-made—and very expensive," says Harald Johnson.

If the arrangement with Botany 500 saved the show's producers a bundle on wardrobe costs, it was also a boon for Dick Van Dyke, who was allowed to take his custom-fitted suits home after he'd worn them on the air. And, recalls Johnson, Van Dyke's personal closet wasn't the only one to reap benefits from this particular perquisite of the Botany 500 setup. Says the costumer, "Part of the deal was that Sheldon Leonard and Carl Reiner also received suits made by the same tailor."

Once Harald Johnson got Van Dyke's wardrobe problems squared away courtesy of Botany 500, the costumer set to work organizing a similar scheme to obtain the steady parade of smart dresses and sporty outfits that would be required to keep Rose Marie and Mary Tyler Moore poised on the cutting edge of the early sixties fashion scene. Using the Botany 500 plan as a guide, the costumer negotiated deals with a variety of California-based women's clothing designers, most of whom were only too happy to loan samples of their latest fashion lines to the show's female stars in exchange for the exposure and—of course—a prominent plug in the show's closing credits.

As Johnson remembers, the only real drawback he encountered in borrowing clothes for the show's female stars was that it occasionally engendered rivalry between them. "There was always jealousy about who got the better things to wear," he recalls. And, according to the costumer, that competition didn't always end in the dressing room.

"They never were close friends," observes Johnson, who insists that he caught the first signs of jealousy between the show's female stars shortly after the show's producers started to feature Mary Tyler Moore more prominently in the series. "In the beginning," explains Johnson, "Rose thought that she would be the female star of the show. Then Mary actually became the female star, because the public just took to her. And Rose Marie fell into second place."

But if a rivalry existed between the show's leading ladies, Rose Marie insists that she was never aware of it. "There was never any problem or anything," says the actress, who nonetheless acknowledges that she and her costar did seem to keep their friendship at arm's length. "We were pleasant enough," she says. "We always got along—but very, very sparingly, so to speak. I don't know why. We just never hit it off."

Carl Reiner dismisses out of hand the notion that jealousy ever played a significant role in the social dynamic of *The Dick Van Dyke Show*, on stage or off. The closest thing to competition that Carl Reiner ever observed on the Van Dyke set came early in the show's run, when Rose Marie and Morey Amsterdam would occasionally lobby for more scenes set in *The Alan Brady Show*'s writers' room, where they had most of their lines. "It's funny," says Reiner, "in their heads, it was a show about a comedy writer. But I never thought it was a show about writers. In my head, it was a show about a husband and father who happened to be a comedy writer. And I had to explain that to them over and over again. They never felt their part was big enough in the first year—but it was just like in any show, everybody wants a bigger part." But if Rose Marie and Morey Amsterdam cheerfully acknowledged their hunger for increased stage time during the show's early days, the producer insists that the pair certainly never let their feathers get in a ruffle over it. "They finally fell into the fact that the show was what it was," says Reiner, "and then they were both very happy."

The fact is, ruffled feathers of any sort were an extremely rare sight on the set of *The Dick Van Dyke Show*. "We never had an argument," observes Van Dyke show director Alan Rafkin. "It was always settled with a laugh, with a smile. Because that was Dick's temperament, and so it became the temperament of the show." Carl Reiner agrees that it was rare that anyone heard the sound of raised voices at a Van Dyke rehearsal— unless they happened to drop by on one of those mornings when he and his executive producer failed to see eye to eye.

"Sheldon and I had a lot of fights," says Carl Reiner. And, according to the producer, the vast majority of their battles were staged at the show's Wednesday morning script readings, where Reiner recalls that he and his "worthy adversary" would frequently lock horns over the finer points of comic theory. "They used to have some wonderful arguments," recollects

Dick Van Dyke. "Sheldon had a background in three-camera, and when it came to story—he was a strict constructionist. But Carl came in with some different ideas about comedy. So they were at odds a lot." And yet, even in combat, Van Dyke insists that his producers were never less than entertaining. "We'd all just sit and listen to them," recalls the actor.

Writer Sam Denoff—who with his partner Bill Persky would eventually write many of the show's finest third-, fourth-, and fifth-season episodes—recalls that he used to watch with nervous fascination whenever his producers engaged in a particularly heated debate. "They would

"There was always a little bit of pandemonium on the set," observes Dick Van Dyke. "Sheldon Leonard used to say we looked like otters playing in a pond."

have these tremendous fights," recalls Denoff. "And Billy and I would sit there in terror. Sheldon would say, 'No, Carl. Don't you see? Goddammit, don't you see?' And Carl would say, 'No, Sheldon, *you're* wrong, for chrissake!' Then Sheldon would say, 'Well, Carl—you're crazy! I don't think it'll work.' And he'd walk out."

Carl Reiner hastens to add that Leonard's abrupt departures from the Van Dyke show set were never the result of pique, but merely the most visible manifestation of his overwhelming workload. "Sheldon always disappeared after the readings," says Reiner. "When you've got five shows on the air, you can't pay attention to the minutiae on every one of them." Naturally, Leonard's habit of making sudden exits was not lost on the Van Dyke show's observant cast, who soon began to view their executive producer's frequent disappearing acts as the stuff of legend. "We used to call him the Shadow," says Mary Tyler Moore, recalling the Lamont Cranston character from the classic radio show. Adds Rose Marie, "We even had a welcome mat made up for Sheldon with the name LAMONT CRANSTON printed on it."

If the Van Dyke show's producers occasionally engaged in a few rounds of spirited verbal sparring during the weekly script meetings, most observers agree that these admittedly blustery debates—which were, after all, invariably waged on the show's behalf—posed little threat to the show's otherwise unflappable creative harmony. In fact, it's one of the minor miracles of the Van Dyke show's production history that the set remained practically free of strife throughout five full seasons of production—a remarkable record, especially considering the extremely diverse and highly opinionated group of talents that assembled there each week.

"Morale was very important on that set," explains Sheldon Leonard, who maintains that he and Carl Reiner worked hard to foster an atmosphere of creative harmony on the Van Dyke show set, if only because they found that a buoyant mood on the set seemed to make for better shows. "If you weren't happy when you came in," notes Leonard, "something would be missing. And it would show up on the screen."

To many observers, the infectious spirits that prevailed on the set could be traced directly to the show's producer, whose own indefatigable personality was legendary even then. "Carl was ebullient," recalls writer Harvey Bullock. "He was open—always jumping around. You could tell he was in love with being there." Camera coordinator Jim Niver seconds that sentiment, adding, "With Carl, it was always like he'd just been let out of a cage. There was always excitement. 'Here!' he'd say, 'here's a new thing! A new idea!' Great enthusiasm—that's Carl."

Reiner was also, according to Niver, a tireless booster of new talent. And, adds Niver, the producer was never so happy as when he was dragging some awestruck young comic or singer he'd just discovered down to the Van Dyke set, where the flabbergasted newcomer would invariably be introduced to the show's entire cast and crew, usually with great fanfare. "Carl was always bringing somebody in," says Niver. "He would walk in like he'd just found a new toy that we all had to stop and listen to," says Niver. "He'd stop rehearsal and we'd all say, 'Oh, what now?' Then he'd say, 'Oh, you gotta hear this person!' Then somebody'd start telling stories."

One of the show's more notable on-set visitors was a talented young comedian named Bill Cosby, who'd been invited by Carl Reiner to drop by the set of *The Dick Van Dyke Show* one afternoon in the show's fourth year. But, though Cosby was still a relatively unknown nightclub comic at the time, Carl Reiner denies that he played more than a passing role in the discovery of the soon-to-be superstar. For that prescient act, the producer gives full credit to his then teenaged son, Rob, who was actually the first to draw his father's attention to Bill Cosby's substantial gifts.

"When [Rob] was about sixteen," as Reiner would recall for an interviewer in 1985, [46] "I came home from the Van Dyke show one night about one in the morning. Rob was awake. I said, 'What are you doing awake? You have school tomorrow.' And he said, 'I just saw the greatest comedian on *The Tonight Show*, a guy named Bill Cosby.' And he proceeded to get out of his bed and do Cosby's whole routine for me, the voices, everything. I just got hysterical." So impressed was the elder Reiner by his teenaged son's facsimile of the comic's act that he finally invited Cosby himself to pay a call to the Van Dyke show set, where the comedian was only too happy to provide a sample of the genuine article for the show's cast and crew. "I invited Cosby to visit us on the set," recalls Reiner. "He was there for the whole Wednesday reading, and we didn't get a bit of work done that day, we were laughing so hard. He did all of his act, and he was hilarious."

"He was just a young guy," remembers Dick Van Dyke, who harbors similarly fond memories of Cosby's unscheduled visit to the Van Dyke set, "but he came in and did this piece about Noah and the Ark—and he absolutely threw us all on the floor." Perhaps no one was more taken with Cosby's electrifying performance than Sheldon Leonard, who declared to all within earshot that they hadn't seen the last of Bill Cosby. And, sure enough, within the year, Sheldon Leonard himself would play an instrumental role in Cosby's eventual transformation from comedian to primetime commodity when he cast the rising comic opposite Robert Culp in

I Spy, an innovative adventure series that Leonard executive produced for NBC beginning in 1965.*

"There was always a little bit of pandemonium on the set," observes Dick Van Dyke, recalling the giddy spirits that occasionally overcame the cast during rehearsals for the show. "Sheldon Leonard used to come down to the set and say we looked like otters playing in a pond." And, it must be admitted, the cast's unflappable esprit de corps did have its mischievous side as well. Dick Van Dyke himself confesses that he certainly wasn't above enlivening a dull rehearsal with a good practical joke, if the opportunity presented itself.

One of Van Dyke's favorite rehearsal pranks was the vanishing cast trick, a bit of organized whimsy that usually began with the star leading the entire cast off the set just split seconds before one of the show's hapless guest stars was scheduled to make his or her entrance. "We'd vacate the studio," explains Van Dyke. Then, hidden at a safe distance, the star and his coconspirators would watch their victim squirm as he or she waited in vain for someone onstage to cue his or her entrance. "We'd leave them standing out there, all alone on an empty soundstage," recalls Dick Van Dyke, "until they finally decided to open the door and find out what the hell was going on."

Ann Guilbert recalls that, despite the good-natured hazing that

---

*By sheer coincidence, Carl Reiner recalls that he was also responsible—in a roundabout way—for Robert Culp's casting in that same series. According to Reiner, Culp was already an established leading man when he approached the producer for advice on breaking into the writing end of the business. "Culp loved the Van Dyke show," explains Reiner, "so he asked me to comment on some writing he'd done." But no sooner had Reiner agreed to read the actor's writing sample than he realized that Culp had written a sample script for an hour-long adventure series—a genre for which Reiner professed little expertise. And so, rather than try to critique it himself, Reiner offered to pass the script along to his partner Sheldon Leonard, who at that precise moment happened to be in the early stages of casting his own hour-long adventure series, *I Spy*. As fate would have it, Sheldon Leonard was far more impressed by Culp's acting skills than his potential as a writer. And so, though he wound up taking a pass on the actor's sample script, Sheldon Leonard did end up signing Robert Culp to a long-term contract to star in *I Spy*, making him the second actor—along with his costar, Bill Cosby—to land a role on the series courtesy of Carl Reiner.

awaited the show's more tolerant guest stars, the Dick Van Dyke stage was still one of the most popular destinations in Hollywood for character actors. "Every actor in town wanted to work our show, because it was so damn much fun," the actress recalls. "They were all such funny people that working there was just a ball." But in spite of the conviviality that the show engendered, Dick Van Dyke recalls that his company's free-wheeling approach to the creative process was not for everyone. "Sometimes we'd have a guest star who just didn't know what the hell to make of us," confesses the star, who cites Robert Vaughn—the actor who played Laura's old flame on episode 59, "It's a Shame She Married Me"—as one of the few Van Dyke show guest stars to cast a scornful eye on the cast's hijinks. "I think our silliness kind of got on his nerves a little bit," says Van Dyke, who recalls that the visiting actor spent most of his week on the set eyeing the cast with a mixture of curiosity and disdain. "He just kind of sat and studied us," recalls Van Dyke. "Like an anthropologist."

Actor Ross Elliott had no such qualms about the highly charged creative atmosphere that he observed on the Van Dyke set. "Rehearsals on that show were a kind of free-for-all," says the actor, who ap-

Amateur cartoonist Dick Van Dyke's lighthearted caricatures frequently popped up on the show, as is apparent in this still from the show's 132nd episode, "Draw Me a Pear," in which Van Dyke's sketch of Mary Tyler Moore threatens to upstage guest star Ina Balin.

peared as a psychiatrist in episode 82, "The Brave and the Backache," and reprised the role two years later in episode 129, "Uhny Uftz." "If anyone had an idea for a line, you threw it in and they'd use it."

"Everybody had input," agrees Ann Guilbert. "Carl was really great about that. Anybody could think up a gag or change their line. Sometimes the new lines were funny, sometimes they weren't. But you always felt as though you were contributing."

Naturally, rehearsals for *The Dick Van Dyke Show* were not all fun and games. As on any TV or movie set, there were the unavoidable hours of waiting for lights to be adjusted, cameras to be blocked, or any one of the ten thousand other details that go into filming a weekly TV series. But, notes actor Frank Adamo, even during these inevitable lulls, the cast had little trouble coming up with diversions to keep themselves occupied. "There was no sitting around," says Adamo. "If we found ourselves just sitting there, we'd be filling our mouths with cookies. You know, knoshing and giggling and scratching." According to Rose Marie, there was rarely a shortage of edibles on the Dick Van Dyke set. "We could've had a party anytime we wanted it," says the actress, who remembers that the show's prop man, Glenn Ross, always kept his office refrigerator well stocked with goodies. "If you wanted a sandwich, you'd say, 'Glenn, I'm hungry. I can't wait for lunch.' He'd say, 'What do you want? Ham and cheese?' He'd have soda and snacks around all the time."

"They had anything you can imagine," echoes Morey Amsterdam. "Sandwiches of all kinds, and coffee and cake and fruit, and everything else." Ironically, in spite of the show's well-stocked cupboard, the actor insists that he actually lost weight over the course of his years on the show—no thanks to Carl Reiner. "Carl was a food tout!" the actor exclaims. "He was always saying, 'Taste this! Taste that!' If I'd let myself go, I'd've gained four hundred pounds!"

Of course, snacking was by no means the only distraction available to actors on the Van Dyke set. Mary Tyler Moore and Ann Guilbert, both fans of a then popular word game called Perquacky, would frequently organize on-set Perquacky tournaments to keep the cast and crew entertained during breaks in the show's rehearsals. Conspicuously absent from the word play would be Dick Van Dyke, who preferred to while away his downtime in pursuit of more contemplative activities, such as sketching or playing the piano. "When we used to rehearse," notes Rose Marie, "Dick would sit in a corner and doodle." An accomplished amateur cartoonist, Van Dyke delighted in skewering his fellow players with exaggerated caricatures, many of which eventually found their way on camera.

The Petrie family portrait that's sketched on the bottom of a turtle shell in episode 73, "Turtles, Ties and Toreadors" is an original Van Dyke; as is the scathing depiction of Mel Cooley that graces Buddy's dart board in show 79, "The Lady and the Tiger and the Lawyer." And the hilarious big-mouthed caricature of Laura in episode 132, "Draw Me a Pear," offers another prime example of the shows resident cartoonist at work.

According to Morey Amsterdam, Dick Van Dyke's passion for cartooning was matched only by the star's devotion to classical music. "He was a very good piano player," says Amsterdam, who recalls that when he wasn't rehearsing or off in a corner sketching, Dick Van Dyke could usually be found noodling away at the keyboard of the studio's practice piano, where the star's tastes ran heavily toward the baroque. "He was a real nut for Bach," notes Amsterdam, a classically trained cellist himself. And Van Dyke was surprisingly reverent in his playing—at least until he came to the end of a piece, when, according to Amsterdam, the star would often pop up from the piano bench and throw himself to the floor, where he would immediately launch into a vigorous calisthenics routine. "He was a tremendous athlete," says Amsterdam. "I've seen Dick do a hundred pushups and get right back on stage and do a scene."

As in any workplace, at the end of the day the show's hardworking actors would happily bid each other adieu before heading off on his or her separate way. For despite the very real affection that they shared on the set each day, the men and women who created *The Dick Van Dyke Show* rarely saw each other outside of the studio. "We never socialized too much or anything like that," recalls Ann Guilbert. And though associate producer Ron Jacobs insists that the show's actors and producers frequently dined together after the show's Tuesday night filmings—at Martoni's on Cahuenga, Friscatti's on Sunset, or any one of a half dozen other local eateries—most observers agree that even these celebratory functions grew increasingly rare after the first few weeks of the show's initial season. "We had a lot of fun on the set," says Ann Guilbert, "and then we'd all get in our cars and go home to our families."

CHAPTER 15
Wednesday Nights

"THE HIGHER THE QUALITY OF A SHOW," SHELDON Leonard is fond of saying, "the longer it will take to catch on with the general public." And, unfortunately, by the middle of the show's first season, *The Dick Van Dyke Show* was well on its way to proving him right. In fact, invoking Leonard's logic, *The Dick Van Dyke Show* must have been of extremely high quality indeed—judging by the amount of time it would take before the general public finally did catch on. In its first season on the air, *The Dick Van Dyke Show* averaged a pitiful Nielsen rating of 16.1, which means that the series was, on average, tuned in by only 16.1 percent of America's television households over the course of the season. By contrast, the year's top-rated series, *Wagon Train*, commanded a whopping year-end average rating of 32.1. By the end of the season, the Van Dyke show was firmly docked in eightieth place, near the very bottom of the A.C. Nielsen Company's year-end ratings chart.

When word of the Van Dyke show's dismal early ratings first reached Sheldon Leonard, he remained remarkably unfazed. Despite the show's initial ratings, Leonard today maintains that he never for a minute thought that the problem lay with the show itself. In his mind, there was nothing wrong with *The Dick Van Dyke Show*—or at least nothing that he and his producer couldn't fix with a little judicious tinkering. No, the real reason they were getting trounced in the weekly ratings was far more prosaic. In Sheldon Leonard's mind, it was their time slot that was killing them.

When *The Dick Van Dyke Show* premiered on October 3, 1961, it had been scheduled to run on Tuesday nights at 8:00 P.M.—a time slot that Sheldon Leonard maintains was far too early in the evening for a show that was supposed to appeal to adults, as he'd hoped theirs would. Furthermore, Sheldon Leonard was convinced that the series would never find its target audience of sophisticated adults as long as it remained saddled with an early evening time slot.

It was a persuasive argument. And when Sheldon Leonard presented it to the programming executives at CBS following the show's first few weeks of lackluster ratings, the network was sufficiently impressed with his logic to order a time change for the series. And so, effective January 3, 1962, CBS moved *The Dick Van Dyke Show* from Tuesdays at 8:00 EST to Wednesday nights at 9:30 EST.

When Sheldon Leonard found out that CBS had agreed to move his show to a more opportune time slot, his sense of relief was laced with apprehension. On the one hand, he was aware that the show's midseason shift to a later time slot represented their first real opportunity to attract the discriminating attention of the intelligent audience of grown-up viewers that had so far eluded them. On the other hand, the producer also recognized that the show had to reel in that larger audience—and fast— or the show's last-minute reprieve could very quickly turn into its last

gasp. And so, hoping to leave little to chance, the show's producers decided to inaugurate their new Wednesday night time slot with an episode that was without question one of the finest half hours they'd yet produced.

The show's producers couldn't have known it then, of course, but "Where Did I Come From?"—

Dick Van Dyke and Mary Tyler Moore mug for the camera in a publicity still designed to alert viewers to the first year's mid-season time change.

which was filmed as the show's nineteenth episode, on November 8, 1961—would prove to be one of the single funniest Dick Van Dyke episodes ever filmed. A charming flashback enlivened by some of the show's most outrageous slapstick, the episode purports to record key events in the life of Rob and Laura Petrie in the final hectic days before their son Ritchie was born. The flashback opens in the Petries' bedroom, where Rob is slowly driving his wife to distraction with his overanxious behavior during the last days of her pregnancy. In his zeal to remain prepared for anything, he climbs into bed wearing jacket and pants, on the off chance he might have to pop up for a middle-of-the-night run to the maternity ward. When Rob finally does drift off to sleep, he keeps his dialing finger poised over the dial on the telephone—just in case of emergency.

Of course, when the stork does comes calling, Rob is caught completely unaware. When Laura calls him at work to announce that her time has arrived, her husband is standing over a tray of prune Danish, clad only in a rumpled shirt and boxer shorts, having dispatched his wrinkled pants and suit to the local dry cleaner for a quick pressing. In a panic, Rob demands that Mel Cooley surrender his pants—a suggestion that the producer rebuffs without hesitation. "I really need my pants today," Mel explains apologetically. "I'm having lunch with the sponsor."

Rob finally arrives home—wearing Buddy's pants hiked high above his ankles—where he succeeds in locking bumpers with the taxicab that's been waiting to whisk Laura off to the hospital. Fortunately, Charlie the laundry man shows up to save the day when he offers to make an unscheduled stop at the maternity ward with Laura in tow. "Honey, you don't mind going in a laundry truck, do you?" Rob asks his long-suffering wife. "No," she replies, "as long as you're with me, darling." And then, turning to the laundry man, she adds, "This is very nice of you!"

"Oh, that's all right," Charlie quips as he escorts the mother-to-be and her nervous husband out to his waiting truck. "You know our motto, 'We pick up and deliver.'"

An undisputed classic in the annals of the Van Dyke show, "Where Did I Come From?" also ranks high on Dick Van Dyke's own list of all-time favorites. "There was an awful lot of slapstick in that one," the star reminisces. "But I had an absolute ball. They let me do everything I wanted to." Director John Rich also counts the episode among his favorites, citing Van Dyke's standout performance as reason enough to treasure the hilarious half hour. As the director observes, "Dick was just superb."

Of course, as the actor cheerfully admits, playing the part of a nervous poppa wasn't exactly a stretch for the real-life father of four. In fact, the actor had just returned from his own most recent excursion to the maternity ward—where his daughter Carrie Beth was born on October 18, 1961—less than a month before this episode was filmed. Naturally, Carl Reiner had no qualms about incorporating the actor's comical perspectives on his own blessed event into the week's script. "Everybody brought up all the crazy things that happened when their kids were born," says Van Dyke, "and we put 'em all in one show."* And, as it turned out, Dick Van Dyke wasn't the only cast member to arrive at the table with an abundance of expectant-parent material—on the night "Where Did I Come From?" was filmed, Ann Morgan Guilbert herself was seven months pregnant.

Ironically, when Ann Guilbert had first become aware of her condition the previous summer, she'd been hesitant to let Carl Reiner in on her secret. And with good reason. Since the show had been in production only a few weeks at that time, Guilbert was understandably concerned that Reiner might decide to replace her with an actress who was not so likely to grow visibly pregnant within a short time. Of course, when the actress finally did summon the courage to break the news to her producer, she was pleased to discover that Reiner had absolutely no intention of replacing one of his key supporting players over a little thing like pregnancy. "He apparently didn't mind having a big, fat neighbor," the actress later joked.[48]

Since it wasn't practical to integrate the actress's real-life pregnancy into the show's ongoing continuity at that late date, Reiner chose instead to mask Ann Guilbert's increasingly visible condition in oversized blouses and A-line dresses for the remainder of her appearances on the series that first year—with the notable exception of "Where Did I Come From?" in which Guilbert's off-screen pregnancy dovetailed perfectly into the story's flashback segment. After the episode was filmed, Guilbert left the series for a temporary, and well-earned, maternity leave. Guil-

---

*Dick Van Dyke would further establish his own paternal credibility a few weeks later when he played host to the annual telecast of *The Wizard of Oz* on CBS, December 10, 1961, along with his three eldest kids, Barry, who was then ten; Chris, then eleven; and Van Dyke's six-year-old daughter, Stacy. According to a report that appeared under Cecil Smith's byline in the *Los Angeles Times* on the day of the broadcast, CBS had been anxious to include Van Dyke's newborn in the telecast as well, as they informed the star on the day Carrie Beth was born. "How d'ya like that?" Van Dyke is supposed to have said. "Carrie was only born three hours ago, and already they want to book her for *The Wizard of Oz!*"[47]

When CBS asked family man Dick Van Dyke to host their annual holiday broadcast of *The Wizard of Oz* in 1961, the star brought three of his real-life brood along for the ride; seated on the bench with Dad are Barry and Stacy, while the star's eldest son, Chris, sits in the foreground.

bert's daughter, Hallie Eckstein—who would eventually launch her own acting career under the stage name Hallie Todd—would be born two months later, in January of 1962.

If Carl Reiner had been able to foresee what he was actually getting himself into when he signed on as producer of *The Dick Van Dyke Show*, he might well have thought twice before he let Sheldon Leonard talk him into taking the job in the first place. But it was only after the series was well into its first season of production that the hapless writer began to get a glimmer of the sheer, unrelenting enormity of his weekly duties on the show.

In addition to his primary responsibilities as the show's chief writer and story editor, Carl Reiner was also responsible for supervising the casting, staging, scoring, and editing of as many as thirty-two entirely new half-hour episodes of the Van Dyke show each season—most of which he also wrote. As incredible as it seems, of the sixty-three scripts filmed in the first two years of *The Dick Van Dyke Show*, Carl Reiner would receive a solo writing credit on no fewer than forty of them—or just slightly less than two-thirds of the entire output of the show's first two seasons. And that's not counting the editing, polishing, and uncredited rewrites that he performed on the remaining twenty-three shows filmed in the Van Dyke show's first two seasons—a prodigious feat by any measure. * As Reiner's friend and longtime manager George Shapiro observes, "To do what he did! Carl's like Lou Gehrig. An iron man!"

"For two solid years, I wrote all day—every day," says Reiner, describing his working method during the show's early days, a routine so relentless that it allowed no time off, not even on weekends. "On Saturday and Sunday I'd work on rewrites to get the show in shape for Monday's rehearsal." And no sooner would the writer polish off one script than he'd start to work on the next week's show. Perhaps the only thing more remarkable than the tireless dedication that Reiner displayed during those first few years of the Van Dyke show was the unending patience that his family exhibited toward their absentee husband and father during that same period. But, as Reiner would later explain to a reporter, he

---

*Incredibly, Reiner also found time to moonlight as an actor in no fewer than four films during his years as producer of *The Dick Van Dyke Show*, logging cameos in *The Thrill of It All* and *The Art of Love*—both of which he also wrote-as well as more substantial parts in *It's a Mad, Mad, Mad, Mad World* and *The Russians Are Coming, The Russians Are Coming*.

made certain that he had his wife's unstinting support well before the show ever hit the air. "Before I started it," said Reiner, "my wife and I agreed I'd have to devote my entire time to it if it was to be the best possible show."49

Given Reiner's near impossible workload, he was constantly on the lookout for freelance scriptwriters to augment his own Herculean efforts on the show. "People would submit scripts to me," says Reiner. "And Sheldon was terrific at finding writers, because he knew a lot of them from his other shows. So he'd bring in people that he knew." Of course, since the vast majority of these outside writers lacked Carl Reiner's own particular insights into the Van Dyke show's unique character and rhythms, most of the scripts they submitted to the show required extensive reworking by Reiner before they were up to his exacting standards for the series. But Reiner was so delighted to be getting any help at all that he didn't mind the extra work that these freelance submissions engendered—at least not at first. "If they could just give me pages to work on, I would be so happy." But, before long, Reiner discovered—to his growing dismay—that rewriting an outsider's script often took him far longer than it did to compose one of his own from scratch. "It took me four to five days to write a script," says Reiner. "But I found myself taking eight days to rewrite someone else's show!"

The worst scripts were those that arrived, as Reiner describes it, "with the bones buried in the wrong place." And, he observes, the task of retooling a structurally unsound script could be a vexing process. "Those were the ones that drove me nuts! I'd have to take *this* out, and when you take *this* out, *that* falls out. I finally decided it's easier to write a show myself. So that's why I wrote forty of the first sixty, because I could work faster that way."

Of course, it would be of no small consolation to Carl Reiner that in writing the lion's share of the show's first two seasons by himself, he had practically guaranteed that the series would remain well within the boundaries of his own unique—and largely autobiographical—vision. "The show was *my* reality," Reiner explains unapologetically. "That didn't mean you got a better reality in my scripts than somebody else might've written. Or that I wrote better than anybody else. But my reality was my reality."

One early Van Dyke show that Reiner maintains fell somewhat short of his own highly specific standards of reality was "The Curious Thing About Women," an episode that many fans of the series regard as a highlight of the show's first season. Written by Frank Tarloff—under the pen name David Adler—the episode revolves around a domestic squabble that erupts after Rob exploits Laura's habit of opening his mail as fodder for a comedy sketch. What's really got Laura steamed is Rob's depiction of her as an incurable snoop, which she feels is an unwarranted accusation. But Laura's resolve is tested a few days later when a mysterious package arrives at the Petrie house addressed to her husband. Not surprisingly, Laura proves unable to restrain herself, and in less than sixty seconds the curious homemaker has unleashed the parcel's volatile cargo: a giant, inflatable life raft, which naturally swells to its full ten-foot length in the middle of the Petries' living room floor just as Rob walks in the door!

The gargantuan life raft—and Mary Tyler Moore's priceless comic reaction as she tries to physically restrain it—provides the episode with one of *The Dick Van Dyke Show*'s more spectacular comic set pieces, a superb example of slapstick mayhem that calls to mind the physical comedy that Lucille Ball had already perfected a decade earlier on *I Love Lucy*. Which might explain Carl Reiner's lukewarm reaction to the episode, whose comic premise undoubtedly hewed a bit too close to traditional sitcom conventions for his somewhat less formulaic sensibilities. "I didn't love the fact that we made Mary so silly that she had to open the package," says Reiner, who confesses that his biggest problem with Frank Tarloff's script was that he simply couldn't imagine his own wife—or anyone else's, for that matter—behaving as Laura Petrie does in the episode. "I made Laura a little sillier than my wife," explains Reiner, "but I was still basing things on Estelle. And I never liked that show particularly, because that wasn't my wife."

Actually, the fact that "The Curious Thing About Women" seems to echo the basic plot mechanics of an *I Love Lucy* episode may not be entirely coincidental. It's a little known fact that Frank Tarloff's script for "The Curious Thing About Women" was actually based on a plotline that the writer first composed for the Joan Davis sitcom, *I Married Joan*, which itself was little more than an *I Love Lucy* knock-off from the Desilu assembly line of the early fifties. "Curiosity"—which was the title of the script that Tarloff penned for the Davis show—was first telecast on December 3, 1952. The *TV Guide* synopsis for the Joan Davis episode—which was co-authored by Tarloff, Arthur Stander, and Phil Sharp—seems to reveal a more than passing similarity to Tarloff's later script for the Van Dyke episode. "Joan's husband forbids her to open his mail," reads the blurb. "She follows his order until the next day, when a large parcel arrives."[50]

Tarloff's relatively mild act of creative larceny was hardly uncommon, especially in an era when situation comedy writers routinely dusted off scripts from as far back as radio in their search for fresh springboards. Ironically, Tarloff today claims that he has almost no recollection of writ-

Dick Van Dyke poses with his rehearsal stand-in, stock player Frank Adamo, who enjoyed the distinction of logging more appearances on the series than anyone outside of the show's central cast.

ing either version of his durable storyline. Speaking of "The Curious Thing About Women," Tarloff confesses, "I saw it about six months ago, and I didn't even remember that I'd written it until I saw my name on it at the end."

Despite Carl Reiner's reservations about "The Curious Thing About Women," practical considerations made it difficult for the producer to take a pass on any material with such obvious comic potential. "I mean, I couldn't say no to it," he acknowledges, "because I needed a show to do." And, once the dust settled, the producer admits that he didn't regret that decision. "It was a very successful show," Reiner allows. "And very funny. But it always bothered me that I would never have come up with that premise. That show was written by another person—it was somebody else's reality. And I didn't like that."

Eagle-eyed Van Dyke show fans will no doubt recognize the delivery boy who drops off Laura's mystery parcel in this episode as Frank Adamo, a gangly character actor who would prove to be a durable addition to the show's unofficial stock company—a select group that also included Ross Elliott, Jamie Farr, Herbie Faye, Jerry Hausner, Allan Melvin, Isabel Randolph, Johnny Silver, Doris Singleton, and Amzie Strickland, among others. But, unlike the other members of the Van Dyke show's loose-knit repertory company, Frank Adamo also enjoyed the rare status of regular employment on the series. For, in addition to the dozens of bit parts, atmospheric roles, and uncredited walk-ons that Adamo contributed during his five seasons on the show, the skinny bit player was also employed as Dick Van Dyke's full-time rehearsal stand-in—a job that came about as the result of Adamo's long-standing friendship with the star, a friendship that predated the Van Dyke show by at least a year and a half.

Frank Adamo was a struggling junior executive in the advertising game when he met Van Dyke during the star's lean years in New York in the late 1950s. "I was working for J. Walter Thompson at the time," recalls Adamo. "And Dick used to come up to J. Walter to rehearse and do Rinso commercials, or some damn thing like that. So we got to be friendly up there." As fate would have it, Adamo found himself out of work a few months later—just as Dick Van Dyke's fortunes were about to take a turn for the better. "I had left J. Walter Thompson," Adamo says, "and I read in the trades that Dick was going to be doing *Bye Bye Birdie.*" Figuring that he had nothing to lose by asking his old friend for a job, Adamo gathered the courage to pay an unannounced call on the fast-rising star. "I knew he was in rehearsal at the Phyllis Anderson Theatre down on Second Avenue," recalls Adamo, "so I went and stood by the stage door. It was a very snowy, cold day. And when Dick came out, I told him very frankly that I needed work." To Adamo's surprise, Van Dyke offered him a job on the spot.

For the next year, the former ad man enjoyed steady employment as Dick Van Dyke's backstage assistant on *Bye Bye Birdie.* "During that year we became very close," recalls Adamo. "Like family. I met Dick's wife, Marge, his grandparents, and his whole tribe of kids. And we all got along like peas in a pod." Naturally, when Van Dyke finally left *Bye Bye Birdie* for the fertile territory of weekly television, he invited his capable assistant to join him. "Dick said to me," remembers Adamo, "very casually, 'Would you like to go to California? I don't know what we can pay.' I said, 'Don't worry about it. I'll just go along on good faith.'" And, once he got to California, that faith was quickly rewarded when Sheldon Leonard—struck by the rail-thin character actor's striking physical resemblance to Dick Van Dyke—immediately offered to put him to work as Van Dyke's rehearsal stand-in.

Of course, the stand-in work—which basically required Adamo to do little more than stand under the set's hot lights in Dick Van Dyke's stead during the show's arduous technical rehearsals—was clearly not the most glamorous job on the show. And so, to break the monotony, Adamo would often sit in on the show's table readings, where he would sometimes be asked to read one of the small parts that hadn't yet been cast. Naturally, when the time finally did come to hire an actor for one of these minuscule parts, the producers often would simply hand the part to the star's eager stand-in. "Sheldon would say, 'Frank's already doing the part, let's just give it to him,'" recalls Adamo. "That's how I ended up doing all the little parts on the show."

And while it's true that most of Adamo's on-camera work on the Van Dyke show flashed across the screen in the blink of an eye, the bit player did manage to take center stage on at least a few occasions. Adamo's personal favorite of all his Van Dyke show bit parts was H. Fieldstone Thorley, the pretentious poet who does his bit to bruise Rob's ego in episode 55, "I'm No Henry Walden!" Equally memorable was Adamo's turn in episode 101, "Romance, Roses and Rye Bread," where he played an actor who brazens his way through a dismal production of an off-Broadway travesty called *Waiting for an Armadillo*. But Adamo's finest moment—or at least the one that drew the biggest laughs—came in the show's eighteenth episode, "Punch Thy Neighbor," where Adamo played the singing telegram man Jerry hires to deliver his scathing assessment of Rob Petrie's writing talent to the unamused writer. "Look how far this man has gotten," Adamo's telegram man sings in a grating monotone, "Writing shows that are really rotten."

CHAPTER 16
Bad Old Days

BY THE FIRST WEEK OF 1962, THE CAST AND CREW OF *THE Dick Van Dyke Show* had returned from a well-earned two-week holiday hiatus to begin work on the show's twenty-fourth episode, "The Twizzle," a show that has the distinction of ranking among Carl Reiner's least favorite Van Dyke shows. "There're about eight shows where one or two or three members of the cast were not happy with it," he confesses. "And 'The Twizzle' was one of them."

Little wonder, since Carl Reiner's offbeat script—which depicts Sally Rogers's improbable discovery of a new singing sensation in a Connecticut bowling alley—reads more like an extended satirical sketch from *Your Show of Shows* than a fully realized Van Dyke show plotline. Reiner today admits that the episode was originally designed as little more than a starring vehicle for a virtually unknown singer named Jerry Lanning, whose main claim to fame was that he happened to be the son of the now all but forgotten fifties pop singer Roberta Sherwood.* "That was one of those things where somebody came to me and said, 'Can you do a show for Roberta Sherwood's son?'" explains Carl Reiner. "It was written for him." But, despite the writer's valiant push, Lanning proved to be no Ricky Nelson, and "The Twizzle" today remains a prime example of that rarest of commodities, a Dick Van Dyke show misfire.

---

*In addition to the small measure of immortality he earned by virtue of his single appearance on the Van Dyke show, Jerry Lanning would resurface in the late 1970s as a regular on the daytime dramas *Search for Tomorrow*, *The Guiding Light*, and *Texas*.

Dick Van Dyke's own candidate for the show's all-time stiff is episode 27, "The Bad Old Days," which was filmed just three weeks after "The Twizzle," on January 30, 1962. "That was the worst one we ever did!" declares Van Dyke, recalling the episode's well-worn plotline, in which Buddy attempts to convince Rob that the modern American male is being systematically emasculated by tyrannical wives like Laura. Gullible husband Rob nearly falls for Buddy's line, until he imagines—via an elaborate dream sequence—just how lousy things really must have been in "The Bad Old Days."

Of course, the idea that a young husband's masculinity might be threatened by his wife's domestic tyranny was already a wheezing premise in 1962—a fact that did not pass Van Dyke's notice. But what really gave the actor heartburn was the episode's dream sequence, a creaky turn-of-the-century costume piece in which the star was forced to don Gay Nineties garb and sport an oversized handlebar mustache, with predictably uneasy results. "It was just awful," sighs the star, "just incredible!" The show's only

A publicity still taken during rehearsals for the show's 27th installment, "The Bad Old Days," the episode that earns Dick Van Dyke's personal vote for worst Van Dyke show ever. "It was just awful," he insists. "I don't know what the hell we thought we were doing. It didn't work, and we all knew it."

saving grace, says Van Dyke, is that production requirements for the dream sequence dictated that it be shot separately from the rest of the episode, thus sparing him and Mary Tyler Moore the indignity of having to perform the travesty in front of an actual audience. "We shot it during the day," Van Dyke recalls, still cringing at the memory. "I don't know what the hell we thought we were doing," he says. "It didn't work, and we all knew it. But by that time we were too far into it to stop!"

When Dick Van Dyke posed for this daylight savings time reminder near the end of the Van Dyke show's first year, the star had every reason to believe that the clock had just about run out on *The Dick Van Dyke Show* as well.

In defense of the show's hard-working cast and crew, it's probably only fair to point out that by the time they began rehearsals for the pair of ill-conceived episodes cited above, the show had already been in active production for well over six consecutive months—an exhausting stretch during which the actors had enjoyed only minimal time off, and writer/producer Carl Reiner none at all. In fact, by the end of January 1962, Carl Reiner had already been producing and writing—and rewriting—an entirely new half-hour Van Dyke show teleplay every week for more than eight consecutive months! Considering the enormity of his task, it's almost a miracle that the show's quality during that season remained as consistent as it did. As the show's third-season story editor Bill Persky would later observe, "Our worst shows were better than most people's best."

Besides, as longtime Van Dyke show writer Sam Denoff contends, with a production schedule that demanded at least thirty new shows every year, no one expected the series to score an out-of-the-park home run with each episode. "Out of twenty-six or thirty shows a year," says Denoff, "you know you're gonna have six that are fantastic, twelve that are pretty good, and three or four clunkers that—for one reason or another—don't work."

But if the Van Dyke company had to contend with one or two "clunkers" as their first year rolled to an end, it was hardly cause for alarm. Far more damaging to the cast's ordinarily buoyant morale was the very real threat that, despite all their hard work and struggle, *The Dick Van Dyke Show* might not be returning for a second season at all. By the beginning of 1962, rumors of the show's imminent demise—spurred on by the show's consistently dismal Nielsen standings—had been circulating for months. As costumer Harald Johnson remembers, "We were sort of, like, walking on grapes the whole first year."

According to Van Dyke stock player Doris Singleton, who logged her first appearance on the series in episode 22, "The Talented Neighborhood," cancellation jitters were already in the air when that episode was filmed during the first week of December 1961. "Everyone was very worried," recalls the actress, "because the show was in trouble at that time." And, in the eyes of many in the Van Dyke show cast that week, Singleton was something of an authority on the subject of premature cancellation, having recently survived the abrupt cancellation of *Angel*, a sitcom on which she'd enjoyed steady employment until it had been axed after a single season on CBS. And, says Singleton, the circumstances surrounding her show's unceremonious cancellation were a topic of especially keen interest to Mary Tyler Moore, who was understandably concerned that the Van Dyke show might face a similarly ignoble end. "Mary asked me, 'When did you know that you were going off the air?'" says Singleton. It certainly didn't lift the young actress's spirits when Singleton informed her that, in her case, the end came swiftly and without warning. "Mary was very depressed," recalls Singleton, "because it didn't look like the Van Dyke show was going to be renewed."

Of course, as the youngest and least established member of the Van Dyke company, Mary Tyler Moore had good reason to be nervous, if only because she had so much to lose. But though the untimely demise of *The Dick Van Dyke Show* would almost certainly have dealt a staggering blow to her burgeoning career, Mary Tyler Moore had equally compelling personal reasons to pray for the show's continued success. In late 1961, the actress and her first husband had filed for divorce, a dissolution that had been finalized in February of 1962. And so, by the time the show's first season rolled to an end that same month, the newly single twenty-five-year-old mother had come to depend on the familial surroundings of the Van Dyke show set for emotional, as well as professional, support. "They

were my family," acknowledges the actress. "They were my first experience with a feeling of family outside of my own blood relations."

In spite of the lingering doubts that hovered over the Van Dyke soundstage during the final weeks of the show's first season, the cast seemed to
have little difficulty rallying their energies for the outstanding two-part
episode that would comprise their penultimate effort for the season: "I
Am My Brother's Keeper" and "The Sleeping Brother." The twin episodes
would also be fondly remembered as the segments that first introduced
the final addition to the show's family tree, Rob's brother Stacey Petrie,
who was played by the star's real-life brother, Jerry Van Dyke.

According to Carl Reiner, that inspired bit of stunt casting was not part
of any great design on his part, but the result of what the producer terms
"one of those happy accidents." As Reiner tells the story, he didn't even
know his star had a younger sibling until Dick Van Dyke happened to
mention in passing that his brother was opening his nightclub act at
Chicago's Playboy Club. "Your brother's a comic?" Reiner asked, already
weighing the fertile creative possibilities in his mind. "Is he funny?"

"Oh, sure. He's very funny," came Van Dyke's reply. Which was, of
course, all Carl Reiner needed to hear.

"Well, then," Reiner proposed, "I'll write a show for your brother. And
then I'll fly him out here to star in it!"

As Reiner recalls it, he went right to work. "Tell me a little about your
brother," suggested the writer, fishing for any clue that might lead to a
suitable storyline. Van Dyke then rattled off a thumbnail profile of his
younger brother, ending with a little tidbit that Carl Reiner found
absolutely irresistible. "Dick said, 'Oh, yeah, as a kid he was a bit of a
somnambulist,'" Reiner recalls. "And I said, 'That's it!' I knew I could
make something out of a brother who walks in his sleep!"

When he got home that night, Carl Reiner sat down and began to work.
In the first half of what the writer would eventually expand into the show's
first two-part saga, Rob's ebullient brother Stacey arrives for an unexpected visit. Although Stacey instantly wins Laura and Ritchie over with
his jokes and confident patter, Rob is less impressed by his brother's irrepressible vitality—a fact that does not go unnoticed by Laura, especially
after Rob begins to treat his brother with a diffidence bordering on open
hostility. Finally, after Stacey is safely sequestered in the family's guest
room, Laura demands an explanation for Rob's inhospitable attitude
toward his only brother. It's not long before Laura comes to understand
the true cause of her husband's strange behavior, at which point she's tak-
en aback. "My brother Stacey has a problem," confesses Rob. "He's a
somnambulist."

"Are you sure your brother can act?" Carl Reiner asked Dick Van Dyke before
the writer scripted the show's first two-parter as a showcase
for Jerry Van Dyke. "Oh, absolutely," came the star's reply. "If he can't,
I'll have to kill him."

And not just any garden variety sleepwalker, Rob explains, but a world class somnambulist—a genuine, bona fide schizophrenic sleepwalker, complete with two entirely independent personalities. "When he's awake he's very shy," says Rob. "But when he's asleep, he's very friendly and outgoing." Suddenly, as if to offer an unprompted demonstration of the curious extremes of his strange malady, Stacey walks into the room, now wide awake and as shy as a door mouse! And it's in this sorry state that Rob's bashful brother finally confesses the secret ambition that has brought him to New York in the first place. "I've been thinking," he stammers, "well, that maybe I'd like to be a...a comedian!"

Rob has his doubts, of course. But he finally sets them aside and agrees to introduce his brother to Mel Cooley and the rest of his friends at a party a few nights later. Naturally, Rob's worst fears come to pass when his brother shows up at the party in a state of somnambulant inebriation—and then proceeds to dazzle every one of the assembled guests with the high-octane charm of his comedy act. When Mel Cooley offers the young comic an audition for *The Alan Brady Show*, it puts Rob in a tight spot, since he knows that his brother will never be able to make it through the audition—unless he happens to be asleep. And it's on that cliffhanger that the show's first installment comes to an end.

Character actor Jay C. Flippen played the title role in "The Return of Happy Spangler," an episode that was anything but happy for the demoralized cast of *The Dick Van Dyke Show*, who were convinced that it would be the show's swan song.

Carl Reiner didn't actually intend to write a two-part episode. But once he sat down at the typewriter, he says, the show's premise quickly expanded beyond the scope of a single script. "I had all this fun stuff," he says, "and I'm not gonna throw it out! So I knew I had to do a second part."

Of course, it was only after he'd polished off the second installment of his ambitious two-parter that it finally dawned on Carl Reiner that he was about to commit two half hours of network prime time to spotlight the singing, acting, and comedic talents of an actor he still hadn't even met! It had been one thing to write the star's brother into a single episode of the show—but now, with two shows suddenly resting on Jerry Van Dyke's still untested shoulders, Carl Reiner suddenly realized that the stakes had just gone up one very large notch. If the star's younger sibling didn't turn out to be everything that Dick Van Dyke had promised, the producer would now have not *one* but *two* very dull episodes of *The Dick Van Dyke Show* on his hands. Finally, if only for the peace of mind it would afford him, Reiner decided to put in an eleventh-hour call to the star himself. "Dick," Reiner began, "are you sure your brother can act?"

"Yeah," Van Dyke responded. "Why?"

"Because the show's hysterical," Reiner replied. "Only it's gonna be a two-parter. So your brother's gotta be a good actor. You're sure he can act?"

"Oh, absolutely!" Van Dyke answered.

"Great," Reiner answered with audible relief. "How can you be so sure?"

"Because," Van Dyke replied, oozing conviction, "if he can't—I'll have to kill him."

Jerry Van Dyke finally did prove worthy of his brother's confidence. But not before he put John Rich through what the director describes as one of the most trying weeks of his entire career. As Rich tells the story, his troubles began at the table reading for "The Sleeping Brother," which is when the director first started to suspect that the star's brother might have gotten in a little over his head. "I can tell this story because Jerry and I are very good friends," says Rich. "He was scared stiff!" That much was clear, says the director, from the younger Van Dyke's line readings, which were stiff and colorless throughout all of the early rehearsals for the episode. "He read his lines without anything on them," says Rich. "Uncurved. Flat."

Carl Reiner also noticed the actor's stiffness at that initial rehearsal, but remained confident that John Rich—who had earned such a glowing reputation for his winning way with actors—would be able to bring the star's brother around with a few days of rehearsal. For his part, the director wasn't so sure, but he finally decided to reserve judgment. "You listen to the first reading," says Rich, "and you say, 'This'll get better.'"

But, to the director's mounting dismay, it didn't get better. By the time John Rich began blocking scenes out on the stage a day or two later, he noticed little improvement in the neophyte actor's shaky confidence level. "We started to put the thing on its feet," recalls Rich, "and Jerry was really a stumbler." By the time the cast broke for lunch on the third day of rehearsal, the director recalls that the other cast members were exchanging glum looks all around. "Taking nothing away from Jerry," says Rose Marie, recalling those early rehearsals for the show's twenty-eighth episode, "he was bad." And, according to Rich, the veteran actress wasn't the only one to hold that opinion at the time. In fact, notes the director, about the only member of the cast who seemed not the least bit concerned about Jerry Van Dyke's flailing performance was his brother, who invariably ended each morning's rehearsal by offering his younger sibling a hearty clap on the back before he calmly led him off to the studio commissary for lunch. "Dick looked very cool," acknowledges Rich, who admits that he, on the other hand, was growing decidedly less so with each passing day.

The turning point finally came after the show's Friday night run-through, a lackluster affair that caused John Rich to embark on a course of action that he'd been hoping to avoid all week. With only two rehearsal days remaining before the Tuesday night filming, the director finally decided that it might be an opportune time to pull Dick Van Dyke aside for a short on-set confab. "I think Jerry might need a little help," the director suggested. And then, having dropped the hint in the broadest terms possible, the director decided that the wisest choice might well be to withdraw, leaving the problem in the capable hands of his star player. "That's all I said," says Rich.

It was enough. "When Jerry came in on Monday, he was a heckuva lot better," recalls the director, who'd been overjoyed to observe the startling progress that had occurred almost overnight. "Suddenly he got it just right," says Rich, "that shy, self-deprecating, lovely quality that was the character." And, notes John Rich, the younger Van Dyke continued to make similar breakthroughs throughout the remaining two days of rehearsals. "By Tuesday night, he was a smash. It was extraordinary. A triumph!"

"I never did ask what happened," says Rich, who swears he still has no idea what Dick Van Dyke might've said or done to inspire his brother after such a slow start. One possible explanation for the younger Van Dyke's turnaround is offered by Frank Adamo, who suggests that Jerry Van Dyke may actually have decided to keep his performance in check in deference to his older brother. "It wasn't Jerry's show," explains Adamo, "and he knew that. So I think Dick finally had to tell him, 'Look Jerry, just go out there and do what you do best. Don't worry about me.'"

With characteristic modesty, Dick Van Dyke dismisses any suggestion that he played a significant role in his younger brother's triumphant debut performance on the show. "He was very nervous," acknowledges the elder Van Dyke. "But his comedy instincts were good, particularly when he had an audience to work with. And by the time we hit the audience, he was doing great."

Dick Van Dyke was by no means alone in his glowing assessment of his younger brother's telegenic promise. "He came in, and he was delightful," recalls Carl Reiner, who was so impressed with the younger Van Dyke's talents that he would eventually try—unsuccessfully—to come up with a series for Jerry Van Dyke. "We tried to do a pilot with him two years later that didn't work."

No matter. In the wake of his debut on *The Dick Van Dyke Show*, Jerry Van Dyke was deluged with TV offers, and—notwithstanding an occasional dry spell or two—he's been hard at work ever since. In 1963, the younger Van Dyke signed on as Judy Garland's second banana for the early episodes of the excitable diva's now legendary CBS variety series. And in the years since then, the popular character actor has logged many, many appearances on television variety shows and situation comedies, including featured roles on *My Mother the Car*, *Accidental Family*, and—more recently—his Emmy award–winning stint as assistant coach Luther Van Dam on the popular ABC situation comedy *Coach*.

On Tuesday, February 20, 1962, the cast of *The Dick Van Dyke Show* filmed "The Return of Happy Spangler," the episode that would mark the end of the show's first full season. To commemorate this milestone in the show's brief but eventful production history, the show's producers had arranged to stage a small on-set wrap party that was scheduled to begin at the conclusion of the night's filming. Unfortunately, by the time "The Return of Happy Spangler" was filmed, no one felt much like celebrating the end of *The Dick Van Dyke Show*'s first season—since by that time most of the show's cast and crew were convinced that there might never be a second.

Only a few days before the episode's February 20 filming date, word had reached the cast that CBS would not be renewing the show's option for a second season. The depressing rumor was soon confirmed by one of Sheldon Leonard's most trusted sources inside the network, who informed the executive producer that CBS President Jim Aubrey had called his top programmers to New York during the week of February 12, 1962, for the purpose of hammering out a preliminary draft of the network's upcoming fall schedule for the 1962 TV season. And for the low-rated *Dick Van Dyke Show*, the news was not good. After noting that the show's much-hyped midseason move to a less competitive time slot had failed to produce even a burp in its paltry Nielsen standings, the network had quietly dropped the series from consideration for a spot on the fall schedule. Which meant that, for all practical purposes, *The Dick Van Dyke Show* was dead.

And so it was that clouds gathered over the normally sunny Van Dyke set as the cast assembled to begin rehearsals for their thirtieth episode on Valentine's Day 1962. And yet, even though most of the show's hard-working cast and crew were convinced that "The Return of Happy Spangler" would mark their swan song as a theater company, fate would soon prove them very, very wrong.

Fate. And Sheldon Leonard.

CHAPTER 17

On the Banks of the Ohio

AS UNSETTLING AS THE RUMORS OF THE NETWORK'S mounting disaffection had been to company morale in the waning days of *The Dick Van Dyke Show*'s freshman year, Sheldon Leonard maintains that he was never particularly troubled by the noises that had been emanating from CBS—at least not at first. After all, in his mind, the network posed little threat to him or the show as long as he remained on good terms with his sponsor/friends at Procter & Gamble, the advertising giant who continued to wield considerable muscle in the network's corridors of power. "With the support of powerful sponsors like Procter & Gamble," Leonard observes, "it was possible to bully and manipulate the networks." Of course, if Procter & Gamble suddenly decided to pull the plug on the series—now, that would be different.

That would be a calamity.

Unfortunately, Sheldon Leonard would have ample cause to find out just how calamitous only a few days later, when he received a singularly distressing call from Lee Rich, the Benton and Bowles Agency vice president who then rode herd on the household products manufacturer's vast media interests. The ad man had called Leonard to relay a progress report on Procter & Gamble's advertising plans for the coming season—and, for Sheldon Leonard, the news was not good. After monitoring *The Dick Van Dyke Show*'s stagnant ratings for the better part of the season, Lee Rich explained, Procter & Gamble's marketing analysts had developed serious doubts about the show's continued viability as an effective advertising vehicle.

"And?" Leonard interrupted, his eyes already fixed clearly on the writing on the wall.

And, the ad man continued, as a result, Procter & Gamble had all but decided to end their sponsorship commitment to *The Dick Van Dyke Show* effective with the show's final first-season broadcast.

As Sheldon Leonard took the words in, his mind began to reel. It was disastrous news, of course. But what made it all the more alarming was the timing—coming, as it did, just as the producer was preparing to go toe-to-toe with CBS over the network's impending cancellation order. Clearly, if *The Dick Van Dyke Show* ever needed the support of Procter & Gamble, it was now. Because without it, as Leonard shuddered to recognize, the show simply didn't have a prayer. "There must be something we can do," Leonard exclaimed, "something we can say to Procter & Gamble to make them change their minds."

"Probably not," came the weary reply from Lee Rich, who suggested that the time to act had already passed. The final decision would be made in just a few hours, he explained, at a high-level meeting of the company's product managers that he was, in fact, scheduled to attend the very next morning in Cincinnati. "In that case," Sheldon Leonard announced decisively, "you'd better save me a seat on the plane. Because I'm going to Cincinnati with you."

It was an outrageous suggestion, as Rich was quick to inform Leonard almost as soon as he'd made it. "I realize," the producer admitted, "that what I'm proposing is unorthodox."

No, protested Lee Rich, it was more than unorthodox. The idea that a television producer would even think of crashing a high-level powwow at his sponsor's corporate headquarters to deliver a personal plea for one of his own shows was—well, it was nothing short of preposterous.

And yet...

After only a few moment's consideration, Lee Rich had to admit that— as outlandish as it was—the producer's scheme was not without a certain roguish charm. And then, too, there was always the chance that it might actually work. It was just possible that the Procter & Gamble executives might be so flattered by the sudden arrival of a bona fide Hollywood celebrity on their corporate doorstep that they would be moved to grant their glamorous visitor an uncommonly sympathetic audience. Besides, the ad man reasoned, if nothing else, Sheldon Leonard could almost certainly be counted on to provide the staid midwestern executives with a show that none of them would soon forget.

And so it was decided. Lee Rich would go along with Leonard's scheme. And a few short hours later, an extra ticket had been booked on the overnight flight from Los Angeles to Cincinnati, where Lee Rich had arranged an audience for Sheldon Leonard with the soap company's top executives for the very next day.

Early the following morning the pair arrived at Procter & Gamble's corporate headquarters, where—still bleary-eyed from the all-night flight—the ad man and the TV producer were quickly ushered into one of the company's wood-paneled boardrooms. And there, standing before a select audience of the company's top marketing executives, Sheldon Leonard reached into his actor's bag of tricks and launched into what would prove to be one of the most important performances of his entire career. "I went back East," as he would later describe it, "got down on one knee, and sang 'Mammy.'"[51]

"Sheldon made a big, long, impassioned speech," recalls Lee Rich, "a typical Sheldon Leonard speech." As Leonard remembers that fateful morning, he kicked off the memorable sales pitch with a confession. "I told them that I knew the show had been a little rusty in its first year," he says, "that it had not yet hit its stride—that it was not the show we knew it could be." And then, after thoroughly disarming his audience with the ingenuousness of this opening gambit, the producer quickly segued into a sincere appraisal of *The Dick Van Dyke Show*, with a marked emphasis on the series' vast and as yet barely tapped potential. "I loved the show," he explains today, "and I loved the material. And I simply explained to them my deep gut feeling that, if given a chance for people to gain some familiarity with the characters, the show would catch on."

But, of course, he didn't stop there. Drawing on skills of persuasion sharpened by more than thirty years as a character actor specializing in con men, touts, and strong-arm characters, Sheldon Leonard charmed, wheedled, and cajoled the roomful of hard-nosed executives until, finally, he had every last one of them nibbling from the palm of his hand.

Or almost every one of them.

Unfortunately, there was a lone holdout. And, as fate would have it, he would prove to be the most troubling exception of all. For of all the executives in the Procter & Gamble boardroom that morning, only Lee Rich himself remained visibly unmoved as Sheldon Leonard wrapped up his pitch. And the ad man's studied neutrality was particularly unnerving to the producer, who knew that without Lee Rich's go-ahead, he was sunk, since Procter & Gamble would be highly unlikely to approve the kind of sponsorship commitment he needed without the consent of their Madison Avenue media guru.

Fortunately, the agonizing suspense would be mercifully short-lived. It was no more than a few seconds before one of Procter & Gamble's management team turned and put the question to Rich directly. "Well, Lee," the executive queried. "What do *you* think? What does Benton and Bowles think we should do?"

Rich paused only an instant before he finally volunteered his opinion, a split second that nonetheless seemed like an eternity to the anxious executive producer of *The Dick Van Dyke Show*. "The Benton and Bowles Agency," Lee Rich finally announced, "recommends that you renew *The Dick Van Dyke Show*." Though the words had been far too long in coming, Lee Rich's declaration sounded like poetry to Sheldon Leonard. And, just as the producer had predicted, Rich's vote of confidence was all that was needed to usher the Procter & Gamble executives firmly into his camp.

"Procter & Gamble agreed to pick up the show for another year," says Sheldon Leonard, who boarded the plane for his return flight to Los Angeles later that same afternoon. But no sooner had that plane touched down in California than Leonard discovered that his travels were not over yet. For there, waiting for him when he got off the plane, was an urgent message from Lee Rich, who had stayed behind in Cincinnati to iron out the remaining wrinkles in the Procter & Gamble sponsorship deal. And

The cast struggles gamely to maintain appearances at the show's first-season wrap party, despite rumors that the show had already been served with a cancellation notice from the network.

judging from the grave tone of this latest dispatch, it was apparent that the ad man had run into some pretty big wrinkles. "I came back to Hollywood very happy," says the producer, "only to learn that Procter & Gamble had had second thoughts. Suddenly they were only willing to sponsor half the program!"

The news came as a particularly devastating blow to Sheldon Leonard, since it meant that, even after all of his efforts of the past twenty-four hours, he was suddenly—for all practical purposes—right back at square one. "I now had to go back out and find another sponsor to pick up the other half of the show," he says. Worse yet, he had to do it fast, before word of his sponsor's defection leaked to the executives at CBS, who would be almost certain to view this latest turn of events as all the justification they needed to proceed with the show's cancellation, which—through some miracle—was still not official. And so, with the clock ticking loudly in his ears, Sheldon Leonard turned around and boarded another jet—this one bound for New York City.

By the time the producer landed at New York's Idlewild airport early the next morning, Sol Leon of the William Morris office had already arranged the first appointment in what promised to be a busy day of meetings. The producer's first pitch had been scheduled at the headquarters of the P. Lorillard Tobacco Company, the makers of Kent cigarettes. "They interrupted a board meeting to bring me in there," insists Leonard, who returned the courtesy by opening his own presentation with a gesture of deference calculated to earn him the instant respect of the roomful of busy executives. "Sheldon took off his gold watch," recalls Grant Tinker, who also happened to be present during Leonard's presentation that morning, "and he put it on the desk. And he said to them, 'How much time do I have?' They said, 'Twelve minutes.' And he said, 'Well, gentlemen, here's what I want to tell you.'"

And with that, recalls Tinker, the producer began pitching his wares in his own inimitable fashion. "He's one of the most articulate guys in the world," says Tinker, who testifies to the peculiar effectiveness of Leonard's trademark Damon Runyon–inflected speech patterns in a straight business setting. "He just said what he had to say so well that it was like music."

True to his word, Leonard wrapped his presentation twelve minutes later, at which point the producer retrieved his watch from the table and hurried on to his next appointment. "We left Lorillard," recalls Sol Leon, "and the executives went back into session by themselves." Meanwhile, Leonard and his agent had already moved on to the offices of the Compton Advertising Agency, where the producer wasted little time launching

To save his beloved *Dick Van Dyke Show* from almost certain extinction,
Sheldon Leonard drew on every ounce of charm he'd polished over three decades
of playing touts, con artists, and strongarm men in Hollywood.

into his by now well-rehearsed presentation for an executive of the Alberto-Culver Company.

As fate would have it, the producer's pitch to the hair products company executive turned out to be the easiest one of all. "I find out that his children are already familiar with the show," the producer recalls, "and he's already strongly biased in favor of it. You know, I've already got him lined up. He's gonna be a cinch." But, in an ironic twist, the eager executive never even got to hear the end of his visitor's spirited sales pitch.

About a minute and a half after he'd started his talk, Sheldon Leonard noticed that his agent, Sol Leon, had suddenly been called to the phone for what was obviously an urgent message. Ignoring his agent's momentary defection, the producer returned to his spiel. But no more than a minute later Sol Leon walked back into the conference room and, smiling broadly, unceremoniously called the meeting to an abrupt finish. "Sol Leon gives me this signal for 'Cut!'" recalls Leonard. "So the only thing I can figure is that it is no longer necessary for me to continue pitching the show, because obviously the phone call had said that Lorillard was gonna buy it. Which is what had happened."

"In the intervening twenty minutes after we left the Lorillard boardroom," confirms Leon, "they had enthusiastically decided to buy the other available half of the show. So that was it."

With P. Lorillard Tobacco and Procter & Gamble now signed to share *The Dick Van Dyke Show*'s advertising tab for the entire season, Sheldon Leonard had good reason to hope that his series would suddenly look a lot more enticing to CBS, who would, he assumed, finally be persuaded to drop their saber-rattling stance and restore the series to a prominent spot on their fall schedule. Unfortunately, such was not the case.

Despite the pair of lucrative sponsorship commitments that Leonard had sewn up for the show's second season, the producer was shocked to discover that the programmers at CBS still seemed completely uninterested in renewing their option for a second year of *The Dick Van Dyke Show*, fully sponsored or not. According to Leonard, the network's official excuse was that there was simply no room for the series on their fall lineup. While the producer had been shuttling back and forth across the country, the programmers explained, they'd been forced to promise the Van Dyke show's time slot to another series, and now the fall lineup was simply booked to capacity.

Or so they said—though Sheldon Leonard didn't buy it for a second. In his opinion, the network's stubborn refusal to budge on the issue of the Van Dyke show's renewal was nothing more than residual fallout from the petty antipathy that network president Jim Aubrey had demonstrated for the series from the very start. But, petty or not, for a few days in the late winter of 1962, that antipathy looked as though it might actually play the deciding role in the fate of *The Dick Van Dyke Show*.

That it didn't was largely due to the timely intervention of Sheldon Leonard's friends from Procter & Gamble, who made short work of the stalemate when they finally stepped in to add their own booming voice to the debate. "The argument from Procter & Gamble to Aubrey was,

'Do you want to keep our daytime business?'" explains Sheldon Leonard, who notes that Procter & Gamble was, then as now, one of the primary sponsors of the network's extremely lucrative daytime lineup. "'Well, if you like our daytime business—the soap operas that are the backbone of your daytime operation—then you'd better find a time spot for Dick Van Dyke!'"

It turned out to be a persuasive argument indeed. A few days later, under the headline, "Van Dyke Show Renewed," the industry trade paper *Daily Variety* carried news of the show's renewal on the front page of its March 21, 1962, issue. "One of the few freshman shows to be renewed for next season," wrote *Variety*, "is the Dick Van Dyke half-hour comedy." [52] The blurb went on to explain that the show would be returning to its old Wednesday night time slot, and concluded with a brief mention of the show's new sponsorship arrangement. "Procter & Gamble," noted the trade paper, "will have Lorillard sharing the tab. [53] And so, it was official at last. *The Dick Van Dyke Show* was back in business.

CHAPTER 18

Never
Name
a Duck

LIKE MOST OF THOSE ON *THE DICK VAN DYKE SHOW'S* FIRST year payroll, Dick Van Dyke had all but written the series off after he'd wrapped up work on the first season's final episode in late February of 1962. "I think most of us just assumed that that was it," he says. "We had pretty much given up hope that there was any recourse." Which is why the actor was so surprised when Carl Reiner called a few weeks later to inform the star that he would indeed have a show to come home to the following season. "I didn't even know that Sheldon had gone to Cincinnati," confesses Van Dyke. "I didn't know that he'd saved our necks until it was over. I had gone into a movie over at Columbia, and I figured that my career was gonna have to go somewhere else."

Not that the star had any reason to worry about his professional prospects beyond *The Dick Van Dyke Show*. If the show's first year had accomplished nothing else, it had established its namesake as a star of the first magnitude—a singing, dancing dynamo whose services were in demand well before the cameras had even stopped rolling on the show's first season. In February of 1962, Van Dyke had spoken to Walt Disney, who was anxious to cast the rising star in one of his pet projects: a musical comedy to be adapted from a series of children's books about a spellbinding English nanny named Mary Poppins. Intrigued, Van Dyke gave Disney an immediate thumbs-up on his involvement, though the star hastened to explain that he wouldn't be able to start work on the project for at least a year, as his feature film calendar for 1962 was already booked solid.

On May 1, Van Dyke reported to Columbia Pictures, where he was set to reprise his stage role in the studio's big-screen adaptation of *Bye Bye*

Birdie, which would be the first film in a nonexclusive five-year, seven-picture contract that the actor had signed with the studio. *Birdie's* three-month shooting schedule would keep Van Dyke hopping through the end of July, leaving him just enough time to shave and shower before he was scheduled to report back to the Desilu Cahuenga lot to start rehearsals for the second year of his own series on August 1.

In spite of the scheduling complications that inevitably resulted, Van Dyke would find time to complete no fewer than five feature film assignments during the four summer breaks in the Van Dyke show five-year production schedule. In addition to *Birdie* and *Mary Poppins*, the star would also log appearances in *What a Way to Go!*, *The Art of Love*, and *Lt. Robinson Crusoe, USN*. But perhaps even more intriguing than the star's actual early sixties filmography is the short but fascinating list of projects that he considered but, for one reason or another, never made. High on this roster of films that never were is *Zoomar*, a comedy that was to have been based on a novel written by the late Ernie Kovacs. Also discussed during Van Dyke's tenure as star of *The Dick Van Dyke Show* was a big-screen biography of Laurel and Hardy, in which Van Dyke would have portrayed his boyhood idol Stan Laurel. The star also briefly entertained the notion of portraying the blacklisted talk-show host John Henry Faulk in a film biography based on Faulk's memoir, *Fear on Trial*, a film that eventually did surface a decade later as a TV movie starring William Devane.

Despite the number of big-screen roles that Van Dyke packed into his resumé during that fertile period, the star made no secret of the fact that he was usually happiest on the set of his own series. "I've found movies the hardest and dullest work," the actor confessed a few weeks after he began work on *Bye Bye Birdie*.[54] And, after viewing the rushes of his first scenes from *Bye Bye Birdie*, the actor came to the surprising conclusion that—in his opinion, anyway—his talents were far better served on his own small-screen series. "I seemed so stiff to myself," as the star would later assess his work in *Bye Bye Birdie*, "and only about sixty percent as effective as I feel I am on my TV show, where I'm relaxed and at home."[55]

A few days after Carl Reiner wrapped up his chores as producer of the first season of *The Dick Van Dyke Show*, the busy writer checked into an office on the Universal-International lot, where he'd been contracted to write *The Art of Love*, which would be filmed—with Dick Van Dyke in a leading role—in 1964. After the nonstop rigors of writing, producing, and story editing the Van Dyke show, Reiner viewed the task of writing a single screenplay almost as a vacation. If so, it would be a short-lived respite. In

May of 1962, with the first production date of the Van Dyke show's second season looming right around the corner, Reiner began splitting his workday between his office at Universal and his writer's cubicle on the Desilu Cahuenga lot, where he would arrive each afternoon at three to start work on one of the twenty-two original Van Dyke show scripts that he would singlehandedly contribute to the series during its second year of production.

But as busy as he was, May also meant the arrival of one Hollywood ritual that Reiner was not about to miss. And so, on May 22, 1962, Carl Reiner took a break from his labors to attend the annual Emmy Awards ceremony, where he and director John Rich had each been nominated for one of the coveted statuettes. While John Rich lost the award for Outstanding Directorial Achievement in the Field of Comedy to *Car 54*'s Nat Hiken that year, Carl Reiner was genuinely stunned to hear his name announced as the recipient of that year's Emmy award for Outstanding Writing Achievement in the Field of Comedy. And the flattered writer didn't attempt to disguise his shock as he stumbled to the dais to deliver a brief acceptance speech that many regarded as the high point of the evening's festivities. "I wish somebody would have told me," Reiner quipped once he got to the podium, his bald pate gleaming under the bright stage lights. "I'd have worn my hair!"

Sheldon Leonard had been predicting that *The Dick Van Dyke Show* was on the verge of a spectacular comeback for months before the show finally made its second-season debut on September 26. But it's unlikely that even the show's unfailingly optimistic executive producer was prepared for the overwhelming audience response that would greet *The Dick Van Dyke Show* in the first weeks of its sophomore season. The show's second season premiere episode garnered the series' highest rating to that time— and that was just the start. By the fourth week of the season, the show finally cracked the Nielsen top ten for the very first time, when the October 17 broadcast leapt into ninth place with a whopping average audience rating of 24.8, the first crest in a ratings tide that would continue to rise right through the end of the 1962–1963 season, when *The Dick Van Dyke Show* would finish the year as ninth-highest rated show in prime time, racking up an impressive average audience rating of 27.1 for the season. Not a bad comeback for a series that finished its first year in eightieth place.

According to Dick Van Dyke, the show's astonishing second year turnaround was at least partly attributable to the legion of new viewers who had discovered the series over the summer, when—at the urging of Carl

Reiner—CBS had agreed to rebroadcast many of the show's first-season episodes. "We did rather well during the summer," explains the star. "They put us into reruns, when we didn't have such stiff competition. And so we hit the air the next fall with a little bit of an audience, which we hadn't had at all in the first year."

But, as effective as the show's summer rerun campaign might have been in attracting new viewers to the show, longtime Van Dyke show observ-

Sheldon Leonard arrives at the show's first-season wrap party with not a moment to spare—within a matter of days, the producer would embark on a cross-country mission to save the show that would take him more than 10,000 miles in less than forty-eight hours. Pictured, from left, are Richard Deacon, costume assistant, Marge Makau, Larry Mathews, script supervisor Marge Mullen, associate producer Ron Jacobs, Morey Amsterdam, Mary Tyler Moore, Dick Van Dyke, film editor Bud Molin, Rose Marie, prop man Glenn Ross, Carl Reiner, director John Rich, assistant director John C. Chulay, composer Earle Hagen, an unidentified visitor, and Sheldon Leonard.

er Jay Sandrich suggests a simpler explanation for the show's sudden surge in popularity. "In the Van Dyke show's second year," says Sandrich, "CBS put a new show called *The Beverly Hillbillies* on in front of it. It was an immediate smash and went straight into the top five. The Van Dyke show followed it—and so it too became an immediate hit."

It might seem hard to fathom that *The Dick Van Dyke Show*—by far the smartest, most sophisticated half-hour comedy of its age—may actually have hitched a ride into the Nielsen top ten on the coattails of *The Beverly Hillbillies*—a series that many prime-time pundits rank as among the least sophisticated shows ever broadcast by the CBS network. But even a cursory scan of the Nielsen charts of the era seems to bear out Sandrich's scenario.

The fact is, based on ratings alone, *The Beverly Hillbillies* wasn't merely a hit—it was a phenomenon. In the weeks following the backwoods comedy's debut in the time slot just before *The Dick Van Dyke Show* on CBS's Wednesday night lineup, *The Beverly Hillbillies* blazed up the Nielsen ratings charts with a speed unmatched by any show before or since. By the close of the Nielsen ratings period ending October 21, 1962, *The Beverly Hillbillies* had grabbed the number-one spot in the weekly Nielsens, making it the first series in prime-time history to hit the top of the ratings chart within five weeks of its premiere. And because viewers in the pre-remote-controlled early sixties were notoriously reluctant to get up and flip the channel once their favorite program went off, *The Beverly Hillbillies*' ratings bonanza came as a godsend to the producers of *The Dick Van Dyke Show*, who stood to inherit a spillover audience of millions from their popular rural lead-in. And, of course, it's a testament to the Van Dyke show's own staying power that the series quickly established a dedicated and highly discriminating following all its own—an audience whose unwavering loyalty to *The Dick Van Dyke Show* was strong enough to ensure the series a steady berth in Nielsen's top twenty for the remainder of its five-year run.

If *The Dick Van Dyke Show*'s producers hoped to attract a broader audience to the series at the outset of their second year on the air, they made a canny choice in scheduling "Never Name a Duck" as the inaugural episode of the show's sophomore season. A funny, tender, and touching entry in the long-running saga of the Petrie family, the bittersweet comedy begins when Rob arrives home with a pair of cute baby ducklings that he presents to Ritchie, despite Laura's pointed objections. "Those cute little balls of fur," she warns, "are going to grow into big, fat, noisy, dirty, dumb ducks!" Sharing few of his mother's concerns, Ritchie promptly christens his new pets Stanley and Oliver, at which point Laura is forced to relent, acknowledging the unwritten rule that a pet, once named, instantly becomes an inseparable member of the family.

Of course, her worst fears come to pass a few weeks later when Oliver dies, leaving Stanley—now fully grown—all alone and looking a bit peaked himself. Fearing that the grief of losing his second pet might be too great for Ritchie to bear, Rob takes the surviving duck to the local veterinarian's office, where he hopes the doctor might be able to work up a cure for the ailing bird.

Arriving at the vet's office, Rob is surprised to find the waiting room teeming with eccentric pet devotees of every possible stripe. On one side of him sits a talkative poodle fancier, and on the other, a cat owner who seems somewhat more down to earth—until she looks Rob in the eye and assures him that, "a duck is a duck, a dog is a dog, and a cat is a *person!*" The slightly befuddled duck owner's visit veers even further into the realm of the surreal when another patron of the doctor's office turns out to be the doting owner of a decidedly recalcitrant, full-grown kangaroo.

In the show's penultimate scene, Rob returns home without the duck and is then forced to explain to his uncomprehending son that he's just set the boy's pet free in the waters of a local pond. "It's very selfish of us to make Stanley stay in that kitchen sink when he'd much rather be in the park with his friends," Rob explains, struggling valiantly to find words to convey a very grown-up set of concepts to a distraught seven-year-old. Rob finally wins the boy over with a bit of anecdotal evidence that seems to indicate that the bird might be okay after all. No sooner had he put the duck in the water, Rob explains, than Stanley spied a beautiful white female duck and promptly took off after her, "like a jet speedboat." Satisfied that nature has taken the proper course, Ritchie resolves to visit the pond bearing a pair of wedding presents for his former pet—a box of oatmeal cookies and a jar of his father's favorite caviar!

"The actual story was absolutely true," insists Carl Reiner, who cites the episode as yet another Van Dyke show inspired by a page in the Reiner family scrapbook—though in this case, the writer admits, the actual circumstances would require a certain degree of poetic license in the retelling. For one thing, the real-life writer had already moved to Beverly Hills by the time he brought home a pair of cute baby ducklings to his own son Lucas, who was at that time still a toddler. "We put them in the sink," says Reiner, "and they ate Rice Krispies." And, like Rob and Laura, Carl and Estelle Reiner soon discovered that even the most adorable baby ducks don't stay cute forever. "They'd go swimming in the pool," Reiner recalls. "And I said, 'Look at that, how pretty! They're swimming in the pool!' Then we looked in the pool, and the bottom of it was cov-

Dick Van Dyke, Larry Mathews, and their feathered costar from "Never Name a Duck," the episode that scored the highest rating of any *Dick Van Dyke Show* up to that time; not coincidentally, it was also the first episode to follow *The Beverly Hillbillies* on CBS's Wednesday night schedule.

ered with shit! Those two ducks shat more than our German shepherd. So we knew we had to get rid of them."

The writer finally decided to set his ducks loose in the waters of Los Angeles' MacArthur Park lagoon, just as he would later have the fictional Rob Petrie set his pet loose in a local pond. But, in stark contrast to the waterside pastoral that Rob Petrie describes to his seven-year-old son on the show, Reiner and his own young son found their encounter with nature a far more harrowing experience. "The other ducks didn't want ours in the pack!" recalls Reiner, who was shocked to observe the fierce territorial behavior exhibited by the swimming flock. "One duck came out of the pack—he was almost flying, with his legs hitting the water. He came over and he grabbed one of our ducks by the neck and shook him like he was gonna knock his head off!"

By then in tears, Reiner's two-year-old son Lucas was practically beside himself at having to witness the cruel pageant of nature that was being enacted before his eyes. Fortunately, the elder Reiner managed to save the day when he tossed a handful of breadcrumbs onto the water, creating just enough of a diversion to give his ducklings time to lose themselves in the center of the flock. "Luckily," notes Reiner, "I brought a lot of bread with me."

Carl Reiner would not be the only Van Dyke show company member to come away from the making of "Never Name a Duck" with a renewed respect for the unpredictability of the animal kingdom. Van Dyke show stock player Jerry Hausner is not likely to forget his own run-in with Duke, the headstrong kangaroo who turned what was supposed to be a simple sight gag in the vet's office into a lively on-set improvisation that pitted actor against animal in a hilarious onstage tug-of-war. But while Hausner acknowledges that the unscripted tussle earned big laughs on the night of the performance, things didn't look nearly so comical from his vantage point on the set. "I was scared to death," recalls the diminutive character actor. "That animal was mean!"

And yet, the actor recalls with a chuckle, everything had gone perfectly well at dress rehearsal. As written, the sight gag was actually quite straightforward—in the original script, Hausner was merely supposed to grab the kangaroo's leash and lead the animal quickly and uneventfully out the door of the veterinarian's office. And that's pretty much how the scene had played in rehearsal that afternoon, when the kangaroo appeared to be calm and exceedingly well behaved. Unfortunately, by the time they let Duke out of his cage for the evening show, the marsupial star emerged in decidedly testier spirits.

"He was angry about something," says Hausner, who first noticed the alarming shift in his costar's disposition only after he got on stage with him. "Suddenly, he was obstreperous," recalls Hausner. "He didn't want to do anything that I wanted him to do." But with the cameras rolling— and the audience howling—the actor had little choice but to play out the impromptu tug-of-war, even if his 185-pound costar did seem to be getting the better of him. "We got big laughs," notes Hausner. "But all I could think of is how they train kangaroos to box in the circus. And how they usually win."

CHAPTER 19
Stumbling

WHEN *THE DICK VAN DYKE SHOW* RETURNED TO THE AIR ON September 26, 1962, fans of the series were no doubt surprised to discover that the show sported an entirely new opening title sequence for its second-season premiere. Gone was the primitive still-photo montage that had run under the opening titles of the first thirty episodes; in its place the producers had substituted a whimsical introductory sequence that would, with slight variation, open each of the show's remaining 127 episodes. In the now-classic opening that debuted that night, Rob Petrie breezes jauntily into his living room, only to take an unplanned nosedive over an ill-placed ottoman that sits squarely in his path.

It was a simple enough gag. And, according to the show's director, no one on the set gave the sequence much thought the night it was filmed, almost an afterthought, at the end of a full day's shooting. And yet, in years to come, that unassuming introductory sequence—and its near twin, in which Van Dyke deftly sidesteps the ottoman at the last second—would become the show's most indelible visual signature.

Ironically, Carl Reiner was initially unconvinced that the show even needed a new title sequence when the idea was broached by one of the show's skittish sponsors a few weeks before the start of the second season. "The sponsors," recalls Reiner, "were always saying, 'We've got to catch them at the beginning. We've got to make sure they stay with you.'" And, in the eyes of the nervous advertisers, the show's original opening titles were simply not visually compelling enough to keep the fickle viewing public glued to their seats through the show's first commercial break.

While Carl Reiner certainly sympathized with his sponsor's desire to rope viewers into the show as quickly as possible, the producer didn't see how he could hope to grab a viewer's interest with something as inherently predictable as the opening titles of a TV show. "I said, 'People are never going to stay with you for the main titles,'" recalls the producer. "'They're the same every week!'"

But, after a few day's deliberation, the solution finally came to him. The best way to keep the show's opening credits sequence compelling from week to week would simply be to film it twice! In the first version, Reiner would shoot his star taking a pratfall over a living room ottoman. And then, just to keep the audience guessing, they would film a second take, nearly identical to the first, in which the star *doesn't* stumble. This second variation would then be substituted in random rotation with the first, so that the audience would never be sure, from week to week, whether Van Dyke was going to take the fall or not. "One week he trips," explains Reiner. "And one week he doesn't. Then the people at home were supposed to say, 'I wonder if he trips this week?' It was silly. I don't think it ever worked. But that was the idea."*

Both variations of the Van Dyke show's celebrated opening sequence were filmed on the evening of August 14, 1962, just a few minutes after the cast had wrapped their thirty-second episode, "The Two Faces of Rob." The two versions of the soon-to-be immortal sequence were filmed in record time, says John Rich, if only because, after a full day's work, none of the show's cast and crew were anxious to hang around the set any longer than they had to. And no one was more eager to wrap the evening's shoot than the director himself, who had already arranged a dinner date for later that night. "I had someone waiting for me in the Pacific Palisades or something," recalls Rich, "and I was irritated, frankly, about having to shoot this thing on a night I didn't want to."

But, with the second-season premiere less than six weeks off, the show's

---

*Just to confuse matters even more, eagle-eyed viewers will note that a third variant of the show's familiar opening title sequence pops up in season three. In this variation—which is easily distinguished from the first two because the cast is wearing slightly dressier formal evening wear in version three—Van Dyke successfully negotiates the troublesome ottoman, only to get tripped up a few steps later when he stumbles and almost falls a second time. Shortly after this third variation was filmed, Carl Reiner finally decided that his game of musical title sequences was having virtually no impact on the show's viewership, and the practice of alternating the show's opening title sequences would be all but abandoned by the end of the third year. During the show's final two seasons, the take where Van Dyke sidesteps the ottoman was used almost exclusively under the show's opening titles.

producers were anxious to get the new title sequence in the can. And so, after discussing the game plan with Carl Reiner, John Rich went right to work. "Okay, let's go," barked the director, rallying his cast and crew to the stage in his best no-nonsense voice. "Can we do this *now?*"

The actors obediently took their places on the set, where—still clad in the outfits they'd worn in the final scenes of "The Two Faces of Rob"—the cast filmed the entire sequence in little more time than it would take to watch the twenty-second clip when it debuted on the show a few weeks later. "I set up a camera very quickly," says Rich, explaining his strategy for the shot. "All I wanted was something where Dick had enough room to come in and trip, and everybody else would have room to cluster around him, so that it made a comfortable shot. And it was set up about as fast as I just said it."

Dick Van Dyke stumbled with such remarkable aplomb that his producers eventually decided to exploit their star's penchant for pratfalls in the show's opening credit sequence.

Not surprisingly, the director made sure that he got everything he needed in the very first take. "Dick came in, fell over the thing, and we shot it. And I said, 'That's fine, let's go home.'" According to John Rich, it was while standing there on the set that Carl Reiner actually came up with the inspiration to film a second, alternate, version of the sequence. "Carl said, 'Hey, wait a minute! Let's do a variation, so that some nights Dick doesn't trip.' I said, 'Oh, good idea.'"*

---

*According to camera coordinator Jim Niver, the final decision of choosing which variation would appear on a given episode was left entirely to film editor Bud Molin. "None of us ever knew whether Dick was going to trip over the ottoman or not until we finally saw it on television," says Niver, "same as everyone else."

At Rich's signal, the actors dutifully repeated the sequence, with Dick Van Dyke substituting a deft sidestep around the ottoman for his earlier pratfall. "We shot it," says Rich, "and I went off on my date. The whole thing took about three minutes. I don't think we gave it any more thought than that. I just set the camera and said, 'Let's go.' Sometimes it works better that way."

And yet, despite the extemporaneous circumstances of its shooting—or, perhaps, as Rich indicates, because of them—the show's classic opening title sequence achieves a casual spontaneity that is entirely appropriate to the material, a quality, moreover, that probably could not have been improved had Rich and his director of photography labored over the sequence for another week. And, of course, much of the credit for the sequence's visual elegance—indeed, for that of the entire series—must go to the show's director of photography, Robert DeGrasse, a veteran of forty years behind the camera who had long since mastered the art of capturing rich and varied visual textures on film with a minimum of fuss.

"Robert DeGrasse was wonderful," gushes Carl Reiner, who considered himself fortunate indeed to have had at his disposal the services of a veteran like DeGrasse, who, as house cinematographer at RKO Pictures during the studio's heyday in the thirties and forties, had distinguished himself as director of photography on many of the studio's most prestigious pictures, including *Stage Door*, *Alice Adams*, and *Carefree*. And yet, despite his gilded resumé as one of the most accomplished cinematographers of Hollywood's Golden Age, DeGrasse had little trouble adjusting to the three-camera television arena, where—as Carl Reiner observes—the medium's inherent technical, budgetary, and time restrictions posed a very different set of challenges than those found on the average feature film set.

"A three-camera set could look very flat," explains the producer. "You didn't have a lot of depth to the set. And here you had three cameras working, so you had to light all three angles at once." And yet none of these potentially daunting technical limitations seemed to deter the show's talented director of photography, who skillfully employed lighting to manipulate the show's black, white, and gray palette to achieve a look of surprisingly rich texture and almost three-dimensional depth. "He was," says Carl Reiner, "the best guy for making a three-camera show look good with shadows and light."

Like most of those who worked behind the scenes on any of executive producer Sheldon Leonard's cost-efficient situation comedy sets, Robert DeGrasse actually split his workweek between two shows. Under an ingenious system that the thrifty executive producer had devised to maximize his studio labor force, DeGrasse would work as director of photography on the Van Dyke show for the first two days of the week only; then, the morning after that show's Tuesday night filming, the cinematographer would shuttle next door to Desilu's stage 9, where he would spend the remainder of his workweek performing similar duties on *The Danny Thomas Show*. All of which kept the sixty-two-year-old cinematographer hopping throughout the three years that both shows were in production on adjoining Desilu soundstages. "We used to walk back and forth between the shows," recalls Jim Niver, who—like DeGrasse and most of the rest of the Van Dyke show's behind-the-scenes crew—also split his own workweek between the two series. "The minute there was a layoff on one show, I'd usually go right over and watch the other show in rehearsal. It was a busy time. But it all worked, quietly and efficiently."

Under the watchful eye of veteran director of photography Robert DeGrasse, even the most mundane scenes were imbued with a rich visual elegance. Says Carl Reiner, "He was the best guy for making a three-camera show look good with shadows and light."

Indeed it did. By the middle of *The Dick Van Dyke Show*'s second season, the show's production machine fairly hummed along, fueled by the dedicated efforts of a crackerjack team of skilled troubleshooters that included the show's associate producer Ron Jacobs, production manager Frank Myers, and assistant director John C. Chulay. Another unsung hero in the weekly production miracle that yielded *The Dick Van Dyke Show* was the show's tireless and highly organized script supervisor, Marge Mullen, who rode herd on each of the 157 *Dick Van Dyke Show* scripts that followed the series' pilot episode.

As *The Dick Van Dyke Show* moved into its second full season of production, it had become clear to producer Carl Reiner that at least one member of his crack creative staff—director John Rich—might not be long for the series. By the end of his first year as house director of *The Dick Van Dyke Show*, John Rich had already begun to attract the attention of some of the biggest producers in Hollywood's feature-film community, most notably Paramount's Hal B. Wallis, who was anxious to sign the director to a long-term pact to make features for him at that studio. And although Rich would not officially leave the series until a few weeks into the show's third season, Carl Reiner could already see that he wasn't going to be able to keep his ambitious young director pinned down to the rigors of a weekly series forever. "We knew John was gonna have to take a rest sometime," says Reiner, "so we started to develop other directors."

Most of the responsibility for recruiting and training new directors for the Van Dyke show fell to executive producer Sheldon Leonard, who accomplished the task—with typical paternal fervor—by establishing an informal apprenticeship program designed to attract talented newcomers. "If Sheldon Leonard saw somebody he thought had good timing," notes Ron Jacobs, "he'd let them come in and observe us." At the end of a reasonable apprenticeship period, during which the novice would watch John Rich or one of the lot's other experienced directors at work, the newcomer would be given a shot at directing an episode or two on his own. "John Rich trained five of us who were essentially out to get his job," observes director Alan Rafkin, an early graduate of Sheldon Leonard's unofficial apprentice program. "There was me," recalls Rafkin, "Lee Philips, Hal Cooper, Jerry Paris, and maybe a couple others."

Ironically, one name conspicuously absent from Sheldon Leonard's list of potential Van Dyke show directors was his very own right-hand man and top assistant director, Jay Sandrich. Although Sandrich would eventually forge a highly distinguished career as the award-winning director of scores of episodes of *The Mary Tyler Moore Show*, *He & She*, *The Cosby Show*, and *Soap*, among many others, he never did get a shot at directing *The Dick Van Dyke Show*—though he insists that it wasn't for lack of trying. "I begged Sheldon to let me direct a couple," he recalls today. "I loved the Van Dyke show. Still do. That was always, to me, a really wonderfully written, very sophisticated show. And that was the show I wanted to direct. But, for whatever reason, Sheldon just never felt that I was ready or capable."

And although Sandrich has long since forgiven his onetime mentor for what must, in retrospect, be viewed as one of Sheldon Leonard's few questionable judgment calls, the former assistant director of the Van Dyke and Danny Thomas shows still remembers how frustrating it was to watch less experienced hands get their shot at directing the Van Dyke show while he was forced to look on from the sidelines. "That was a hard thing," says

Sandrich. "A lot of directors were coming in who didn't understand how to do cameras, or they didn't understand the show, or whatever."

Fortunately, director-trainee Alan Rafkin wasn't one of them. A former stand-up comic, Rafkin had actually played second banana to Dick Van Dyke on an ill-fated variety show pilot that the star shot in the late fifties—an experience that undoubtedly gave the director a head start when he was finally assigned to direct the show's thirty-seventh episode, "My Husband Is Not a Drunk."

Carl Reiner (top, center) leads his production staff in a chorus of "Danny Boy" in playful tribute to studio patriarch Danny Thomas in this crew photo taken during production of the show's second season. Pictured in the row immediately below Carl Reiner are, from left, stand-in Frank Adamo, director Jerry Paris, assistant director Johnny Chulay, CBS publicist Bruce Pennington, and second assistant director Bud Messinger; in the middle row stand makeup artist Tom Tuttle, music editor Donn Cambern, camera co-ordinator Jim Niver, director of photography Robert DeGrasse, Dick Van Dyke, and Morey Amsterdam; and, finally, kneeling in the foreground are camera operator Harry Webb and costume supervisor Harald Johnson.

Another Van Dyke show classic, "My Husband Is Not a Drunk" features a welcome reprise of the inebriated husband character that Dick Van Dyke had played to such riotous effect early in his career. The episode's clever storyline describes the complications that ensue after Rob falls prey to a posthypnotic suggestion that he become a falling-down drunk every time he hears a bell ring. "It was just a magnificent piece of material," enthuses Rafkin, who remembers that Van Dyke kept him in stitches all week long. "Every time that bell went off and Dick would get drunk again, I'd get hysterical," Rafkin confesses. "I mean, it just made me laugh every time. And it never stopped making me laugh. He could do it for me tonight—in my living room—and I would still laugh."

Carl Reiner was an equally enthusiastic fan of Van Dyke's drunk husband character, the trademark comic premise that the star introduced in *The Girls Against the Boys* on Broadway in 1959 and later revived for a short comic interlude in the Van Dyke show pilot. In fact, it was after see-

ing his star perform the character in the show's pilot that Reiner first became determined to bring the hilarious characterization back at the earliest opportunity. The question then became how to depict Rob Petrie in a state of public drunkenness without betraying the integrity of the character, who was, of course, firmly established as an upstanding husband, father, and all-around pil-

A posthypnotic suggestion provided a socially acceptable excuse for the normally straitlaced Rob Petrie to appear in a state of comic inebriation throughout most of the show's thirty-seventh episode, "My Husband Is Not a Drunk."

lar-of-the-community type. In other words, not the sort of guy who could spend the better part of an episode in a drunken state, no matter how comical. Unless...

Unless Rob only *thought* he was drunk, but was in fact under the influence of hypnosis. It was the perfect solution. By letting Rob slip into a posthypnotic trance at the top of the show, the writer had created the ideal rationale for putting his straitlaced star into a drunken stupor without having him touch so much as a drop of booze. "That's how we got away with me playing a drunk," observes Dick Van Dyke.

Like most of the directors who got their start behind the camera on *The Dick Van Dyke Show*, Alan Rafkin would parlay his early experience on the show into a long and profitable career as a prolific director of half-hour comedy. In addition to directing three additional Van Dyke show episodes and numerous installments of *The Andy Griffith Show*, Rafkin would eventually serve as house director on a number of other highly regarded shows, including *The Bob Newhart Show*, *One Day at a Time*, and, in more recent years, *Coach*.

Even so, it should be noted that not every recruit to Sheldon Leonard's apprenticeship system experienced quite so smooth a transition from novice to full-fledged director as did Al Rafkin. "It's always difficult for a new director to come in and direct a show that's already established," observes Ron Jacobs. And one problem that frequently presented itself to anxious young directors eager to strut their stuff on the Van Dyke show was how to deal with a cast who were already so fully confident in their roles that they were essentially capable of directing themselves. "You didn't have to tell that cast what to do," says Jacobs. "Rosie would already know if she had to get up and go to the desk on this line, or that she had to stand up on that line." The real secret to directing the Van Dyke show, notes Jacobs, was simply knowing when to get out of the way and let the show's remarkably instinctive performers fly.

One freshman director who learned that lesson the hard way was Coby Ruskin, a Sheldon Leonard protégé who came on board to direct the show's fortieth episode, "The Secret Life of Buddy and Sally." Though Ruskin would go on to establish a respectable career at the helm of multiple episodes of *The Andy Griffith Show* and *Gomer Pyle, USMC*, the novice director's first week on the Van Dyke show would amount to nothing less than a trial by fire. As Morey Amsterdam tells it, the director's troubles began at the show's very first rehearsal, when Ruskin, anxious to flex his directorial muscles, rather courageously dared to second guess one of Amsterdam's own line readings. The line in question came early in the episode, during a short exchange where Buddy is supposed to be protesting the idea of having to work late at the office. Apparently, after watching a preliminary run-through of the sequence, Ruskin decided that the scene could use a little more pizzazz. "He stopped me," recalls Amsterdam, "and he said, 'You're not aggravated enough. Jump up and down! You're furious this happened! You're a disgruntled citizen!'"

That would be a problem. Like every other actor on the show, Amsterdam had come to view himself as the gatekeeper of his character's reality. And, as the actor politely informed the director, the overblown reaction that Ruskin seemed to be asking for simply didn't fit the actor's conception of Buddy's reality. "I can't do that," replied Amsterdam. "I wouldn't know how. I've never been a disgruntled citizen in my life."

But Ruskin was insistent. And, finally, the actor reluctantly agreed to give the suggestion a try—with one caveat. "I'll do it your way," Amsterdam volunteered. "But," he warned, "when Carl and Sheldon come down to watch the run-through, I don't know what they're gonna think."

They would both find out soon enough. The cast staged their first run-through for the show's producers just a few days later, and when Amsterdam got to the scene that had earlier caused so much controversy, he played it with wild-eyed abandon—just as he'd been directed. And, just as he'd anticipated, Sheldon Leonard took one look at the scene and stopped the rehearsal cold.

"Morey!" the executive producer exclaimed. "What are you doing?" As Amsterdam recalls it, he quickly assumed his straightest poker face and explained that he was simply playing the scene as if he were a disgruntled citizen. "That's ridiculous!" came Leonard's retort. "You've never been a disgruntled citizen in your life!" Needless to say, the apprentice director restaged the scene later that same afternoon, this time taking full advantage of his actor's instinctive reactions.

When Ann Morgan Guilbert left *The Dick Van Dyke Show* for an extended pregnancy leave midway through the show's first season, the actress had been far from certain there would be a job waiting for her when she was ready to come back to work a few months later. "When I left, I didn't even know if the show was going to get picked up for another year," she says. "And when it did, I didn't know if they were going to use me again."

But, according to Carl Reiner, there was never any doubt that he would always find room on the show for Ann Guilbert, whose role in the show's ensemble was, in his mind, unassailable. As proof, the producer offered to sign her to a long-term employment contract within a few days of her return to the show in October of 1962. There's no question it was an attractive offer—in exchange for her commitment to continue with the series each year through the end of its run, the proposed contract would guarantee the actress steady employment in a specified number of episodes each season. Which was a considerable improvement over the status Guilbert had labored under during the show's first year, when she simply had been called in to work on a show-by-show, as-needed basis. But despite the obvious advantages outlined in the proposed contract, Ann Guilbert left her producer somewhat astonished when she informed him that she actually preferred working without any contract at all.

"With two youngsters at home, I didn't want to work all the time," she acknowledges today. "I was happy doing about as much as I did. I thought, if I'm under contract, I'll just have to come in and sit around to do two or three lines. And for a three-camera show, you've got to come in and work for four or five days, even if it's just a little bitty scene." On the other hand, the actress reasoned, if she continued to book her appearances on the series on a show-by-show basis, her producers would almost certainly make better use of her time. "If they have to hire me as a guest star every time they use me," she surmised, "they'll only call me in when they really want to use me."

Looking back, Guilbert is convinced that she made the correct decision. "It worked out fine for me—I don't think the pay scale was that different whether you were a continuing character or a recurring character, like I was."* And as far as the actress could tell, her freelance status had little or no impact on the frequency of her appearances on the series. "They used me a lot," she says, "because my character figured in the house scenes. Dick had Morey and Rosie to talk to in the office scenes, but Mary needed someone to talk to—and that's why Millie was always there."

But if, as Guilbert suggests, Millie Helper's status as Laura Petrie's best friend and chief sounding board guaranteed the actress playing her a consistent visibility, Guilbert was equally aware that the role of next-door neighbor imposed its own set of limitations as well. "I was the door opener and door closer," the actress admits with bemused detachment. "I'd stick my head in, and they'd say, 'Go home, Millie!' or something like that. It was always in and out—in and out." Equally frustrating for the actress

---

*Like most of the show's cast, Guilbert was paid rather modestly for her work. In her recollection, her shooting fee at the series' start in 1961 was a mere five hundred dollars per episode, though the actress recalls that that figure would finally be doubled by the time the Van Dyke show left the air in 1966.

were those scenes where her character seemed to appear mainly as a device to keep the show's plot purring along. "I hated the part where I had to sit around the living room and say, 'And then what happened, Rob?'"

But, if the character of Millie Helper was occasionally employed more sparingly than Ann Guilbert might've preferred, the actress would presumably have little complaint with the show's forty-first installment, in which Millie takes center stage in the somewhat unlikely role of the lone adult witness to an aerial attack perpetrated by a giant woodpecker!

The decidedly nondisgruntled Morey Amsterdam in a publicity still from one of the show's early episodes.

CHAPTER 20
Sneezing Funny

THE SERIES OF GIANT WOODPECKER ATTACKS THAT PRO-
pel the plot of episode 41, "A Bird in the Head Hurts," must surely rank
as one of the most outlandish comic premises to surface on an episode
of *The Dick Van Dyke Show*. And yet, as implausible as it sounds, Carl
Reiner insists the episode's absurd storyline was drawn practically verbatim from a true-life tale that was described to him by Millie Helper's
real-life counterpart, Millie Schoenbaum of New Rochelle, New York.

"Nobody's gonna believe it!" Reiner told his former New Rochelle
neighbor when she called him in Beverly Hills to share the harrowing tale
of how an oversized woodpecker had taken to attacking her son. "The
kid wouldn't go to school, because every day a bird pecked his head!"
swears Reiner. "When she told me that story, I said, 'Write it up, Millie.'
I'll use that one on the show."

The script that Carl Reiner finally drafted from his former neighbor's
notes turned out to be one of the writer's best, a bizarre foray into suburban surrealism rendered all the more fantastic simply because it was
based on the truth. In the episode's opening scenes, Rob and Laura scoff
at Ritchie's frantic claim that he's been singled out as an object of attack
by a giant woodpecker. The skeptical parents are fully prepared to dis-
miss the boy's outrageous tale as the fanciful product of an overstimu-
lated imagination, until Millie arrives to report that she's actually
witnessed one of the attacks with her very own eyes. That's when the
Petries decide it's time to call in an expert.

Unfortunately, the concerned parents derive little satisfaction from the
Westchester County game warden, who arrives to inform them that the
county's animal protection laws are biased overwhelmingly in the bird's

favor. Eschewing the animal specialist's flip suggestion that they send the boy to school in pith helmet and sunglasses, Rob eventually deduces that it might not be Ritchie that the woodpecker is after but the boy's hair, which—as Rob cleverly surmises—the bird has somehow identified as an ideal nesting material. Finally, using a few hairs from his son's comb as bait, the resourceful father successfully lures the bird into captivity. And by episode's end, the once-troublesome predator has found a new and far safer home in the aviary of the Bronx Zoo.

"All of that really happened," says Carl Reiner, who was surprised to discover how little embellishment was actually required to craft a comic restaging of his neighbor's anecdotal account. In fact, the writer insists that at least one scene in his script was transcribed almost verbatim from the actual event. "Those were the game warden's actual lines," says Reiner, noting the similarities between the Schoenbaums' real encounter with the local game warden and his fictional re-creation of the same event. "He told them, 'There are no woodpeckers in New Rochelle.' Then, when they saw the bird, he said, 'You're not allowed to shoot it.'" Finally, adds Reiner, when the distraught Schoenbaums inquired what they might do to protect their child, the real-life game warden answered exactly as the writer would later portray it in his script. "He told them, 'Have your kid wear a pith helmet!'"

Of course, it wasn't every week that one of Carl Reiner's friends was kind enough to phone up with as rich a story premise as the one that inspired "A Bird in the Head Hurts." Most weeks the producer was forced to look elsewhere for comic stimulation. According to Reiner, one of his most fertile sources of inspiration was Dick Van Dyke himself, whose own inventive improvisations provided the comic fodder for more than one classic Van Dyke episode. One memorable example was "Gesundheit, Darling," the episode where Rob develops an apparent allergic reaction to his wife and child—a storyline that Reiner insists was inspired by nothing more than his star's unique ability to sneeze funny.

"I loved the way he sneezed!" exclaims Reiner, who recalls that he first became aware of Van Dyke's theretofore unknown sternutatationary skills when he noticed the star regaling the crew with an impromptu demonstration of a dozen or more comical sneezes during a lull in rehearsal one afternoon. Within a week's time, Carl Reiner had written "Gesundheit, Darling," an entire half-hour script designed to capitalize on what must surely qualify as one of Dick Van Dyke's most unusual abilities.

But Van Dyke's uncanny facility for sneezing funny would not be the only previously unheralded talent to emerge from one of the star's frequent on-set improvisations. "Dick could do pantomimic things that

Rob falls prey to a TV hatchet man played by Gene Lyons in the show's forty-eighth episode, "Ray Murdock's X-Ray," the first Van Dyke show to carry the credit "directed by Jerry Paris."

nobody else in the world could have done," says Carl Reiner, who delighted in testing the limits of his star's capabilities at every possible opportunity. "Just to see if he could do it," says Reiner, "I once challenged Dick to sneeze, cough, belch, fart, and hiccup—to do everything that the human body could possibly do—all within one second! And he did it! All at once. 'Ugh-da-cough-wheez-hick-ah-bloo!'"

"They were always coming up with stupid physical ideas," recalls Dick Van Dyke, who insists that Carl Reiner wasn't the only member of the show's writing staff to derive pleasure from this particular form of benign torture. "One time," recalls Van Dyke, "Sam Denoff said, 'You're a tap dancer, but you've got a broken leg and you've got to do a number. Let me see you do that!'" "And then," adds Bill Persky, who swears he was present at the rehearsal where Dick Van Dyke attempted to conquer that particular challenge, "Dick did a guy tap dancing with a broken leg on a shot of novocaine! I mean, you would just throw this stuff at him, and he would then do it. You'd give Dick a challenge like that, and he just couldn't resist."

"It was just fun," allows the star. "That's the whole idea. I think that's why the show worked so well, because—on top of the good writing and everything else—we had such a good time."

In a town where the frequency and volume level of a star's on-set temper tantrums are often viewed as the most reliable barometer of his or her celebrity standing, Dick Van Dyke's unfailing congeniality on the set of his own series was viewed with an almost reverential awe by many Hollywood observers. "Dick was a doll," observes character actor Jerry Hausner, a regular member of the show's unofficial stock company.

"He never seemed to worry about anything," echoes director John Rich, who claims he never heard a single harsh word emanate from the star's lips in all their years together. According to Rose Marie, "Dick just sort of relaxed and did what he wanted to do." "He never got angry," concurs writer Bill Idelson. "Dick just sort of floated above it all."

But, according to the star's own recollections, that's not exactly true. As Dick Van Dyke reluctantly confesses, his legendary patience *was* tried to the breaking point on at least one occasion. As Van Dyke recalls it, this rare display of pique occurred early in the show's second year, shortly after he made the ill-considered decision to appear in a commercial that touted the virtues of Kent cigarettes. According to Van Dyke, he'd originally agreed to appear in the spot after Sheldon Leonard approached him and requested his participation as a favor for one of the show's more loyal sponsors. But though the actor willingly agreed to participate, it was a favor he would soon come to regret.

Despite Dick Van Dyke's eventual misgivings about the thirty-second Kent cigarette pitch that he and Mary Tyler Moore filmed during the show's second season, the commercial remains one of the most fascinating bits of Van Dyke show arcana ever recorded. Essentially little more than an extended product endorsement, the bizarre spot—which was filmed on the Van Dyke set—purports to capture New Rochelle's favorite suburban couple in a moment of domestic relaxation, as Rob and Laura lounge around their familiar living room extolling the virtues of Kent cigarettes in dialogue so stilted that it could not possibly have been written, supervised, or edited by Carl Reiner.*

---

*In fact, executive producer Sheldon Leonard takes full credit for the content, script, and direction of the Kent spot, which—like similar integrated commercials that the executive producer prepared on behalf of General Foods for his Andy Griffith and Danny Thomas shows—was produced largely as a gesture of goodwill toward the show's loyal sponsor, who paid little or no additional cost for the cast's custom-made endorsement. "I did integrated commercials free," boasts Leonard. "I made them up, wrote the commercial, used my cast of characters and crew. I gave the sponsor a complete one-minute commercial—and it never cost them a dime."

"I have the two things that would make any man happy," boasts Rob Petrie in the almost surreal exchange of dialogue that opens the spot. "A gorgeous wife, and I'm smoking a Kent!" When Laura inquires which of the two he prefers more—her or the cigarette, Rob's answer comes without a moment's hesitation. "Let me see..." he says. "For cooking and for dancing and kissing—you satisfy best. But, for filter and taste, Kent satisfies best!" "I'll accept that," Laura replies—somewhat improbably—before she, too, relaxes into an easy chair to enjoy the soothing taste of her own freshly lit cigarette. And, on that oddly disconcerting image, the commercial fades out.

"We only did that once," declares Dick Van Dyke, who claims that he found the spot so singularly disturbing after he finally saw it on the air that he was moved to put his foot down for the first and only time during the entire run of the series. "I told Sheldon, 'This is a family show. Kids are watching, and I just cannot be telling kids to smoke cigarettes.'" According to Van Dyke, the executive producer offered no argument, and the spot was pulled from the air shortly thereafter. "And," assures Van Dyke, "we never did another one."

The star's principled reaction to his on-air endorsement of their sponsor's product was particularly ironic in light of the fact that he and Mary Tyler Moore were both heavy smokers throughout the years *The Dick Van Dyke Show* was in production—though, it must be admitted, neither of them favored their sponsor's brand. "Mary smoked Pall Malls," recalls costumer Harald Johnson. "I know, because she was always bumming cigarettes from me, and I smoked Pall Malls."

But, while Kent may not have been the preferred brand for either of the show's stars, Johnson insists that that didn't stop them—or any of the other smokers on the show's staff, himself included—from accepting the free cartons of Kents that the sponsor willingly supplied to the show's cast and crew. The fact that Kent was not the brand of choice for most of them made little difference, according to Johnson, who recalls that he and his backstage coconspirators devised a highly effective way around that little obstacle. "I'd take my carton of Kents down to the local market and exchange them for Pall Malls," confesses the costumer, who insists that he wasn't the only perpetrator of this minor scam at his sponsor's expense. "Mary did the same thing," says Johnson, "and so did Dick."

And, sure enough, after more than three decades, Mary Tyler Moore—now a confirmed nonsmoker—cheerfully confesses to her own participation in the petty larceny that Johnson describes. "Oh, exactly!" she admits. "I used to take mine to my local market and just automatically trade 'em in."

"Dick just sort of relaxed and did what he wanted to do," recalls Rose Marie; here, the star impersonates a new car in an extended pantomime from episode 49, "I Was a Teenage Head Writer."

After more than a decade of toiling in the vineyards of episodic television, John Rich finally got his shot at the majors in the closing weeks of 1962, when Hal B. Wallis closed a deal to secure the director's services for a five-picture contract to direct movies for his unit at Paramount Pictures. But though Wallis's offer looked like a once in a lifetime opportunity to the ambitious director, John Rich was also aware that accepting the movie deal would mean leaving *The Dick Van Dyke Show* once and for all. And that, insists Rich, was not an easy decision to make. "I was very happy there," says the director, recalling his days on the Van Dyke show. "But the fact is, I had a chance to do films."

The director's first film for Paramount would be the Van Johnson–Janet Leigh comedy, *Wives and Lovers,* which was set to go before the cameras in the early months of 1963. In all, Rich would direct four more features over the next four years—*The New Interns, Boeing, Boeing,* and the Elvis Presley vehicles *Roustabout* and *Easy Come, Easy Go*—but, ironically, after spending a few years in the supposedly greener pastures of feature filmmaking, the veteran TV director admits that he finally couldn't wait to get back to the bustling world of weekly television. "Films bored me," says Rich, who found the tedium of feature-film production especially frustrating after the breakneck pace he'd maintained as director of *The Dick Van Dyke Show.* "I was used to going so fast with them—it was all snap-snap-snap! In five days, you knew what you had. On a film, you'd work for a year—and by the time you were done, whatever was funny initially would quickly grow stale."

Although Carl Reiner and Sheldon Leonard knew they had little choice but to grant their director's request for an early release from his contract with the show, the producers were understandably concerned about the potentially deleterious impact that Rich's sudden departure might have on company morale. "John was like the father figure on the set," observes Reiner. "When he left, everybody was afraid we couldn't do it without him."

But John Rich harbored no such fears for the show's future, as he explains in his own fabled account of how he came to appoint actor Jerry Paris to be his successor. "Carl and Sheldon were worried about what would happen to the show," he explains. "But it was already firmly on the tracks. The cast and the writing were so solid, I told them, that anyone could direct the show—I turned around, and Jerry happened to be standing there—even *him*." In Rich's recollection of the events that followed, he summoned the slightly startled actor over and tendered a job offer on the spot. "I said, 'Jerry, you want to be a director?' And Jerry says, 'Yeah, I guess so, why?' So I turned to Carl and said, 'How about if Jerry watches me very carefully as a director for the next six weeks?' Carl said, 'If you think he can do it.' And, of course, he turned out great. So Jerry became a director because I needed an out to do a film."

Though few would deny that John Rich spins an entertaining tale, Carl Reiner takes exception to at least a few of the particulars in the director's account of how Jerry Paris came to discover his calling as director of *The Dick Van Dyke Show*. Despite Rich's assertion that serendipity played a primary role in the future director's big break, Reiner insists that the decision to move Jerry Paris behind the cameras in the Van Dyke show's second season was hardly an arbitrary choice. In fact, notes Reiner, Jerry Paris had been lobbying for the chance to direct an episode of *The Dick Van Dyke Show* practically from the day he arrived. "Jerry Paris bothered me to become a director for two years," says Reiner. According to Paris's friend Ann Guilbert, the actor's ambition to direct had been so strong that he even attempted to make it a condition of his employment to work as an actor on the show. Before Paris agreed to play Jerry the dentist, insists Guilbert, "he told Sheldon Leonard, I'll do the part, but only if you'll let me direct later."

But despite the actor's single-minded determination to move behind the scenes, Carl Reiner was not entirely convinced that directing a weekly TV series was the best job for a man of Jerry Paris's wide-ranging temperament. "Jerry was so flaky," the producer admits with a laugh. "No one thought he'd be very good as a director. We said, 'Oh my God, they're not gonna listen to you!'"

Though Carl Reiner insists that he also took the actor's considerable strengths into account—"He was hilarious," acknowledges Reiner, "and very bright"—in the end, it was the actor's unwavering confidence in his own abilities that would sway the producer most decisively. "Anybody who wants to direct that badly," says Reiner, "you know he's going to be able to direct. So I said, 'We'll give him a shot.'"

Of course, even after Carl Reiner set his own misgivings aside, Jerry Paris still had to prove himself on the set, where the former actor's credibility remained a topic of concern among his fellow company members well into his first few days on the job. "Nobody came up to my office and said, 'Hey, what are you doing?'" recalls Reiner. "But there was talk. 'Hey,' they'd whisper, as they took you aside. 'Is this gonna work?' And I'd say, 'I dunno, let's take a chance. We'll see.'"

To those who knew Jerry Paris well, there was never any doubt that the actor had found his true calling at last. "Jerry loved directing," observes Bill Idelson, who'd known Paris since the late forties, when the pair had attended acting classes together in New York. "Jerry loved being in control of people," says Idelson. "He would take over. He told you what to do, he told you what to wear. You went to a party, he directed the party. If you had him at your wedding, he would direct your wedding. He would direct anything. He was a natural born director."

And Paris's natural affinity for the job soon became apparent to the show's cast, who would eventually develop a fierce loyalty to their new coach. "Jerry loved actors," says Idelson, "and actors always felt comfortable with him, because they knew he loved them. He was with you every second. He got very involved—he was *in* your body. He could tell you to jump through a wall and you'd try it, because you knew that it might be funny." "Jerry was our greatest audience," concurs Dick Van Dyke, who credits the director with inspiring him to new heights of slapstick invention on more than one occasion. "He invented a lot of good moments on the show."

And, as Carl Reiner observes, Paris wasn't shy about taking credit for those comic moments that bore his particular signature. "When we'd watch the rehearsals," recalls Reiner, "Jerry would say, 'Did you see that? I put that joke in.'" Finally, after a few week's exposure to Paris's relentless self-promotion, the producer felt obliged to bring his overeager director into check. "I finally said, 'Jerry, don't say, "I put that in." Because if you say, "I put that in," that's *all* I'll think you put in! If you don't tell me every time you put something in, I will give you credit not only for that, but for everything that happened on the stage that Dick put in, or that Mary put in!' And he said, 'Yeah, you're right! You're absolutely right.'"

But despite his overbearing personality, the show's cast couldn't help

Jerry Paris logs one of his increasingly infrequent forays before the cameras in the show's fifty-second episode, "Don't Trip Over That Mountain."

but notice how Jerry Paris invariably approached his work with intelligence and an infectious enthusiasm, and it wasn't long before he'd earned the loyalty and respect of the show's entire staff, including many of those who'd been among his most skeptical detractors. "Jerry did better than anyone dreamed," acknowledges Carl Reiner. "He finally surprised us all." And as proof of their confidence, the show's producers would assign the journeyman director to helm no fewer than ten second-year episodes, at least a few of which would one day number among the show's all-time classics, including "Ray Murdock's X-Ray," "I Was a Teenage Head Writer," "Give Me Your Walls," "I'm No Henry Walden," "When a Bowling Pin Talks, Listen," and a curious little science fiction parody that bore the unlikely title, "It May Look Like a Walnut!"

CHAPTER 21
Nuts

IN THE YEARS BEFORE HIS DEATH IN 1986, JERRY PARIS invariably cited "It May Look Like a Walnut!" as the debut episode of his tenure as director of *The Dick Van Dyke Show*. But, while that's not strictly true—Paris actually received his earliest director's credits on "Ray Murdock's X-Ray" and "I Was a Teenage Head Writer," two episodes that were filmed weeks before "It May Look Like a Walnut" finally went before the cameras on January 15, 1963—it's not hard to see how the walnut show might have eclipsed its more mundane predecessors in the director's recollection. With its half-dozen interweaving plotlines, a handful of the show's most elaborate sight gags, and a classic cameo appear-

"I was doing my version of *The Twilight Zone*," says Carl Reiner, recalling the show's unforgettable fifty-first episode, "with seventeen hundred walnuts."

ance from none other than Danny Thomas himself, "It May Look Like a Walnut" easily ranks as one of the most unforgettable episodes of *The Dick Van Dyke Show* ever committed to film.

"I was searching for things to do to stay current," explains Carl Reiner, recalling the genesis of his script for the walnut show, "and I loved *The Twilight Zone*." And so, for the Van Dyke show's fifty-first episode, the writer concocted a surrealistic takeoff that drew liberally from Rod Serling's classic science-fiction TV anthology series as well as from a number of other sources, most notably Don Siegel's classic 1956 sci-fi shocker, *Invasion of the Body Snatchers*, which was scripted by Daniel Mainwaring from a novel by Jack Finney. In Reiner's spoof, Rob Petrie wakes up one morning to find himself surrounded by extraterrestrials from the planet Twilo, who have somehow taken on the physical forms of his best friends in their nefarious quest for world domination, an invasion that's led by a general who just happens to bear an uncanny resemblance to *The Dick Van Dyke Show*'s own co-executive producer, Danny Thomas. "I was doing my version of *The Twilight Zone*," insists Carl Reiner, "with seventeen hundred walnuts."

And there's no doubt that walnuts would play a key role in the episode's brazenly silly plotline, which opens in the Petrie bedroom, where Rob is gradually reducing Laura to a nervous wreck with his scene-by-scene reenactment of the creaky plotline from a late-show thriller in which aliens plot to take over the world by tampering with the earth's walnut supply. Rob's chilling blow-by-blow account sends Laura to bed scared out of her wits, but in the end it's he who has the nightmare—or so it would appear when Rob awakes the next morning to find his house strewn with walnuts. At first, the hapless husband assumes that his wife is simply playing a joke on him, but he's forced to think twice when he arrives at work and Buddy offers him a snack from his sack of...walnuts!

Things go from weird to worse for the beleaguered comedy writer when his co-workers and Mel Cooley begin to pace around the office like a trio of mindless zombies. When they're joined by a Danny Thomas lookalike who is introduced as Kolac, the evil emissary from the planet Twilo, Rob becomes convinced that he must be having a bad dream. Hoping to jostle himself awake, he rushes home—only to confront the most bizarre sight of all. For no sooner does he go to hang up his coat than his wife comes sliding headfirst from the hallway closet, grinning malevolently from atop a mountain of thousands and thousands of...walnuts! Suddenly, from out of nowhere, Buddy, Sally, and Mel appear, flanked by the alien Danny Thomas—forming a tableau so fearsome that it forces the drowsing writer from his slumbers once and for all. Once awake, Rob barely has time to regain his composure before he makes the rather startling discovery that Laura has shared almost the exact same dream!

Reiner's script for "It May Look Like a Walnut" was, of course, an exercise in silliness from the very first page. Even so, the show's cast members were savvy enough to appreciate the comic potential in the writer's broad parody from their very first reading of the script. Which was more than could be said for Sheldon Leonard, who emerged from that same reading somewhat less taken with Reiner's tongue-in-cheek parody. "Sheldon didn't like that one," recalls Dick Van Dyke. "He thought it was a little too bizarre, and he didn't think it would be funny."

"Sheldon and I had a big argument about that show being no good," concurs Reiner, who recalls that his executive producer pronounced the script unsalvageable after a single table reading. "It was," notes Reiner, "the only time we had one of those arguments." But Carl Reiner held firm, and finally—after the requisite amount of around the table haggling—the executive producer gracefully bowed to his producer's instincts. And when Leonard finally saw how well the episode played before the audience at the show's Tuesday night filming, he was the first to admit he'd obviously misjudged the effort.

"I was 100 percent wrong," the executive producer would later observe, "and Carl was 100 percent right on that one." [56] "Sheldon was terrific," recalls Reiner, "a mensch. He just said, 'You were absolutely right!'"

According to Van Dyke show writer Sam Denoff, Leonard's handling of the debate that surrounded the walnut show provides a revealing glimpse of the executive producer's evenhanded managerial style in action. "Sheldon was really the boss," says Denoff. "But he never, ever, said, 'You do it my way.' All of his producers would fight with him, and he'd always say, 'Okay, if that's the way you wanna do it. But I'm telling you it's gonna stink.' And when it didn't stink, he'd admit it didn't stink. He was that kind of gracious man."

From their very first reading of the script, the cast fully expected to have a ball during the rehearsal and filming of the walnut show. And, by all accounts, they did—despite the somewhat complicated technical setup that was required to facilitate Laura's unforgettable third-act entrance from atop the monstrous pile of walnuts that pours forth unexpectedly from the Petries' front-hall closet. According to Michael Ross—the son of Van Dyke show prop man Glenn Ross—that memorable sight gag was accomplished using real walnuts. Sacks and sacks and sacks of them, in fact, which were poured into the closet a few hours before showtime through a chute that had been specially rigged above the set. "We packed the closet with walnuts before the show," explains Ross, who was no more than a teenager when he arrived on the set to help his father assemble the mechanics of the sight gag in 1963.

On the night of the filming, Mary Tyler Moore sat perched on a back-stage ladder, from which she was to leap onto the waterfall of walnuts at the precise split second that Van Dyke unleashed them onto the stage. On another ladder stood an additional pair of stagehands, whose job it would be to drop a few hundred additional walnuts into the mix, for good measure, once the closet door was opened. It was a complicated setup, but—to everyone's amazement—when the moment of truth finally arrived, the sight gag went off without a hitch. As soon as Van Dyke opened the closet door, the walnuts came tumbling out right on cue, and Mary Tyler Moore slid onto the stage from atop an enormous pile of hard-shelled walnuts to make one of the grandest comic entrances in television history.

And if you've ever wondered whatever became of all those walnuts after the episode was filmed—according to at least one firsthand observer, the ones that didn't crack went right back to the store! Or so claims the show's film editor, Bud Molin, who insists that once the episode was shot, the show's pennywise producers had made arrangements to return any undamaged walnuts to the nut wholesaler from whom they were pur-

Mary Tyler Moore makes the grandest entrance in the history of situation comedy; once the episode wrapped, many of those same walnuts eventually found their way onto the produce shelves of southern California supermarkets.

chased in the first place! "The deal was," explains Molin, "they could return the ones that weren't broken and get their money back." By Molin's reckoning, the unbroken walnuts eventually found their way back to the shelves of local supermarkets and, it might be safely assumed, were finally purchased and consumed by southern California nut aficionados—few of whom, presumably, had the slightest notion of their snack's highly distinguished pedigree.

According to Dick Van Dyke, more than a few of these tasty morsels were also consumed by the show's hungry cast and crew, many of whom had been snacking freely on the walnuts all week—at least until it finally dawned on someone that a surfeit of walnuts just might have an adverse effect on their digestive tracts. But, says Van Dyke, by then it was too late. "We all got really bound up," the star confesses. "The entire cast and crew were constipated—we were in bad shape for days."

When the words "It May Look Like a Walnut" appeared on television screens during the opening title sequence of *The Dick Van Dyke Show*'s February 6, 1963, broadcast, it would mark the first time the title of an episode of *The Dick Van Dyke Show* actually appeared on the air, though it would certainly not be the last. According to Carl Reiner, he would have begun the practice of running on-screen titles even earlier if the idea had only occurred to him. "The titles were always on the scripts," he explains. But it was not until the cast was reading "It May Look Like a Walnut" around the rehearsal table, maintains Reiner, that "some smart person said, 'This is a funny title. Why not put it on the air?'" The producer instantly agreed, and it was decreed that, effective immediately, the titles for that and all subsequent episodes of *The Dick Van Dyke Show* would be offered up for public consumption. "And we did it till the end," says Reiner. "It was like an extra bit of entertainment."

For *The Dick Van Dyke Show*'s fifty-fourth episode, "The Sam Pomerantz Scandals," Carl Reiner returned to that most durable of Van Dyke show formats, the comedy-variety episode. "Those musical shows were always easier on my heart," explains Reiner, who had discovered early on that it took considerably less time to craft a script in which Rob, Laura, Buddy, and Sally spend the better part of the episode singing, dancing, and telling old jokes—whether at a party, a neighborhood variety show, or an old friend's Borscht Belt nightclub—then it did to write an entirely new plot-driven episode from scratch. "It was a pleasure when we did those shows, because I didn't have to write a forty-page show," observes Reiner. "I could write a twenty-two-page show, since I knew there were gonna be three musical numbers."

But as effective as the show's musical-variety format could be in helping the writer meet his annual script quota in the show's first two or three seasons, Reiner also recognized that it was a device best used sparingly. "You couldn't do 'em too often, or it would turn into a musical show," says Reiner. "But I knew that once every thirteen weeks or so I could do a musical show." And so it was that Reiner dropped Rob, Laura, Buddy, and Sally into the Borscht Belt for the show's fifty-fourth episode, which is set in a Catskills resort managed by Rob's old army buddy Sam Pomerantz.

As "The Sam Pomerantz Scandals" opens, Rob, Laura, and the rest of the gang arrive for what they fully expect to be a leisurely vacation in the mountains. But all thoughts of a relaxing weekend are dashed after Rob accidentally incapacitates the club's headliner in a tennis match, and he, Laura, Buddy, Sally, and Mel are drafted into service as the featured entertainment in the club's main room. Sally rises to the challenge with a rousing rendition of Johnny Mercer's "I Wanna Be Around." Next, Buddy provides a few minutes of comic relief before he introduces Rob and Laura, who wow the audience with an impromptu soft-shoe to the tune of "Carolina in the Morning." For their big finale, the cast regroups on stage to perform "The Musicians," the classic bandleader number that would be reprised memorably a few months later on the Van Dyke show's Christmas episode.

But as far as Dick Van Dyke was concerned, the real highlight of the episode was the show's Laurel and Hardy sketch, an extended pantomime in which the star got to play Stan Laurel to costar Henry Calvin's Oliver Hardy—a piece that was quite clearly intended as a heartfelt tribute to one of Dick Van Dyke's most esteemed boyhood idols. "Stan Laurel was my hero," says Dick Van Dyke, who counts among his most cherished memories the afternoon he finally got a chance to meet the former silent film star at Laurel's home in Santa Monica, an event that took place not long after Van Dyke first moved to California.

"When I started the series," Van Dyke reminisces, "I asked a lot of people whatever became of Stan. But nobody was sure where he was." Then, one day, Van Dyke recalls, as he was looking up a phone number in the Santa Monica city directory, he happened across a listing for a Stan Laurel. Van Dyke nervously dialed the number and was thrilled when the voice at the other end turned out to be Stan Laurel himself.

As Van Dyke began to stammer out a halting introduction, he was greatly relieved to discover that the screen star already knew who he was. "He was familiar with the show," says Van Dyke, "and he said he liked my work." Before the call ended, Stan Laurel had invited his enthusiastic fan to drop by for a visit the following Sunday afternoon. "He lived in an apartment on Ocean Avenue in Santa Monica," remembers Van Dyke. "I just went over there, knocked on the door, and couldn't believe I was in

Before Dick Van Dyke dared to impersonate Stan Laurel on the show's fifty-fourth episode, "The Sam Pomerantz Scandals," the star called his boyhood idol for pointers; also pictured, Henry Calvin.

his presence." The two comic actors exchanged small talk for no more than a few minutes before the conversation finally—and inevitably—turned to the business of comedy. "Of course, all I did was pump him with questions," confesses Van Dyke. "We talked about physical comedy a lot."

As Van Dyke rose to leave at the end of the afternoon, the aging comedian extended his hand in friendship and offered a compliment that the younger comedian would never forget. "He said," recalls Van Dyke, "'If anybody ever decides to do a film on my life, I would like you to play me.' It was the greatest compliment I'd ever had in my life. That made my day."

Van Dyke finally got his opportunity to return the compliment with the homage that he and Henry Calvin performed on the Van Dyke show's fifty-fourth episode. Surprisingly, Van Dyke insists that until the night he filmed "The Sam Pomerantz Scandals" he'd never performed his impression of Stan Laurel in public—a fact that made the actor only that much more anxious to hear the great man's response to his tribute, which arrived a few minutes after "The Sam Pomerantz Scandals" received its first network broadcast on March 6, 1963.

"I called him as soon as the show went off the air," Van Dyke would later recall.[57] As the star relayed the conversation to Bob Thomas of the Associated Press, Stan Laurel had been extremely complimentary, finally offering the younger comedian, in Van Dyke's words, "25 minutes of notes and criticisms."[58] Curiously, the only element of Van Dyke's act that the screen legend found amiss was the actor's choice of hat, which, in Laurel's opinion, curled a little too sharply at the brim for authenticity's sake. "I did everything I could to get a flat brim like Stan's," Van Dyke observed at the time, "even had the brim pressed out. But it still didn't look right, and Stan said so. 'I would have loaned you mine,' he said. That just killed me."[59]

Van Dyke would stay in frequent contact with his idol until Stan Laurel's death in February of 1965, at which time Dick Van Dyke was asked to prepare a eulogy for the legendary screen star—a task that he undertook with an understandable mixture of sadness and pride. Later that same year, Van Dyke was again called upon to pay tribute to Stan Laurel when he hosted a CBS television special honoring Laurel and Hardy—to benefit the Motion Picture Relief Fund—that was broadcast on November 23, 1965.

After an eight-month stretch that would see the creation of thirty-three entirely new episodes of *The Dick Van Dyke Show*, the show's cast and crew finally wrapped their second production season on April 9, 1963, with the filming of the show's sixty-third episode, "All About Eavesdropping."* But, even though the Van Dyke show's cameras had finally shut down for the summer, there would be little rest for the show's star player. A few days later, Dick Van Dyke was scheduled to report to the Walt Disney studios in Burbank, where the actor would spend the better part of the late spring and summer filming his scenes as Bert the chimney

---

*Although it was filmed as the last episode of the show's second season, "All About Eavesdropping" would be held over for broadcast until the following year, an efficiency measure designed to give the busy company a one-episode head start when they reported back for the hectic beginning of the fall season a few months later. This scheduling sleight of hand would be repeated to similar effect at the end of the show's third and fourth seasons as well, when the show's ninety-fifth episode, "My Two Show-offs and Me" and episode 127, "A Farewell to Writing," would each be filmed at the end of their respective production years and be broadcast in the following season.

sweep in Disney's musical fantasy *Mary Poppins*, which costarred Julie Andrews.

While many of the show's hardworking cast and crew viewed the show's springtime hiatus as the start of a well-deserved rest from the relentless pressures of putting on a weekly television series, nothing could be further from the truth for the child actor who played Ritchie Petrie. On the contrary, for young Larry Mathews, the show's final day of shooting marked the start of a routine that he found far more stressful than acting in a weekly network television series: public school. For a youngster who enjoyed the luxury of his own on-set tutor for eight months out of each year, the thought of being thrust back into the world of hallway passes, absence notes, and regimented recess for the final six weeks of each school year was nothing short of demoralizing.

"You go back into school," says Mathews, "and all of a sudden there's a teacher hassling you. When you have a private tutor, one-on-one, it's real easy to learn, and you can learn quickly. It's much easier than being in a classroom of forty or fifty kids." And the fact that Mathews had skipped a grade didn't make the child actor's annual readjustment to public school any easier. "I went from first to third grade," recalls Mathews, "so I was always coming back to children that were older than me in age. And yet, I felt like I was older than them." And, as Mathews observes, the most difficult challenge of returning to school may have been relearning how to talk to kids his own age. "Every so often I would not be able to relate to the kids in my class, simply because I spent most of my year around adults. And when I would get back in a school situation, it was like regressing."

By the time the membership of the Academy of Television Arts and Sciences gathered to pass out their annual Emmy awards on May 23, 1963, they'd already bolstered the spirits of the Van Dyke show's cast and crew with award nominations in almost every major category for which the show was eligible. And before the night was over, Carl Reiner would accept two statuettes, including the Emmy for Outstanding Program Achievement in the Field of Humor, as well as his own second consecutive Emmy for Outstanding Writing Achievement in the Field of Comedy. And, after being left standing at the altar the previous year—when he'd been nominated, but did not win, in the director's category—John Rich was especially gratified to accept the evening's Emmy for Outstanding Directorial Achievement in Comedy.

In the acting categories, Dick Van Dyke was nominated for, but did not receive, the award for Outstanding Continued Performance by an

Despite the tutoring he received on the set of the Van Dyke show, former child star Larry Mathews recalls that he was required to return to regular public school classes at the conclusion of the show's production season each year.

Actor in a Series, which went to E. G. Marshall for his work on *The Defenders*. Mary Tyler Moore also nabbed a nomination for the top acting trophy for an actress, though the Emmy for Outstanding Performance by an Actress in a Series would be won by *Hazel*'s Shirley Booth. Also nominated for an acting trophy that evening was Rose Marie, who faced especially stiff competition in the supporting actress category, where the comedic actress was at a distinct disadvantage in a field dominated by actresses in traditionally showy dramatic roles. But though Rose Marie could take pride in the fact that she'd been the only comedy performer to earn a nomination in the extremely competitive supporting actress category, the award for Outstanding Performance in a Supporting Role by an Actress would go to Glenda Farrell, who was recognized for her dramatic turn as a guest star on an episode of *Ben Casey*.

CHAPTER 22
Unlikely Saviors

BY THE START OF THE SHOW'S THIRD YEAR, THERE COULD be little doubt that Carl Reiner's tireless efforts as the head writer, producer, story editor, and resident genius behind *The Dick Van Dyke Show* had paid off in handsome dividends. By its third season of production, *The Dick Van Dyke Show* had already achieved a degree of success of which its creator could hardly have dreamed when he sat down to pound out the first draft of his *Head of the Family* pilot on Fire Island five summers before.

After spending its first season as a dark horse in the weekly Nielsen sweepstakes, *The Dick Van Dyke Show* had bounded into the top twenty near the start of its second year, where it would remain throughout the rest of its five-year run. Even more impressive was the fact that, after two years on the air, *The Dick Van Dyke Show* had earned the near-unanimous endorsement of television critics across the land, many of whom took pleasure in citing the show as the leading exemplar of that rarest of prime-time programming forms: a situation comedy for grown-ups. Equally heartening to the show's creator/producer was the unstinting support he'd received from his peers within the industry, who had thus far honored his show with four Emmy Awards—the first of many more to come.

But, while Reiner's ceaseless devotion to *The Dick Van Dyke Show* during its first two years of life had resulted in a rosy outlook for the series, the toll of those same efforts on his personal well-being had not been nearly so salutary. In fact, in later years, Reiner would submit that the stress of having to perform so many duties on the show practically singlehandedly for two years very nearly killed him. "If I hadn't found someone to help me in that third year," he says today, "I wouldn't be here. I would've had a heart attack."

All of which goes a long way toward explaining why Carl Reiner ascribes such importance to the addition of a pair of writers named Bill

Persky and Sam Denoff to his staff at the start of the Van Dyke show's third season—an arrival that the producer says came not a moment too soon. "Bill Persky and Sam Denoff," asserts Reiner, "saved my life." And yet, as Carl Reiner is first to admit, the young writers seemed an unlikely pair of saviors the day they arrived on his doorstep, sample script in hand, in 1962. In fact, when Bill Persky and Sam Denoff first approached the producer with their earliest Van Dyke show sample script late in the show's second season, the pair had never even written a situation comedy before—or much of anything else, for that matter.

Bill Persky and Sam Denoff first teamed up in the late fifties, after meeting at New York's WNEW radio, where they had both worked in the programming department. Like many comedy writers of the late fifties, the pair got their start as joke writers, contributing material and routines to Don Rickles and other nightclub comics of the era. Lured to California by the promise of staff writing jobs on Steve Allen's short-lived 1961 variety show, the pair would spend the next two years drifting through a wide array of short-term assignments, including a one-season stint as sketch writers on NBC's *Andy Williams Show*. "We had some odd jobs," says Sam Denoff, recalling their early years in Los Angeles, "and stood in a lot of unemployment lines."

Considering their skimpy professional resumés, it's a wonder that Persky and Denoff managed to get in to see Carl Reiner at all. But then, it probably didn't hurt that the team's agent at the Morris office happened to be Carl Reiner's close friend, adviser, and nephew by marriage, George Shapiro, an aggressive

Bill Persky and Sam Denoff, the writers Carl Reiner credits with saving his life, pictured in the cramped quarters they shared on the Desilu lot; Denoff is seated at the typewriter.

booster of talent who was not above using his privileged position to land his young clients a meeting with the busy producer. "You're gonna love these guys," Shapiro promised Reiner as he handed him a Van Dyke show script that the team had written on spec. "They've written a funny, funny script."

"All right," sighed Reiner, who decided to reserve judgment until he'd read the sample script himself. Not that he had any reason to doubt Shapiro—but, after two years of combing through freelance Van Dyke show submissions, experience had taught the producer not to expect much. And, alas, Persky and Denoff's initial submission hardly gave Carl Reiner cause to revise those expectations.

"They wrote a show that was so wrong," observes Reiner, recalling Persky and Denoff's earliest writing sample for the series. "It was a battle of the sexes kind of thing," he elaborates, "and it wasn't funny—at least not my kind of funny. And, if it wasn't my kind of funny, I didn't care how funny it might be to someone else—it wasn't right for the show." But

despite his harsh judgment of their work, Reiner agreed to meet Persky and Denoff, if only as a favor to George Shapiro. Even so, it would not be a long conference. In the producer's recollection, his first meeting with Persky and Denoff consisted of little more than a couple of handshakes and a few polite words of rejection. "I just said, 'No, it's not right for us,'" says Reiner.

The cast brushes up on their bidding techniques in a still from "The Masterpiece," the second Van Dyke show script to come from the busy typewriter of writers Bill Persky and Sam Denoff.

As Sam Denoff recalls it, Carl Reiner's summary dismissal of their earliest attempt at writing a situation comedy came as a particularly painful blow, especially since—after nearly two years of irregular employment as variety show writers—Persky and Denoff had been anxious to make the leap to the more respectable arena of situation comedy. "We wanted to be more like real writers," remembers Denoff, "rather than sketch guys."

Deciding that there was little they could do but attempt to learn what they could from their mistakes, the writers finally sat down to analyze their rejected Van Dyke show script—and soon came to the sobering conclusion that Carl Reiner's dim assessment of their work had probably not been far off the mark. "Basically," admits Sam Denoff, "it was a stupid script." Their biggest mistake, recalls Denoff, was that their sample script had simply failed to capture the very specific comic rhythms and tone of *The Dick Van Dyke Show*. "That's what happens with a lot of writers," he observes. "They look at something on television and they say, 'Oh, this is what it is!' But they miss the point." Which is exactly the trap that Denoff and his partner fell into when they set out to write their initial Van Dyke show sample. "We didn't understand what they were going for on that show."

But that would not be a problem for long. Beginning with the very next broadcast of *The Dick Van Dyke Show*, Persky and Denoff began watching the program with a concentration that bordered on scientific. Sitting quietly in front of their television sets each Wednesday night, they studied the show's storylines, dissected the jokes, and analyzed the dialogue until they were almost as familiar with *The Dick Van Dyke Show*'s characters and setting as Carl Reiner himself.

Concurrent with their ongoing study of the Van Dyke show, Persky and Denoff continued to hone their situation-comedy writing skills by taking on freelance assignments from a wide range of half-hour comedies of the era, including *McHale's Navy* and *The Joey Bishop Show*, among others. But, although the writers were happy to get the work, they couldn't help but notice that none of the half-hour comedies they were writing for strove for even a fraction of the wit, intelligence, and craft that could be found on any episode of the Van Dyke show. Finally, the team's frustration grew so great that they concluded that it was high time they gave the Van Dyke show another shot. "We decided," says Denoff, "why write for these other kinds of shows? We wanted to write for Dick Van Dyke. So we decided that we would try and go back to Carl again." And so, armed with the hard-earned insights they'd gleaned from their intensive study of the show, the writers called George Shapiro.

Who called Carl Reiner.

"George came to me," recalls Reiner. "And he said, 'They watch the show, they know what your sensibility is now. They know who your people are. And they got a great idea for a show. Promise me you'll go talk to them.'"

"So we got a meeting with Carl," Denoff continues. "And we went in with a shopping list of ideas." But, as it turned out, Carl Reiner was hooked on their very first pitch. "We want to do a flashback episode," Persky proposed, before launching into a detailed outline of a story that takes place in the days immediately following Ritchie's birth, a comedy of errors in which Rob becomes convinced that he and Laura have been given the wrong baby. "I don't remember where the mixed-up babies idea came from," recalls Denoff. "But Carl liked the idea." "They came in with the baby show," concurs the producer, "and I said, 'Oh boy! This is heaven!'"

A few days after Reiner gave the story his go-ahead, Persky and Denoff reconvened in the producer's office for what would be their first full-fledged story conference with Carl Reiner and Sheldon Leonard. And it was there that the freshman writers began their education in comedy writing, Dick Van Dyke style. "Bill and I started pitching how we would do the story," recalls Denoff, "and then Carl and Sheldon broke the story down, scene by scene by scene by scene. We weren't talking dialogue—unless, once in while, a joke or an idea would come up, and then we'd write it down." But, as Reiner reminded them more than once that afternoon, the purpose of that initial session was simply to hammer out a road map for the writers to follow once they went off to start writing the script on their own. "And," says Denoff, "we didn't leave the office until Carl and Sheldon were satisfied that we had that structure."

With their story outline in hand, Persky and Denoff went right to work, driving directly from the Desilu Cahuenga lot to their office, which in those days was a tiny cubicle that the pair rented in a rundown West Hollywood office building at 8228 Sunset Boulevard. "Neither of us could ever write at home," explains Denoff, who still chuckles at the thought of the abysmally cramped quarters of their first office, a windowless room whose most arresting feature was a wall-sized mural of Japan's Mount Fuji that was mounted behind a set of venetian blinds, presumably to give the impression that the volcano was just outside the nonexistent window. Although the room was barely wide enough to contain their single desk and chair, the young writers took solace in the fact that their office was one of the few in the building to boast its own private bathroom—which Persky and Denoff soon came to view as an extension of their hopelessly inadequate workspace. "One of us literally had to sit in the bathroom while the other one sat at the desk typing," recalls Denoff.

"Sam sat at the typewriter," reminisces Bill Persky, picking up his partner's description of their early work routine. "And we'd talk through the script. We'd play all the parts—just talking it out, back and forth, like a conversation. We'd type stuff, and then we'd go back and fix it." "And," adds Denoff, "after we wrote it, we rewrote it. And rewrote it. With all the great pain that you go through when you're trying to get something right that you want to be right. We just stayed in that room and wrote the script—with one guy sitting at the chair and the other guy in the bathroom."

After three or four weeks of these painstaking labors, Persky and Denoff finally finished a script that they felt was good enough to submit to Carl Reiner. The only problem was that their completed draft ran long by about ten or twelve pages. "We knew it was too long," notes Sam Denoff, "but we didn't know what to cut. We wanted to leave in all this wonderful stuff that we wrote." After their initial attempts at editing proved futile, the writers finally decided to turn it in as it was and let their producer decide what to delete. And so, on May 22, 1963, the proud writers delivered their slightly long first draft of the script that they'd finally titled "That's My Boy???"

Then came the hard part.

Rob and Laura arrive home with their new baby—or is it?—in "That's My Boy???," an episode that seems to have found its way onto the all-time ten-best lists of almost everyone involved with the series.

"We sat in our office and waited," recalls Sam Denoff. "And we waited. And waited. We were going crazy, just waiting to find out whether Carl liked it." But finally, says Denoff, after two or three days that seemed endless at the time, the phone rang.

"I remember it like it was yesterday," says Persky, recalling that phone call. "Sam sat at the little typewriter table, and I was sitting in the hall." A few seconds after Denoff picked up the receiver, he threw a glance at his partner. "It's Carl!" he whispered. "And he's read the script!"

"We both held our breath," continues Persky. "And then Sam started to smile, and he said, 'Oh my God! That's great!'" Sam Denoff claims he still remembers Reiner's exact words. "Carl said, 'Fellas, it swings! It's terrific!'" Within seconds, the jubilant Denoff had hung up the phone and leapt to his feet to embrace his partner in a celebratory hug. "We laughed," says Denoff, "and then we did whatever dance we could do in that limited space."

Carl Reiner would not be alone in his admiration for "That's My Boy???," which is one of those Van Dyke episodes that seems to have found its way onto the all-time ten-best lists of almost everyone involved with the series. A no less discerning critic than John Rich—who had returned to the series to direct this and the following three episodes as his valedictory bow on the show—lists "That's My Boy???" among the top two or three Van Dyke shows of all time. And it's not hard to see why. An unofficial sequel to the saga of Ritchie's birth that was outlined in the show's nineteenth episode, "Where Did I Come From?," "That's My Boy???" traces Rob and Laura's adjustment to parenthood in the days that follow Laura's arrival home from the maternity ward.

The comic complications set in almost immediately, as Rob gets it into his head that, owing to a clerical mixup at the hospital, he and Laura have somehow arrived home with someone else's baby. And, try as she might, there's nothing Laura can do to dissuade her husband from his preposterous assumption. "Do you know that one out of every fifty million women has the wrong baby?" Rob asks his skeptical wife. "That's a cute trick," she answers, unfazed. "How does she manage it?"

Rob doesn't get his comeuppance until later that evening, when he finally comes face to face with Mr. and Mrs. Peters, the couple whose child he's convinced the hospital has switched with their own. But it's only after they arrive at his doorstep that Rob recognizes the magnitude of his error. For, as becomes obvious the minute the visiting couple walks into his living room, there's simply no way the hospital could've gotten their baby confused with Rob's—if only because Mr. and Mrs. Peters are black!

"Why didn't you tell me on the phone?" Rob stammers to his guest, who's clearly enjoying the spectacle of Rob's embarrassed reaction. "And miss the expression on your face?" replies Peters, savoring the moment to the last.

And there's no question that Rob's stunned reaction to his guests' arrival was a sight to be savored. The tortured take that Dick Van Dyke summoned for the black couple's climactic entrance would stand as one of the actor's crowning achievements—a brilliantly modulated reaction in which the character's protean foolishness is revealed in the actor's deft combination of shock, relief, and—finally—utterly bewildered embarrassment. And, judged purely on the basis of the length of the riotous ovation that greeted the entrance of actors Greg Morris and Mimi Dillard on the night the show was filmed, many Van Dyke show staffers insist that the scene easily qualifies as the funniest single moment of the entire series. "That," maintains Dick Van Dyke, "to my recollection, is by far the longest laugh we ever got."

And yet, according to Sheldon Leonard, until just a few hours before show time, it looked doubtful that the scene would make it before the cameras at all. For, in one of the strangest behind-the-scenes ironies of the entire series, the sight gag that would provide *The Dick Van Dyke Show* with its longest single laugh was filmed despite loud cries of protest from the show's sponsor and the CBS network itself.

"Procter & Gamble had been very frightened about that episode," observes Sheldon Leonard, who recalls that he got his first whiff of an impending storm at the show's Friday night run-through, which was, as always, attended by representatives of the show's sponsors. As Leonard recalls the events of that evening, his actors had barely left the stage before an emmissary from Procter & Gamble approached him to voice grave reservations about what he'd just seen. According to Leonard, the sponsor's worries were well intentioned, if somewhat misguided.

After watching the show's climactic twist, the sponsor was convinced that viewers might misinterpret the producer's intentions and assume that the black couple was being used as the butt of a joke. "It's gonna look like we're making fun of the black man," Leonard recalls the sponsor complaining. To which the executive producer quickly replied, "No, it's not! It's gonna look like we're making fun of Van Dyke, because he's an idiot! The black man is smarter, more self-contained. And, he has more dignity."

Leonard's reasoned argument seemed to placate the sponsor for the time being, and it was finally decided that Procter & Gamble would defer to the producer's judgment. Thinking the issue settled, Leonard went on to other matters. But, as the executive producer might have guessed, the

Though "The Musicians" became a Van Dyke show signature tune, the number actually originated on an obscure children's record that Dick Van Dyke had unearthed some ten years earlier when he was hosting an afternoon kid's show in Atlanta.

controversy surrounding the episode was not fated to vanish that easily. That much would become clear the following Tuesday afternoon, when—with only hours to go before the show was to be filmed—Sheldon Leonard heard from an anxious CBS executive who'd developed a bad case of cold feet of his own. "Won't people think we're ridiculing the black couple?" the well-meaning network executive queried.

With time running short, Sheldon Leonard decided not to argue the point, but instead offered a compromise that he hoped would settle the matter once and for all. Why not, he proposed, let the audience be the judge? It was Leonard's suggestion that they simply let the cast go ahead and film the show as written when the audience arrived in the studio that evening. If at that time, he proposed, even *one* member of the show's in-house audience failed to embrace the show's closing gag—if anyone in the stands let out so much as a single groan when Greg Morris and Mimi Dillard made their scheduled entrance—the executive producer promised to reshoot the entire ending, at his own expense, in any fashion the network dictated.

With showtime looming ever closer, the network agreed to accept the terms of Leonard's compromise, and the climax of "That's My Boy???" was filmed, exactly as written that night. And, just as Sheldon Leonard had predicted, not one member of the audience groaned, moaned, or otherwise complained. But they did laugh. And laugh. And laugh, until they'd registered what many feel was the show's longest laugh on record. And no one from the network ever again mentioned Leonard's offer to reshoot the ending.*

Director John Rich claims that he never had a moment's doubt that the sight gag that ends "That's My Boy???" would deliver a whopping response—a confidence that was readily apparent from the last-minute instructions he offered to Greg Morris and Mimi Dillard a few hours before the episode went before the cameras. "I told Greg and Mimi to wait for the laugh," recalls the director. "I said, 'Just walk in, let Dick do the take, and then stand there.' And I told Greg Morris, 'The only mistake you can make is to speak too soon after Dick's initial reaction.'"

It was good advice. According to Rich, the prolonged ovation that followed the entrance of the black actors was like nothing he'd ever heard. "First there was a gasp," he recalls. "Then there was a laugh. And then

---

*Ironically, though the network acquiesced to the executive producer's wishes on the racial gag, director John Rich remembers another joke—equally innocuous by today's standards—that failed to make it past the show's various censors in 1963. The gag in question originally occurred during the exchange where Rob is chiding Laura for trying to do too much as they're preparing to leave the hospital. "Honey, you shouldn't exert yourself," he cautions, reaching for the babe in arms. "You'd better not carry the baby." In the version that was shot, Laura dutifully hands the infant over. But, in the episode's original script, Laura's response to her husband's solicitousness is far more pointed—and much funnier. "I carried him for nine months," Laura answers. "I think I can carry him out of the building." But, though the line got a resounding laugh at every one of the show's early run-throughs, it was finally deemed unacceptably suggestive by the CBS Standards and Practices Department, which insisted that the line be dropped entirely before the episode was filmed—a suggestion to which Reiner and his writers reluctantly complied.

protracted applause. And that applause was the most gratifying sound I'd ever heard in my life. It was just wonderful. It was quite a piece of vindication."

In Van Dyke's recollection, the laughter went on so long that he began to feel the queer sensation, in his own words, of "being suspended in time." "They would not stop laughing," he recalls. "We stood there forever." The audience's thunderous ovation went on so long, in fact, that film editor Bud Molin insists that he had to cut it down for the finished episode. Apparently, the laughter that was actually shot that night was so protracted that it threw the show's timing off, with the result, says Molin, that he was forced to lop a few precious seconds of laughter from the show's finished track in order to squeeze the scene to fit the finished episode's extremely tight running time. And so, ironically, when viewers at home finally got a chance to see the episode on the air, they were treated to *The Dick Van Dyke Show*'s longest laugh ever...give or take a few seconds.

CHAPTER 23
Changing of the Guard

CARL REINER KNEW THE MINUTE HE READ PERSKY AND
Denoff's first draft of "That's My Boy???"that the writers had crafted a
first-rate script. The plotting was good, the jokes were clever, and the
script's style and pacing were right on the money. But what had impressed
the producer more than anything else was how closely Persky and
Denoff's script resembled one of his own. And for the overworked story
editor, producer, and chief scriptwriter of *The Dick Van Dyke Show*, that
was cause for celebration.

It was like a dream come true. After two years of trolling through freelance story submissions to dredge up raw material for the show; after the
countless story conferences that had been required to structure and polish that material; and after the dozens of last-minute rewrite sessions that
had been required to get those scripts into shape for the show—the weary
producer's prayers had been answered. Here, at last, was a pair of writers who could craft a workable *Dick Van Dyke Show* script from the very
first draft! But even more significantly, in Bill Persky and Sam Denoff,
Carl Reiner recognized a pair of young, hardworking writers who could—
with a little faith, patience, and guidance from him—be trained to serve
as full-time writers for *The Dick Van Dyke Show*. Which is exactly what
he had in mind.

As Bill Persky remembers it, the producer left little doubt that he had
big plans for his fledgling writers. "Carl told us our first script was great,"
recalls Persky. "And then he asked us to write as many shows for him as
we could handle. And that's when everything changed for us."

As Carl Reiner laid it out, the initial terms of Persky and Denoff's
employment on the series would actually be quite modest. As the pro-

ducer explained it at one of their earliest meetings, his budgetary restrictions were such that he couldn't afford to pay them any sort of weekly salary or retainer beyond the script fees they would earn for each episode they actually wrote.* Even so, the producer promised, if the writers were willing to hang around the studio and listen and learn as much as they could about the show and the way it was put together, he could guarantee them a rent-free office on the lot, and as many script assignments on the show as they could handle.

Were they interested?

It took the writers all of two hours to move their typewriter over from the cubicle they rented on Sunset Boulevard to their brand-new office on the ground floor of the Desilu Cahuenga studio's Building A. Ironically, it was only after they'd already taken up residence on the lot that it dawned on the writers that their new space wasn't really much of an improvement over their former digs. "The office they gave us was from, like, 1920," recalls Sam Denoff, exaggerating by no more than a few decades—the structure that Persky and Denoff moved into had actually been constructed during the studio facelift that Desi Arnaz had engineered in the early fifties. "It was painted a dingy green," Denoff continues. "And everything stunk. It smelled like some silent movie star had died in there."

But, as the writers cheerfully acknowledged, whatever their new office may have lacked in the way of amenities was more than mitigated by its opportune proximity to Carl Reiner's own office, which was directly upstairs. And, as Reiner observes, that geographical proximity was no accident, since from the very start it had been his intention to situate his apprentice writers where he could keep a close watch on their progress. "I put them next door to me," says Reiner, "so I would be able to walk in the

---

*Incredible as it seems—considering the amount of material that Persky and Denoff would generate during the show's final three seasons—the writers would not actually work under contract to the show until well into the series' fifth year, when they were engaged to fill in as producers during a brief leave of absence by Carl Reiner. Prior to that time, the pair were paid on a per-script basis, at prevailing fees that hovered in the neighborhood of $3000 for a finished first-draft script, with an additional $1500 for a second-draft rewrite or final polish of their own or another writer's script. Of course, like any other Van Dyke show writer—including Carl Reiner—Persky and Denoff would also collect nominal residual payments for the initial rerun cycles of those episodes that carried their names as primary writers.

room every day and stop them if they started going in the wrong direction."

And, as Bill Persky observes, he and his partner certainly had no qualms about working under the watchful eye of so generous a mentor as Carl Reiner. "It was a wonderful education," notes Persky, who looks back on his years as a writer and story editor of *The Dick Van Dyke Show* as the most rewarding period of his career. It's a sentiment that's echoed by his former writing partner. "It was utopia," observes Sam Denoff. "A situation comedy writer's utopia."

In one of those ironies that is all too common in the mercurial world of television, Bill Persky and Sam Denoff would begin their long and fertile association with *The Dick Van Dyke Show* in August 1963, the very same month that marked the final flowering of John Rich's own long and equally fruitful tenure as the show's director. Rich, who had left the series some months earlier to pursue opportunities in the feature-film arena, had taken advantage of a four-week gap in his movie directing activities to direct his last four episodes at the start of the show's third year.

By an odd coincidence, the director would film his final Van Dyke show episode, "Very Old Shoes, Very Old Rice," on August 27, 1963, the night before his first feature film, Paramount's *Wives and Lovers*, had its world premiere in New York City. "That last episode was particularly emotional," says Rich. "I knew that I had done very nice work with a very extraordinary group of people. And now I was leaving them."

Dick Van Dyke lures a stunned John Rich into the surprise party the cast threw for their departing director after his final night on the show. "When I came through that door with Dick," recalls John Rich, "my mouth dropped open four feet."

The cast, who shared Rich's melancholy on the eve of his departure, decided to commemorate the occasion by surprising their departing general with a top-secret send-off party at the end of his final night of service. But according to John Rich's account of that memorable evening, his actors may have been more successful in their efforts to surprise him than they'd dreamed. As the evening's filming drew to a close, the director—still without a clue to the revelries that his cast had planned for him later that night—found himself feeling more than a little bruised by his cast's apparent lack of emotion on what was, for him, a very difficult night. "I said, 'Cut! That's a wrap,'" recalls Rich, "and then everybody just kind of drifted away. There were a lot of quick, 'G'bye, g'bye's,' and then suddenly, I was alone on the stage."

By then thoroughly confused by his cast's unexpected diffidence, the director resigned himself to the inevitability of a bittersweet exit and began gathering his personal belongings from the now deserted soundstage. "I thought, 'Gee, everyone's gone home, and we never got a chance to mark the occasion,'" the director recalls. "It was sad. But, that's show business." Then, just as the director's melancholia threatened to get the better of him, Dick Van Dyke stepped out from the shadows of the darkened studio—right on cue.

"Dick came out of his dressing room," Rich continues, "and he said, 'Hey, John, you still here?' I said, 'Yeah, yeah. I'm feeling a little nostalgic.' He said, 'Yeah, me too. You want to go across the street and have a beer?' Naturally, I jumped at the chance."

A few minutes later, recalls the director, the pair arrived at a neighborhood watering hole not far from the studio. "When I came through that door with Dick," exclaims Rich, "my mouth dropped open four feet." For there, jammed elbow to elbow into every available corner of the tiny neighborhood tavern stood the entire cast and crew of the Van Dyke show—along with a few dozen other well-wishers—all gathered together with their mugs raised high in cheerful salute to their beloved director. "It was a remarkable send-off party," Rich observes, and a perfect capper to two of the director's most rewarding years in television. "Those were really among my happiest days," notes Rich, "I must say, in the theater."

With John Rich's departure now official, Sheldon Leonard and Carl Reiner began to give serious thought to choosing his permanent replacement. With ten first-rate episodes already under his belt by the start of the show's third year, Jerry Paris seemed the obvious choice to inherit the mantle from John Rich. Or so thought the show's cast, who made no secret of their preference for Jerry Paris when the time came to pick a successor for the departed director. "They used to complain whenever we brought anyone else in to direct," recalls Carl Reiner, who was more than happy to accede to his acting company's consensus. And so, a few weeks into the show's third season, Jerry Paris finally landed his sought-after appointment as the second—and, as it would turn out, final—house director of *The Dick Van Dyke Show*.

No one was more pleased to see Jerry Paris finally achieve his due than his longtime supporter and Pacific Palisades neighbor Ann Guilbert, who recalls that the only downside to Paris's promotion was that it cost her a car-pooling partner. "When we were both just acting, we'd be in the same scenes," recalls the actress, "so I would usually drive down with Jerry." But once Paris took on the far more labor-intensive duties of director, the actress found herself making the thirteen-mile trek into Hollywood on her own. "Sometimes Jerry would have to stay late," says Guilbert. "And I just didn't feel like hanging out."

In the second week of November 1963, the cast of the Van Dyke show put a fresh spin on the show's tried and true variety-show format when they filmed their first—and only—holiday episode, "The Alan Brady Show Presents." In the clever show-within-a-show premise that writers Persky and Denoff concocted for the episode, Alan Brady decides to turn

The cast cuts the cake at John Rich's farewell party, which was convened on August 27, 1963, immediately following the filming of the director's valedictory episode, "Very Old Shoes, Very Old Rice."

the asylum over to the inmates when he invites Rob and his staff—aided and abetted by Laura, Mel, and Ritchie—to create and stage the holiday edition of "The Alan Brady Show" entirely on their own. And, though it may not have been the most complex plotline ever devised for a Van Dyke show episode, it was enough to provide the show's talented cast with an excuse to take center stage for one of the series' most completely satisfying variety-show outings.

Drawing on the skills they'd honed during their year as musical-variety writers for Andy Williams, Persky and Denoff rose splendidly to the challenge of crafting an entire half hour's worth of specialty material for the show's versatile cast—including a handful of songs that the writers composed especially for this episode. "It was a welcome change from the ordinary half-hour show," says Sam Denoff. Curiously, although Persky and Denoff were accorded a rare on-screen credit as composers of the show's entire program of songs, the writers freely admit that they had nothing whatsoever to do with the composition of the episode's rousing finale, "The Musicians"—or, as the tune would become more commonly known to legions of Van Dyke show fans, "We All Are Fine Musicians."

The delightful musical number—in which each of the cast members, in turn, takes on the persona of an instrument in a marching band—had actually made its Van Dyke show debut some nine months earlier, when it provided the finale for the show's fifty-fourth episode, "The Sam Pomerantz Scandals." But, according to Dick Van Dyke, the origin of the song actually goes back even further than that.

"I suggested that song," recalls Van Dyke, who insists that he'd actually discovered the catchy little ditty more than a decade earlier, on an obscure children's record he ran across in 1953 while he was scouting for material to perform on a local kid's TV show he was hosting in Atlanta. "I did little mimes and sketches on the show," the star explains. "And I had a little band, and we used to do that song." And so it was that a decade later, when the star found himself struggling to come up with a suitable finale for the Van Dyke show's fifty-fourth episode, he suddenly remembered the bouncy little tune. The song was originally composed by the team of Glazer and Grean, a pair of composers who were no doubt thrilled to see their obscure children's song achieve instant immortality by its inclusion in not *one* but *two* different episodes of *The Dick Van Dyke Show*. "It's funny how long that little song has lasted," observes Van Dyke, "*everybody* knows that song."

Another fascinating sidelight to the filming of the Van Dyke show's Christmas installment is that—despite the camera crew's diligent efforts to re-create the live ambience of a TV variety spectacular in the shooting

Despite the frolicsome tone of the show's seventy-eighth episode, the cast was practically in shock when they gathered to film "Happy Birthday and Too Many More" four days after the Kennedy assassination in November 1963.

of the episode—"The Alan Brady Show Presents" was, ironically enough, one of the few episodes of *The Dick Van Dyke Show* to be filmed without any audience at all. With six full-costume musical numbers and a flashback scene set in the writers' office, the Van Dyke show producers recognized that it would be difficult, if not impossible, to film such a technically demanding episode straight through before a live audience. And so the decision was made to shoot the episode scene-by-scene, with no audience present. "That one was shot piecemeal on a different stage," recalls Larry Mathews, "because of the way we had to edit the show together."

Though the cast had no way of knowing it then, "The Alan Brady Show Presents" would not be the last Van Dyke show to be filmed sans a studio audience. In fact, just two weeks later, the company would decide to perform yet another episode to an empty house, though in that case the decision would be made under far more sobering circumstances.

Three days into rehearsals for the episode titled "Happy Birthday and Too Many More," the entire world was rocked by the news that the thirty-fifth president of the United States had been shot to death in a Dallas motorcade. Not surprisingly, by the time the company regrouped to film the episode four days later, they were hardly shocked to discover that nobody was in much of a mood for laughing—onstage or off.

CHAPTER 24

Playing to an Empty House

WHEN THE NEWS OF THE KENNEDY ASSASSINATION reached the cast of *The Dick Van Dyke Show* on the morning of November 22, 1963, they were already on stage rehearsing the opening scenes of "Happy Birthday and Too Many More," an elaborately silly exercise that revolved around Rob and Laura's efforts to keep sixty-three unruly kids entertained at Ritchie's birthday party. As Carl Reiner remembers it, the cast had just started to run through a scene when Glenn Ross, the show's prop man, emerged from his backstage office, ashen-faced and sweating.

"He's been shot..." Ross announced in slow, even tones addressed to no one in particular.

"What?" asked Carl Reiner, looking up from his script. "*Who?* Who's been shot?"

"The president..." came the prop man's response. "Kennedy."

Audible gasps swept through the studio, as the cast instinctively moved toward the closest radio, which was still playing just offstage in the prop man's tiny office. And there, crowded shoulder to shoulder amidst the incongruous clutter of party hats and tin horns that the prop man had already gathered for the show's upcoming birthday party episode, the cast of *The Dick Van Dyke Show* stood in horrified silence as the announcer intoned the devastating details of the tragedy in Dallas. "The guy on the radio said the president had died at one o'clock," recalls Rose Marie. "And then we all just looked at one another."

After a very long pause, Carl Reiner broke the stony silence when he dropped his copy of the week's script onto the prop man's cluttered desk. "Well, that's it for today," he announced. "Ain't no one gonna get any more work done. Let's go home."

"I called my husband," says Rose Marie, remembering the overpowering sense of desolation that gripped the entire company at that instant. "I told him, 'I'm coming home.' And then everybody drove home crying."

In one of the day's stranger ironies, director Jerry Paris had already planned to take the afternoon off. Earlier that week, Paris had cast his seven-year-old son, Tony, in a bit part as one of the kids at the party in that week's episode—and, by pure coincidence, the director had already set the remainder of that Friday afternoon aside to register Tony with the Social Security office in preparation for his first day of work that Monday. "It was the first job I'd ever had," recalls Tony Paris, who confesses that he'd been far too young to grasp the significance of the day's events at the time. "My dad was obviously shaken when he picked me up at school," recalls the younger Paris. "And the next thing I knew, we were driving around Hollywood, getting all this business stuff taken care of with Social Security, and joining the Screen Actors Guild and all that. I just remember my dad taking me down to this office where you had to sign all these papers. And all I knew was that something really horrible had happened that day."

In the wake of the tragedy, the Van Dyke show's producers were understandably concerned that the events that transpired in Dallas might have a less than salutary effect on their audience's morale at the

Dick Van Dyke and Mary Tyler Moore in "Happy Birthday and Too Many More," one of only a handful of Van Dyke shows to be filmed without a live studio audience in attendance.

filming that was still scheduled for the following Tuesday night. And, for a few minutes during the long weekend that followed the Kennedy assassination, Reiner and Leonard considered canceling the week's episode altogether. But, finally, invoking the oldest show business maxim of all, Carl Reiner and his producing partner decided that the show would go on—though, under the circumstances, it was decided that it would go on without the benefit of a live studio audience in attendance. And as much as he bristled at the thought, Carl Reiner reluctantly agreed to use canned laughter on the episode's soundtrack, the assumption being that even pre-recorded laughs would be preferable to the shell-shocked response they were likely to get from a live audience in the wake of the recent events.

On the Monday morning following the Kennedy assassination, the cast and crew regrouped to resume rehearsals for "Happy Birthday and Too Many More." And, as anyone who was there will attest, the show's final two days of rehearsal were certainly no party. "We just sat around all week in a stupor," recalls Dick Van Dyke. "There *was* a pretty somber mood on the set," concurs Tony Paris. But even discounting the cast's emotional state that week, Paris insists that "Happy Birthday and Too Many More" would have been a difficult shoot under even the best of circumstances. "There were forty kids on the set that day," explains Paris, indicating the overwhelming number of child extras who'd been brought in for the episode's birthday party scene. "And almost all of them were really high strung."

Given the generally high level of hyperactivity shared by the cast of underaged extras, recalls Tony Paris, his father certainly didn't have to push very hard to motivate them to the state of pandemonium that was required for the sequence where the kids were supposed to run rampant through the Petrie household at the peak of the party's frenzy. In fact, according to Paris, at least one of the show's high-spirited extras spent the better part of his two days on the set in seeming preparation for that very sequence. "There was this one kid who just kept running around the set screaming," says Paris. "Literally screaming! I really grew to hate that kid."

"The show didn't turn out that badly on the air," maintains Dick Van Dyke, offering an even-handed assessment of "Happy Birthday and Too Many More" that would not be shared by many others in the show's cast and crew, most of whom were only too eager to put the show's ill-fated seventy-eighth episode far, far behind them. "That was a pretty bad episode," acknowledges Tony Paris. "But even if Kennedy hadn't been killed," he adds, "it probably still would have been a pretty bad show."

After the logistical trials of the Christmas episode and the tumultuous complications that attended the filming of the birthday party show a few weeks later, the company was greatly relieved to discover that their very next episode would be a mercifully straightforward comedy of domestic manners titled "The Lady and the Tiger and the Lawyer." The episode's brisk storyline pits Rob against Laura in an ill-fated competition to find a suitable mate for the seemingly perfect bachelor who's just moved in down the street, with Laura siding with her maiden cousin, Donna, while Rob submits Sally Rogers as the natural matrimonial choice. A somewhat awkward romantic triangle results when the bachelor appears to be equally taken with both of them—an intriguing dilemma that is resolved rather abruptly when the bachelor confesses that he won't be calling either woman again, on doctor's orders. "I have this bad, bad temper," he confesses. "I'm prone to hit people that I love." And until he gets his problem under control, he explains, his therapist has suggested he never date any woman more than once.

The episode's somewhat offbeat ending aside, what makes "The Lady and the Tiger and the Lawyer" a particularly noteworthy entry in the annals of *The Dick Van Dyke Show* is that it was the inaugural script from Garry Marshall and Jerry Belson, two writers who would eventually have a substantial impact on the series. Like many of the other outstanding comedy writing talents of their era, Belson and Marshall had earned their stripes in the situation comedy field at the thriving comedy factory that Sheldon Leonard ran on the Desilu Cahuenga lot throughout the early 1960s. Garry Marshall hailed from New York, where he'd earned a respectable living as a joke writer for Jack Paar and some of the era's more popular nightclub comics, including Joey Bishop. In 1962, Bishop lured Marshall to the West Coast with a job offer to write for *The Joey Bishop Show*, which just happened to be filmed on the Desilu Cahuenga lot. It was there that Marshall was first teamed with Jerry Belson, a would-be comedy writer in his early twenties who'd earned his entrée onto the lot on the strength of a sample script he'd pitched over Sheldon Leonard's transom in the early months of 1962. According to legend, it was Sheldon Leonard's inspiration to pair Belson and Marshall as a team. But, says Jerry Belson, after all these years, he's forced to admit that that's not exactly true.

"Garry and I already knew each other," Belson confirms. In fact, says the writer, he and Marshall had already decided to form a writing partnership when the producers of *The Dick Van Dyke Show* brought them together for what they assumed would be the future team's first meeting—an illusion that the writers did little to dispel. "Sheldon and Carl wanted it to seem like they put us together," explains Belson, "so we pretended like we'd never met.

But whatever the circumstances of that initial meeting, the teaming of Belson and Marshall would prove to be a most fortuitous pairing. Over the course of the Van Dyke show's final three seasons, Garry Marshall and Jerry Belson would contribute no fewer than eighteen scripts to the show, including the texts for such classic episodes as "Talk to the Snail," "Odd But True," "No Rice at My Wedding," "Baby Fat," and at least a half dozen other shows that would rank high among the series' all-time brightest half hours. "They were really funny, brilliant guys," observes

Rob Petrie comes slightly unhinged in Red Hook, New Jersey, in Carl Reiner's script for the third-season classic, "Who and Where Was Antonio Stradivarius?"; pictured with Van Dyke is costar Sallie Janes.

Carl Reiner, who admits that Belson and Marshall's only real shortcoming as writers was that they shared a common weakness for good old-fashioned one-liners.

"They loved jokes," remarks Reiner, who was never quite sure if the team's dazzling facility for the one-two comic punch was an asset or a liability on his character-driven series. "You had to watch them," says Reiner, "because they could slip in a joke that would destroy your character in a minute. And we had to be very careful of that." When Reiner did run across something that he deemed inappropriate in one of their scripts, notes Belson, the producer could be almost ruthlessly direct in communicating his displeasure. "When Carl didn't like something in your script," says Belson, "he'd write 'RR' next to the joke." And as Belson discovered shortly after he got one of his own early scripts back from the producer and noticed the curious annotation scrawled liberally throughout the margins, the dreaded initials turned out to be Carl Reiner's shorthand for "*rotten 'riting.*" "It meant you'd written a bad joke," says Belson, who admits that he would cringe whenever the mark appeared on one of his and Marshall's submissions. "Carl was such a nice guy, he'd never tell you that you stunk. That's why we always hated to see that little 'RR' in the margin when we got our scripts back from Carl."

Belson recalls that another one of the producer's favorite self-coined literary appellations was "the realie," a term that, as defined by Carl Reiner, basically referred to any one of the countless moments of carefully observed reality that the producer insisted his writers include as often as possible in their scripts. "He was always saying, 'We need more realies! Give me more realies!'" says Belson. "Carl would ask us, 'How do you use that rubber thing on the end of a toothbrush? Well, put that in the show!'" And, as Belson soon discovered, his producer's thirst for such privileged moments of reality was all but unquenchable. "Carl didn't care about funny," insists Belson, "he wanted realies. If you sat down with Carl, instead of saying, 'What's funny?' he would sit you down and say, 'Okay, what happened to you this week? What'd you fight with your wife about?' And those things that happened to you were the realies that Carl wanted. And so we were always searching for more realies."

Despite the addition of Garry Marshall and Jerry Belson to Carl Reiner's short list of favored Van Dyke show freelancers, the producer's own script contributions decreased only slightly in the show's third year, when his byline would still appear on close to a quarter of the season's total production output. Even so, the producer viewed having to script only a fourth of the year's Van Dyke shows as a picnic compared to the Herculean schedule he'd been forced to maintain during the show's first two seasons.

By the middle of the show's third year—as Persky and Denoff began to relieve Carl Reiner of at least part of the burden of the show's all-consuming scripting and story editing chores—the producer suddenly found himself with a virtual surfeit of time to devote to his own contributions to the series. And it's obvious that Reiner put this extra time to good use, as his later Van Dyke show scripts reflect a richness of style, content, and subtext that simply was not apparent in the writer's earliest scripts for the series.

One particularly noteworthy example of Reiner's evolving maturity is a third-season episode that bore the ungainly title "Who and Where Was

Antonio Stradivarius?" In Reiner's script for this classic episode, he employs a hokey—if eminently satisfying—amnesia plotline in which we are given to imagine what might happen to a staid suburban husband were his moral bearings suddenly to become unhinged by an unexpected thump on the head. For Rob Petrie, anyway, what results is a hilarious "lost weekend" in which his deepest subconscious impulses are played out with a dolefully trusting blonde named Graciella in the unlikely environs of Red Hook, New Jersey.

A few episodes later, Reiner provided equal time for Mrs. Petrie in his script for the show's eightieth episode, "The Life and Love of Joe Coogan," in which Laura ponders a few of her own roads not taken after Rob runs into a handsome stranger from her past. In the episode's touching climax, Laura discovers that her onetime suitor has come to rededicate his life to the priesthood. And in a poignant twist, she and Rob are soon moved ro reexamine one of the cleric's old love poems in spiritual terms. Rob's oddly tender reading of the sonnet sets the stage for the episode's effective—and affecting—closing moment, which offers a sweet meditation on the fleeting quality of youthful desires and the basic unpredictability of all human yearning.

It is perhaps not surprising that in later years Carl Reiner would cite his script for "The Life and Love of Joe Coogan" as among his all-time favorites, in large measure because of the poem that he composed to anchor the episode's deeply felt ending scene. "I don't write poetry," he explains. "But I wrote that poem. And I had to write it so it had a double meaning, since the priest was talking about God, but Laura thought he was talking about love between a man and a woman. Took a long time. I fussed with that an hour or so. And then I got it right."

Carl Reiner's outstanding roster of bylined third-year scripts also included another installment in the writer's ongoing saga of the military courtship and early married life of Army Staff Sergeant Rob Petrie and the former Laura Meehan, who finally consummate their nuptial vows—or attempt to, anyway—in the show's eighty-fifth episode, "Honeymoons Are for the Lucky." Like the previous chapters in Reiner's continuing show-within-a-show saga, this flashback is set against the backdrop of Camp Crowder, Missouri, where Rob and Laura's honeymoon plans are severely cramped after Sergeant Petrie's wedding furlough is canceled unexpectedly. Finally, undaunted by official orders, Rob concocts a foolproof—if foolhardy—scheme to get off the base. And so, under cover of darkness late that night, Rob sets off across the drill field in a disguise that includes Laura's black chiffon dress, a pair of white sneakers, and a set of false eyelashes that the hapless soldier has unwittingly affixed wifh a permanent adhesive.

Like the earlier flashbacks that made up Carl Reiner's long-running saga of Rob and Laura's romantic history, the plotline of "Honeymoons Are for the Lucky" was borrowed from the annals of the writer's own early days of marriage to the former Estelle Lebost—right down to the absurd details of Rob's AWOL scheme. "That stuff where he wears eyelashes—I didn't do that," assures Reiner, "but I did sneak out over a fence. And a guy caught me." And, once caught, Reiner tried his best to talk his way out of the fix, much as his fictional alter ego would do in Reiner's retelling of the incident two decades later. "The guy didn't believe me," insists Reiner. "So I went around the drill field."

In Carl Reiner's fictional treatment, the honeymoon couple finally ends up in a ramshackle boardinghouse where, as the landlady explains, the wedding suite is so-named because "it's the only room that people don't have to go through to get to their own rooms." And, incredible as it seems, Reiner insists that the spartan accommodations that he depicts in his script describes almost exactly the cramped quarters where he and his wife spent their own honeymoon, including the sign that prohibited the couple from using a rocking chair after 8:00 P.M. ! "We got a room in an apartment that had three rooms in a row," explains Reiner, recalling his own early days of marriage during a military housing crunch. "The toilet was out in the hall, so people were coming through our room all night. Actually, they were very nice. They made sure they only came through once the whole night. But we kept a screen around our bed anyway."

Of course, by the end of Reiner's script, the landlady has had a change of heart, and everything finally works out for nexvlyweds Rob and Laura, who enjoy their first night of wedded bliss in the relative seclusion of the apartment manager's private room. And as for the real-life couple? Carl and Estelle Reiner celebrated their fiftieth wedding anniversary in 1993, which means that they've already outlasted the five-year run of their fictional counterparts by some five decades. And counting...

CHAPTER 25
Picturing Mary Naked

BY THE END OF THEIR FIRST SEASON AS *THE DICK VAN DYKE Show*'s de facto writing staff, newcomers Bill Persky and Sam Denoff had already more than fulfilled Carl Reiner's early confidence in their promise. In the show's third year alone, the prolific team's byline would appear on no fewer than a dozen scripts, including such hardy Van Dyke show perennials as "Big Max Calvada," which featured Sheldon Leonard's only on-screen appearance on the show, playing—no surprise here—a gangster; "The Pen Is Mightier than

Carl Reiner, playing artist Serge Carpetna, reveals his scandalous portrait of Laura Petrie in "October Eve." "I figured that everybody wanted to see Mary naked," explains the episode's co-writer, Sam Denoff, "because I certainly did."

the Mouth," in which Sally departs *The Alan Brady Show*'s staff for a brief stint as second banana on Stevie Parsons's late-night talk show; and "October Eve," an episode that Persky and Denoff rank high on their own list of personal favorites. Persky and Denoff's pride in "October Eve" is understandable—if the writers had done nothing else to merit their mentor's faith during their first season on the show, their script for "October Eve" alone would probably have been enough to justify their fees for the entire year.

In the episode, Laura is forced to confront a long-forgotten skeleton in her closet when a nude oil portrait that she apparently posed for in the early days of her marriage suddenly surfaces in a prominent midtown gallery. The awkward circumstances surrounding the creation of the incriminating portrait are revealed by Laura in a flashback that takes place eight years earlier. The scene shifts to the studio of a petulant painter named Serge Carpetna—who is played, with appropriately hammy gusto, by Carl Reiner*—where Laura has come to have her portrait painted as a keepsake for Rob. But, while Laura has a nice, representational portrait in mind, the artist clearly has other ideas—as she discovers when she finally gets her first glimpse at the artist's canvas. Only then does she see, to her horror, that the painter has taken it upon himself to render her stark naked. "How dare you!" Laura gasps. "That's not me! That's not the way I was standing there!"

"I painted you as a goddess," Carpetna counters, "and you're acting like a peasant!" When Laura protests that she would've been perfectly happy with a more conventional portrait, the artist grows incensed. "For *that* kind of a picture," he shouts, "you take a camera, you go to Central Park, you get on a pony, and snap your brains out!" Finally, in a pique, Carpetna sends the ungrateful philistine back to New Rochelle—without the painting.

Which brings us back to the present, where Carpetna, now a darling of the art world, has renamed Laura's fifty-dollar commissioned portrait

---

*"I loved that part," confesses the producer, who recalls that writers Persky and Denoff conceived the role with him in mind. "They said, 'You gotta play this guy!'" he remembers. "I guess they thought I was going to do it as well as anybody else." Reiner's own modest appraisal aside, the show's associate producer, Ron Jacobs, insists that the producer's choice to cast himself in the part represented nothing less than impeccable judgment. "Carl's such a good comic actor, how could you not use him? He would have to be a bad producer not to hire Carl Reiner the comic actor."

"October Eve," and upped its price to $5,000 in the bargain. Of course, once Laura finally confesses all to Rob, he's able to straighten everything out with a quick visit to Carpetna's Greenwich Village studio. There, after a brief round of negotiations, Rob convinces the artist to sell the painting to a reclusive South American millionaire, who will presumably display the work in a less visible venue than the main room of a Madison Avenue Gallery.

When Persky and Denoff dreamt up "October Eve," they were no doubt aware that prevailing standards of taste would never allow them to show Laura's revealing portrait on the air. In fact, according to Dick Van Dyke, the painting never actually existed at all. "That's right," admits the star, "there was nothing there." On the night the show was filmed, says Van Dyke, the actors played their scenes to a prop painting that was, in reality, a completely blank canvas. And yet, it's a testament to the show's artful direction—and equally artful misdirection—that viewers would end up conjuring up a far more vivid picture of the painting in their imaginations than anything the show's producers could have depicted in the first place. As Dick Van Dyke tells it, the sleight of hand employed in the episode may actually have been more convincing than anyone dreamed. "People *swear* they saw that painting," the star observes. "There were a number of shows we did where the audience would insist they'd seen something they hadn't, and that was one of them. People think they saw the painting, but nobody ever saw it—that was just artful writing."

For their part, Persky and Denoff confess that the challenge of persuading the show's vast viewing audience to picture Mary Tyler Moore posed in the altogether never struck them as a particularly daunting task. "I figured that everybody wanted to see Mary naked," admits Sam Denoff, "because I certainly did."

The Dick Van Dyke Show wrapped its third production season with the filming of the show's ninety-fifth episode, "My Two Show-Offs and Me," on April 3, 1964. A few days later, Dick Van Dyke boarded a plane for London, where he and his wife Marjorie hoped to squeeze in a three-week vacation—their first in four years—before the actor was due to report to Paris for location shooting on *The Art of Love*, a Universal Pictures comedy written by Carl Reiner, who would also log a cameo role in the film himself.

Van Dyke's already flourishing big-screen career would get another boost later that summer, when *Mary Poppins* finally opened to widespread acclaim—and highly favorable box office—after a star-studded world premiere at Grauman's Chinese Theatre on August 27, 1964. The runaway success of the Disney film cemented Van Dyke's reputation as a bona fide movie star, and also sent his fee—which was reportedly $100,000 for the Disney film—soaring to a then staggering $250,000 per picture. By comparison, the actor's Van Dyke show salary at the start of the show's fourth season was a relatively paltry $5,000 a week.

Carl Reiner also stayed busy during the four-month hiatus that fell between the show's third and fourth seasons. After completing work on his script for *The Art of Love*, the hyperactive writer immediately signed a contract to write three more comedies for Universal Pictures over a four-year period. In April, Reiner also began hosting *The Celebrity Game*, a weekly panel show that ran on the CBS network's prime-time schedule throughout the summers of 1964 and 1965. When the *Hollywood Reporter's* Hank Grant wondered if the producer might not be spreading himself a bit thin by adding an emcee assignment to his already teeming workload, the writer-producer-actor–game-show host dismissed the

columnist's concerns out of hand. "Every other Friday night I tape two shows within three hours at CBS," Reiner quipped. "This is work?"[60] And, as if he weren't already busy enough that summer, Reiner also found time to produce a comedy album called *The First Nine Months*, which was written by Bill Persky and Sam Denoff. The record offered a

"He would have to be a bad producer not to hire Carl Reiner the comic actor," says Ron Jacobs, recalling producer Carl Reiner's decision to cast himself as "October Eve's" bohemian artist, Serge Carpetna.

Laura appears unmoved by her husband's excuses in this publicity still from "Dear Mrs. Petrie, Your Husband Is in Jail," the second script from soon-to-be Van Dyke show stalwarts Garry Marshall and Jerry Belson.

comedic look at the trials of pregnancy and parenthood, an arena that had, of course, proved quite fertile for the writers when they penned "That's My Boy???" a year or so earlier.

As in previous years, the cast and creative staff of *The Dick Van Dyke Show* once again assumed a high profile at the Emmy awards ceremonies for the 1963–1964 season, which were held on May 25, 1964. For the second year in a row, the series dominated the Television Academy's comedy awards categories, with a total of six nominations. By evening's end, Van Dyke personnel would walk away with no fewer than five of the coveted statuettes, including the series' second consecutive Emmy for Outstanding Program Achievement in the Field of Comedy. In his second consecutive nomination in the top actor's category, Dick Van Dyke picked up his first Emmy for Outstanding Continued Performance by an Actor in a Series, an honor that was echoed by Mary Tyler Moore, who picked up her own Emmy for Outstanding Continued Performance by an Actress in a Series in her second nomination in the category. Also honored that night were Jerry Paris, for Outstanding Directorial Achievement in Comedy, and Bill Persky and Sam Denoff, who shared an Emmy with Carl Reiner for Outstanding Writing Achievement in Comedy or Variety.

The evening's only disappointment came when Rose Marie, nominated for the second year in a row, was once again shut out in the fiercely competitive supporting actress category. In a field once again dominated by actresses nominated for showy dramatic performances, the award for Outstanding Performance in a Supporting Role by an Actress was given to Ruth White, for her dramatic supporting role in a Hallmark Hall of Fame special.

The loss of an Emmy Award that year seemed a matter of very small consequence to Rose Marie, who was at that moment still recovering from the devastating loss of her husband, trumpeter Bobby Guy, who had died of natural causes earlier that month. The news of Guy's death came as a particular blow to members of the Van Dyke show cast, who had come to know the musician through his frequent stints as a player in the show's onstage combo. Rose Marie was so torn by grief that she actually considered retiring from the entertainment field altogether. "I was devastated when he passed away," explains the actress, who had taken stock of her life in the wake of her tragedy and arrived at the sobering conclusion that show business suddenly seemed very unimportant to her. "I can't sing anymore," she remembers telling friends at the time, "and I can't go back to work." Finally, after some very painful soul-searching, she called her friend John Rich to break the news that she was considering leaving *The Dick Van Dyke Show* before the show's fourth season of production got underway in late July.

John Rich was understandably taken aback by the news. As the Van Dyke show's founding director, he understood as well as anyone how vital Rose Marie's contribution was to the show's delicate chemistry, and he was also well aware of how potentially devastating her departure would be for the series. And, of course, the director also recognized what a vital role *The Dick Van Dyke Show* played in Rose Marie's life—even if the actress had temporarily lost sight of that fact herself. "Rosie," the director beseeched her. "Please don't make any final decisions until I have a chance to talk to you."

As Rose Marie tells it, the director arrived at

Though Rose Marie and Morey Amsterdam were each nominated for Emmy's for their work on the series, neither of them ever won the award, owing largely to complicated Emmy nomination procedures of the era that tended to favor dramatic actors in the supporting actor categories.

her house that very evening, determined to persuade her to rethink her position on the enormous decision she was about to make. The marathon conversation that followed lasted far into the night, until Rose Marie's mother finally tiptoed in at two the next morning to bring the talk to a close. "My mother came into the living room," recalls Rose Marie, "and she said to John, 'You oughta go home now.'" At which point, says the actress, the director dutifully rose from his chair to leave. But before he got to the door, John Rich turned to ask his old friend one final question. "He said, 'Rosie, have I convinced you to stay with the show?'" she recalls. "And I said, 'Yes.' And then John said, 'Then I've done my job.' And he left."

Rose Marie finally returned to the Van Dyke set in the last week of July 1964, as the cast gathered to start rehearsals for the show's fourth season.

The Van Dyke family as they appeared in a photo taken during rehearsals for episode 110, "Brother Can You Spare $2500?"; pictured, clockwise from left, are guest stars Tiny Brauer and Jimmy Cross, director Jerry Paris, Rose Marie, Mary Tyler Moore, Dick Van Dyke, guest star Gene Baylos, story editor Sam Denoff, Carl Reiner, story editor Bill Persky, script supervisor Marge Mullen, guest star Sheila Rogers, Morey Amsterdam, second assistant director Bud Messinger, and guest star Herbie Faye.

According to the actress, Richard Deacon was so concerned that she be spared any emotional awkwardness on her return that he took it upon himself to deliver a short pep talk to the rest of the cast a few moments before she arrived. "Whatever you do," Deacon cautioned, "don't make a big fuss when Rosie walks in. What she really wants is for everyone to treat her the same as always." Most important of all, the actor added, the cast was to avoid indulging in any overt displays of sentimental affection. "If everyone puts their arm around her," the actor warned, "she'll only start crying."

The cast listened politely to their colleague's well-intentioned instructions, and then proceeded to disregard every single one of them the minute Rose Marie walked onto the set. When the actress suddenly found herself surrounded once more by the gentle laughter and warmth of her beloved company, she made little attempt to stem the flow of tears. Nor did anyone else, for that matter—least of all Richard Deacon himself. "When I got back they were so wonderful," says Rose Marie. "They were truly, truly a family that really cared. Every one of them."

In the months to come, the actress would be no less touched by her company's ongoing regard for her still-tender emotions. "They used to take things out of the scripts that they thought might upset me," she recalls. Nor did that concern end at the studio gates. As the actress would later recall, Dick Van Dyke frequently took it upon himself to check in with her once she got home in the evening. "Sometimes when I'm home at night," as the actress told a reporter in early 1965, "he'll call and say, 'What are you doing?' And I'll say, 'The dishes.' And he'll say, 'Why don't you come over and have a drink? We're just sitting around.' If you can say you love somebody without being mushy, I say we all love that man."61

"We shut up a lot in the beginning and just watched," says Bill Persky, recalling his early days of apprenticeship with Sam Denoff on the staff of *The Dick Van Dyke Show*. "But," he adds, "by the end of our first season, we pretty well knew what we were doing." It was an opinion shared by Carl Reiner, who rewarded the team's diligence with a promotion at the start of the show's fourth season, when Persky and Denoff were appointed *The Dick Van Dyke Show*'s official story consultants, a post they would hold throughout the show's fourth and fifth seasons.

It would be a busy two years. As the show's officially designated story editors, it would be Persky and Denoff's job to generate a brand-new script every week, either by writing it themselves or by assigning a story idea to one of the show's ever-increasing stable of freelance contributors. Once a script's first draft was complete, it would then be up to the story editors to hone and polish it, or, in some cases, totally rewrite it—until that early draft was as close to perfect as humanly possible—before they delivered it up for the company's scrutiny at the show's Wednesday morning table reading. And, of course, it was at that initial reading that the story editors' real work began.

"We'd go through the whole script very slowly," explains Rose Marie, describing the reading that would take up the better part of the show's first rehearsal session each Wednesday morning. "Word for word. And we'd make all the little changes. Morey would say, 'I can get a better joke in here, let me try something!' And we'd all have something to say."

"We'd spend the whole afternoon rewriting, really," adds Dick Van Dyke. "Everybody got the chance to throw their two bits' worth in." And, of course, at this stage of the weeklong rehearsal process, it was understood that nothing in the script was carved in stone—a factor that many cast members found quite liberating. "The loosest part of the rehearsal was probably that first reading," notes writer and sometime Van Dyke show performer Bill Idelson, "because nothing was at stake. You knew damn well none of the lines were gonna be there when you performed the show, so you'd kid around and have coffee and donuts."

While Bill Persky allows that the peculiar form of creative democracy practiced at the Van Dyke show's weekly table reading could indeed be beneficial to a script—"The show often got better," he says, "because everybody was pretty intelligent"—the story editor maintains that all that cross-table kibbitzing had a downside as well. "There was always a tendency to fix and potchkeh around," he says. "It was like a disease. I used to call it rewrite-itis." And it was a malady that the writer found particularly vexing, especially since it frequently resulted in more work for him and fellow story editor Sam Denoff. "The flexibility to change anything was so ingrained in us," observes Persky, "that sometimes no one bothered to look at what was really there before they started looking to improve it."

By way of example, Persky describes one particularly maddening script session where the enthusiastic company spent the better part of an entire rehearsal struggling to improve a single joke line—only to discover that the setup already had a perfectly good rejoinder lurking on the following page. "Somebody read a line that happened to fall at the bottom of a page and said, 'Ooh, I'll bet we can find something funny to put here!'" And in their enthusiasm to come up with a new punchline, says Persky, the company spent what seemed like forty-five minutes pitching brand-new jokes before somebody finally flipped the page and found the already-scripted comeback waiting for them at the top of the next page! "No one had even bothered to see that the end of the joke had already been written!"

The second episode filmed in the show's fourth production season saw the cast returning to *Twilight Zone* territory for the haunted house parody, "The Ghost of A. Chantz."

Of course, the story editor's ultimate nightmare is the chilling prospect of hosting a table reading so disastrous that an entire script has to be scrapped. But, according to Dick Van Dyke, that dreadful calamity only occurred once on *The Dick Van Dyke Show*. "The script was called 'Art vs. Baloney,'" says Van Dyke, "and I cannot remember anything about it, except that it was unsalvageable. Ungodly! Just awful. We finished it in dead silence." As Van Dyke recalls, the script—which had been written by a freelancer whose name has long since faded from memory—was deemed so odious that the company felt they had little choice but to pitch all surviving copies into the nearest wastebasket at the conclusion of a single reading. "I just took my script and threw it," says Van Dyke. "And everybody said, 'Yep, that's it. Out it goes.' That was the only time in five years that I ever threw a script."

The Van Dyke company's decidedly fluid approach to the written word was by no means limited to the show's early script conferences. "Our show was just one big rewrite," notes Dick Van Dyke, who recalls that Carl Reiner and his story editors thought nothing of fine-tuning a script right up to showtime. "We'd never stop," says Van Dyke. "We'd have a dress rehearsal, and then we'd go and have dinner while the audience came in. But, if Carl or someone had a brainstorm at the dress rehearsal, we'd spend that dinner hour rewriting while we were eating."

It was during these eleventh-hour rewrite sessions that the show's cast and crew came to truly appreciate the wizardry of their script supervisor, Marge Mullen, whose job it was to keep track of every single revision, addition, or deletion that the show's script would undergo over the course

"When you see the guy with the nice hair and the suit become a total schmuck," says Sam Denoff, "that's funny." Pictured, Van Dyke and a pair of unidentified extras in a still from the show's 100th episode, "The Man From Emperor."

of the average rehearsal week. And, according to no less an authority than Carl Reiner, Marge Mullen was very, very good at her job. "You'd tell her, 'Change this, we'll do this. And, oh, yeah, let's change this line to this,'" recalls Reiner, "and she'd be writing." Then, while the company paused to take a break or have dinner, Mullen would take the latest changes and have them typed, mimeographed, collated, and back on the stage before rehearsal resumed. "And," adds Reiner, "the script would always come back exactly right."

One of Mullen's more formidable duties was to keep track of the show's rejects—all those stray jokes, unused sight gags, and rejected one-liners that, for one reason or another, failed to make it into the show's final shooting script. "Whenever we had to take out a joke," explains Sam Denoff, "or a scene that was really terrific but didn't fit—for length or whatever—we would put it in a book so it could be used at a later time." Before long, all of these unused jokes and ill-fitting scenes would find their way into a looseleaf folder that Mullen kept near the set, a compendium of rejected material that came to be known as Marge's S.O.S. file—S.O.S. being the writers' acronym for "some other show." "If we ever needed a joke someday," explains Carl Reiner, "then Marge would be able to pull one from the back of her S.O.S. book."

At least that was the idea. But, according to Sam Denoff, in five years of production there was not one occasion where he or any of his colleagues ever drew even a single line of dialogue from their script supervisor's emergency inventory. "We never, ever used any of them!" the writer exclaims. The end result of Mullen's efforts, recalls Bill Persky, was a notebook of unused Van Dyke show material that was a full six inches thick by the time the show went out of production in 1966. "We always meant to use them," says Persky, who half-jokingly suggests one possible use for the Van Dyke show's cast-offs. "That file was so thick, you probably could have done another entire series using just the stuff in that book."

In addition to performing her duties as script supervisor, Marge Mullen also served—in a strictly uncredited capacity—as the show's final arbiter of what was, and was not, funny. "Marge would watch the run-through," says Reiner, "and if she didn't react, we'd say, 'Oh, oh! Marge doesn't like it.' And we knew we were in trouble. She wasn't always right, but she was a very, very solid indicator."

On the evening of August 4, 1964, the company kicked off the start of their fourth production year with the filming of the show's ninety-sixth episode, "My Mother Can Beat Up My Father," a nearly flawless slapstick exercise in which Laura reveals a heretofore unknown talent for judo after she's called upon to defend her husband against the threats of an abusive drunk in a Manhattan bar. But even though Laura finally succeeds in saving her husband's hide, her spontaneous act of gallantry eventually causes no small amount of damage to her husband's fragile male pride. As a result, Rob is reduced to spending the rest of the classic episode engaged in a series of fruitless attempts to reestablish his manly preeminence over his surprisingly capable wife.

While Persky and Denoff's buoyant script provides another ideal showcase for Dick Van Dyke's virtuoso physical prowess, writer Denoff insists that the real fun of this episode comes in watching the show's leading man fall apart, piece by piece, over the course of the show's half-hour running time, until, by the end of the episode, he's completely undone by his own stubborn pride. The theme of pride coming before a fall—illustrated quite literally in "My Mother Can Beat Up My Father"—was a favorite of writers Persky and Denoff. "Rob was always funniest when he was being a schmuck," says Denoff. "His humor came from a real man who at times is a very loving husband and father but can also be a schmuck, because he can't handle jealousy or whatever." And, adds Denoff, with his good looks and upstanding demeanor, Dick Van Dyke made the perfect fall guy. "When you see the guy with the nice hair and the suit become a total schmuck, that's funny."

CHAPTER 26

Tempest in a Bathtub

ONE OF THE UNFORESEEN ADVANTAGES OF CARL REINER'S decision to shift much of his weekly workload onto the capable shoulders of Persky and Denoff in the show's fourth year was that it allowed the producer to spend more time in front of the cameras during the show's final two seasons. It was a benefit that began to yield dividends with the show's 104th episode, "Three Letters From One Wife," which featured Carl Reiner's first full-frontal assault in the role of Alan Brady.

Of course, Carl Reiner had actually logged a handful of appearances as Rob Petrie's blustery employer before he strode on camera in "Three Letters From One Wife." But most of those performances qualified as little more than cameos, since the actor's face was invariably blocked by a conveniently placed high-backed chair, or hidden from view behind a Santa Claus beard, or beneath a barber's steam towel—intentional visual dodges that were part of a carefully orchestrated, if rarely successful, campaign to keep the identity of the actor playing Alan Brady a secret from the audience. It was a conceit that Reiner insists was born out of his early insecurity that viewers would simply refuse to accept a lowly character actor like him playing a star of Alan Brady's magnitude. "I said, 'They know who I am,'" recalls Reiner. "'I'm the second banana from *Your Show of Shows*. Nobody's gonna think I'm a big star.' So I used to turn myself around and hide."

Reiner claims that he briefly considered bringing in some other actor to play the character, but finally decided against that once it dawned on him that he wasn't likely to find the kind of actor he was seeking in the listings of Central Casting. "I wanted the audience to think of Milton Berle or Danny Thomas," he would later recall, "not some guy I hired for six hundred dollars."[62]

The producer's modest assessment of his own abilities aside, a more plausible explanation for Alan Brady's shadowy presence in the show's first two or three years was that Carl Reiner simply couldn't spare the time required to rehearse anything more complicated than a cameo appearance in the role—at least not as long as he was also responsible for writing, producing, and story editing each episode of the show as well. But, with story editors Persky and Denoff available to man the rudder in season four, Alan Brady was finally allowed to step into the foreground and assume his rightful place among the show's enduring cast of characters.

Carl Reiner confirms that the blossoming of Alan Brady in the show's last two years was not part of any grand design, but a classic case of the tail wagging the dog. "We wrote a couple of shows where the character had to do more complicated things," he explains. "And I said, 'We're not being fair to the writer, because there's so much more you can do if you can see the character's face.' So we turned him around." And, as Sam Denoff observes, it was a long overdue adjustment. "You couldn't make the conceit of never seeing Alan Brady last too long," notes the writer. "So we just said, 'Let's see Alan Brady—and let's make him a funny guy.'"

It's generally assumed that Carl Reiner based his characterization of

Mary Tyler Moore's Laura awaits rescue from a most embarrassing predicament in "Never Bathe on Saturday," the Van Dyke show classic that provided the backdrop for one of the show's most notorious backstage skirmishes.

The Alan Brady Show's vain and hot-tempered headliner on Sid Caesar, the notoriously volatile star of *Your Show of Shows*. But, according to Denoff, there were any number of equally tempestuous role models from television's Golden Age who fit the Alan Brady mold just as well—if not better—than Reiner's former employer. "Carl wasn't doing Sid, really," insists the writer. "The stars of *all* those early variety shows were crazy. And for legitimate reasons. They were on live every week. And it was terrifying. The stress made them crazy."

According to many firsthand observers, the most amazing aspect of Carl Reiner's portrayal of the egomaniacal Alan Brady may have been how little the character actually had in common with the actor who played him. But despite the obvious delight that Carl Reiner took in bringing Rob Petrie's vain, abusive, and short-tempered employer to life, it's generally conceded that it would have been difficult to find a star in Hollywood who less resembled the show's hot-headed tyrant than Carl Reiner himself. In fact, according to those who worked most closely with Reiner on the Van Dyke set, the producer never so much as lost his temper in five years of production.

Except once.

The only recorded instance of Carl Reiner blowing his stack on the set of the Van Dyke show occurred on February 12, 1965, midway through rehearsals for the series' 121st episode, "Never Bathe on Saturday." And no one who was present is likely to forget that day, if only because it also marked the first—and only—time that one of the show's actors actually stormed off the stage and out the studio gates in a huff.

Ironically, the episode that provided the backdrop for the show's most notorious skirmish is regarded today as one the series' most celebrated entries, if for no other reason than Carl Reiner's provocative premise, in which Laura finds herself trapped in a bathroom after she somehow manages to get her toe stuck in the bathtub waterspout. In Reiner's nearly faultless script, the hapless housewife announces her unlikely predicament from behind the locked bathroom door of a luxury hotel suite, where—until that moment—she and Rob had hoped to spend a romantic weekend. In fact, Rob has just donned his most debonair smoking jacket when his wife summons him to the bathroom door to explain that her toe has become stuck in what she erroneously describes as the bathtub faucet, "the little pipe that the water comes out of."

"That's not the faucet, honey," Rob corrects. To which Laura replies, "I don't care what you call it, my big toe is stuck in it." When Rob asks how she managed such a feat, Laura spells it out for him with mounting exasperation. "I was playing with a drip!"

Despite her husband's best intentions—he tries everything he can think of to break her out, including a valiant, if foolhardy, attempt to crash in the door with his shoulder—there Laura stays, locked behind a thick wooden door for the better part of this very funny episode. When the hotel detective finally offers to shoot the lock off, Rob insists on performing that task personally, since, as he explains, "Only a husband can blow the lock off a bathroom with his wife in the bathtub with nothing on and her toe stuck in a pipe."

Like Persky and Denoff's treatment for the earlier "October Eve," Carl Reiner's script for "Never Bathe on Saturday" stands as another masterpiece of sitcom sleight of hand—given the show's playful premise, what we *don't* see is naturally far funnier than anything that the show's actors, producers, or set decorators could possibly have conjured up. Reiner understood this, of course, and he was justifiably proud to have created a situation so charged with comic potential that his leading lady would be able to command show-stopping laughs without having to set foot on stage for more than half of the episode's running time. Which might explain why the writer got so upset when, halfway through rehearsals for the episode, that same leading lady stormed off the set after declaring that she had no intention of playing the role as written.

"Mary walked out in the middle of a rehearsal," recalls Bill Idelson, who played the hotel bellboy in the episode. "She didn't want to do that show, because she said the camera was never on her."

But though Mary Tyler Moore might have been physically out of sight throughout much of the episode, Sam Denoff maintains that the actress was hardly ever out of mind—at least not so far as the show's many millions of male viewers were concerned. "Mary didn't get the idea," observes Denoff, "that during that whole episode, people in America were fantasizing seeing Laura Petrie naked in sudsy water in a bathtub! Whatta picture! But she didn't get that." Even so, it was an image whose potency was certainly not lost on Carl Reiner. "I remember in writing it," Reiner has observed, "I fantasized a woman naked."[63]

While Carl Reiner might have been content to let his audience conjure the visual portion of his leading lady's performance, the actress explains that she had good reason to approach that particular episode with vastly different expectations. And for that, the actress maintains, Carl Reiner would have only himself to blame. "He kept talking about this show that was coming up that featured me," says the actress, recalling the somewhat misleading buildup that her producer had unwittingly given her in the weeks before he finally brought in his script for "Never Bathe on Saturday." "He kept talking about how it was gonna be all about me! So I had this show built up in my mind, and I was just waiting for it so excitedly."

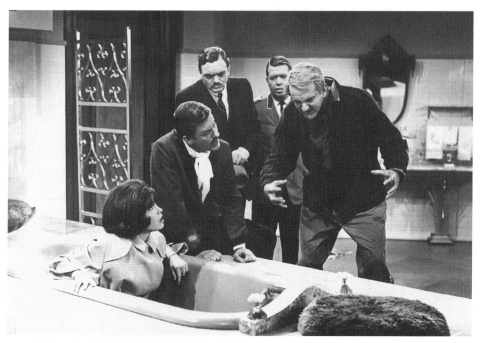

When she first read Carl Reiner's script for the episode, Mary Tyler Moore was convinced that "Never Bathe on Saturday" put her at a distinct disadvantage as an actress, despite Sam Denoff's assurance that all of America would spend most of the episode imagining her floating "naked in sudsy water."

Of course, the actress would have good reason to revise those expectations once she finally had an opportunity to read her producer's much-heralded script at the episode's first rehearsal. "When I read it," reports Mary Tyler Moore, "I saw that I was off-camera the whole time! Everybody was talking about me—but the actress didn't have a thing to play!" And yet, as distressed as Mary Tyler Moore might have been to discover that she would be playing her biggest scene of the entire season from five feet offstage, the actress insists that not even that dismaying news would have been enough to send her over the brink had it been *any* other week.

As fate would have it, the week Carl Reiner finally brought in his script for "Never Bathe on Saturday" just happened to be the same week that Mary Tyler Moore had decided to quit smoking. And, as Dick Van Dyke suggests, the fallout from Mary Tyler Moore's decision to kick her cigarette habit cold turkey may have been far more contributory to her foul spirits that week than any reservations she may have had about the episode's shooting script. "I think it was more nicotine withdrawal than anything else," says Van Dyke, "because I never saw her complain before." And, as the actor recalls, the symptoms of his costar's withdrawal only seemed to grow worse over the course of the rehearsal week. "I watched her get a little paler each day," he observes, "and the circles under her eyes get a little deeper. The poor girl was beside herself."

By the end of the week, it had become clear to Dick Van Dyke that Mary Tyler Moore was nearing her breaking point. "She was a nervous wreck," he recalls. "Everything upset her."

"I was snapping and snarling at everyone all week," the actress concurs. "All because I was trying to quit smoking."

As Bill Persky recalls it, the actress first voiced her mounting apprehensions at one of the episode's earliest rehearsals. "She couldn't understand how she could be funny in this part. And Carl said, 'Are you kidding? Everybody in the world wants to see you naked. And here's their chance.'"

But if, as Persky implies, it had been Carl Reiner's intention to disarm his leading lady's anxiety with that flip observation, the producer obviously hadn't judged the true depth of her feelings. "I was terribly upset," she recalls, "and I guess I must have said so to Carl." And, though no one seems to remember the exact words that Mary Tyler Moore chose to express her dissatisfaction during those early rehearsals, her comments were—by her own admission—incendiary enough to cause a sizable rift between her and the producer. "We ended up not speaking for a couple days," the actress admits, "which was rather impudent of a little twenty-something-year-old novice comedian."

"She was just being a brat," observes Sam Denoff, who confesses that he was also perplexed by the actress's untoward behavior at the time, since it was, as he recalls, "the first show of temperament we ever saw from Mary or any of them." Which goes a long way toward explaining why Carl Reiner maintained such a tolerant attitude to the actress's unusually temperamental display for as long as he did. But, finally, after he'd watched his leading lady sulk for the better part of the rehearsal week, the normally mild-mannered producer had all but exhausted his reserves of patience.

"The blowup finally came on Friday night," remembers Bill Persky. And, as Sam Denoff makes clear, the producer's abrupt outburst did not exactly go unnoticed on the set. "Carl let her have it," adds Denoff. "I don't remember many other times that he lost it. But Carl yelled at her that day."

"That was the only time I've ever seen Carl mad on stage," concurs the show's film editor, Bud Molin, who—almost three decades later—can still recall the exact wording of the lecture that Reiner delivered to his recalcitrant leading lady that night. "Carl said, 'This show will work! I would never ask you to do a show that I didn't think would work! Do you think I'd send you out in a leaky crate? If I didn't think this show was good for you, I wouldn't do it!'" But despite the angry tone, Molin insists that Reiner fully expected that he might yet bring the actress around and be able to continue the evening's rehearsal. Unfortunately, by that point it was obvious to most observers that tempers had already flared far beyond the point of no return. "Mary walked out of the rehearsal," recalls Bill Persky. "The only time she ever did that. She walked out and went home."

Of course, the actress was barely out the studio gate before she began to regret her hasty actions. And by the time she arrived at the Studio City house she shared with her young son and then-husband Grant Tinker, the actress was practically overcome with remorse over what she had finally come to see as a terribly ill-considered temper tantrum. That night, the actress began the process of mending her fences with an apologetic phone call to Carl Reiner, who she reached at home a few hours later.

"What bothered Mary most," recalls Reiner, "was that I'd blown my stack in full view of the sponsors and all the network people. When she called me she said, 'How can I come back to work? The sponsors know you never explode, so now I must look really terrible!'" Caught up in the spirit of the moment, the producer ended up tendering an apology of his own. "I told Mary, 'I've never blown up in five years, give me this one time.' And then she apologized to me a few days later when it turned out to be such a good show."

And, sure enough, when "Never Bathe on Saturday" was finally committed to film the following Tuesday night, Mary Tyler Moore—in a far more compliant mood—turned in one of her most memorable performances, reading her lines, as written, from behind a bathroom door. "*And*," the actress adds sardonically, "I was back smoking again."

CHAPTER 27
Practice Makes Perfect

FOR A SERIES THAT HAD ALREADY LOGGED UPWARDS OF 125 mostly remarkable episodes, the Van Dyke show seemed exceptionally spry in the waning days of its fourth, and penultimate, year on the air—a remarkably fertile period that would see the creation of many of the show's most outstanding efforts. In addition to "Never Bathe on Saturday," other notable fourth-year entries in the Van Dyke show canon include episode 119, "Your Home Sweet Home Is My Home Sweet Home," which reveals the comic details surrounding Rob and Laura's purchase of their house, the only suburban split-level in New Rochelle to come equipped with its own geological rock formation in the cellar; and "100 Terrible Hours," the show's 122nd episode, in which Rob describes the comical complications that resulted when he arranged his first job interview with Alan Brady on the heels of an on-air radio promotion that had required him to broadcast live for four straight days without sleep. Equally memorable was the show's 123rd episode, "A Show of Hands," a comedy of errors in which Rob and Laura accidentally dye their hands black on the very night that Rob is scheduled to accept a racial tolerance award on behalf of *The Alan Brady Show*.

But of all the shows filmed during the closing weeks of the Van Dyke show's fourth year, the best of the lot may well have been episode 124, "Baby Fat," a searing parody of backstage life from writers Garry Marshall and Jerry Belson that chronicles Rob Petrie's brief and debilitating career as an uncredited script doctor for one of Alan Brady's ill-fated theatrical ventures. Packed with knowing theatrical in-jokes, clever literary illusions, and irresistible scenes of pure farce, "Baby Fat" easily ranks among the show's very best—if most frequently overlooked—efforts.

"I had no recollection of that one at all," admits Dick Van Dyke, who confesses that he had rediscovered "Baby Fat" only recently, when he happened to catch the episode in reruns as he was flipping through the channels at home one night. "And I was impressed by it," he says. "It was a bit of a farce, but it had a certain touch of sophistication that none of our other shows had." Oddly enough, in talking to Carl Reiner a few days later, the star discovered that his former producer had also stumbled across that same broadcast, and had been no less impressed by his own rediscovery of the nearly forgotten classic. "Neither of us had seen that one in at least twenty years," recalls Reiner, "and then we both just happened to see it that night. Dick told me he'd been laughing out loud, and I said, 'Me, too!'"

On Tuesday, March 30, 1965, the Van Dyke company filmed "There's No Sale Like Wholesale," which would be broadcast as the final episode of the show's fourth season. But, as in previous years, the company would cram one extra show into the season's production year—episode 127, "A

Farewell to Writing"—which would be held for broadcast the following September. Of course, with the entire cast and crew anxious to get started on their long-awaited summer hiatus, no one was eager to linger on the lot any longer than they had to. As a result, "A Farewell to Writing" was filmed on a special accelerated rehearsal schedule of only three days from start to finish.

In the episode's storyline, Rob makes the decision to sequester himself in the peaceful surroundings of a friend's remote cabin for a few days, hoping that the enforced solitude might inspire him to finally sit down and finish his long-planned memoirs. But the would-be author soon discovers that a lit-tle bit of peace and quiet goes a long way, and by the time he returns to civilization, Rob has logged more time playing with a pair of six-shooters and brushing up on his paddleball stroke than sitting behind the type-writer.

It's probably no coincidence that the spare production requirements of "A Farewell to Writing" made it an ideal episode to film on the show's temporarily abbreviated production schedule. If nothing else, the episode would require minimal rehearsal, since much of its running time was devoted to Dick Van Dyke's extended monologue in the cabin. In fact, according to Van Dyke, his solo turn in "A Farewell to Writing" was filmed with practically no formal rehearsal at all.

"They had three cameras, and the place was full of props," says the actor, "so they just let me go—which I loved to do. I had an awfully good time with that one." Caught up in the spirit of improvisation, the star recalls that during the actual performance he ended up filming far more material than could be squeezed into the running time of the finished episode. "I don't know how many pieces of shtick I did that were never in the show," he says, "'cause I just got going and kept going. We never worried about editing it, since it was on film, and could always be edited down to time later."

Despite Dick Van Dyke's proven knack for on-camera spontaneity, the actor insists that he would most often begin visualizing his sight gags and physical routines for a given episode as early as the very first script read-ing. "That's when a lot of my physical pieces would come to me," he says. "Anytime I could find an opening for a piece of physical business, I'd put it in, because I loved to do it." Even so, the star acknowledges that he was usually at his most inventive during the show's second and third rehearsal days, when he could finally set his script aside and begin actually acting out all the physical gags and routines that he'd visualized earlier in the week. "My creative heat hit when we were on our feet actually rehearsing the movement," says Van Dyke. "That's when things would kind of instinctively happen to me. A lot of times those little flashes of inspiration would hit right in the middle of a scene, and then you'd just have to try it."

But, according to Rose Marie, on those rare occasions when Van Dyke lacked a suitable inspiration, the actor would simply substitute perspira-tion and hope for the best. The actress recalls many afternoons when she'd spot the star off in a quiet corner of the stage, diligently sweating out the choreography of a sight gag or bit of physical shtick until he finally had it polished to his satisfaction. Of course, as Rose Marie recalls, the spectacle of Dick Van Dyke at work was a sight that rarely failed to attract a crowd—even in a busy rehearsal studio. And so, more often than not, by the time Van Dyke had perfected his latest flip, fall, or double take, he could count on finding himself surrounded by a small throng of delighted cast and crew members, many of them doubled over in laughter. "Then," recalls Rose Marie, "Dick would say, 'Is that funny?' I'd say, 'Funny? It's hysterical! Leave it in!'"

And if it didn't turn out to be so hysterical? Well, explains Van Dyke, that's what rehearsals were for. "Nobody was ever squelched for brainstorming an idea," the star explains. "We all felt free to do anything that came to us. That was the great part of it." "These people knew how to rehearse," insists John Rich, who helped instill that discipline during his early years as the show's director. "Our show was very, very carefully rehearsed."

That statement might have come as news to Guy Raymond. As Van Dyke's guest star on "A Farewell to Writing," it was the hapless actor's misfortune to arrive on the Van Dyke set during the one week when the show's normally dedicated cast seemed devoted to nothing more serious than getting through their final three days of work as quickly and painlessly as possible. "We were like kids getting ready for vacation," explains Ann Guilbert. "Who wants to study for exams? We just wanted to split. Guy came ready to bust his butt, and everybody else just wanted to play and get out of there."

"Nobody was paying much attention to anything," says Raymond, who recalls that he could barely get Dick Van Dyke to rehearse their scenes together more than once or twice during the entire three days he was on the set. "Everyone was in such a hurry to get out of there that there wasn't time for rehearsal or anything."

After his first dispiriting morning on the Van Dyke set, Guy Raymond recalls that he wandered into the Desilu commissary, where he was heartened to discover that costar Ann Guilbert had been thoughtful enough to save him a seat in the cramped lunchroom. "She was kind to me," says the actor, still thankful for the gracious gesture that the actress extended nearly three decades ago. "She showed me compassion."

Such displays of courtesy were not uncommon for Ann Guilbert, who admits that she frequently took it upon herself to make visiting performers feel at home on the Van Dyke set. "I always felt sorry for the people who were guest stars on the show," she explains. "When you go to a new set every time you do a show, you have to get reacquainted with all new people. You never know who to eat with." To Guilbert, who grew up as the nomadic daughter of a Veterans Administration doctor whose job required frequent reassignment, getting acquainted with strangers—and putting others at ease in strange surroundings—was practically second nature. "Having moved around all the time as a kid, I always felt compassion for whoever was a new kid on the block."

In a sweet—if largely coincidental—real-life postscript to the Van Dyke show's 127th episode, Ann Guilbert and guest star Guy Raymond would become reacquainted in a lasting friendship that would one day blossom into romance and, finally, marriage. But despite the circumstances of their first meeting, Guilbert explains that their eventual union was hardly the result of an on-set infatuation. In fact, the actress admits that she and Raymond actually lost touch after his ill-fated Van Dyke show appearance, only to become reacquainted in the late sixties, when both were members of a local theater group. By that time, both were sin-

gle—though it was not a status they were destined to maintain for long. "We struck up a friendship," says Guilbert, "which turned into matrimony."

On September 12, 1965, Carl Reiner continued what had by then become an annual tradition when he accepted, for the third year in a row, the Emmy award for Outstanding Program

Rob contemplates a life on the open road in a still from the show's 125th episode, "Br-rooom Br-rooom."

Achievement in Entertainment on behalf on *The Dick Van Dyke Show*. Dick Van Dyke also made a return trip to the dais when he picked up the Television Academy's top acting award for the second year in a row. Carl Reiner's script for "Never Bathe on Saturday" also earned an Emmy nomination that year, though the Academy's sole writing award that season went to dramatic writer David Karp for his work as author of an episode of *The Defenders*.

Even as the Van Dyke show continued to make its impact felt at the industry's most important year-end awards ceremony, the series maintained its impressive showing on the popular front as well. When the A.C. Nielsen ratings service published the year-end averages for the 1964–1965 season, *The Dick Van Dyke Show* ranked as the seventh-highest-rated prime-time series for the year. The show's average audience rating of 27.1 for the fourth season put the series just a few points behind its all-time third-season peak, when *The Dick Van Dyke Show* ended the 1963–1964 season with an eye-popping year-end average rating of 33.3, making it the third-highest-rated prime-time program of that entire year.

By the end of the Van Dyke show's fourth season, it had been almost exactly seven years since Carl Reiner sat down in his Fire Island study to write the thirteen half-hour comedy scripts that would eventually change his life. In the years since then, the writer had weathered his share of storms. But now, four seasons and untold man hours later, Carl Reiner's acclaimed *Dick Van Dyke Show* seemed poised at the very pinnacle of its creative and commercial potential. Indeed, any other producer in Reiner's enviable position—with a critically lauded, and still relatively youthful, series firmly anchored in the Nielsen top ten—would no doubt have been working very hard to capitalize on his show's current critical and popular standing by trying to lock the series into a lucrative long-term production deal.

Instead, Carl Reiner was already planning his exit.

CHAPTER 28
Curtain Calls

DICK VAN DYKE CLAIMS THAT CARL REINER NEVER INTENDED *The Dick Van Dyke Show* to run forever. "He'd said at the outset," reports the actor, "that if the show went five years, that would be plenty." And though neither Van Dyke nor anyone else connected with the series seems to recall exactly when Carl Reiner first declared his plan to end the show once its original five-year contract with CBS expired in 1966, the producer had been promising as much since at least the middle of season four.

"Carl says there is no possibility the show will go beyond its fifth year," noted the *Los Angeles Times*'s Cecil Smith in that paper's entertainment column on December 28, 1964. "Dick Van Dyke has a handsome movie career awaiting him, and Mary Tyler Moore is en route to movies."[64] And as *Daily Variety*'s Dave Kaufman pointed out a few months later, Carl Reiner was equally anxious to move beyond the confines of the small screen. "They're breaking up that gang," wrote Kaufman in late 1965, "because the series has done so well most everyone connected with it wants to go into other fields."[65]

Well, not quite everyone. It's worth noting that there was also a highly vocal contingent of the Van Dyke show's cast who made it clear that they were actually quite happy just where they were. "It was a shame we didn't go on for another couple years," says Rose Marie, who recalls that she—along with Morey Amsterdam and Richard Deacon—lobbied long and loud on the show's behalf throughout the early months of 1965. "We told Dick and Carl, 'We think you're making a mistake,'" the actress recalls. "And they said, 'Naw, let's finish up on top.' They didn't want to go on—they figured that we had done the best show that we could, and they didn't want to fall down."

But, according to Morey Amsterdam, the most fervent opponent to Carl Reiner's plan to shut the series down was none other than the show's executive producer himself. "Sheldon was very, very upset," recalls Amsterdam. "He told Dick, 'Are you crazy? CBS would've taken us for another five years! You could have backed up the Brink's truck right here and had them unload as much money as you wanted!'"

"No question about it," acknowledges Sheldon Leonard, who confirms that the CBS network made no secret of their desire to renew the show's contract well beyond the five-year mark. "We were offered a very fat deal for the three years to follow." And, as Leonard recalls trying to explain to the show's principal players at the time, their own bargaining positions could not have been stronger. "Just tell them what you want!" Leonard recalls advising Mary Tyler Moore, Carl Reiner, and Dick Van Dyke. "Tell them you want three times your present salary. Or four times—five, ten times! Whatever you want. If you're looking to solidify your future, you can write your own ticket!"

To illustrate his point, the executive producer invoked the name of their Desilu Cahuenga neighbor, Andy Griffith, who had quite successfully renegotiated the contract for his own Sheldon Leonard–produced series less than a year earlier. "Andy Griffith was faced with the same situation at the end of five years," Leonard explained to his stubborn stars and producer. "They came to him hat in hand. And Andy was amenable, and he wrote his own ticket—and it was a very rich ticket. And you people can do the same thing!" Finally, as Leonard tells it, he singled out the producer for one final pitch. "If you go to color," the executive producer told Carl Reiner, "you could have five more years!"*

But despite the passion of his arguments on the show's behalf, Sheldon Leonard confesses that he knew even then that he was pleading a lost cause. "The issue was settled before the question even arose," Leonard admits today. "The morale to go on with the show just wasn't there. Dick

---

*Although Reiner chose not to heed his executive producer's advice to keep the series on the air, Reiner insists that both he and Sheldon Leonard *had* given serious thought to filming *The Dick Van Dyke Show* in color as early as the show's third season. But, says Reiner, the plan was quickly abandoned as soon as they discovered that filming the show in the more expensive color process would have added about seven thousand dollars to their weekly budget. "It didn't seem to make any sense at the time," explains the producer. "There was no big argument. It was like, 'What do we do? It'll cost us seven thousand dollars a week more to go to color.' 'Oh. Well, in that case, let's not.'"

Van Dyke was being courted by everybody in the business. Carl Reiner was anxious to get out from behind his desk and become a director. And Mary Tyler Moore knew that there was a big contract waiting for her at Universal. They all felt that they were wasting their time in television—and here Universal and all of these people were throwing money at them in great, large gobs."*

But even if the offers tendered by the studios hadn't been quite so irresistible, Carl Reiner maintains that the departure of Dick Van Dyke and Mary Tyler Moore for the big-screen arena was inevitable—if only because they were both still relatively young. "You have to remember," explains Reiner, "that in the days before our show, most of the big sitcoms were cast with people who had all had careers in movies—Andy Griffith, Lucille Ball, Danny Thomas—and most of them were perfectly happy to have found a niche in television and to just stay there." But now, notes Reiner, Dick Van Dyke and Mary Tyler Moore were being offered a chance to turn the tables—to become the first stars to make the transition from small screen to big, instead of the other way around. Who could blame them for wanting to give it a shot? "If we had been older folk, we probably would have let the show go on past the five years," he observes. "But Mary and Dick really wanted to move on. And so did I. We all wanted to do movies."

And yet, despite Carl Reiner's assertions to the contrary, Dick Van Dyke steadfastly insists that he would have been delighted to continue starring in his series well beyond the term of his original five-year contract—as long as his producer agreed to stick around as well. "I don't think any of us wanted in the least to quit," says Van Dyke. "It really was the most pleasant way to make a living I've ever discovered. It was a real

---

*As Leonard suggests, neither of the show's two leading players would suffer financially in the years following the show's demise in 1966. Universal Pictures was the winner in the spirited bidding to lure the services of Mary Tyler Moore, who finally signed a seven-year, ten-picture contract with the studio at a reported fee of $100,000 per film. As for Dick Van Dyke—whose own per picture fee had reportedly ballooned to five times that amount by 1966—the star would walk away from the series with a pair of multipicture deals in place at Disney Studios and Columbia that would keep him busy through the end of the decade. In 1965, Van Dyke had also negotiated an exclusive television contract with CBS that called for the star to headline a series of three annual specials for the network—the first to appear in 1967—all of which would be produced by Van Dyke's own Lotus Productions.

home." But, he observes, as far as he was concerned, the show's fate was sealed the day Carl Reiner announced that he would not be returning as the show's producer beyond season five. "No one would have dreamed of going on without Carl. It just wouldn't have been the same show without him."

Sam Denoff also dismisses the commonly held view that Dick Van Dyke's career ambitions—or anyone else's, for that matter—played a significant role in the show's premature demise. "It wasn't a matter of everyone wanting to go do movies or anything like that," Denoff maintains. "Dick already had a movie career!" The real reason the show left the air when it did, says Denoff, was Carl Reiner's and Dick Van Dyke's shared desire to end the series while the audience was still laughing. "Dick and Carl decided basically that they did not want to have the show go downhill. A lot of us felt that it could've gone on—I think we could have. But Dick and Carl wanted to bring it to an end, so they did."

If nothing else, Carl Reiner's decision to retire the series at the close of its fifth season provided his staff with a renewed creative incentive as they gathered to start work on the show's fifth year in the last week of July 1965. "Everybody was aching to do the best fifth year we could possibly do," observes Reiner. And so, their creative edge honed by an awareness of the show's impending curtain call, the cast and crew of the Van Dyke show embarked on their fifth and final year together, determined to create their best season yet.

It would be a tall order, of course. And if in the final analysis the show's creators fell slightly short of their admittedly lofty goal of carving out the series' finest season yet, it wouldn't be for lack of effort. But, as Carl Reiner himself acknowledges, after five seasons, it was perhaps inevitable that the series would finally begin to reveal a few signs of age in its final year. "We tried to do something new with every show," says Reiner, "but after a certain number of years it's very hard to come up with something different every single week."*

But despite the pressure of having to compete with the creative legacy of their own first four seasons, the cast and crew of *The Dick Van Dyke Show* still managed to craft a fifth season of thirty-one half hours that would include many of the series' most fondly remembered episodes, beginning with the season's very first entry, "Coast to Coast Big Mouth." Based on a script that would eventually earn writers Bill Persky and Sam Denoff their second Emmy for the series, the episode details the hilarious complications that ensue after a glib quiz-show host tricks Laura into blurting out, on national television, the scandalous fact that her husband's boss wears a toupee. "That was Mary at her best," notes Denoff, who cites the scene where Laura finally tenders her sheepish apology to a glowering Alan Brady as one of the best-performed set pieces of the entire series. As the scene begins, Laura shyly approaches Brady, who is seated behind his massive desk, surveying the line of wig stands that display his now obsolete toupee collection. "Fellas," he says, addressing the wigs, "there she is! There's the little lady who put you out of business."

"Alan," she protests, "it was an accident!"

"So was Custer's last stand!" Brady shouts, clutching one of the pathetic hairpieces in his hand. "Would you like a scalp for your belt?" When

---

*Astute viewers will find plenty of evidence to back up Reiner's assertion in the striking number of fifth-season Van Dyke shows that borrow themes, settings, or—in some cases—entire plot elements from earlier shows. To name a few of the more notable examples: the dire straits in which Laura finds herself after she speaks out of turn on television in the fifth season's "Coast to Coast Big Mouth" recalls the strikingly similar plight that befell Rob after he found himself seated in Ray Murdock's hot seat for the show's forty-eighth episode, "Ray Murdock's X-Ray"; the plotline of season five's "The Ugliest Dog in the World," in which the Petries take a troublesome canine into their home, bears distinct echoes of Rob and Laura's earlier frustrations with Buddy's German shepherd in the show's seventh episode, "The Unwelcome Houseguest"; and finally, the garish brooch that forms the centerpiece of season five's "The Curse of the Petrie People" bears a striking resemblance—thematically, at least—to the bauble that Rob presented to his wife in the show's thirteenth episode, "Empress Carlotta's Necklace."

Laura tries to convince the star that he might actually be more attractive without a toupee, the quick-tempered egoist mocks her transparent insincerity by tossing the wigs onto his scalp, one atop the other. "*That's* the receding hairline job," he exclaims, indicating a wig that's designed to make people think he's losing his hair slowly; next, he points out his crewcut model, designed for summer wear; and, finally, Brady plunks an intentionally disheveled toupee on top of his head, explaining that it's his "Alan-you-need-a-haircut" model. "What, do you suggest I do with all of these now?" he asks her at last. Well, Laura volunteers, ever helpful, "There must be *some* needy bald people."

Arriving in the very nick of time, Rob rushes in to rescue Laura just as his employer appears to undergo a sudden—and quite unexpected—change of heart. "I've decided to be adorable about this mess," Brady volunteers, suddenly turning philosophical about his baldness. "I'm not twenty-nine anymore. I'm an established genius," he admits. "Sooner or later it was bound to come out. And this way I'm getting a lot of sympathy—not to mention the publicity."

And so, all's well that ends well. Or so it seems, until Laura—giddy with relief—riles the tyrant all over again with her playful suggestion that she might actually garner even greater publicity for the star by revealing another of his best-kept secrets to the media. "Maybe I oughta go on television and tell them about your nose!" she blabs. At which point Rob wisely—and swiftly—entices her to beat a hasty retreat before the final fade-out.

When "Coast to Coast Big Mouth" was filmed as *The Dick Van Dyke Show*'s fifth-season opener on August 3, 1965, it's unlikely that any of the show's returning cast was as happy to be back at work as Dick Van Dyke, who'd just spent a less than stimulating summer shooting the undistinguished *Lt. Robinson Crusoe, USN* for Disney, the first feature in the star's four-film commitment to the studio. Despite the fact that the film had been directed by Van Dyke's friend and manager, Byron Paul, the star was less than thrilled by the results—an opinion that he was only too happy to share with his trusted colleagues on the Van Dyke show set once he returned to work. "That was the year," recalls Rose Marie, "Dick came in and said, 'If you're a friend of mine, you won't go see the picture.'"

As the cast of the Van Dyke show regrouped to begin their fifth year together, they would bid a fond farewell to the show's longtime film editor, Bud Molin, who left the show after four seasons to assume editing chores on *I Spy*, a lighthearted adventure series that was the latest brainchild of producer Sheldon Leonard. Although Molin viewed the transition as nothing more than a practical career choice—the Van Dyke show was, after all, on its way out, while *I Spy* offered the promise of continued employment—Carl Reiner viewed his long-established editor's departure as tantamount to treason.

"Carl got real annoyed," recalls Molin. "I didn't think it was such a bad thing. I just figured Van Dyke was gonna be folding, so I signed on to do *I Spy*. I just thought it would be fun to do another show. But Carl was a little hurt." Even so, there was little Reiner could do to prevent the defection, especially since it was his own executive producer who was responsible for luring the editor to another show in the first place. And so, for the show's final season, Molin's longtime assistant editor, Beryl Gelfond, moved behind the Van Dyke show's editing table—leaving it to Reiner and Molin to patch up their differences at a later date. Which they eventually did, with spectacular results. After a creative collaboration that has already lasted more than thirty years, Bud Molin continues to edit every feature film that carries the credit "directed by Carl Reiner," just as he's done since 1969's *Where's Poppa?*

In the show's final year of production, Sheldon Leonard would become another increasingly shadowy presence on the set of *The Dick Van Dyke Show*. By 1965, the executive producer was spending much of his time out of the country, tending to the production demands of *I Spy*, a series that was frequently shot in far-flung locations around the globe. Even so, Leonard was hardly worried about the effect his absence would have on the Van Dyke show. After five years of production, the executive producer recognized that his own guiding presence on the set was no longer the crucial factor it had once been in

Dick Van Dyke stretches his range to play Rob's late Uncle Hezekiah in the fifth-season episode "The Great Petrie Fortune."

the show's weekly routine. In fact, the show's well-oiled production machine was operating so smoothly by season five that the cast and crew had by then managed to knock a full day off their previous five-day rehearsal schedule. "We got so good at it in the last year or so," observes Carl Reiner, "that we could do the show in four days. We knew who we were by then."

Of course, it probably didn't hurt the show's efficiency rating that Carl Reiner had in his employ a pair of story editors as talented, diligent, and tireless in their labors as Bill Persky and Sam Denoff, who had, in the space of two short years, risen from the status of freelance writers to become indispensable cogs in the show's weekly production apparatus. And the team's sterling capabilities were scarcely lost on Carl Reiner. On the contrary, when the producer announced that he was taking a leave of absence a few weeks into the show's fifth year, he would pay his capable assistants the ultimate compliment of handing them the keys to the store.

CHAPTER 29
Shenanigans

GIVEN CARL REINER'S DOGGEDLY PATERNAL ATTITUDE toward *The Dick Van Dyke Show*, the decision to take an out of town acting job at the height of the show's final production cycle could not have been easy to make. In fact, says Reiner, when director Norman Jewison first called to offer him a choice role in *The Russians Are Coming, The Russians Are Coming*, his first impulse had been to turn the offer down flat.* "I said no to *The Russians Are Coming* five times!" recounts Reiner. "I told them, 'No, I can't leave the show, it's my baby. And we're almost at the end of the tunnel.' I wanted to go out big." Reiner finally relented—but only after he'd extracted an ironclad guarantee from the film's producers that he would be required to spend no more than twelve weeks on the film's northern California location. "I told them," says Reiner, "'I'll do the movie, but only if I can get twelve Van Dyke shows down on paper before we start shooting.'"

And so it was that Reiner spent the better part of the summer of 1965 cramming with Persky and Denoff to get a dozen Van Dyke show scripts in shape before his upcoming hiatus from the show. But finally, on September 11, 1965—a few days after the Van Dyke company had wrapped their 133rd episode, "The Great Petrie Fortune"—Carl Reiner flew to Ft.

---

*Although Reiner insists he was originally offered the part of the Russian sailor, Rozanov—the role eventually played by Alan Arkin—he opted instead to play the film's straight lead, Walt Whittaker, a Manhattan TV writer whose peaceful summer on a small resort island is disrupted by the unexpected arrival of an offshore Soviet submarine.

"Morale was very important on that set," says Sheldon Leonard. "If you weren't happy when you came in, it would show up on the screen."

Bragg in northern California to begin principal photography on what would be his most substantial acting role in five years. There, sequestered in what he would describe as "a charming town with one theater, a bowling alley, and a stoplight,"[66] Reiner would spend the better part of the next twelve weeks in self-imposed exile from his beloved *Dick Van Dyke Show* for the first—and only—time in the show's five-year life span.

It would be of no small consolation to Reiner that he'd left the show in the capable hands of Bill Persky and Sam Denoff, who had been promoted to the status of full-fledged producers for the duration of his absence. "I trusted that the guys knew my sensibilities," Reiner observes. "They knew what I hated." But, though Persky and Denoff were flattered by their mentor's confidence in their abilities, they would soon discover that the show's cast was not so easily convinced. "The cast trusted us," explains Bill Persky, "up to a point."

As Persky himself is quick to acknowledge, the challenge of stepping into Carl Reiner's shoes—even as understudies—was no easy trick. "There never has been a guy as important to a show as Carl was on that show. *He* was the real star, and I think Dick would be the first one to acknowledge that. So, when Carl left, everybody in the cast felt betrayed. And the first show we did where Carl wasn't there, they were scared. We were like this loving family, and suddenly Daddy was gone and we were now on our own." Dick Van Dyke is even more succinct in his appraisal of those first few rehearsals without Carl Reiner. "We were lost," says the star.

And it's unlikely that Van Dyke would've gotten much argument from Persky and Denoff had he voiced that assessment at the first script meeting convened following Reiner's departure—a tense gathering that Persky and Denoff approached with understandable trepidation. But, despite the sense of foreboding that hung over the studio as the fledgling producers passed the week's scripts around the table, the pair forged gamely ahead. "Page one!" announced Bill Persky, doing his best to sound commanding despite the self-consciousness he felt repeating the phrase that Carl Reiner had intoned at each of the show's 132 previous script sessions.

The panic that had been steadily mounting in the studio seemed to ease up momentarily when the actors flipped their scripts open and began to read aloud. But though the novice producers were heartened by the sounds of laughter that greeted the show's opening scene, their relief would be short-lived. A few pages later, the actors hit a slight snag in the script, and suddenly the dark clouds that had been hovering over the soundstage seemed to grow even thicker. "There was a problem in one scene, and a major problem in another scene," notes Persky, who emphasizes that discovering a rough patch or two in an early draft of a Van Dyke show script was certainly not unusual. "It needed the usual rewrites," sighs the writer, recalling the almost palpable dread that seemed to grip the actors as they continued to trudge their way through the troubled script. "You could tell that they were worried."

Even so, the actors were not entirely unsympathetic to their understudy producers' plight—as Bill Persky discovered a few moments later, when his acting company willingly dropped their guard to share a moment of spontaneous comic relief with their beleaguered producers. As Persky recalls, the agonizing tension was finally broken when the studio phone began to ring right in the middle of the ill-fated reading.

"Yes?" answered Richard Deacon, who happened to be sitting closest to the phone when it rang. Then, as Persky recalls, after a short pause, the flamboyant actor turned and handed the receiver to him with a grand flourish. "They want to talk to the *producer*," Deacon announced, placing an unmistakably acid emphasis on the final word.

"Richard Deacon was a particularly acerbic kind of guy," explains Persky, who recalls that he could tell by the wicked glint in the actor's eye that he was up to something—though exactly what, Persky wasn't quite sure. Warily, the stand-in producer took the receiver in hand, and—his nerves already badly frayed from the trial of the morning's reading—barked a gruff salutation into the phone.

"Yeah?" demanded Persky. At which point the person on the other end of the line chirped in a voice that was clearly audible to most of those sitting at the table. "Is this Carl Reiner?" the caller asked, somewhat confused.

"No, it's *not!*" snapped Persky, without missing a beat. "But I'm doing the best I can."

There was something so simple, honest, and appropriate about Persky's almost confessional response to the caller's innocent query that most of those gathered around the table couldn't help but find it funny. And in no time at all the entire company burst into an unrestrained round of laughter— a tonic that would prove a welcome antidote to the glum spirits that only moments before had blanketed the studio like a plague. When the reading finally resumed a few minutes later, it was blissfully free of all visible signs of angst. "They were insecure that first week," concludes Persky. "But they got over that as soon as they saw that we knew what we were doing."

If further proof that Persky and Denoff knew exactly what they were doing was required, ample evidence would be displayed in the first show to be filmed under their auspices, "Odd But True." In the episode's almost deliriously offbeat storyline, Rob Petrie achieves a dubious notoriety after it's discovered that the freckles on his back can be connected to form a reasonable facsimile of the Philadelphia Liberty Bell—a premise that Carl Reiner insists could only have come from the twisted sensibilities of writers Garry Marshall and Jerry Belson. "That was Belson and Marshall," observes Reiner. "They always came up with crazy, wonderful things which stretched our show."

"I've always been obsessed with Ripley's *Believe It or Not*," confirms co-writer Jerry Belson, who hastens to add that "Odd But True" was one of the few Van Dyke scripts that was most definitely *not* inspired by any real-life incident. "That never happened to any of us," says Belson. But whatever their inspiration, Belson and Marshall's penchant for the offbeat served the writers especially well when they sat down to script the episode's climactic sequence, a surreal confrontation that takes place in the waiting room outside the *Odd But True* offices. There, Rob and Laura unwittingly instigate a battle royal whose participants include a woman who swears that her pet dachshund has been fasting for a decade, a man who brandishes a potato that bears an unlikely resemblance to a one-eyed duck, and an unusually industrious gent who claims that he's just hiked all the way from Buffalo to Manhattan—on his hands. "We had a lot of fun when we did that story," says Belson. "That was just me and Garry going nuts."

Buoyed by the audience's favorable reception to "Odd But True"—which proved beyond a doubt that it *was* possible to get through an entire episode of *The Dick Van Dyke Show* without Carl Reiner, if just barely— the cast approached rehearsals for the following episode with a far more relaxed attitude. Maybe a little too relaxed, as Dick Van Dyke explains. "We got a little carried away on that one," says Van Dyke, remembering the boisterous rehearsals that took place a few days before the cast shot episode 135, "Viva Petrie." "We were having so much fun that we got a little undisciplined, I'm afraid." Indeed, notes the star, things finally got so out of hand that it took nothing less than a stern reprimand from Sheldon Leonard to bring the errant company back in line.

According to Van Dyke, their troubles began a day or two into rehearsals, after the cast began to uncover flaws in the episode's storyline, a trifle in which Rob and Laura play reluctant hosts to an itinerant bullfighter of dubious pedigree. "The show was not

Carl Reiner crammed to get a dozen Van Dyke show scripts in shape so that he could take time off to act in *The Russians Are Coming, The Russians Are Coming* near the top of the show's fifth season. Pictured with Reiner on one of the film's northern California locations is Eva Marie Saint, who played his wife in the film.

working," observes Van Dyke. "It simply wasn't there." But rather than work themselves into a lather trying to repair the troublesome script, the company decided that a light approach might yield better results. "Whenever a show wasn't quite working, we found that just by staying loose and clowning around and having fun with it, we usually found something."

Usually. But not always.

Finding little inspiration in the episode's admittedly thin plotline, the cast—led by Van Dyke and guest star Joby Baker—instead turned their attentions to the staging of a mock bullfighting tournament. The only problem was that, although the company's antics struck most of those gathered on the set as wildly amusing, the horseplay had almost nothing to do with the episode as written. "We were having so much fun that we never did get around to putting the show together," recalls Van Dyke. Which was a subtlety not lost on Sheldon Leonard, who—with his characteristically impeccable timing—happened by the Van Dyke stage at the very height of the cast's boisterous shenanigans.

"Sheldon walked in on us," confesses Van Dyke, "and we all had a bad case of the sillies. He looked at the show, and he saw that, obviously, it was not working, and we were doing nothing to repair it. And, for the first time I can recall, Sheldon lost his temper. He really screamed at us. It was two days before showtime, and he just couldn't believe that we were letting things fall apart the way we were." Suitably chastened, the actors returned to work on the spot. "Oh, boy," says Van Dyke, "you could've heard a pin drop! To get dressed down by Sheldon is an experience, I'll tell ya. He's worse than a high school principal."

Not surprisingly, the show was in far more presentable shape by the time it went before the cameras the following Tuesday evening. "I don't know how good the show turned out to be," confesses the star, "but at least we made *something* out of it." At the conclusion of that evening's dress rehearsal, Sheldon Leonard made a point of wandering backstage to give his cast an approving nod—a gesture of benevolent acceptance that was greeted with audible sighs of relief from the actors. "Sheldon didn't mind our having fun," notes Van Dyke, "as long as we had a good episode."

For the fun-loving star of *The Dick Van Dyke Show*, the shenanigans didn't stop once he left the set—as any one of his four now fully grown children will attest. Ironically, when the irrepressible star finally did get a rare day off from work, he would often grab his kids and his home-movie camera and head right back to the studio, where he and his brood frequently shot their own 8mm home-movie epics on the idle soundstages and backlot streets. In one of the Van Dyke gang's more elaborate mini-epics—a Western spoof entitled, "Hide! It's Noon!"—Dad played a marshal named Shorty, while his two teenaged boys, Barry and Chris, donned black hats to play the film's outlaw gang.* An even more ambitious project was "The Beast that Ate Encino," a sci-fi parody that was set in and around the rambling San Fernando Valley house at 4869 Encino Avenue that also served as home to the Van Dyke clan.

And for a few heady years in the midsixties, that Encino address was also the site of the San Fernando Valley's most spectacular Halloween attraction. For it was there, each October 31, that Dick Van Dyke—aided and abetted by a small army of the neighborhood's more industrious children—would transform his sprawling front yard and driveway into a homemade Halloween spook factory. "It was like a carnival," recalls Tony Paris, the son of Van Dyke director Jerry Paris, who was all of nine years old when his father first took him to see the Van Dyke family's annual Halloween spectacular. "Dick had a mechanical Frankenstein coming out of the ground," says Paris. "And a Dracula, and vampires, and mechanical men. It was the most impressive thing I'd ever seen one man do by himself." Nor was Tony Paris alone in his admiration for Van Dyke's Halloween handiwork. "It was the biggest thing in the Valley," he observes. "There was always a long line of cars waiting to get into his driveway on Halloween night."

"I'd get anywhere from three to five thousand people every year," boasts Van Dyke. "It finally got to the point where I had to hire two off-duty cops just to handle all the traffic." The star also took it as a point of pride that the vast majority of rubberneckers who drove through his driveway each year seemed completely unaware that the curator of the display also happened to be the star of the country's top situation comedy. Which was just fine with Van Dyke, who maintains that he created the neighborhood attraction purely for the fun of the undertaking.

---

*Perhaps inspired by his dad's 8mm epics, Dick Van Dyke's son Barry would finally turn to acting full-time in the late seventies. After logging a string of one-shot roles on *Mork and Mindy*, *The Love Boat*, and *Remington Steele*, among others, Barry Van Dyke finally landed recurring roles on *Galactica 1980* and *Airwolf*, as well as costarring stints on his father's 1988 series, *The Van Dyke Show* and, beginning in 1993, *Diagnosis: Murder*. The younger Van Dyke also logged at least one appearance on the original *Dick Van Dyke Show*, in 1962, when he and his brother Chris played cameo roles as two of the kids in the show's twenty-second episode, "The Talented Neighborhood."

"Richard Deacon was a particularly acerbic kind of guy," says writer Bill Persky, who came by that knowledge firsthand when he found himself on the receiving end of one of the actor's well-timed jests.

"It all started out with a Frankenstein monster I built one year and stuck out in front. And it was such a big hit that the next year I made a Dracula. And then a Mummy. And every year I'd add a few more. Finally I had a crew of teenage kids who helped me. Over the years, I built about thirty monsters out in the yard. Halloween used to be quite a big deal around my house."

Though his cherished Van Dyke company performed their labors far from Carl Reiner's sight during the dozen weeks the producer spent filming *The Russians Are Coming, The Russians Are Coming* in northern California in late 1965, they were by no means out of his mind. But, outside of a few short hops home—and, of course, the producer's daily phone calls to Persky and Denoff—Reiner's most significant contact with *The Dick Van Dyke Show* for the better part of those three months came when he watched the show on television, along with the rest of America, each Wednesday night. And, not surprisingly, the producer proved to be one of the show's greatest fans. "Some of the shows they did while I was gone were as good as any we did together," Reiner says today. In fact, of all the episodes that were produced by Persky and Denoff during his leave of absence, Carl Reiner recalls only one that gave him even the slightest cause for worry—episode 141, "Who Stole My Watch?"

In the episode's storyline, Rob and Laura are stymied when Rob's expensive new watch comes up missing after a birthday celebration at the house. At his wit's end, Rob is finally forced to consider the possibility that one of his friends may have taken the timepiece from his house. And it was that somewhat shaky conjecture that made Carl wince. "There's no chance on God's earth Rob would ever think that Buddy or Sally would steal from him!" exclaims Reiner, who, even after five years' worth of Van Dyke shows, continued to judge the characters' behavior by the strict yardstick of his own personal code. "Would *I* ever think Mel Brooks took a watch from *my* house?" Reiner asks rhetorically. "Of course not!" After seeing the episode, the producer was outraged; and he didn't hesitate to share his umbrage with his understudy producers the next morning. "Hey," he remembers asking them, "how could you let that go?"

"We thought we dealt with that," explains Sam Denoff. "We thought we covered that with a line where Rob says, 'This is impossible. None of my friends could have done that.' But these things are very subjective, and I guess Carl didn't agree." In any event, Reiner admits that his momentary disenchantment with his substitute producers was hardly significant in light of their far greater achievements during his leave of absence. "In all those shows they did, they missed that *one* little thing," Reiner says today. "One little thing. But the rest of them were terrific."

Carl Reiner finally wrapped his scenes in *The Russians Are Coming* in early December of 1965, just in time to report back to the Van Dyke show set to supervise the filming of the show's 145th episode, "The Curse of the Petrie People," which was filmed on December 14. Another of the show's undisputed classics, "The Curse of the Petrie People" turns a comic lens on the nearly unendurable mortification Laura suffers after Rob's mother presents her with a garish heirloom brooch that's shaped like the continental United States, a family memento that's been passed down by Petrie wives for generations. With great effort, Laura feigns gratitude for the monstrosity. But the doting in-laws have barely made it out the door before Laura accidentally drops the irreplaceable heirloom down the garbage disposal—thus invoking an ancient Petrie family curse. Whether Laura's action is motivated by accident or Freudian intent is never really made clear, which only adds to the fun.

Initially hoping to fool the in-laws, Laura commissions a jeweler to cast a new brooch. Naturally, sharp-eyed Clara Petrie spots the fake at once. But in the episode's surprise twist, the mother-in-law announces that she finds Laura's futile attempts to replace the lost heirloom far more meaningful than the object itself. Before long the mother-in-law has confessed that, like Laura, she too has secretly detested the brooch since the very first day it was handed to her by her own mother-in-law. And by episode's end, the pair conclude that the only true Curse of the Petries was the one that befell the wives who were forced to wear the garish family heirloom for all those years.

The episode's wildly inventive script sprang from the fertile minds of Carl Kleinschmitt and Dale McRaven, a pair of journeymen writers who had been discovered on the Desilu lot less than a year earlier by Persky and Denoff. After laboring for a spell as uncredited script doctors on *The Joey Bishop Show*, the ambitious team would quickly establish first-rate credentials on the Van Dyke show, where they would contribute eight of the show's final thirty-one scripts. Kleinschmitt and McRaven's impressive portfolio of fifth-year Van Dyke scripts would include "Uhny Uhftz," a science-fiction-themed episode in which Rob has an apparent close encounter with a UFO; "Body and Sol," a flashback episode that explores Rob's brief career as Pitter Patter Petrie, middleweight champ of Company A; and, most memorably, the show's 153rd episode, "Obnoxious, Offensive, Egomaniac, Etc.," which describes a writer's nightmare in which the working draft of Rob, Buddy, and Sally's latest script accidentally finds its way to Alan Brady before the writers have had a chance to delete all the nasty comments they included in the script for their own private amusement.

Proud papa Dick Van Dyke poses for a publicity still with his son Chris, who would graduate from a cameo appearance in a first-year Van Dyke show, "The Talented Neighborhood," to costarring roles in 8mm Van Dyke family epics with titles like "Hide, It's Noon!" and "The Beast That Ate Encino."

"That actually happened to us," says Dale McRaven, who confesses that when he and Kleinschmitt were on *The Joey Bishop Show*, they frequently slipped blatantly unprintable stage directions into their first-draft scripts as a means of venting their frustrations toward the show's star. "Joey Bishop was not a nice person to writers," says McRaven. And so, to get back at him, the scribes would simply describe him in the unkindest terms imaginable in early drafts of the scripts they wrote for his show. Of course, the writers got the fright of their lives the week they discovered that they'd accidentally submitted their latest script to the studio typist before they'd had a chance to white out the expletives.

A sleepless night followed, but—unlike Rob, Buddy, and Sally—McRaven and Kleinschmitt were spared the indignity of having to climb through their boss's window to retrieve the incriminating script. The next morning, the writers were relieved to discover that their producer had caught their error and pulled the script from circulation before it could do any harm. "We came to work the next day and found out he'd saved our ass," says McRaven. "Otherwise it might've been a very interesting table reading—for *some* people."

CHAPTER 30
The Last Chapter

AS THE VAN DYKE SHOW'S FINAL PRODUCTION SEASON rolled to its inevitable end, the show's producers decided that a few curtain calls might be in order. And so, during the show's last thirteen weeks, Carl Reiner and head writers Persky and Denoff contrived to spotlight each member of the show's colorful supporting cast in at least one show before the curtain rolled down for the last time.

And so it was that Richard Deacon's Mel Cooley finally got to stand up to his domineering brother-in-law in the show's 146th episode, "The Bottom of Mel Cooley's Heart," which concludes with the optimistic suggestion that *The Alan Brady Show*'s beleaguered producer may finally have earned some small measure of respect from his tyrannical employer. Similarly, Sally Rogers's oft-stalled search for romance reaches a tentative denouement in the show's 148th episode, "Dear Sally Rogers," when the writer's televised plea for a husband attracts a mountain of marriage proposals—including one surprisingly poignant declaration that arrives from the pen of her own long-suffering boyfriend, Herman Glimsher. And, though her character doesn't undergo any particularly earth-shattering changes, Millie Helper finally gets a chance to shine when she shares the spotlight with Laura in episode 150, "Long Night's Journey into Day," in which the two wives spend an eventful night protecting the Petrie house from all sorts of imagined disasters while their husbands are away on a fishing trip.

But none of the show's extended family would receive a more definitive send-off than Buddy Sorrell, whose character would literally undergo a sacred rite of passage in the bar mitzvah sequence that closed the show's 149th episode, "Buddy Sorrell, Man and Boy," which was scripted by Ben Joelson and Art Baer. One of Morey Amsterdam's all-time favorite Van Dyke shows, it's the actor's recollection that the show's classic bar mitzvah episode was inspired by a stray comment he dropped one afternoon, after he happened to overhear Carl Reiner and some of the show's other writers swapping tales of their own bar mitzvahs.

"Carl said to me, 'What happened at your bar mitzvah?'" recalls Amsterdam. "And I said, 'Nothing. I was never bar mitzvahed. We didn't have the money. In those days my folks couldn't afford to be Jewish.' And Carl started to laugh. He said, 'Well, you're gonna be bar mitzvahed now!'"

Co-writer Art Baer recalls a somewhat different origin for the bar mitzvah episode, which he claims was actually inspired by a comment uttered in passing by his mother. Like Morey Amsterdam, Baer had somehow missed out on having a bar mitzvah when he was a youngster. But on his fortieth birthday, the writer recalls, his mother called to propose that it still wasn't too late to have a bar mitzvah. Baer didn't take her up on the suggestion, though he did bring the idea into his next story meeting for *The Dick Van Dyke Show*. "I mentioned it to Carl," says Baer, "and he thought it was funny, and that it would work for the show. And we worked it out on the spot."

In the episode, which was filmed on January 18, 1966, Rob and Sally begin to suspect that Buddy might be stepping out with a woman other than his wife, Pickles, after he begins leaving work early to keep a string of mysterious appointments. Of course, once Rob finally confronts Buddy with his suspicions, the older writer finally comes clean. He hasn't been seeing another woman, explains Buddy—he's been seeing a rabbi! And though he admits that he'd been far too embarrassed to tell anyone sooner, he finally confesses that he's been secretly cramming to stand up for the bar mitzvah ceremony that he'd missed out on some thirty years earlier. Of course, with his secret now out in the open, Buddy approaches the ceremony with renewed confidence. And, by episode's end, surrounded by friends and well-wishers, Buddy Sorrell accepts the ancient rite of passage of his faith, finally declaring to one and all, "Today I am a man."

In an effort to preserve a suitably pious atmosphere in the show's closing scene, the producers hired an actual cantor to sing the traditional prayers that open the episode's bar mitzvah sequence. But although cantor Arthur Ross-Jones was brought in to lend gravity to the proceedings, Morey Amsterdam recalls that the religious singer was certainly not immune to the allure of the show's bright lights and glamor.

According to the actor, the cantor was supposed to sing a brief passage of prayer, in Hebrew, at the top of the bar mitzvah scene. But, while the cantor performed his task perfectly well at the show's afternoon dress rehearsal, Amsterdam reports that the steady glow of the show's spotlight seemed to go to the singer's head about the time the show's cameras were finally moved into place. "When he saw there were about three hundred people in the audience," notes the actor, "he got drunk with power." By the time the director shouted "Action" that night, says Amsterdam, there was no stopping the starstruck cantor. "He just kept on singing and singing, for maybe five or ten minutes."

As Amsterdam recalls, he finally took the wind out of the cantor's sails the minute he paused to take a breath. Without missing a beat, Amsterdam stepped forward, did a double take at the cantor, and then cried out, "One more time!" Needless to say, another take of the scene was quickly arranged. And this time, the cantor wisely chose to stick with the original script.

After the uncharacteristic reverence of "Buddy Sorrell, Man and Boy," the company moved back to more familiar ground for their 151st episode, "Talk to the Snail," a scathing show-business satire that offered solid evidence—as if any were needed—that *The Dick Van Dyke Show* was in little danger of losing its comic edge as the series lurched toward its final fade-out a few weeks hence. In the episode, which was written by Jerry Belson and Garry Marshall, Rob and the gang are moved to consider their employment options beyond *The Alan Brady Show* after they uncover a classified network memo that seems to call for an immediate reduction in the size of the show's writing staff. With the threat of midseason unemployment looming, Rob secures a job interview with TV ventriloquist Claude Wilbur, a slightly schizophrenic puppeteer who insists on conducting the interview in front of his puppet podium. There Rob meets Wilbur's alter ego, a mean-spirited puppet named Jellybean the Snail. Before long, as Jellybean comes to dominate the increasingly surreal proceedings, Rob begins to wonder who's actually in charge, Wilbur or the Snail. "Don't talk to *him*," Jellybean instructs Rob, "*I'm* asking the questions."

Once Jellybean takes over, the interview quickly disintegrates into a slapstick free-for-all. When Rob dares to speak out of turn, the sadistic snail rewards the writer's hapless insurgence with a brisk smack to the side of the head. "*I'll* decide what's funny," the arrogant puppet commands. After Rob absorbs a few more well-placed smacks to the head, he finally decides to stand up to the snail. "He better not hit me again," the writer informs the sympathetic ventriloquist, even as the puppet continues to eye Rob with suspicion. "And I'm not kidding!"

Eventually, Rob wins the snail's grudging respect, as well as a firm job offer. But, fortunately, Alan Brady intervenes before his star writer is forced to accept the position, and Rob finally turns the schizophrenic puppeteer down. When the crafty snail asserts that it's too late for the writer to back out, since they've already shaken on the deal, Rob counters with an argument based on biological grounds. "A shake with a snail is not binding," the writer declares, citing no less an authority on the subject than Walt Disney.

Like most of Jerry Belson and Garry Marshall's best work for the series, "Talk to the Snail" combines a wildly offbeat premise with gut-wrenchingly funny gags, sharply drawn characterizations, and an unerring eye for the absurd. According to Belson—who numbers this episode among his own all-time favorites—Garry Marshall's early experience as a writer for puppeteer Shari Lewis served as the episode's springboard. Though, Belson is quick to add, the perky puppeteer most certainly did not serve as the model for their demented ventriloquist. "She wasn't mean like this guy was," the writer asserts.

For his role as Walt Whittaker in Norman Jewison's *The Russians Are Coming, The Russians Are Coming*, Carl Reiner recalls that he spent twelve weeks of the show's final year on location in Ft. Bragg, California, "a charming town with one theater, a bowling alley, and a stoplight."

Nor did the show's actual guest star resemble the schizophrenic pup-peteer he portrayed in the episode. If anything, Paul Winchell demon-strated his own good-natured sense of humor by his willingness to spoof his own well-established persona as America's preeminent television ven-triloquist of the fifties and sixties. But, as the cast of the Van Dyke show would discover, Winchell's talents were by no means limited to the field of puppetry.

By the mid-sixties, Winchell had for some time been pursuing a sec-ond passion as a self-taught medical researcher and scientific inventor—a field in which the famous ventriloquist had already earned some renown. In 1965, Winchell had developed and patented his own design for an arti-ficial human heart, a fact that had stunned Dick Van Dyke when he first discovered that tidbit on the set of *The Dick Van Dyke Show* in 1966. "I remember listening to Paul Winchell talk all that week," recalls Van Dyke. "I was fascinated to hear how this ventriloquist had come up with an arti-ficial heart. It just floored me that he had been that creative."

In February and March of 1966, the Van Dyke company rounded out their final six weeks of production with a mixed-bag of a half-dozen episodes that—regardless of their relative standing on the show's long and illustrious honor roll—would forever be remembered as the last batch of wine from a very sweet vintage.

In the first of this final six, "A Day in the Life of Alan Brady," pande-monium erupts when narcissistic Alan Brady horns in on Millie and Jer-ry's anniversary party with a full documentary camera crew in tow. Rob goes undercover in the show's 154th entry, "The Man from My Uncle," in which G-Man Harry Bond, played by a deadpan Godfrey Cambridge, sets up a surveillance station in Ritchie's room. And Rob Petrie makes his feature-film debut—opposite a scorching Italian starlet—in the gritty underground film that plays a key role in the plot of the show's 155th episode, "You Ought to Be in Pictures," which was filmed on March 8, 1966. Finally, Jerry and Millie grow jealous when Rob and Laura devel-op a burgeoning friendship with a pair of exciting new neighbors in episode 156, "Love Thy Other Neighbor," which was filmed on March 15, 1966.

A few minutes after the cast finished shooting "Love Thy Other Neigh-bor," the company regrouped on the set to film the new scenes that would be used in the framing sequence of their 157th episode, "The Last Chap-ter," which would be largely devoted to a reprise of classic clips from past episodes. But despite the fact that the episode existed as little more than a showcase of the show's most outstanding moments, few fans of *The Dick*

Van Dyke Show would be disappointed when "The Last Chapter" was aired—slightly out of order—on June 1, 1966, as the show's final episode.

As the title suggests, the episode was designed to suggest a denouement in the long-running saga of Rob and Laura Petrie and their extended family of friends, neighbors, and co-workers. Not surprisingly, the crafting of this climactic episode was a task that writers Carl Reiner, Bill Persky, and Sam Denoff approached with their customary wit and warm affection. In the episode's storyline, Rob offers Laura an early peek at the just-completed manuscript of his long-awaited autobiography, *Untitled: A Series of Terribly Important Events in the Fairly Unimportant Life of Robert S. Petrie.*

As Laura flips excitedly through the pages of Rob's memoir—a comical look at the life and times of a TV writer and his loving wife—viewers are treated to flashbacks of key moments in the epic chronicle of Rob and Laura Petrie as it unfolded over the five years of *The Dick Van Dyke Show.* We watch Rob's stuttering marriage proposal in an open jeep at Camp Crowder, Missouri; and we witness his faltering stumble down the aisle on the day the pair are finally wed. We relive Laura's eventful trip to the maternity ward, and we laugh once again at the postnatal jitters that have Rob convinced that their infant was switched at birth. But finally, the episode—and the series—ends as it began, when Carl Reiner's Alan Brady announces that he plans to produce and star in a TV series based on the real-life saga of a TV comedy writer.

Sound familiar?

"That was a very easy show to come up with," says Carl Reiner, who recalls that he and his story editors knocked out the script for "The Last Chapter"'s wraparound sequences in the space of a few hours, just weeks before the episode was due to go before the cameras. "We said, 'What are we gonna do for the last one?' And I said, 'Well, let's do this!' It seemed a very logical thing to do."

Ironically, *The Dick Van Dyke Show*'s final episode had not yet aired when the Academy of Television Arts and Sciences passed out their Emmy Awards for the 1965–1966 season on May 22, 1966. Even so, the Academy had been impressed enough with what they'd already seen of the show's fifth year to reward the series with eight nominations, out of which the show would earn four awards. Dick Van Dyke and Mary Tyler Moore each would add another Emmy to their growing collections—it would be his third award in the leading actor category, her second. Two of Bill Persky and Sam Denoff's fifth-season scripts earned nominations in the Academy's writing category that year: "The Ugliest Dog in the World," and the show that would finally earn the writers their second Emmy, "Coast to Coast Big Mouth." And, in an award presentation that must have surprised no one, Carl Reiner accepted his fourth consecutive Emmy in recognition of *The Dick Van Dyke Show*'s status as the year's Outstanding Comedy Series.

Shut out that evening was Jerry Paris, who was nominated for his second Emmy in the director's category, with the award going to William Asher, the director of *Bewitched*. And though he'd been nominated in the supporting actor category, Morey Amsterdam would go home empty handed after the Emmy for Outstanding Performance by an Actor in a Supporting Role in a Comedy went to *The Andy Griffith Show*'s Don Knotts. And, finally, in her third nomination in the supporting actress category, Rose Marie seemed like the odds-on favorite to finally receive long overdue recognition for her work on the series. In her two previous nominations, the actress had been aced out of the award by dramatic actresses who—perhaps unfairly—had shared the supporting category with comedic actresses. But, as the Academy had finally changed their nominating rules to give supporting comedy performers their own separate categories that year, Rose Marie looked to be a shoo-in to win the honor at last. Alas, it simply wasn't meant to be. In an ironic twist of fate, the supporting actress Emmy that year went to the one actress who had a stronger lock on the Academy voters' sympathies than even Rose Marie: Alice Pearce—the original Mrs. Kravitz on *Bewitched*—who had died only two months before the awards were handed out.

The title of *The Dick Van Dyke Show*'s final episode was actually a misnomer. For though "The Last Chapter" would be aired as the show's swan song on June 1, 1966, it was not the last *Dick Van Dyke Show* filmed.* That honor would go to "The Gunslinger," a whimsical spoof that imagines what life might have been like for Rob and Laura and their friends had they lived in the wild and wooly west. In Persky and Denoff's fanciful script for the episode that was filmed on March 22, 1966, Rob plays a retired gunslinger turned small-town sheriff—or, more precisely, "a slinger-turned-singer-turned-dancer-turned-rancher-turned-parson-turned-sheriff"—who is forced to pick up his six-shooters one last time for a showdown with his archnemesis, Big Bad Brady, in the barroom of Miss Sally's saloon.

---

*Nor is "The Last Chapter" generally shown as the final episode in the show's syndicated rerun package, which follows the show's original production sequence.

Sam Denoff admits that having the opportunity to make a real Western—even a parody Western—was, for most of the company, a dream come true. "Every guy fantasized about being a cowboy star—me, a Jewish guy from Brooklyn; Persky, a Jewish guy from Atlantic City; and Dick, a small-town boy from Danville, Illinois. So we decided we'd do a cowboy show." As icing on the cake, Persky and Denoff even wrote themselves into the episode. The writers appear in a brief cameo as a pair of skeptical cowpokes who cast disapproving glances at Sheriff Rob near the top of the episode. Jerry Belson and Garry Marshall also got to don sideburns and six-shooters and join the show's star-studded cast of extras—Marshall plays the barkeep at Miss Sally's Saloon, and Belson is the unfortunate gambler who catches one of Sheriff Petrie's stray bullets during a card game. Not surprisingly, Denoff reports that he and his fellow writers had a smashingly good time playing cowpokes for the cameras. "We got to dress up as cowboys. What's more romantic than that?" asks the writer. "I still have the hat!"

When the cast of *The Dick Van Dyke Show* lined up for their 158th and final curtain call at the end of that night, the ovation that greeted them was overwhelming. And though each of the company's actors understood that that moment would mark the last time they would appear on stage as a company, none of them was eager to prolong the bittersweet moment. And so, with the sound of the applause still ringing in their ears, the actors took one last bow before making their final, graceful exit from the stage.

A few minutes later, the cast regrouped on another part of the lot for what would constitute their last official gathering—the show's closing-night wrap party. A noisy and wildly celebratory affair, *The Dick Van Dyke Show*'s closing night bash would be one party that would not soon be forgotten by any of those in attendance. "It was," in the words of Van Dyke writer Dale McRaven, "a very *up* party."

And yet, observes Carl Reiner, beneath the surface of boisterous back-slapping and jubilant congratulations, the evening was also marked by a poignant undercurrent of sadness as well. "We'd gotten to really like each other," notes Reiner, "and—in some cases—adore each other. And then, suddenly, we were splitting up. We all cried a lot that night."

"We were all a little in shock," agrees Morey Amsterdam. "We knew we were breaking up a family."

"I don't think any of us realized how tough it was going to be to break it up," observes Ann Guilbert, who acknowledges that when the end of *The Dick Van Dyke Show* finally came, it took her—as it did most of the cast—

completely by surprise. For Guilbert, the first real pangs of regret had surfaced suddenly, and quite unexpectedly, only a few weeks earlier, during an informal lunch she shared with the rest of the show's cast at a local eatery near the studio. "Instead of going to the commissary for lunch," she reminisces, "we all went out to a restaurant that day." And it was there, as the actress took in the easy laughter and casual chatter that surrounded her at the table, that it suddenly struck her for the first time that the day was not far off when this remarkable group of people would no longer be together. "That was, for me, the beginning of really starting to miss the camaraderie. And, in little ways like that, it began to creep up on all of us that it really was ending."

And, says Guilbert, it was perhaps inevitable that the cast's mounting sadness would finally surface in the soft glow of the Hawaiian lanterns that illuminated the show's closing night party. "I think it sort of all came down that last night," she says. "Until that moment, I don't think any of us really realized that it really was, just...*over.*"

Perhaps hoping to stave off the moment of final departure, many of the show's cast members lingered at the closing-night party well after the throng of well-wishers had thinned out to only a hearty few. Although none of them wanted to be first to leave, Frank Adamo recalls, it was Richard Deacon who finally broke the spell when—unable to face the unbearable task of voicing individual farewells to each of his beloved friends and colleagues—he simply slipped away from the party unannounced. "Richard Deacon couldn't handle it, God bless him," recalls Adamo. "So he just walked away. That was his way of dealing with it."

In the moments that followed Deacon's quiet, dignified exit, the rest of the cast soon followed suit, each in his or her own fashion. Some slipped off, as Deacon had done, without saying a word, while others chose to make their departure in a hail of hugs and laughter. But either way, notes Frank Adamo, it was not an easy exit for any of them. "Everybody had a very difficult time saying goodbye to each other," the actor recalls. "A *very* difficult time."

Perhaps more difficult for some than others, notes Bill Persky, who maintains that, though the end of *The Dick Van Dyke Show* was an emotional event for all concerned, the prevailing emotions as the final curtain rang down were relief and celebration rather than tears and regret. "I think everyone realized they'd been a part of something special," he observes, "but, in my mind, there was not a lot of sadness. We were looking to the future. Most of us—certainly Dick and Mary and Carl and Sam and myself—when we came off that show had something big to go to. The feeling at the time was that the show had been wonderful. But, now, whatever came next was gonna be wonderful, too."

And yet, as those most intimately involved in the show's creation and execution would soon discover—Bill Persky among them—those five brilliant seasons of *The Dick Van Dyke Show* would be a very, very tough act to follow. "Only in retrospect," reflects Persky, "did we realize what a special time we had on the show. And that it was never gonna be recaptured."

EPILOGUE

ON MAY 16, 1992, MOREY AMSTERDAM, ROSE MARIE, MARY Tyler Moore, Dick Van Dyke, and Carl Reiner were reunited on the stage of Hollywood's Universal Amphitheatre for their first televised appearance together in twenty-six years. The occasion was Comic Relief V, the HBO cable network's fifth annual all-star comedy benefit to aid the homeless, and the cast of *The Dick Van Dyke Show* had been scheduled to appear as guests of honor. And although some of the biggest names in comedy were slated to appear on the Universal Amphitheatre's stage over the course of the four-hour event, the riotous ovation that greeted the entrance of television's Rob, Laura, Buddy, and Sally—along with their creator—left little doubt that they were indeed the evening's main event.

After the stunning spectacle of their entrance, the cast—perhaps wisely—remained low-key for the duration of their brief ceremonial appearance. Once the tumultuous applause finally died down, the company took center stage to volunteer a few sober remarks in support of the evening's worthy charitable cause. And then, with little more than a nod to the familiar characters with whom they'd become so closely identified over the last thirty years, they were gone.

As brief as it was, the Van Dyke show cast's appearance on Comic Relief V is probably as close as diehard fans of the series will ever come to a bona fide *Dick Van Dyke Show* reunion. After enduring countless requests that they stage a comeback, the show's producers and most of its surviving cast members have steadfastly insisted that they'd just as soon let Rob, Laura, Buddy, and Sally live on in the perpetual sheen of our black and

white memories. But, though Dick Van Dyke and his television family have thus far resisted all attempts to lure them back together for a formal reunion, they have come awfully close on at least a few occasions.

The idea of a Van Dyke show reunion was first broached as early as 1968, when Jerry Paris suggested it as a potential premise for Dick Van Dyke's second CBS special, which Paris directed. "At one point," Paris told a reporter in 1968, "some of us did think of doing an hour-long version of the old *Dick Van Dyke Show*. But Dick didn't want to do it this time."[67]

But despite Van Dyke's early resistance to the notion of a reunion, by the late seventies the actor's resolve had softened to the point where he did agree to revive Rob Petrie for a brief tongue-in-cheek send-up that he and Mary Tyler Moore performed as a sketch on the March 25, 1979, installment of *The Mary Tyler Moore Hour*. But other than that largely forgotten cameo appearance, none of the show's cast has been seriously tempted to revive the characters that they so lovingly brought to life more than three decades ago.

Though much has been made of the spectacular big-screen contracts that awaited Dick Van Dyke and Mary Tyler Moore after the Van Dyke show left the air in 1966, it's worth noting that life after *The Dick Van Dyke Show* was scarcely an ordeal for the other members of the show's acting ensemble, most of whom found no shortage of work waiting for them in the wake of the show's highly publicized demise.

Always popular with casting directors, Richard Deacon would continue to log an impressive array of credits in his post–Van Dyke show career, including continuing roles on *The Pruitts of Southampton, The Beverly Hillbillies,* and *The Mothers-in-Law.* Though Deacon invariably found himself cast in acerbic roles on screen, the character actor's offscreen kindnesses were legendary among members of Hollywood's acting community, many of whom would openly mourn the beloved character actor's passing in 1984, when he died unexpectedly at the age of sixty-two.

The years since *The Dick Van Dyke Show* have been no less kind to Ann Guilbert, who has racked up an equally substantial list of credits over the past few decades, including memorable guest appearances on *Dragnet, Barney Miller,* and *Newhart,* among dozens of other situation comedies, miniseries, and hour-long dramas. Guilbert also performed continuing roles on *Hey, Landlord!*—a 1966 series that was written and created by Jerry Belson and Garry Marshall—as well as on Andy Griffith's short-lived 1971 comeback series, *The New Andy Griffith Show.* Though the actress has chosen to focus her energies on her stage career in recent years, Guilbert was lured back to the small screen to play Theresa Fanelli, the matriarch on *The Fanelli Boys,* a situation comedy that had a brief run on NBC in the 1990-91 season.

Although Jerry Paris continued to accept occasional acting assignments until shortly before his untimely death in 1986, his activities as a director kept him far busier behind the cameras than in front of them in the years following *The Dick Van Dyke Show.* Though Paris directed a handful of feature films in the late sixties—including the Jerry Lewis vehicle *Don't Raise the Bridge, Lower the River; How Sweet It Is,* which starred Debbie Reynolds; and *The Grasshopper,* from a script by Jerry Belson—he would discover far more lasting success in television, where the director's long list of credits includes episodes of *The Mary Tyler Moore Show* and *The Odd Couple,* as well as a ten-and-a-half-year run as house director of *Happy Days*, which was created and produced by Garry Marshall. When *Happy Days* finally left the air in 1984, Jerry Paris returned to the feature-film arena. Sadly, the director had just completed work on his eighth film, *Police Academy 3*, when he died at the still relatively youthful age of sixty.

Unlike most of his Van Dyke show colleagues, child actor Larry Mathews chose to return to civilian life after the series folded up shop in 1966. After resuming his life as just another ordinary southern California kid, Larry Mazzeo reclaimed his given name and eventually graduated from UCLA with a degree in Theater Arts in 1976. Though Mazzeo has spent the better part of his adult career working behind the scenes in television production, he was briefly reunited with his TV dad not long ago, when the former child star contributed a cameo to *The Chairman's Choice*, a 1993 cable TV special that Dick Van Dyke hosted to promote reruns of *The Dick Van Dyke Show* on the popular *Nick at Nite* cable network.

In the years after the curtain rang down on *The Dick Van Dyke Show*, Morey Amsterdam remained ubiquitous on our home screens in countless guest star and supporting parts on comedy and variety shows, as well as in his frequent role as resident quipster on celebrity panel shows like *The Match Game* and *Hollywood Squares*. He was briefly reunited with Richard Deacon and Rose Marie for an episode of *The Love Boat*, and he also played opposite Rose Marie in a 1985 installment of Showtime's *Brothers*.* As fate would have it, the comedian was again paired with Rose Marie for what would prove to be his final appearance in prime time, when the two old friends were cast as a married couple on an episode of *Caroline in the City* that aired a few months before Amsterdam's death in 1996. In the wake of his passing, the legendary comic was eulogized by his show business peers in a loving—if irreverent—memorial service that Rose Marie insists was the funniest she ever attended. "Every comic in town was there," she recalls. "It was hilarious. And, you know, I'm pretty sure that's the way Morey would've wanted it."

After the Van Dyke show left the air in 1966, Rose Marie secured her reputation as one of TV's most reliable character players with a succession of comic and dramatic guest-starring roles on a wide array of episodic series, including *The Virginian, Hey, Landlord!, The Monkees, Kojak,*

---

*By odd coincidence. Ann Guilbert's youngest daughter, Hallie Todd, was one of the featured players on *Brothers*. Todd was, of course, the baby that Ann Guilbert was carrying during early episodes of *The Dick Van Dyke Show*.

and *Cagney and Lacey*, to name but a few. Like her old friend Morey Amsterdam, Rose Marie also found many years of profitable employment as one of the wisecracking stars of *The Hollywood Squares*, where she commanded her own cubicle from 1966 until well into the early 1980s.

The Dick Van Dyke Show's players were by no means the only members of the show's distinguished alumni to make good on the promise they demonstrated on the award-winning series. In the months after it was announced that *The Dick Van Dyke Show* would be shuttered, Bill Persky and Sam Denoff found themselves deluged with job offers to write for practically every half-hour series on television. But, after sizing up the various proposals, the team decided that the time had come for them to create a series of their own. The result of their subsequent brainstorms was *Good Morning World*, which finally premiered—with Sheldon Leonard and Carl Reiner as executive producers—on CBS in the fall of 1967. Based very loosely on Persky and Denoff's own early days in radio,

"We had so much fun," notes Dick Van Dyke, "that I knew even then that things would never get any better. And, as a matter of fact, they didn't."

the series—which bore distinct echoes of the Van Dyke show in both style and structure—featured Joby Baker and Ronnie Schell as a pair of early-morning LA disc jockeys.

Before the pair started work on *Good Morning World*, Persky and Denoff were also approached by Danny Thomas, who wanted the talented writer-producers to work up a series for his daughter Marlo, who was at that time still a struggling actress with very few credits. It was an assignment, explains Sam Denoff, that the team undertook only with great reluctance. "We weren't very familiar with Marlo's work," explains Denoff, "so when Danny said, 'Why don't you do a show for my daughter?,' we said, 'Uh...' As very often happens, we thought that *Good Morning World* would be the big hit."

But that was not to be the case. As it turned out, Marlo Thomas proved to be an exceptionally capable comic actress, and *That Girl*—the series that Persky and Denoff created to showcase those talents—would finally enjoy a prosperous run of five seasons on ABC. *Good Morning World*, on the other hand, debuted the following year on CBS and barely made it though the season, despite the presence of an equally winning actress named Goldie Hawn in the supporting cast. After *That Girl* finally left the air in 1971, Persky and Denoff would collaborate on a handful of other original half-hour comedies—including *Big Eddie*, *Lotsa Luck*, and *The Montefuscos*—though none of these would capture the spark of their earlier collaborations. Although Persky and Denoff amicably disbanded their durable partnership in the late seventies, Bill Persky resurfaced a few years later as executive producer of the popular and critically acclaimed CBS situation comedy *Kate and Allie*.

Sheldon Leonard was already well into his first season as executive producer of *I Spy* by the time the Van Dyke show wound to its inevitable end in 1966. After shepherding *I Spy* through three prime-time seasons, the executive producer finally turned his energies back to situation comedy in 1969, when he executive-produced *My World and Welcome to It* for NBC. A half-hour situation comedy based on the life and works of James Thurber, the series would be widely hailed for its innovative premise—though low ratings would force it off the air within the year. In 1975, the legendary producer returned once again to the half-hour form with *Big Eddie*, a situation comedy that would reunite Leonard with Bill Persky and Sam Denoff, who would create, write, and produce the short-lived series that brought Leonard back to prime time as an actor in the distinctly Runyonesque role of a reformed big-city gangster. When *Big*

Eddie was canceled after three months, Sheldon Leonard retired from television to devote himself to his family and his work with the Directors Guild. He died in 1997, having lived a long and wonderful life indeed.

The studio that Sheldon Leonard presided over during the glory days of *The Dick Van Dyke Show* is still in operation at 846 Cahuenga Boulevard, though these days it goes by a new name, the Ren-Mar Studios. And although the former Desilu Cahuenga studio has seen a few lean years—during one extended production slump in the early seventies, the lot actually functioned as a health club, its legendary soundstages reduced to light duty as indoor tennis and racquetball—courts the lot today is again one of the busiest production facilities in Hollywood. In recent years, the former Desilu soundstages have played host to a formidable list of long-running comedies, including *Soap*, *The Golden Girls*, and *Empty Nest*—all of which originated from the creative braintrust behind the Witt-Thomas-Harris production company, one of whose principals just happens to be Tony Thomas, son of Danny Thomas.

Still one of comedy's most prolific Renaissance men, Carl Reiner has enjoyed his most consistent employment in the years since the Van Dyke show as a director of big-screen comedies. Since inaugurating his movie directing career with *Enter Laughing* in 1967, Reiner has amassed an impressive list of credits that includes *The Comic*, *Where's Poppa?*, and *Oh, God!*, as well as most of Steve Martin's early film vehicles, including *The Jerk*, *The Man with Two Brains*, *Dead Men Don't Wear Plaid*, and *All of Me*. And yet, even with a resumé that's by now grown almost as thick as some small-town phone directories, Carl Reiner still points proudly to his five years as creator, writer, and producer of *The Dick Van Dyke Show* as the crowning achievement of a long and immensely rewarding career.

While most of the principal players in the Van Dyke show saga managed to forge long and successful careers after they left the series in 1966, few of them would claim many later accomplishments that might arguably rival the enormous impact of the Van Dyke show's five esteemed seasons. Not so Mary Tyler Moore, whose own 1970 comeback series would blaze a prime-time trail every bit as bright as that burned by its illustrious predecessor.

And yet, as Sam Denoff points out, the groundbreaking achievement of *The Mary Tyler Moore Show* owed no small debt to its star's formative years in the cast of *The Dick Van Dyke Show*. "The success of Mary's own series came as a result of her doing the Van Dyke show for five years," states Denoff, "and seeing how a well-run, homogeneous company should work." Grant Tinker, the former advertising executive who would mastermind his former wife's own series, as well as the vast MTM empire that would rise up in its wake, has long acknowledged that he kept the creative framework of the old Van Dyke show in the forefront of his mind when he assembled the creative team of actors, writers, and directors who would eventually sustain *The Mary Tyler Moore Show* through seven critically acclaimed seasons.

Mary Tyler Moore portrays associate news producer Mary Richards in an early seventies pose from *The Mary Tyler Moore Show*. "The success of Mary's own series came as a result of her doing the Van Dyke show for five years," says Sam Denoff, "and seeing how a well-run, homogeneous company should work."

But the magical chemistry that Mary Tyler Moore shared with her former Van Dyke show costar played an even more fundamental role in the actress's 1970 comeback. Indeed, there might never have been a *Mary Tyler Moore Show* at all had it not been for *Dick Van Dyke and the Other Woman*, the well-regarded 1969 CBS television special that reunited Van Dyke and his former TV wife for the first time since 1966. And, as the actress would no doubt be the first to admit, that providential reunion—and the creative rejuvenation that arose from their pairing—came not a moment too soon.

By 1969, Mary Tyler Moore's much-ballyhooed leap into feature films had proven to be a washout In the space of only three short years, the actress's once-promising career had somehow been stymied by a string of flops that included *Thoroughly Modern Millie*, *What's So Bad About Feeling Good*, and—the absolute nadir of her big-screen career—*Change of Habit*, an Elvis Presley vehicle that featured the actress in the unenviable role of a nun who's forced to choose between Elvis and the church. Nor had the actress fared much better when she ventured onto the Broadway stage in 1966, as the title character in *Holly Golightly*, a little-remembered musical retelling of Truman Capote's novella *Breakfast at Tiffany's*. And so, when Dick Van Dyke called to invite the star to join him for a one-shot reunion on his 1969 variety-show special, the actress was more than prepared to give the small screen another tumble.

It probably didn't hurt that *Dick Van Dyke and the Other Woman* also reunited the stars with writers Bill Persky and Sam Denoff, whose script for the special was perfectly tooled to show off the multitalented actress to her best advantage. That opinion was obviously shared by the executives at CBS, who wasted little time signing the actress to the contract that led directly to *The Mary Tyler Moore Show* in 1970. Seven years and a record number of Emmy Awards later, *The Mary Tyler Moore Show* left the air voluntarily—like its illustrious predecessor—as one of the most honored television series of its time.

By the time Mary Tyler Moore engineered her spectacular television comeback in 1970, Dick Van Dyke had reached a creative impasse of his own. Like his former costar, Van Dyke had been highly disillusioned by his own foray into the feature-film arena in the years following the Van Dyke show. After a promising start in features, the actor soon found himself bogged down in a long succession of largely undistinguished roles in films like *Fitzwilly*, *Lt. Robinson Crusoe*, and *Chitty Chitty Bang Bang*—none of which seemed to deliver even remotely on the promise that Dick Van Dyke had demonstrated so effortlessly week after week on his own series.

In fact, the star didn't find a truly suitable feature-film vehicle until 1969, when Carl Reiner brought him *The Comic*, the story of an aging silent-screen comedian that the writer—working with Van Dyke's old friend Aaron Ruben—had handcrafted for Dick Van Dyke. But despite its first-class creative pedigree, *The Comic* met with little more than a yawn at the box office. In the face of this latest resounding failure, Van Dyke began to eye the relative security of weekly television with a renewed interest.

And, after watching Mary Tyler Moore effect such a graceful transition back to the small screen in 1970, Dick Van Dyke was inspired to entertain offers for a comeback series of his own. The result was *The New Dick Van Dyke Show*, which reunited the star with his original TV mentor, Carl Reiner, who signed on to create, write, and produce the new series, just as he had the original. When the series premiered on Saturday, September 18, 1971—fittingly, in the time slot immediately preceding Mary Tyler Moore's own immensely popular half hour—television pundits predicted immediate and long-lasting success for the series. But, just three years later, it had become obvious to all concerned that *The New Dick Van Dyke Show* was not likely to rekindle the magic of the old, *Dick Van Dyke Show*, and the show quietly left the air at the end of the 1973 season.

Although Van Dyke has remained a highly visible presence on our home screens over the years, with scores of appearances in specials, guest shots, and the occasional TV movie—including his return to prime time in 1993's *Diagnosis: Murder*, which would lead to a series of the same name—the star would have little luck in traditional comedy settings. In 1976, he headlined *Van Dyke and Company*, an Emmy-winning variety show that had a brief run on NBC. Five years later, Van Dyke shot a pilot that never sold for a series called *Harry's Battles*, a proposed ABC situation comedy that would have paired the star with Connie Stevens had the show ever made it to the air. The star's luck wasn't much better when Grant Tinker teamed him with his son Barry for *The Van Dyke Show*, a troubled CBS situation comedy that ran for a few months in 1988. Ironically, none of the star's latter-day comeback attempts would finally generate nearly the excitement that greeted the return of his original series to national prominence as part of cable TV's *Nick at Nite* lineup in February 1992.

But if Dick Van Dyke has found it increasingly difficult to step out of Rob Petrie's shadow in recent years, the star today seems almost cheerfully, resigned to the fact that—whatever else he has done or may do—he will always be identified, first and foremost, with the series that bears his name. In fact, a few weeks after *Nick at Nite* added Van Dyke's vintage series to its schedule, the popular rerun network elevated the star to the status of elder statesman when they drafted him to portray *Nick at Nite's* ceremonial "Chairman of the Board" in an entertaining series of on-air promotional spots. Almost immediately, the star's smiling countenance would once more become synonymous with quality television, as Van Dyke introduced the distinct charms of *The Dick Van Dyke Show* to a new generation of viewers, many of whom had not even been born when the series first premiered in the dark ages of the early 1960s.

When *The Dick Van Dyke Show* voluntarily ceased production in 1966, the series was already being hailed as a modern television classic, a lone beacon of light in the vast wasteland of early sixties television. The show's unique blend of wit and warmth would prove beyond any argument that a situation comedy could be sophisticated and urbane—and still deliver a sizable audience. In the space of only five years, Carl Reiner and his company of actors, writers, and fellow producers had succeeded in creating a work of such consistent intelligence and invention that it would set a new standard for quality television—a standard that still serves as a benchmark for primetime comedy to this day. As few television shows had done before, and very few have done since, *The Dick Van Dyke Show* would forever alter the way we watch television.

Although the Van Dyke show may be long gone, the magic that was shared by a loving company of friends on a tiny Hollywood back lot more than thirty years ago will always be with us, if only in reruns. And there, captured for all eternity in crisp images of black and white, the often strange and always wonderful world of *The Dick Van Dyke Show* will no doubt continue to delight audiences for as long as there are television sets on which to tune it in—and people willing to share in the laughter.

Perhaps Morey Amsterdam summed it up best when he addressed a group of fans at a television seminar in Los Angeles some twenty years after the series ceased production. Toward the end of the evening, someone asked the character actor if working on *The Dick Van Dyke Show* for all those years had really been as much fun as it appeared. The aging performer leaned back in his chair and smiled before finally tendering an answer. Then, after a brief pause, he leaned forward again, suddenly beaming. "It was," he intoned, "like going to a lovely party that you never wanted to end."[68]

THE DICK VAN DYKE SHOW LOG
A COMPLETE VIEWER'S GUIDE
TO ALL 158 EPISODES OF
THE DICK VAN DYKE SHOW
including the Pilot Film for Head of the Family

Regular Cast and Characters:

Rob (Robert) Simpson Petrie	Dick Van Dyke
Laura Meeker/Meehan Petrie	Mary Tyler Moore
Ritchie (Richard) Rosebud Petrie	Larry Mathews
Sally Rogers	Rose Marie
Buddy (Maurice) B. Sorrell	Morey Amsterdam
Mel (Melvin) Cooley	Richard Deacon
Dr. Jerry (Gerald) Helper	Jerry Paris
Millie (Mildred) Krumbermacher Helper	Ann Morgan Guilbert
Alan Lester Brady	Carl Reiner

Supporting Cast and Characters:

Stacey Petrie (Rob's brother)	Jerry Van Dyke
Herman Glimsher	Bill Idelson
Sol Pomeroy	Marty Ingels (1961–1962)
Sam Pomerantz (Sol in later episodes)	Henry Calvin (1963), Allan Melvin (1963–1966)
Pickles (Fiona) Conway Sorrell	Barbara Perry (1961–1962), Joan Shawlee (1963)
Edward Petrie (Rob's father)	Will Wright (1961)
Sam Petrie (Rob's father)	J. Pat O'Malley (1962, 1964), Tom Tully (1964, 1966)
Clara Petrie (Rob's mother)	Carol Veazie (1961), Isabel Randolph (1962, 1964, 1966)
Alan Meehan (Laura's father)	Carl Benton Reid
Mrs. Meehan (Laura's mother)	Geraldine Wall
Freddie William Helper	Peter Oliphant
Ellen Helper	Jennifer Gillespie (1961), Anne Marie Hediger (1962)

Stock Players:

Frank Adamo, Eleanor Audley, Arthur Batanides, Tiny Brauer, Jane Dulo, Ross Elliott, Jamie Farr, Herbie Faye, Bernard Fox, Dabbs Greer, Jerry Hausner, Peter Hobbs, Jackie Joseph, Ray Kellogg, Sandy Kenyon, Ken Lynch, Allan Melvin, Isabel Randolph, Patty Regan, Bert Remsen, Johnny Silver, Doris Singleton, Amzie Strickland, Herb Vigran, Geraldine Wall, Len Weinrib, Howard Wendell, Valerie Yerke

1958–1960
THE *HEAD OF THE FAMILY* PILOT

The pilot film for Carl Reiner's *Dick Van Dyke Show* prototype is filmed—with Reiner himself in the lead—a few weeks before Christmas 1958 at New York's Gold Medal Studios.

Complete Credits:

Written and Created by	Carl Reiner
Produced by	Stuart Rosenberg and Martin Poll
Directed by	Don Weis
Music Composed and Conducted by	Bernard Green
Director of Photography	Charles Harten
Film Editor	Angelo Ross
Sound by	Edward J. Johnstone
Art Director	Leo Kerz
Production Manager	Anthony LaMarca
Sound Editor	A. H. Pesetsky

Pilot) **Head of the Family** Airdate: 7/19/60
WRITER: Carl Reiner / DIRECTOR: Don Weis

Cast: Robert Petrie—Carl Reiner, Laura Petrie—Barbara Britton, Ritchie—Gary
Morgan, Sally Rogers—Sylvia Miles, Buddy Sorrell—Morty Gunty, Allan
Sturdy—Jack Wakefield, "Snappy," The Snappy Service Delivery Man—Milton Kamen, Mrs. Harley—Jean Sincere, Teacher—Nancy Kenyon, Roy—Joey
Trent, Freddie—Mannie Sloan

Filmed in December 1958.

Television writer Robert Petrie is determined to convince his son the value of
comedy writing after he discovers that the six-year-old is embarrassed to tell his
friends what his father does for a living.

Behind the scenes: The unsold *Head of the Family* pilot was originally aired at
9:30 P.M. on Tuesday, July 19, 1960, on *Comedy Spot*, a CBS anthology series that
served as a clearing house for unsold TV pilots...Director Don Weis would later
distinguish himself as a house director on some of TV's classiest comedies, including *The Andy Griffith Show* and *M*A*S*H*...In the late 1980s, New York's Museum of Broadcasting—now the Museum of Television and Radio—added a copy of
Carl Reiner's personal 16mm print of the *Head of the Family* pilot to their permanent collection. But, according to Carl Reiner's longtime friend and manager
George Shapiro, that print—which at the time was thought to be the only surviving copy of Reiner's historic telefilm—very nearly didn't make it to the museum at
all. As Shapiro describes it, the night before he was set to drop off the film, he discovered—to his absolute horror—that his car had been stolen, with Carl Reiner's
irreplaceable pilot film in the trunk! "I can't tell you how upset I was," Shapiro
recalls. "I didn't care about the car. I would have made a deal to leave the car
stolen—plus my next *five* cars—just to get that film back!" Shapiro assumed that
his worst fears had been realized when the police called a few days later to report
that they'd recovered his car—or what was left of it. "It was found abandoned and
stripped," remembers Shapiro. "I never saw such a stripped car. They even stripped
the bumpers off! I had old jackets and towels in the trunk. And they took the towels! They took everything in sight." Or almost everything, as Shapiro discovered
once he finally gathered the courage to peek into the ravaged car's trunk. "But
there, in the bottom of the trunk, was the film!" he says. "It was the *only* thing left
in the whole car! They took my dirty towels—but they left that little 16mm film
case!" After that scare, Shapiro admits that he was loath to let the film out of his
sight. "I slept with it next to me until they picked it up and took it to the Museum
of Broadcasting. And only then did I tell Carl what had happened."

WINTER 1961
THE DICK VAN DYKE SHOW PILOT
"The Sick Boy and the Sitter"

The pilot episode for the revamped *Dick Van Dyke Show* is filmed—with Dick Van Dyke installed in the role of Rob Petrie—on January 20, 1961, at Hollywood's Desilu Cahuenga Studios.

Complete Credits:

Written, Created, and Produced by	Carl Reiner
Directed by	Sheldon Leonard
Associate Producer	Ronald Jacobs
Music Composed and Conducted by	Earle Hagen
Director of Photography	Robert DeGrasse
Art Director	Kenneth A. Reid
Film Editor	Leon Selditz
Production Manager	Frank Meyers
Assistant Director	Jay Sandrich
Production Supervisor	W. Argyle Nelson
Prop Master	Stuart Stevenson
Camera Coordinator	James Niver
Casting	Ruth Burch
Script Continuity	Rosemary Dorsey
Set Decorator	Ken Swartz
Rerecording Editor	Edward Sandlin
Recorded by	Glen Glenn Sound Co.
Costumes	Harald Johnson
Makeup	Lee Greenway
Hairstylist	Irma Kusely
Sound Engineer	David Forrest
Music Coordinator	Walter Popp
Executive Producer	Sheldon Leonard in association with Danny Thomas

Mr. Van Dyke's Wardrobe Furnished by Botany 500

1) The Sick Boy and the Sitter Airdate: 10/3/61
WRITER: Carl Reiner / DIRECTOR: Sheldon Leonard

Supporting cast: Mel Cooley—Richard Deacon, Dottie—Barbara Eiler, Woman at Party—Eleanor Audley, Janie—Mary Lee Dearing, Sam—Michael Keith, Dr. Miller—Stacey Keach, Sr., Man at Party—Fred Sherman

Filmed on January 20, 1961. Songs: "The Sidewalks of New York" (Lawlor, Blake); "Hello, Hello" (Amsterdam); "I Wish I Could Sing Like Durante" (Wyle, Pola)

Rob talks Laura into going to a party at Alan Brady's penthouse, even though she'd rather stay home and look after their ailing five-year-old.

Episode 1, "The Sick Boy and the Sitter."

1961–1962
THE DICK VAN DYKE SHOW
Season One

The triumphs and struggles of TV writer Rob Petrie and his wife Laura are chronicled in a first season of exceptional scripts written or supervised by Carl Reiner, who will shepherd the series through its first three seasons as the show's triple-threat head writer, story consultant and producer. Sheldon Leonard serves as executive producer throughout each of the show's five seasons, and Ron Jacobs is associate producer for the entire run. And, as of the show's third episode, John Rich would climb on board as the show's regular director.

First Season Credits:

Created and Produced by	Carl Reiner
Associate Producer	Ronald Jacobs
Music	Earle Hagen
Director of Photography	Robert DeGrasse, A.S.C.
Art Director	Kenneth A. Reid
Film Editor	Bud Molin, A.C.E.
Production Manager	Frank Meyers
Assistant Director	(episodes #1–2)Jay Sandrich
	(episodes #3–30) John C. Chulay
Production Supervisor	W. Argyle Nelson
Prop Master	Glenn Ross
Camera Coordinator	James Niver
Casting	Ruth Burch
Script Continuity	Marjorie Mullen
Set Decorator	Ken Swartz
Rerecording Editor	Edward Sandlin
Recorded by	Glen Glenn Sound Co.
Story Consultant	Carl Reiner
Costumes	Harald Johnson
Makeup	Tom Tuttle
Hair	Elenore Edwards
Sound Engineer	Cam McCulloch
Music Coordinator	Walter Popp
Executive Producer	Sheldon Leonard in association with Danny Thomas

Dick Van Dyke's Wardrobe Furnished by Botany 500
Women's Fashions provided by Fabiola by David Barr, Lill-Ann,
William Pearson, Ann Arnold of Beverly Hills, and Gino Paoli

2) The Meershatz Pipe Airdate: 11/28/61
Writer: Carl Reiner / Director: Sheldon Leonard

Supporting Cast: Mel Cooley—Richard Deacon, Elevator Operator—Jon Silo, Alan Brady—Carl Reiner (uncredited voice-over)

Filmed on June 20, 1961.

Rob frets over his job security after Buddy and Sally prove themselves perfectly capable of polishing off an entire script in his absence.

Behind the Scenes: Carl Reiner makes his first appearance as Alan Brady in an uncredited off-screen voice-over that can be heard near the end of this episode...Sharp-eyed viewers will note evidence of a bit of minor on-set mischief in the short scene that takes place in the hallway outside the writers' room, where a sign listing the floor's other tenants can be glimpsed—a roster that includes the show's prop master, Glenn Ross, as well as the show's set decorator, who appears on the address plate as Ken Swartz, MD.

3) Jealousy! Airdate: 11/7/61
Writer: Carl Reiner / Director: Sheldon Leonard

Supporting Cast: Mel—Richard Deacon, Jerry—Jerry Paris, Millie—Ann Morgan Guilbert, Valerie Blake—Joan Staley

Filmed on June 27, 1961. Songs "Say Goodbye for Charlie Jones" (Amsterdam)

Laura's jealousy gets the better of her when Rob starts working late hours with a gorgeous guest star of *The Alan Brady Show*.

Behind the Scenes: This landmark episode marks the first appearance of Rob and Laura's next-door neighbors, dentist Jerry Helper and his wife Millie.

4) Sally and the Lab Technician Airdate: 10/17/61
Writer: Carl Reiner / Director: John Rich

Supporting Cast: Thomas Edson—Eddie Firestone, Charlie, the Snappy Service Man—Jamie Farr

Filmed on July 5, 1961.

Laura plays matchmaker for Sally—with disastrous results—when she pairs the talkative comedy writer with her shy cousin, Thomas, the pharmacist.

Behind the Scenes: The first episode directed by John Rich, who would be a series mainstay for the better part of the show's first two years...This episode also introduced *The Alan Brady Show*'s secretary, Marge—named after Dick Van Dyke's real-life wife—who would remain an offstage presence throughout the show's run...Jamie Farr makes the first of a handful of appearances in the bit role of *The Alan Brady Show*'s coffee man. The actor would achieve far greater prominence a decade later, when a similar bit role he played on an episode of *M*A*S*H* blossomed into eleven seasons as the cross-dressing Corporal Klinger on CBS's long-running antiwar comedy.

5) Washington vs. the Bunny Airdate: 10/24/61
WRITER: Carl Reiner / DIRECTOR: John Rich

Supporting Cast: Mel—Richard Deacon, Man on Plane—Jesse White, Snappy
  Service Man—Jamie Farr

Filmed on July 11, 1961. Song: "You're the Top" (Porter)

Rob is plagued by fatherly guilt when he's forced to take a business trip on the
night of Ritchie's debut as a bunny in the school play.

Behind the Scenes: Carl Reiner confesses that his rationale for inserting a dream
sequence in this episode—in which Rob imagines Laura, dressed in a bunny suit,
haranguing him for parental malfeasance—was purely prurient. "I did that because
I wanted to see Mary's legs in a bunny suit," he admits...Dick Van Dyke's on-set
stand-in, Frank Adamo, is briefly visible as one of the passengers on Rob's air-
plane—it would be the first of many cameo appearances from the show's most frequently seen bit player.

Episode 5 "Washington vs. the Bunny."

6) Oh How We Met the Night That We Danced Airdate: 10/31/61
WRITER: Carl Reiner / DIRECTOR: Robert Butler

Supporting Cast: Sol—Marty Ingels, Mark Mullen—Glenn Turnbull, Marcia
Rochelle—Chickee James, Ellen Helper—Jennifer Gillespie, Dancer—Pat
Tribble (uncredited)

Filmed on July 18, 1961. Songs: "You, Wonderful You" (Warren, Brooks, Chaplin); "French-Fried Blues" (Hagen)

Rob recalls his frustrated attempts to date Laura when she was a USO showgirl
and he was an overeager staff sergeant in the army's special services division.

Behind the Scenes: The first of many flashback episodes that would trace the
continuing saga of Rob and Laura's courtship, this was also one of the few Van
Dyke show episodes to be filmed without so much as a token appearance from
Buddy and Sally...Rob's wife-to-be is introduced as Laura Meeker, a behind-the-
scenes reference to Mary Tyler Moore's then-husband Richard Meeker...Rob's side-
kick, Sol, was based on Carl Reiner's real-life army chum, Sol Pomerantz, a name
that would pop up—often with slight variation—throughout the life of the series.

Episode 6, "Oh, How
We Met the Night
That We Danced."

7) The Unwelcome Houseguest Airdate: 11/21/61
WRITER: Carl Reiner / DIRECTOR: Robert Butler

Filmed on July 25, 1961. Song: "Brahms' Lullaby" (arranged by Hagen)

Laura's plans for a quiet weekend in the country are spoiled when Buddy suckers Rob into looking after his family pet, a giant German shepherd named Larry.

8) Harrison B. Harding of Camp Crowder, Mo. Airdate: 11/6/61
WRITER: Carl Reiner / DIRECTOR: John Rich

Supporting Cast: Harrison B. Harding—Allan Melvin, Evelyn Harding—June Dayton, Police Officer #27809—Peter Leeds

Filmed on August 1, 1961.

Rob is too embarrassed to confess that he can't recall ever having met a mysterious stranger who arrives at his house claiming to be an old army pal.

*Behind the Scene*s: By coincidence, character actor Allan Melvin would later appear as Rob's army buddy Sol Pomerantz in numerous subsequent episodes. Melvin had previously held down a long-running role as one of Sergeant Bilko's recruits on *The Phil Silvers Show*, and would eventually log numerous appearances as one of Jim Nabors's barracks buddies on the long-running *Gomer Pyle, USMC*. The popular character actor would also play Sam the butcher on *The Brady Bunch*, as well as Archie Bunker's friend Barney Hefner on later seasons of *All in the Family* and its spin-off, *Archie Bunker's Place*...Character actor Peter Leeds's unnamed police officer would return to the show for a second bit part, as Officer Jack Bain, in episode #18, "Punch Thy Neighbor."

9) The Blonde-Haired Brunette Airdate: 10/10/61
WRITER: Carl Reiner / DIRECTOR: John Rich

Supporting Cast: Millie—Ann Morgan Guilbert; Pharmacist—Benny Rubin

Filmed on August 15, 1961.

Laura dyes her hair blond in an ill-conceived effort to rekindle Rob's interest after she becomes convinced that the romance has faded from their marriage.

Behind the Scenes: Though it was originally filmed as the series' ninth show, the producers scheduled this episode to be broadcast as the second show in order to better spotlight the rapidly emerging talents of Mary Tyler Moore.

10) Forty-Four Tickets Airdate: 12/5/61
WRITER: Carl Reiner / DIRECTOR: John Rich

Supporting Cast: Mel—Richard Deacon, Jerry—Jerry Paris, Millie—Ann Morgan
Guilbert, Mrs. Billings—Eleanor Audley, Cop—Paul Bryar, Scalper—Opal
Euard, Man in Battered Hat—Joe Devlin, Usher—Frank Adamo (uncredited)

Filmed on August 22, 1961.

Rob turns to scalpers as a last resort after he forgets to reserve forty-four *Alan
Brady Show* tickets for a PTA group from Ritchie's school.

11) To Tell or Not to Tell Airdate: 11/14/61
WRITER: David Adler / DIRECTOR: John Rich

Supporting Cast: Mel—Richard Deacon, Snappy Service Man—Jamie Farr

Filmed on August 29, 1961. Songs: "You Gotta Start Off Each Day with a
Smile" (Amsterdam); "Mambo Jambo" (Prado)

Rob worries that Laura might be tempted back into show business after Mel
offers the former USO hoofer an opportunity to fill in for an ailing dancer on *The
Alan Brady Show*.

Behind the Scenes: The first of three Van Dyke show scripts written by the pseu-
donymous David Adler, the pen name of Frank Tarloff, a writer Carl Reiner first
met in the Catskills in the early forties. Unable to work under his own name after
he defied the House Un-American Activities Committee in the early fifties, Tarloff
had found a good living writing—under his assumed name—for *The Danny Thomas
Show* and other comedies produced by Sheldon Leonard on the Desilu lot. Adler
tells a fascinating story about the difficulties he had concocting a comedy-writing
pseudonym after Leonard requested that the writer find himself a nom de plume
that would attract as little attention as possible. "I struggled for a new name," recalls
Tarloff. "Not an easy thing really." He initially settled on the rather fanciful pen
name of Erik Shepard, though the writer today insists that Sheldon Leonard rejected that one on the grounds that it simply didn't sound Jewish enough to be convincing. "At that time almost all comedy writers were Jewish," Tarloff explains.
"So Sheldon told me to forget Erik Shepard, and to find a name that sounds like
every other comedy writer—a Jewish name! So I came up with David Adler. And
that one got through without a question." Though Tarloff would be one of the few
Van Dyke show freelancers to exhibit any real promise in the show's early days, the
writer's tenure on the show would finally be curtailed by his decision to leave the
country in pursuit of the more favorable job climate that existed in Great Britain
in the early sixties.

12) Sally Is a Girl Airdate: 12/19/61
WRITER: David Adler / DIRECTOR: John Rich

Supporting Cast: Mel—Richard Deacon, Ted Harris—Paul Tripp, Pickles—Barbara Perry, Snappy Service Man—Jamie Farr

Filmed on September 5, 1961.

Buddy and Mel jump to hasty conclusions after Rob suddenly starts treating Sally like a lady.

Behind the Scenes: This episode features a rare on-screen appearance by Buddy's wife, Pickles, who—despite the efforts of two different actresses to breathe life into the character—would finally prove far more durable as an off-screen presence...Speaking in the pages of the December 1981 issue of *American Film Magazine*, Carl Reiner recounted a salty anecdote involving Selma Diamond that may well have served as the inspiration for this episode. Recalling the outspoken actress and *Caesar's Hour* writer who would serve as his primary model for Sally Rogers, Reiner said, "Selma Diamond is the one who actually said one day in a writers' conference, 'Why don't we go out and find some girls and get laid?' She's not a lesbian. She just said it because she felt like one of the guys."

Episode 12,
"Sally Is a Girl";
Rose Marie and
Paul Tripp.

13) Empress Carlotta's Necklace Airdate: 12/12/61
WRITER: Carl Reiner / DIRECTOR: James Komack

Supporting Cast: Mel—Richard Deacon, Jerry—Jerry Paris, Millie—Ann Morgan
   Guilbert, Maxwell—Gavin MacLeod, Edward Petrie—Will Wright, Mrs.
   Petrie—Carol Veazie

Filmed on September 12, 1961.

Rob surprises Laura with an unexpected gift—a thoroughly tasteless necklace
that she's loath to wear in public.

Behind the Scenes: This episode marks one of the earliest directorial efforts of
James Komack, who would enjoy his greatest success in the seventies, when he
would produce a long string of popular TV comedies including *The Courtship of
Eddie's Father*, *Welcome Back, Kotter*, and *Chico and the Man*, among
others...Guest star Gavin MacLeod would also discover far greater fame in seventies television. In 1970, the actor began a seven-year run as *The Mary Tyler Moore
Show*'s quick-witted newswriter, Murray Slaughter, a role that the actor would follow up with a nine-year stint as *The Love Boat*'s genial skipper, Captain Merrill
Stubing.

14) Buddy, Can You Spare a Job? Airdate: 12/26/61
WRITER: Walter Kempley / DIRECTOR: James Komack

Supporting Cast: Mel—Richard Deacon, Jackie Brewster—Len Weinrib

Filmed on September 19, 1961.

After Buddy's plan to desert *The Alan Brady Show* for greener pastures backfires, Rob and Sally face the difficult task of convincing Mel to let him return.

Behind the Scenes: According to Carl Reiner, the part of insult-comic Jackie
Brewster had originally been conceived for Don Rickles, who finally turned out to
be unavailable the week the episode was filmed. The part was then offered to nightclub comic Shecky Greene, who actually rehearsed the role for three days before
personal problems forced him to back out as well, just two days before the episode
was to be shot. Finally, at his wit's end, the producer called in Len Weinrib, a young
comic actor Reiner had first spied in the company of *The Billy Barnes Revue*—a
casting decision that proved most fortuitous. "We put Lennie on his marks and he
learned it overnight," recalls Reiner. "And he was sensational." In an ironic postscript, the producer remembers that after the show finally aired, he actually got a
complaint from Shecky Greene. "I get a call from Shecky," recalls Reiner. "I'm
sure he's going to say, 'Gee, you know, it turned out good anyway.' But he says,
'You stole some of my lines!'" According to Reiner, the lines in question had been
an ad lib that Greene added during his three days of rehearsal on the show—a script
improvement that Reiner naturally assumed was fair game after the actor voluntarily walked away from the role. "I couldn't believe it," notes Reiner. "I thought
he was joking. I said, 'What?' And he says, 'You stole a line from me!'"...This
episode would mark the final appearance of the original fanfare arrangement of

the show's opening theme song. Beginning with the next episode, the more familiar "three-chord" arrangement of *The Dick Van Dyke Show* theme song—which had until then been heard exclusively under the show's end titles—would be moved to the top of the show as well.

15) Who Owes Who What? Airdate: 1/24/62
WRITER: Carl Reiner / DIRECTOR: John Rich

Supporting Cast: Mel—Richard Deacon, Jerry—Jerry Paris, Fight Announcer— Carl Reiner (uncredited voice-over)

Filmed on October 10, 1961.

Buddy remains oblivious to Rob's efforts to collect an old debt.

16) Sol and the Sponsor Airdate: 4/11/62
WRITER: Walter Kempley / DIRECTOR: John Rich

Supporting Cast: Sol Pomeroy—Marty Ingels, Henry Bermont—Roy Roberts, Mrs. Bermont—Isabel Randolph, Arlene—Patty Regan

Filmed on October 17, 1961. Songs: "Frère Jacques" (traditional); "You, Wonderful You" (Warren, Brooks, Chaplin)

Rob can't quite bring himself to tell a boisterous old army buddy that he's not welcome at a fancy dinner party that the Petries are hosting to impress one of Rob's sponsors.

Behind the Scenes: This would be the second and final Van Dyke show appearance of Marty Ingels, who departed the recurring role of Sol Pomeroy to costar with John Astin in *I'm Dickens, He's Fenster*, a short-lived ABC sitcom that would premiere the following September. Allan Melvin would assume the role of Rob's army pal in later episodes.

17) The Curious Thing About Women Airdate: 1/10/62
WRITER: David Adler / DIRECTOR: John Rich

Supporting Cast: Jerry—Jerry Paris, Millie—Ann Morgan Guilbert, Delivery Man—Frank Adamo, Alan Brady—Carl Reiner (uncredited voice-over)

Filmed on October 24, 1961.

Unable to control her curiosity, Laura can't resist opening a mysterious package that arrives addressed to Rob—an act of impetuousness that she comes to regret shortly after she discovers that the parcel actually contains a large, self-inflating life raft.

Behind the Scenes: Writing once again under the pen name of David Adler, Frank Tarloff based his script for this episode on a remarkably similar idea he and fellow writers Arthur Stander and Phil Sharp had worked up almost a decade earlier for the December 3, 1952, episode of the Joan Davis sitcom *I Married Joan*...Though no reference was made to it in the episode, actress Ann Guilbert was actually seven months pregnant when this show was filmed—a condition, she reports, that caused her no small amount of discomfort when she filmed the show's closing scene, in which Millie and Jerry are supposed to laugh uproariously after they discover Laura with the fully inflated life raft. "Jerry and I came in and didn't say anything," recalls Guilbert, "'cause we were just supposed to get into hysterical laughter. But it's very hard to laugh like that when you're seven months pregnant!"

18) **Punch Thy Neighbor** Airdate: 1/17/62
WRITER: Carl Reiner / DIRECTOR: John Rich

Supporting Cast: Jerry—Jerry Paris, Millie—Ann Morgan Guilbert, Officer Jack Bain—Peter Leeds, Vinny, the Milkman—Jerry Hausner, Freddie—Peter Oliphant, Singing Telegram Man—Frank Adamo

Filmed on November 1, 1961. Song: "Twinkle, Twinkle, Little Star" (traditional, arrangement by Hagen)

Rob gets miffed when Jerry begins broadcasting his low opinion of *The Alan Brady Show* throughout the neighborhood.

Behind the Scenes: When Rob deciphers the acronymical name of Alan Brady's production company, Jeffgregbarbloubenraypolly Productions, he reveals the following elusive, if utterly useless, data on his employer's personal life: Jeff and Greg are Alan Brady's kids; his wife's name is Barb; Ben is his lawyer; Ray is his brother; Lou, his manager; and Polly, it turns out, is the name of Alan Brady's parrot.

19) **Where Did I Come From?** Airdate: 1/3/62
WRITER: Carl Reiner / DIRECTOR: John Rich

Supporting Cast: Mel—Richard Deacon, Millie—Ann Morgan Guilbert, Willie, the Coffee Man—Herbie Faye, Charlie, the Laundry Man—Jerry Hausner, Cabbie—Tiny Brauer, Dry Cleaning Man—Frank Adamo

Filmed on November 8, 1961.

Rob recalls the final frantic days of Laura's pregnancy—a tumultuous time that culminated with her arrival at the maternity ward in a laundry truck.

Behind the Scenes: "Bedlam," is how Rose Marie describes the conditions that surrounded the shooting of the climactic scene where Rob convinces Buddy to surrender his trousers to him. "When Buddy took off his pants," she says, "the audience went crazy." As the actress recalls, the ovation was so sustained that her topper line—"Isn't anybody gonna ask me to turn around?"—was completely lost in the din. "I held it as long as I could," she says, "and then I finally just threw away the line." Director John Rich was forced to shoot the scene a second time just to get a clear take of Rose Marie's line—and it was this take that finally made it into the finished episode. In spite of the confusion that attended its shooting, John Rich cites this episode as among the series' best. "That," says the director, "was my all-time favorite show."

20) The Boarder Incident Airdate: 2/14/62
WRITERS: Norm Liebmann and Ed Haas / DIRECTOR: John Rich

Filmed on November 14, 1961.

Rob invites Buddy to spend a few days at his house while Pickles is out of town.

Behind the Scenes: Co-writer Norm Liebmann had been friendly with Dick Van Dyke since the late fifties, when the scribe served as a staff writer for *Flair*, a short radio program that Van Dyke recorded for daily broadcast during the late fifties and early sixties.

21) A Word a Day Airdate: 2/7/62
WRITER: Jack Raymond / DIRECTOR: John Rich

Supporting Cast: Mel—Richard Deacon, Rev. Kirk—William Schallert, Mrs. Kirk— Lia Waggner

Filmed on November 29, 1961.

Rob and Laura are disturbed to discover that Ritchie's vocabulary has suddenly expanded to include a small glossary of four-letter words.

Behind the Scenes: Guest star William Schallert's on-screen spouse is played by his real-life wife, Lia Waggner.

Episode 21, "A Word a Day."

22) The Talented Neighborhood Airdate: 1/31/62
WRITER: Carl Reiner / DIRECTOR: John Rich

Supporting Cast: Mel—Richard Deacon, Jerry—Jerry Paris, Mrs. Kendall—Doris
Singleton, Mr. Mathias—Ken Lynch, Martin Mathias—Michael Davis, Kenneth
Kendall—Jack Davis, Phillip Mathias—Barry Livingston, Ellen Helper—Anne
Marie Hediger, Cynthia—Ilana Dowding, Annie Mathias—Kathleen Green,
Frankie—Christian Van Dyke, Florian—Barry Van Dyke, Neighborhood
Child—Cornell Chulay (uncredited), Alan Brady—Carl Reiner (uncredited
voice-over)

Filmed on December 6, 1961. Songs: "America, the Beautiful" (traditional); "La
Ci Darem La Mano" (Mozart)

Rob is besieged by would-be child stars and their pushy stage mothers after Alan
Brady announces a juvenile talent competition on his show.

Behind the Scenes: Dick Van Dyke's two young sons—Barry and Chris—have
bit parts as neighborhood children, as does assistant director John Chulay's daughter, Cornell. Also recognizable in the show's large juvenile cast is young Barry Livingston, who would shortly land the long-running part of Ernie Douglas on *My
Three Sons.*

23) Father of the Week Airdate: 2/21/62
WRITERS: Arnold and Lois Peyser / DIRECTOR: John Rich

Supporting Cast: Mel—Richard Deacon, Mrs. Given—Isabel Randolph, Allan—
Allan Fielder, Floyd Harper—Patrick Thompson, Candy—Cornell Chulay

Filmed on December 12, 1961.

Rob is crushed to discover that Ritchie has been putting off inviting him to speak
to his class on career day because the boy is afraid that his father might embarrass
him.

Behind the Scenes: At first glance, this episode appears to be little more than a
rewrite of Carl Reiner's pilot script for *Head of the Family.* But, according to co-
writer Arnold Peyser, the episode's genesis was not nearly so simple. The premise
came to him, he recalls, after he organized a father-of-the-week tribute for the scout
troop that his two sons belonged to. Peyser was gratified when all of the boys in
the group seemed more than happy to invite their fathers to describe what they did
for a living—with the curious exception of a boy named Peter Nye, who happened
to be the son of the well-known entertainer Louis Nye. "He was always saying that
his father had a cold," recalls Peyser, "or that Louis was going out of town." After
three or four weeks of these excuses, says the writer, the poignant truth dawned
on him and his wife, Lois, who would finally co-write the episode with him. "I realized that Peter was embarrassed," the writer continues. "He didn't know what his
father might do. And he was afraid that everybody would laugh at him. And we
thought that might make a good story." When the writers brought the idea to Carl
Reiner as a possible Van Dyke show premise, the producer snapped it up. It was
Carl Reiner's inspiration to meld the Peysers' storyline with the plot of his *Head of*

the Family pilot, and to add the ending in which Rob offers the kids in Ritchie's class an impromptu comedy lesson, a slapstick sequence that would prove a perfect complement for Van Dyke's physical abilities. "It was the same story," says Reiner, comparing "Father of the Week" with his earlier *Head of the Family* pilot. "But Dick doing a show for the kids was so much better," he concludes, "because we knew Dick would add things to it, even if it wasn't in the script, and make it his."

24) The Twizzle Airdate: 2/28/62
WRITER: Carl Reiner / DIRECTOR: John Rich

Supporting Cast: Mel—Richard Deacon, Randy "Twizzle" Eisenbauer—Jerry Lanning, Mr. Eisenbauer—Jack Albertson, Counter boy—Tony Stag; Freddie Blassie—himself

Filmed on January 9, 1962. Songs: "The Twizzle" (David, Livingston); "This Nearly Was Mine" (Rodgers, Hammerstein)

Sally drags Mel and the writing staff to a bowling alley to show off her latest discovery—a reluctant pop singer who's invented a new dance craze called "The Twizzle."

Behind the Scenes: "The Twizzle" was actually written by pop tunesmiths Mack David and Jerry Livingston...Originally conceived as a showcase for Jerry Lanning, who was the son of pop vocalist Roberta Sherwood, the episode is probably more fascinating to current viewers for the appearance of character actor Jack Albertson, who would achieve far greater fame a few years later when he accepted the 1968 Academy Award for Best Supporting Actor for his performance in *The Subject Was Roses*. Albertson would also collect an Emmy for his role as junk man Ed Brown on prime time's *Chico and the Man*, which costarred the late Freddie Prinze...According to Carl Reiner, "The Twizzle" bears the dubious distinction of being one of the cast's all-time least favorite episodes.

25) One Angry Man Airdate: 3/7/62
WRITERS: Leo Solomon and Ben Gershman / DIRECTOR: John Rich

Supporting Cast: Marla Hendrix—Sue Ane Langdon, Juror—Patsy Kelly, Cab-driving Juror—Herbie Faye, District Attorney Mason—Lee Bergere, Defense Lawyer Berger—Dabbs Greer, Juror—Herb Vigran, Bailiff—Doodles Weaver, Honorable Judge George M. Tyler—Howard Wendell

Filmed on January 16, 1962.

Laura is convinced that a pretty face has tipped the scales of justice when Rob—on jury duty—sides with the attractive defendant.

Behind the Scenes: This episode is an affectionate takeoff on screenwriter Reginald Rose's award-winning TV drama, *Twelve Angry Men*, which was adapted for the big screen by director Sidney Lumet in 1957.

26) **Where You Been, Fassbinder?** Airdate: 3/14/62
WRITER: John Whedon / DIRECTOR: John Rich

Supporting Cast: Mel—Richard Deacon, Leo Fassbinder—George Neise, Pickles—
Barbara Perry

Filmed on January 23, 1962.

Sally pins her romantic dreams on the arrival of a mysterious suitor who bears
the unlikely name of Leo Fassbinder, an old acquaintance whom she hopes will
brighten an otherwise lonely birthday celebration.

Behind the Scenes: On the first day of rehearsal for this episode, Rose Marie
recalls that director John Rich asked her to show up on the set more than an hour
early so that he could help her find the proper frame of mind to play the episode's
moodier moments. "It was really fabulous," she recalls. "I walked through the
apartment to see where I might do this line or that scene. John wanted me to do
that just so I'd be more comfortable."

27) **The Bad Old Days** Airdate: 4/4/62
WRITERS: Norm Liebmann and Ed Haas / DIRECTOR: John Rich

Supporting Cast: Jerry—Jerry Paris

Filmed on January 30, 1962. Song: "A Bird in a Gilded Cage" (Lamb, Von Tilzer)

Rob rebels against what he perceives as Laura's domestic tyranny after Buddy
convinces him that he's become hopelessly henpecked.

Behind the Scenes: Due to the technical demands imposed by the episode's
extended Gay Nineties costume fantasy sequence, this show would be one of the
very few Van Dyke episodes to be filmed without a live audience in attendance.

28) **I Am My Brother's Keeper** Airdate: 3/21/62
WRITER: Carl Reiner / DIRECTOR: John Rich

Supporting Cast: Mel—Richard Deacon, Stacey Petrie—Jerry Van Dyke

Filmed on February 6, 1962. Song: "Hello, Sunshine, Hello" (Tobias, Murray,
Tobias)

Rob assumes something's wrong when his brother arrives telling jokes and
singing songs—shy, retiring Stacey Petrie acts that way only when he's sleepwalk-
ing!

Behind the Scenes: Though the spelling differs slightly, Stacey Petrie was named
after Dick Van Dyke's real-life six-year-old daughter, Stacy…The first half of the
series' inaugural two-parter, the original broadcast of "I Am My Brother's Keeper" ended with a filmed teaser—which still survives on most of the prints current-
ly in syndication—in which Dick Van Dyke addresses the camera in a direct appeal
to the show's viewers. "I hope you'll be with us next week," the actor implores,
"when my brother wrestles with the problem of auditioning for a television program while he's wide awake! Well, see ya next week!"

29) The Sleeping Brother Airdate: 3/28/62
WRITER: Carl Reiner / DIRECTOR: John Rich

Supporting Cast: Mel—Richard Deacon, Jerry—Jerry Paris, Alan Brady—Carl Reiner, Stacey Petrie—Jerry Van Dyke

Filmed on February 13, 1962. Songs: "Hello, Sunshine, Hello" (Tobias, Murray, Tobias); "Bill Bailey" (traditional, arrangement by Hagen); "By the Light of the Silvery Moon" (Edwards, Madden); "Crying My Heart Out For You" (Johnson, Hopkins); "Mountain Greenery" (Rodgets, Hart); "Banjo Rock" (Jerry Van Dyke); "I Wish My Heart Would Keep Its Big Mouth Shut" (Amsterdam)

Rob's somnambulant brother lands an audition for *The Alan Brady Show,* and Rob begins to wonder how Stacey will ever get through the tryout if he happens to be awake at the time.

Behind the Scenes: Although the part of Alan Brady is playfully credited to one "Alan Brady" in the show's closing credits, Carl Reiner Contributes his first on-camera cameo in the role in this episode.

30) The Return of Happy Spangler Airdate: 4/18/62
WRITER: Carl Reiner / DIRECTOR: John Rich

Supporting Cast: Mel—Richard Deacon, Happy Spangler—Jay C. Flippen, Customer–Frank Adamo (uncredited)

Filmed on February 20, 1962.

Rob runs into the old-timer who gave him his first break in show business, and then makes the mistake of trying to return the favor.

Behind the Scenes: The monologue in which Rob describes why pain is funny is one of director John Rich's favorite moments. "I was always looking for something that would cause Dick pain," the director confesses, "because pain can be funny, if it's done properly by a comic. So we used to look for what we called 'the pain take.' Dick would come in and inadvertently put his hand on the stove and dance around, saying, 'Why did I do that?' When he did a whole lecture on why pain was funny—where he was stabbing himself with prop scissors—he was really talking about what was true in his own comedy."

1962–1963
THE DICK VAN DYKE SHOW
Season Two

Carl Reiner continues as the series' producer, story consultant, and chief writer in year two, contributing twenty-two of the thirty-two scripts that would be produced in the show's second—and longest—production season. He would get a welcome assist from the freelance writing team of Sheldon Keller and Howard Merrill, who would contribute four scripts over the course of the year. John Rich returns as the show's house director, and John C. Chulay continues as the show's assistant director—a position he would maintain for the remainder of the show's run.

Second-Season Credits:

Created and Produced by	Carl Reiner
Associate Producer	Ronald Jacobs
Music	Earle Hagen
Director of Photography	Robert DeGrasse, A.S.C.
Art Director	Kenneth A. Reid
Film Editor	Bud Molin, A.C.E.
Production Manager	Frank E. Meyers
Assistant Director	John C. Chulay
Prop Master	Glenn Ross
Camera Coordinator	James Niver
Casting	Ruth Burch
Script Continuity	Marjorie Mullen
Set Decorator	Ken Swartz
Rerecording Editor	Richard LeGrande
Story Consultant	Carl Reiner
Hairstylist	Donna McDonough
Makeup	Tom Tuttle
Costumes	Harald Johnson
Sound Engineer	
(episodes #32–45, 47–62)	Cam McCulloch
(episode #46)	Frank Webster
Music Coordinator	Walter Popp
Recorded by	Glen Glenn Sound Co.
Executive Producer	Sheldon Leonard in association with Danny Thomas

Mr. Van Dyke's Wardrobe Furnished by Botany 500
Women's fashions provided by E.T. Jr., Los Angeles; William Pearson; Walter Bass of Beverly Hills; Peggy Hunt; Emerson's of Studio City; Arbe Originals; Mr. Mort; Gino Paoli Knits; Gibi Knits of Italy; Marjolaine Colberti Knits; Dee Dee Johnson; Lill–Ann of San Francisco; Dorothy O'Hara; White Stag Sportswear; Mr. Jules of California; Ann Arnold, Beverly Hills

31) **Never Name a Duck** Airdate: 9/26/62
WRITER: Carl Reiner / DIRECTOR: John Rich

Supporting Cast: Mel—Richard Deacon, Mr. Fletcher—Jerry Hausner, Miss Singleton (poodle owner)—Jane Dulo, Miss Glasser (cat owner)—Geraldine Wall, Veterinarian's Assistant—Frank Adamo

Filmed on August 7, 1962.

Rob tries to console Ritchie after he's forced to set the boy's pet duck free in the town pond.

Behind the Scenes: This episode features the first on-air appearance of the show's classic opening title sequence, in which Rob trips over an ill-placed ottoman. The sequence was filmed on the night of August 14, 1962, following the filming of episode 32, "The Two Faces of Rob."

32) **The Two Faces of Rob** Airdate: 10/3/62
WRITERS: Sheldon Keller and Howard Merrill / DIRECTOR: John Rich

Supporting Cast: Millie—Ann Morgan Guilbert, Deli Man—Herbie Faye, Game Show Host—Carl Reiner (uncredited voice-over)

Filmed on August 14, 1962. Songs: "All of Me" (Simons, Marks); "Santa Lucia" (traditional, arrangement by Hagen)

Posing as a mysterious stranger, Rob calls Laura and asks for a date—a prank that backfires when she eagerly accepts his invitation.

Behind the Scenes: The first Van Dyke show script written by Sheldon Keller and Howard Merrill, a freelance writing team who would contribute many scripts in the show's middle years. Keller and Carl Reiner had spent time together in the writers' room on *Caesar's Hour* in the mid-fifties, and before that, at Camp Crowder, Missouri, where they both served in the armed forces during WW II... "I used to love writing one-sided phone calls for Dick," says Carl Reiner, who claims that this classic episode was actually inspired by Dick Van Dyke's almost uncanny ability to convincingly act out one half of a telephone conversation. "I would swear there was somebody on the other end of the line!" notes Reiner. "Every good actor can do it—Mary did it almost as well. But Dick did it better than everybody. He was the master."

33) Bank Book 6565696 Airdate: 10/17/62
WRITERS: Ray Allen Saffian and Harvey Bullock / DIRECTOR: John Rich

Supporting Cast: Jerry—Jerry Paris

Filmed on August 21, 1962.

Rob's imagination runs wild after he discovers that Laura has stashed a sizable sum of cash in a secret bank account.

34) The Attempted Marriage Airdate: 10/10/62
WRITER: Carl Reiner / DIRECTOR: John Rich

Supporting Cast: Doctor—Sandy Kenyon, Chaplain—Dabbs Greer, Corporal—Ray Kellogg

Filmed on August 28, 1962.

Rob recalls the disastrous circumstances that led up to his beleaguered arrival at his own wedding—battered, bruised, and three hours late.

35) Hustling the Hustler Airdate: 10/24/62
WRITER: Carl Reiner / DIRECTOR: John Rich

Supporting Cast: Mel—Richard Deacon, Blackie Sorrell—Phil Leeds

Filmed on September 4, 1962. Song: "Moonlight Bay" (Wenrich, Madden)

Buddy suspects his brother's motives when the supposedly reformed pool shark challenges Rob to a friendly game of Eight Ball.

Behind the Scenes: According to editor Bud Molin, the amazing pool shot that Mary Tyler Moore negotiates at the end of this episode—in which she sinks every ball on the table with a single flick of the cue—was actually the result of a happy accident. Though the trick shot had been carefully laid out by a pool expert beforehand, no one actually expected the actress to make the shot in her first try—if at all. "We had it rigged," notes the editor, "so that she just had to hit the balls in the right general direction." Of course, to get an actual take of the difficult shot, director John Rich was fully prepared to reshoot the scene in close-up, with the pool expert standing in for the actress. But, to the utter amazement of everyone on the set, the actress managed to nail the shot in her first take. "It was just luck," says Molin. "She hit it, and she dropped every ball! And we were able to use the shot, because Dick and Mary didn't go to pieces after she finally got it."

36) What's in a Middle Name? Airdate: 11/7/62
WRITER: Carl Reiner / DIRECTOR: John Rich

Supporting Cast: Mr. Meeker—Carl Benton Reid, Mrs. Meeker—Geraldine Wall, Sam Petrie—J. Pat O'Malley, Mrs. Petrie—Isabel Randolph, Grandpa Petrie— Cyril Delevanti

Filmed on September 11, 1962.

Rob reveals the mysterious saga of how Ritchie was given the middle name "Rosebud" in order to settle a family feud.

Behind the Scenes: Ritchie's middle name is revealed to be an acronym made up of the first letters of the names Robert, Oscar, Sam, Edward, Benjamin, Ulysses, and David.

Episode 36, "What's in a Middle Name?"; Cyril Delevanti, Dick Van Dyke.

37) **My Husband Is Not a Drunk** Airdate: 10/31/62
WRITER: Carl Reiner / DIRECTOR: Al Rafkin

Supporting Cast: Mel—Richard Deacon, Jerry—Jerry Paris, Millie—Ann Morgan Guilbert, Glen Jameson—Charles Aidman, Mr. Boland—Roy Roberts

Filmed on September 8, 1962.

Rob suffers from a posthypnotic suggestion that forces him to act hopelessly inebriated every time he hears a bell ring.

Episode 37, "My Husband Is Not a Drunk"; Charles Aidman, Morey Amsterdam, Rose Marie.

38) Like a Sister Airdate: 11/14/62
WRITER: Carl Reiner / DIRECTOR: Hal Cooper

Supporting Cast: Mel—Richard Deacon, Ric Vallone—Vic Damone

Filmed on October 2, 1962. Songs: "Santa Lucia" (traditional), "The Most Beautiful Girl in the World" (Rodgers, Hart)

Rob is concerned that Sally might be developing romantic delusions when she develops a crush on the show's guest star, the handsome singer Ric Vallone.

39) The Night the Roof Fell In Airdate: 11/21/62
WRITER: John Whedon / DIRECTOR: Hal Cooper

Supporting Cast: Millie: Ann Morgan Guilbert

Filmed on October 9, 1962.

Rob and Laura recount vastly different versions of a marital spat that sent Rob storming out of the house in a huff.

40) The Secret Life of Buddy and Sally Airdate: 11/28/62
WRITER: Lee Erwin / DIRECTOR: Coby Ruskin

Supporting Cast: Mel—Richard Deacon, Waiter—Phil Arnold, Herbie "Hiawatha" Harris—Carl Reiner (uncredited voice-over)

Filmed on October 16, 1962. Songs: "Gilbert and Solomon" (Amsterdam); "Hungarian Folk Dance" (traditional); "Come Rain or Come Shine" (Mercer, Arlen); "Hello, Hello" (Amsterdam); "Harmony" (Burke, Van Heusen)

Rob suspects that Buddy and Sally may be up to a little hanky-panky after he discovers that the pair have been disappearing together each weekend without explanation.

41) A Bird in the Head Hurts Airdate: 12/5/62
WRITER: Carl Reiner / DIRECTOR: John Rich

Supporting Cast: Millie—Ann Morgan Guilbert, Game Warden—Cliff Norton

Filmed on October 23, 1962.

Rob and Laura worry that Ritchie may be suffering from a hyperactive imagination after he claims he's been attacked by a giant woodpecker.

Behind the Scenes: Based on an idea contributed by Carl Reiner's friend and former New Rochelle neighbor Millie Schoenbaum, who was also the real-life model for the show's Millie Helper.

42) Gesundheit, Darling Airdate: 12/12/62
WRITER: Carl Reiner / DIRECTOR: John Rich

Supporting Cast: Jerry—Jerry Paris, Millie—Ann Morgan Guilbert, Allergist—Sandy Kenyon

Filmed on October 30, 1962.

A sudden fit of uncontrollable sneezing has Rob worried that he's developed an allergic reaction to Laura.

#043) **A Man's Teeth Are Not His Own** Airdate: 12/19/62
WRITER: Carl Reiner / DIRECTOR: John Rich

*Supporting Cas*t: Mel—Richard Deacon, Jerry—Jerry Paris, Millie—Ann Morgan Guilbert

Filmed on November 6, 1962. Song: *Hungarian Dance #5* (Brahms)

Rob is afraid Jerry will never forgive him after he lets another dentist perform emergency work on his teeth.

#044) **Somebody Has to Play Cleopatra** Airdate: 12/26/62
WRITER: Martin A. Ragaway / DIRECTOR: John Rich

Supporting Cast: Jerry—Jerry Paris, Millie—Ann Morgan Guilbert, Harry Rogers— Bob Crane, Mrs. Billings—Eleanor Audley, Shirley Rogers—Shirley Mitchell, Cynthia Harding—Valerie Yerke

Filmed on November 13, 1962. Songs: "True, Man, True" (Amsterdam); "The Flowers That Bloom in the Spring" (Gilbert, Sullivan)

Rob has his hands full directing the latest edition of his neighborhood's annual variety show, especially after he discovers that none of the husbands are too keen on letting their wives play the show's romantic leading role.

Behind the Scenes: Not long after his appearance here, guest star Bob Crane would move into a regular spot on *The Donna Reed Show*, and, eventually, the lead role in CBS's wartime sitcom *Hogan's Heroes.*

Episode 44, "Somebody Has to Play Cleopatra"; Valeri Yerke, Dick Van Dyke.

45) The Cat Burglar Airdate: 1/2/63
WRITER: Carl Reiner / DIRECTOR: John Rich

Supporting Cast: Jerry—Jerry Paris, Millie—Ann Morgan Guilbert, Police Lieu-
tenant—Barney Phillips, Photographer—Johnny Silver

Filmed on November 20, 1962. Song: "Glow Worm" (Lincke, Robinson)

Rob and Laura are puzzled by the mystery of how a cat burglar stole their living room set without leaving a single clue behind.

Behind the Scenes: Van Dyke recalls that this episode was inspired by a real-life
incident that happened to him and his wife a few years earlier. "I remember one
night in Long Island," says the star, "my wife and I thought there was a burglar in
the house. I had a little .25 automatic that I kept in the drawer. And I got it out,
but it was empty. I said, 'Where are the bullets?' And my wife said, 'They're in my
jewelry box!' So I opened the jewelry box—and it starts playing 'The Blue Danube
Waltz.' It was so funny that we built a show on that."

Episode 97, "The Ghost of A. Chantz."

46) The Foul Weather Girl Airdate: 1/9/63
WRITER: Carl Reiner / DIRECTOR: John Rich

Supporting Cast: Janie Layton—Joan O'Brien, Mel—Richard Deacon, Alan Brady—Carl Reiner (uncredited voice-over)

Filmed on November 27, 1962. Song: "Get Out in the Sun" (ad lib), "Just in Time" (Styne, Comden, Green)

The TV weather girl from Rob's hometown asks for his help in landing a role on *The Alan Brady Show*—a proposition that Laura eyes with suspicion.

#047) Will You Two Be My Wife? Airdate: 1/16/63
WRITER: Carl Reiner / DIRECTOR: John Rich

Supporting Cast: Millie—Ann Morgan Guilbert, Sam—Allan Melvin, Captain—Ray Kellogg, Dorothy—Barbara Bain

Filmed on December 4, 1962.

Rob faces the fury of a woman scorned in a flashback that recounts how he lowered the boom on his hometown sweetheart after he got engagd to Laura.

Episode 47, "Will You Two Be My Wife?"; Dick Van Dyke, Barbara Bain.

48) Ray Murdock's X-Ray Airdate: 1/23/63
WRITER: Carl Reiner / DIRECTOR: Jerry Paris

Supporting Cast: Ray Murdock—Gene Lyons, Stage Manager—Jerry Hausner, Assistant—Frank Adamo (uncredited), Announcer—Carl Reiner (uncredited voice-over)

Filmed on December 11, 1962.

Laura feels betrayed when Rob confesses to a talk-show host that his own wife is the real-life inspiration for most of the outlandish domestic sketches featured on *The Alan Brady Show.*

Behind the Scenes: Jerry Paris began his long tenure as the primary director of *The Dick Van Dyke Show* with this episode...Carl Reiner confesses that he was never fully satisfied with the resolution that he worked out for this particular show, which depicts Laura's sudden infatuation with the glamorous notoriety that comes with being identified as Rob Petrie's nutty wife. "For her to be proud of the fact that they called her a stupid idiot on the air is just kind of silly," Reiner admits today. "But, we had to finish the show, so that was the ending we did. Today, I don't know if I would've done the same thing."

49) I Was a Teenage Head Writer Airdate: 1/30/63
WRITERS: Sheldon Keller and Howard Merrill / DIRECTOR: Jerry Paris

Supporting Cast: Mel—Richard Deacon

Filmed on December 18, 1962.

Rob recalls the trials of his early days as head writer of *The Alan Brady Show.*

50) My Husband Is a Check-Grabber Airdate: 2/13/63
WRITER: Carl Reiner / DIRECTOR: Al Rafkin

Supporting Cast: Jerry—Jerry Paris, Pickles—Joan Shawlee, Herman Glimsher— Bill Idelson, Anatole—Phil Arnold

Filmed on January 8, 1963.

The Petries' latest skirmish springs from Rob's annoying habit of always picking up the check when they're out with friends.

Behind the Scenes: "That one was on my desk for years," explains Carl Reiner, who recalls that this was the last script to be adapted from the storylines he worked up for *Head of the Family* in 1958. "I had it written as part of the original thirteen, but we couldn't figure out how to make it into a good three-camera show. It never went anywhere 'cause it was flawed." According to Reiner, it was Sheldon Leonard who finally diagnosed that the problem with the script was not the story at all, but its theme. "Sheldon said, 'Money is a bad subject. People don't like shows about penuriousness or money.' And I said, 'Yeah, but this is an honest and true subject. I'll beat it!' And I had it on my desk for about two years. It was always there. Then, one day I was upstairs, and I said, 'I got it! It's a flashback!'" Once he'd solved his story problem, Reiner promptly retooled the script for use on *The Dick Van Dyke Show,* where it remains one of the strongest episodes of the series.

51) It May Look Like a Walnut! Airdate: 2/6/63
WRITER: Carl Reiner / DIRECTOR: Jerry Paris

Supporting Cast: Mel—Richard Deacon, Kolac—Danny Thomas (uncredited cameo), Horror Movie Victim—Carl Reiner (uncredited voice-over), Exercise Show Host—Jerry Paris (uncredited voice-over)

Filmed on January 15, 1963.

A late-show thriller gives Rob a nightmare about a world domination scheme cooked up by an alien who looks exactly like Danny Thomas.

Behind the Scenes: The first show to feature the episode's title as part of the show's opening credits...A few days after this classic episode was filmed, departing director John Rich would report to Paramount studios to start work on his first feature, *Wives and Lovers,* which would begin shooting, after a week of rehearsals, on January 28, 1963.

Episode 50, "My Huband Is a Check Grabber."

52) Don't Trip Over That Mountain Airdate: 2/20/63
WRITER: Carl Reiner / DIRECTOR: Coby Ruskin

Supporting Cast: Jerry—Jerry Paris, Millie—Ann Morgan Guilbert, Nurse—Jean Allison, Doctor—Ray Kellogg

Filmed on January 22, 1963.

Anticipating disaster, Laura warns Rob not to go on a weekend skiing trip—only to blame herself for the inevitable accident that results.

53) Give Me Your Walls! Airdate: 2/27/63
WRITER: Carl Reiner / DIRECTOR: Jerry Paris

Supporting Cast: Vito Giotto—Vito Scotti

Filmed on January 29, 1963.

Laura hires a flamboyant artist to paint her living room, and then has second thoughts when the ingratiating painter begins to take over the entire household.

Episode 53, "Give Me Your Walls!"; Vito Scotti, Dick Van Dyke.

54) The Sam Pomerantz Scandals Airdate: 3/6/63
WRITER: Carl Reiner / DIRECTOR: Claudio Guzman

Supporting Cast: Sam Pomerantz—Henry Calvin, Mel—Richard Deacon, Pickles—Joan Shawlee, Danny Brewster—Len Weinrib

Filmed on February 5, 1963. Songs: "I Wanna Be Around "(Mercer, Vimmerstedt); "Carolina in the Morning" (Donaldson, Kahn); "The Nutty Song" (Livingston); "The Musicians" (Glazer, Grean)

Rob convinces Laura, Buddy, Sally, and Mel to take part in a variety show at an old pal's resort in the Catskills.

Behind the Scenes: The show's bandleader finale, "The Musicians," would be memorably reprised a few months later on *The Dick Van Dyke Show*'s Christmas episode ...The extended Laurel and Hardy pantomime that Van Dyke performs with Henry Calvin was an homage to Van Dyke's longtime idol, Stan Laurel. The star had never performed with guest star Calvin before this episode...Comic Len Weinrib, who plays Danny Brewster, had portrayed the same basic character in the show's fourteenth episode "Buddy, Can You Spare a Job?" though he was called Jackie in the earlier show...Weinrib's comic impression of then President John Kennedy stands as an uncharacteristic example of topical humor on the Van Dyke show.

Episode 54, "The Sam Pomerantz Scandals"; Dick Van Dyke, Henry Calvin.

55) I'm No Henry Walden! Airdate: 3/27/63
WRITER: Carl Reiner/Story by: Ray Brenner and Jack Guss /
DIRECTOR: Jerry Paris

Supporting Cast: Henry Walden—Everett Sloane, Mel—Richard Deacon, Mrs. Huntington—Doris Packer, Yale Sampson—Carl Reiner, Mrs. Felicia Fellowes—Betty Lou Gerson, Dr. Torrance Hayworth—Howard Wendell, Miss Thomas Evelyn—Roxanne Berard, H. Fieldstone Thorley—Frank Adamo

Filmed on February 12, 1963.

Rob feels self-conscious when he discovers he's the only comedy writer at a literary gathering.

Behind the Scenes: Carl Reiner logs his first guest-starring role on the show, playing Yale Sampson, an English philosopher prone to double-talk...Guest star Everett Sloane had been a respected character actor dating back to his days with Orson Welles's *Mercury Theatre of the Air* in the thirties.

56) The Square Triangle Airdate: 3/20/63
WRITER: Bill Idelson / DIRECTOR: Jerry Paris

Supporting Cast: Jacques Savon—Jacques Bergerac, Mel—Richard Deacon, Millie—Ann Morgan Guilbert

Filmed on February 19, 1963. Song: "I Only Have Eyes For You" (Warren, Dubin)

Buddy and Sally are puzzled when they notice that Rob seems to vanish each time the show's handsome French guest star walks in.

Behind the Scenes: The first Van Dyke script from writer Bill Idelson, who frequently portrayed Sally's sad-sack boyfriend, Herman Glimsher, on the series. Idelson got his start as a child star in radio, where he was featured in the cast of the long-running comedy series *Vic and Sade*. In later years, Idelson would forge a long list of comedy-writing credits, including numerous scripts for *The Andy Griffith Show*, as well as logging a stint as a writer and producer of *The Bob Newhart Show* in the early seventies.

57) Racy Tracy Rattigan Airdate: 4/3/63
WRITERS: Ronald Alexander and Carl Reiner / DIRECTOR: Sheldon Leonard

Supporting Cast: Mel—Richard Deacon, Tracy Rattigan—Richard Dawson

Filmed on February 26, 1963.

Alan Brady's summer replacement star is Tracy Rattigan, a lecherous flirt who quickly sets his sights on the head writer's wife.

Behind the Scenes: Though guest star Richard Dawson would discover his greatest fame as emcee of *Family Feud*, his work as an actor would also include a long-running role on *Hogan's Heroes* in the late sixties, as well as a brief run in the cast of *The New Dick Van Dyke Show* in 1973.

58) **Divorce** Airdate: 4/10/63
WRITER: Carl Reiner / DIRECTOR: Jerry Paris

Supporting Cast: Pickles—Joan Shawlee, Steve Longfellow, the Bartender—Charles Cantor, Sheila—Marian Collier, Sheila's Date—Arthur Batanides, TV Defense Lawyer—Carl Reiner (uncredited voice-over), Mr. Thompson—Jerry Paris (uncredited voice-over), Floyd B. Bariscale—Sheldon Leonard (uncredited voice-over)

Filmed on March 5, 1963.

Rob plays amateur marriage counselor after Buddy threatens to divorce Pickles over a silly misunderstanding.

Behind the Scenes: Executive producer Sheldon Leonard turns in an off-camera cameo as the blackmailer, Floyd B. Bariscale...This episode would mark the final on-camera appearance of Buddy's wife Pickles, who would fade into off-screen limbo for the remainder of the show's run. According to director John Rich, the char-

acter was dropped to make more room for the show's already populous supporting cast. "You can only write for so many characters on a continuing situation comedy," says Rich, who notes that the show's central cast—including Ritchie, Mel, Jerry, and Millie—already numbered no fewer than eight continuing characters. "To service eight people effectively every week is a big chore," says Rich. "So you try very hard to not use everybody all the time. And Buddy's wife just wasn't an essential character for the comedy."

Episode 58, "Divorce";
Joan Shawlee,
Morey Amsterdam.

59) It's a Shame She Married Me Airdate: 4/17/63
WRITERS: Sheldon Keller and Howard Merrill / DIRECTOR: James Niver

Supporting Cast: Mel—Richard Deacon, Jerry—Jerry Paris, Millie—Ann Morgan Guilbert, Jim Darling—Robert Vaughn, Edward—Frank Adamo (uncredited cameo)

Filmed on March 12, 1963.

Rob makes a fool of himself when he attempts to outshine one of Laura's dashing old flames.

Behind the Scenes: Camera coordinator Jim Niver made his bow as a director with this episode. And, as he recalls, his first week on the job was an eventful one. "I broke my leg the first day," says Niver. "I was reaching up from the first row of the balcony down to the floor to get something, and my foot slipped off. I fell off the edge and cracked it. I remember Dick looked up from the stage and said, 'What was that sound?' And I said, 'I think it was my leg.' But I didn't go to the doctor until Monday. It was just a fracture."

60) A Surprise Surprise Is a Surprise Airdate: 4/24/63
WRITER: Carl Reiner / DIRECTOR: Jerry Paris

Supporting Cast: Mel—Richard Deacon, Jerry—Jerry Paris, Millie—Ann Morgan Guilbert

Filmed on March 19, 1963. Song: "For He's a Jolly Good Fellow" (traditional)

Rob tries to second-guess Laura's plan to surprise him on his birthday.

Behind the Scenes: In the episode, Sally teases Rob's amateur detective activities by referring to him as Sebastian—a now-obscure reference to the actor Sebastian Cabot who had recently starred as an ace criminologist on *Checkmate,* a popular detective series of the early sixties.

61) Jilting the Jilter Airdate: 5/1/63
WRITER: Ronald Alexander / DIRECTOR: Jerry Paris

Supporting Cast: Freddy White—Guy Marks, Mel—Richard Deacon

Filmed on March 26, 1963.

Sally's latest heartthrob is a stand-up comic who's badly in need of a new writer, which is exactly what Rob and Buddy suspect he's really after.

Episode 61,
"Jilting the Jilter"; Guy Marks, Rose Marie.

62) **When a Bowling Pin Talks, Listen** Airdate: 5/8/63
WRITER: Martin A. Ragaway / DIRECTOR: Jerry Paris

Supporting Cast: Mel—Richard Deacon, Willie, the Deli Man—Herbie Faye, Barber—Jon Silo, Alan Brady—Carl Reiner (uncredited), Uncle Spunky—Jerry Paris (uncredited voice-over)

Filmed on April 2, 1963. Song: "Beautiful Dreamer" (Foster)

Hoping to help his dad through a temporary bout of writer's block, Ritchie inadvertently inspires Rob to plagiarize a sketch idea from a TV kid's show.

63) **All About Eavesdropping** Airdate: 10/23/63
WRITERS: Sheldon Keller and Howard Merrill / DIRECTOR: Stanley Cherry

Supporting Cast: Jerry—Jerry Paris, Millie—Ann Morgan Guilbert

Filmed on April 9, 1963. Song: "Go Tell Aunt Rhody" (traditional)

The Petries get an earful after they accidentally overhear Millie and Jerry on Ritchie's toy intercom.

Behind the Scenes: Although filmed as the final entry in the show's second season, this episode would not be broadcast until the following October. Curiously, when the episode finally did appear—as the fifth episode of the show's third season—it would sport the inaugural appearance of yet a third version of the show's familiar opening title sequence. In this seldom seen variant, Rob avoids tripping over his troublesome ottoman, only to stumble in his tracks a few steps later—an alternate version of the opening credits that would appear only sporadically in the show's final seasons.

1963–1964
THE DICK VAN DYKE SHOW
Season Three

Carl Reiner's creative team expands in the show's third season with the addition of writers Bill Persky and Sam Denoff, who—along with Van Dyke show stalwarts Martin S. Ragaway and the team of Jerry Belson and Garry Marshall—would make their first significant story contributions to the show. The new writers work under the close supervision of Carl Reiner, who will continue to serve as the show's producer, story consultant, and head writer throughout season three. Jerry Paris succeeds John Rich as the series' regular director, a position that Paris will maintain throughout the show's final three years.

Third-Season Credits:

Created and Produced by	Carl Reiner
Associate Producer	Ronald Jacobs
Music	Earle Hagen
Director of Photography	Robert DeGrasse, A.S.C.
Art Direcor	Kenneth A. Reid
Film Editor	
(episodes #64–69)	Alan L. Jaggs
(episode #70)	James Ballas
(episodes #71–95)	Bud Molin, A.C.E.
Assistant Director	John C. Chulay
Prop Master	Glenn Ross
Camera Coordinator	James Niver
Casting	Ruth Burch
Script Continuity	Marjorie Mullen
Set Decorator	Ken Swartz
Rerecording Editor	
(episode #65)	Richard LeGrande
(episodes #64, 66–95)	Robert Reeve
Story Consultant	Carl Reiner
Hairstylist	Donna McDonough
Makeup	Tom Tuttle
Costumes	Harald Johnson
Sound Engineer	Cam McCulloch
Music Coordinator	Walter Popp
Recorded by	Glen Glenn Sound Co.
Executive Producer	Sheldon Leonard in association with Danny Thomas
Production Supervisor	Ronald Jacobs
Production Manager	Frank E. Meyers

Mr. Van Dyke's Wardrobe Furnished by Botany 500

Women's Fashions by William Pearson; Gino Paoli; Ida K's, Wilshire; Helga; Laura Aponte of Rome; Ann Arnold; Mr. Mort; Nan Link, Beverly Hills; Sydney North; Peggy Hunt; Marjolaine Colberti; Norma Morgan; Walter Bass; Geno

64) That's My Boy??? Airdate: 9/25/63
WRITERS: Bill Persky and Sam Denoff / DIRECTOR: John Rich

Supporting Cast: Jerry—Jerry Paris, Millie—Ann Morgan Guilbert, Maternity Ward Nurse—Amzie Strickland, Mr. Peters—Greg Morris, Mrs. Peters—Mimi Dillard, Mel—Richard Deacon

Filmed on August 6, 1963.

Rob recalls his early days of parenthood, including a complicated series of mixups that had him convinced he'd brought the wrong baby home from the hospital.

Behind the Scenes: The first script from writers Bill Persky and Sam Denoff, who would eventually become—after Carl Reiner—the show's most prolific contributors...Beginning with this episode, series regular Richard Deacon would receive a more prominent "single-card" credit in the show's closing titles.

Episode 64, "That's My Boy???"

65) The Masterpiece Airdate: 10/2/63
WRITERS: Sam Denoff and Bill Persky / DIRECTOR: John Rich

Supporting Cast: Ernest Holdecker—Howard Morris, Auctioneer—Alan Reed, Competitive Bidder—Amzie Strickland, Competitive Bidder's Husband—Ray Kellogg

Filmed on August 13, 1963.

The Petries become instant art collectors after Rob inadvertently places the high bid on a painting at an auction.

Behind the Scenes: This episode reunites producer Reiner with his old friend Howard Morris. The pair began their long personal and professional association as fellow GIs in Maurice Evans's special services unit during WW II. After the war, Morris and Reiner shared the stage in the cast of Broadway's *Call Me Mister.* A few years later, the pair would be teamed most memorably in the casts of both *Your Show of Shows* and *Caesar's Hour.* Morris would later direct five episodes of *The*

Dick Van Dyke Show...Though it was supposedly the work of Frank Sinatra, the Artanis original that appears in the episode was actually painted by the show's art director, Ken Reid, who created most of the art props that appeared on the show over the years. The painting today resides in the collection of writer Sam Denoff, who says he rescued the prop from the studio trash bin shortly after the episode wrapped in 1963...Guest star Alan Reed also provided the voice for Stone Age breadwinner Fred Flintstone on TV's pioneering prime-time animated sitcom, *The Flintstones.*

66) Laura's Little Lie Airdate: 10/9/63
WRITERS: Carl Reiner and Howard Merrill / DIRECTOR: John Rich

Supporting Cast: Ed Rubin—Charles Aidman

Filmed on August 20, 1963.

The Petries discover that their marriage is not legally binding after Laura confesses that she lied about her age on their marriage license.

Behind the Scenes: The first of two parts.

67) Very Old Shoes, Very Old Rice Airdate: 10/16/63
WRITER: Carl Reiner / DIRECTOR: John Rich

Supporting Cast: Millie—Ann Morgan Guilbert, Judge Krata—Russell Collins, Dodo Parker—Madge Blake, Donald Lucas Parker—Burt Mustin, Mel—Richard Deacon

Filmed on August 27, 1963. Song: "I Wonder What's Become of Sally" (Ager, Yellen)

Rob and Laura renew their marriage vows in a hastily arranged ceremony, despite the fact that they are barely on speaking terms.

Behind the Scenes: At the conclusion of filming this episode, the cast staged a surprise party for departing director John Rich.

68) Uncle George Airdate: 11/13/63
WRITER: Bill Idelson / DIRECTOR: Jerry Paris

Supporting Cast: Uncle George Petrie—Denver Pyle, Mrs. Glimsher—Elvia Allman, Herman Glimsher—Bill Idelson, Mel—Richard Deacon

Filmed on September 3, 1963. Song: "Buffalo Gals" (traditional)

Rob's exuberant Uncle George comes to New York expecting to find a wife, and quickly sets his sights on Sally Rogers.

Behind the Scenes: "Dick hated that one," observes Carl Reiner, who recalls that his star's distaste for the episode was motivated largely by the fact that he had so little to do in it. "When Dick had something really to do, he was a very giving guy. But everybody's still an actor. And when the fun thing you come to work for is not in there, you're not so crazy about the show. Now, in retrospect, every time we see one of these shows that we thought were terrible, we say, 'They're not so bad!' It almost always had something in it that you could point to with pride."

69) Too Many Stars Airdate: 10/30/63
WRITERS: Sheldon Keller and Howard Merrill / DIRECTOR: Jerry Paris

Supporting Cast: Jerry—Jerry Paris, Millie—Ann Morgan Guilbert, Anita Lebost—
Sylvia Lewis, Mrs. Billings—Eleanor Audley, Howard Lebost—Eddie Ryder,
Freddy, the Grocery Man—Jerry Hausner, Mel—Richard Deacon

Filmed on September 9, 1963. Songs: "My Heart" (Gelbart, Keller); "Blue Tail
Fly" (traditional); "Cielito Lindo" (Fernandez, arranged by Hagen); "A Doo-
dlin' Song" (Coleman, Leigh)

Rob has to choose between Laura and a beautiful new neighbor for the lead role in the annual PTA revue.

Behind the Scenes: English teacher Howard Lebost and his wife Anita were named in honor of Reiner's wife, the former Estelle Lebost...Millie's audition piece, identified in the show as "A Sentimental Love Song, words and music by Mildred Helper," was actually a ditty called "My Heart" that Sheldon Keller and his occasional writing partner Larry Gelbart had composed sometime earlier...According to Carl Reiner, the PTA variety show episodes that were a staple of the series were inspired by his friend Mel Brooks, who, along with his wife, Anne Bancroft, was

constantly being drafted into performing in benefits at their child's school. "To this day, they're always in the yearly shows," says Reiner, who confesses that when it came to his own participation in his children's school benefit shows, he was only slightly more enthusiastic than his on-screen alter ego Rob Petrie. "I was called upon very often to do benefits and things," notes Reiner, "and I was always turning them down. Or I'd do them, but they were always a pain in the A! I mean, I knew you had to turn things down."

Episode 69, "Too Many Stars."

70) **Who and Where Was Antonio Stradivarius?** Airdate: 11/6/63
WRITER: Carl Reiner / DIRECTOR: Jerry Paris

Supporting Cast: Mel—Richard Deacon, Graciella—Sallie Janes, Aunt Mildred—Amzie Strickland, Uncle Edward—Hal Peary, Red Hook Party Hostess—Betty Lou Gerson, Party Host—Chet Stratton

Filmed on September 17, 1963. Songs: "Caissons Go Rolling Along" (Gruber, arranged by Hagen); "Mambo Jambo" (Prado)

During a temporary bout with amnesia, Rob finds himself the life of the party in Red Hook, New Jersey, while Laura waits up nervously in New Rochelle.

Behind the Scenes: This episode's unlikely storyline was actually inspired by an accident that befell Dick Van Dyke's father, Cookie Van Dyke, who once embarked on a mysterious sojourn not unlike Rob Petrie's after suffering a blow to the head during a family gathering. "It was Fourth of July," recalls Dick Van Dyke. "He was about sixty-four at the time, and he'd been showing off for the grandkids and did a back flip off the diving board." "He dives in the pool," continues Carl Reiner, "and he hits his head on the way out. And he gets up. He's fine. Next thing you know, he gets dressed and he gets in his car and he leaves. And he ends up in Palm Springs!" And, as Reiner describes it, it was in this slightly discombobulated state that the senior Van Dyke eventually found himself entertaining a party of total strangers. "He parked the car and he saw a backyard party," says Reiner. "And he's a friendly guy, Cookie Van Dyke, so he goes in and sits with these people. So now he's at a second party, only it's two hundred miles away, and he's got temporary amnesia!" Naturally, when the younger Van Dyke relayed the strange tale of his father's amnesia at work the next day, Reiner wasted little time seizing the story's possibilities. "I said, 'Boy, is that a show for us!'"

71) **Big Max Calvada** Airdate: 11/20/63
WRITERS: Bill Persky and Sam Denoff / DIRECTOR: Jerry Paris

Supporting Cast: Max Calvada—Sheldon Leonard, Bernard—Arthur Batanides, Kenny Dexter—Jack Larson, Mrs.Calvada—Sue Casey, Louie—Tiny Brauer, Waiter—Johnny Silver, Night Club Emcee—Carl Reiner (uncredited voice-over)

Filmed on October 8, 1963. Song: "*I Love to Hear You Say 'Encore'* " (Denoff, Persky)

Rob, Buddy, and Sally's latest assignment finds them under the gun—perhaps literally—when a mobster asks them to pen a comedy routine for his nephew.

Behind the Scenes: Executive producer Sheldon Leonard was a natural for the role of Big Max, having played scores of similar Runyonesque tough guys in his years as a Hollywood character actor. The mobster's imposing vocabulary—at one point he describes Rob, Buddy, and Sally's work as "neither too esoteric nor too mundane. Pragmatically speaking, it hits me right in the gut"—was also intended as a good-natured spoof of Leonard, whose own weakness for five- and ten-dollar words was legendary. Even the character's name was an in-joke; Calvada was, of course, the registered name of the corporate entity that produced *The Dick Van Dyke Show*.

72) The Ballad of the Betty Lou Airdate: 11/27/63
WRITER: Martin A. Ragaway / DIRECTOR: Howard Morris

Supporting Cast: Jerry—Jerry Paris, Millie—Ann Morgan Guilbert, Coast Guard Sailor—Danny Scholl

Filmed on October 15, 1963. Song: "Blow the Man Down" (traditional, arranged by Hagen)

Landlubber Rob is thrilled to go in on the purchase of a sailboat with his neighbor Jerry, until their petty squabbles threaten to run the entire operation aground.

Behind the Scenes: According to his son Andy, this was one of the late actor/director Jerry Paris's all-time favorite episodes. "That was my dad's biggest acting part on the show," observes the younger Paris, "the one that he really felt proudest of."

73) Turtles, Ties, and Toreadors Airdate: 12/4/63
WRITER: John Whedon / DIRECTOR: Jerry Paris

Guest Stars: Maria—Miriam Colon, Immigration Officer—Alan Dexter, Cab Driver—Tiny Brauer

Filmed on October 22, 1963.

Rob decides to bring in a maid to help out around the house, but only succeeds in complicating Laura's life further when the domestic he hires proves utterly incompetent.

Behind the Scenes: At the end of the episode, Maria offers the Petries the gift of a box turtle with the family's caricature painted on its shell—a cartoon that was in fact the handiwork of Dick Van Dyke himself.

74) The Sound of the Trumpets of Conscience Falls Deafly on a Brain That Holds Its Ears Airdate: 12/11/63
WRITERS: Bill Persky and Sam Denoff / DIRECTOR: Jerry Paris

Supporting Cast: Officer Nelson—Bernie Hamilton, Lt. Yarnell—Ken Lynch, Witness—Edward Holmes, Intimidating Hoodlum—Alan Dexter, Police Officer—Ray Kellogg, Nervous Witness—Frank Adamo

Filmed on October 29, 1963.

Rob can't decide whether to testify when he discovers that he's the lone witness to a jewelry store holdup.

75) The Third One from the Left Airdate: 1/1/64
WRITER: John Whedon / DIRECTOR: Jerry Paris

Supporting Cast: Mel—Richard Deacon, Ernie Murphy—Jimmy Murphy, Joan Delroy—Cheryl Holdridge

Filmed on November 5, 1963.

Rob seeks Laura's advice when he finds himself the reluctant object of an enthusiastic young dancer's affections.

#076)   The Alan Brady Show Presents Airdate: 12/18/63
WRITERS: Sam Denoff and Bill Persky / DIRECTOR: Jerry Paris

Original Songs: Denoff and Persky

Supporting Cast: Mel—Richard Deacon, Little Girl—Cornell Chulay, Little Boy—Brendan Freeman, Alan Brady—Carl Reiner (uncredited), Announcer—Jerry Paris (uncredited voice-over)

Filmed on November 12, 1963. Songs: "Anthem to Alan Brady" (Persky, Denoff); "Deck the Halls" (traditional, arranged by Hagen); "Santa, Send a Fella" (Persky, Denoff); "Jingle Bells" (traditional, arranged by Hagen); "I Have Everything But You" (Persky, Denoff); "Little Drummer Boy" (Davis, Onorati, Simeone); "The Musicians" (Grean, Glazer)

Alan Brady revamps his Christmas show into a yuletide extravaganza starring Rob, Laura, and the rest of his show's talented writing staff.

Behind the Scenes: When Persky and Denoff first pitched the idea of a holiday episode, Carl Reiner recalls that he was initally cool to the notion, fearing that the episode would have little value as a summer rerun. According to the producer, he only reconsidered after it dawned on him that he could rerun the holiday episode at least once each year for the remainder of the show's run. "Okay," he remembers telling Persky and Denoff, "we'll do one Christmas show for the whole five years." Due to the unusually high number of costume and set changes, the episode would be filmed over the course of two days, without a studio audience in attendance...The episode's format was inspired by Persky and Denoff's days as writers on *The Andy Williams Show*, whose star frequently invited his own staff and their families to join him on stage for his annual holiday show.

77) My Husband Is the Best One Airdate: 1/8/64
WRITER: Martin A. Ragaway / DIRECTOR: Jerry Paris

Supporting Cast: Mel—Richard Deacon, Diane Moseby—Valerie Yerke, Waiter—Frank Adamo, Alan Brady—Carl Reiner (uncredited)

Filmed on November 19, 1963.

Rob faces a frigid reception from his co-workers after Laura convinces a visiting journalist that her husband is, in fact, the primary creative force behind the *The Alan Brady Show*.

Behind the Scenes: Writer Martin S. Ragaway's fourth script for the series would win the Writers Guild of America Award for Best Episodic Comedy script for 1963.

78) Happy Birthday and Too Many More Airdate: 2/5/64
WRITERS: Bill Persky and Sam Denoff / DIRECTOR: Jerry Paris

Supporting Cast: Pony delivery man—Johnny Silver, Ritchie's Party Guests—Brendan Freeman, Cornell Chulay, Michael Chulay, Tony Paris

Filmed on November 26, 1963. Songs: "Old Macdonald's Farm" (traditional); "The Circus Comes to Town" (Andrew, Denoff)

After Rob scotches Laura's elaborate plans for Ritchie's birthday party, he faces the challenge of entertaining sixty-three screaming kids in the Petrie living room.

Behind the Scenes: Owing to circumstances beyond their control—the episode was filmed a mere four days after the assassination of President John F. Kennedy—the producers opted to shoot this episode without a live studio audience in attendance...Included among the large cast of extras at Ritchie's birthday party are assistant director John C. Chulay's real-life son and daughter, Michael and Cornell Chulay, as well as director Jerry Paris's seven-year-old son, Tony Paris.

79) The Lady and the Tiger and the Lawyer Airdate: 1/15/64
WRITERS: Garry Marshall and Jerry Belson / DIRECTOR: Jerry Paris

Supporting Cast: Arthur Stanwycke—Anthony Eisley, Donna Palmer—Lyla Graham

Filmed on December 3, 1963.

The Petries stage a matchmaking competition to see whether a new bachelor in the neighborhood prefers Sally or Laura's cousin Donna.

Behind the Scenes: The first *Dick Van Dyke Show* episode written by Garry Marshall and Jerry Belson.

80) The Life and Love of Joe Coogan Airdate: 1/22/64
WRITER: Carl Reiner / DIRECTOR: Jerry Paris

Supporting Cast: Mel—Richard Deacon, Millie—Ann Morgan Guilbert, Joe Coogan—Michael Forest, Country Club Waiter—Johnny Silver

Filmed on December 10, 1963.

Rob is overcome with jealousy when he meets one of Laura's old beaus at a country club.

Behind the Scenes: Carl Reiner recalls that he named this episode's title character after one of his old army buddies.

81) A Nice, Friendly Game of Cards Airdate: 1/29/64
WRITER: Ernest Chambers / DIRECTOR: Howard Morris

Guest Stars: Jerry—Jerry Paris, Millie—Ann Morgan Guilbert, Lou Gregory— Edward C. Platt, Beth—Shirley Mitchell

Filmed on December 17, 1963.

Rob is the big winner in a neighborhood poker game, though it nearly costs him a few friendships after it's discovered that he's been dealing from a marked deck.

82) The Brave and the Backache Airdate: 2/12/64
WRITERS: Sheldon Keller and Howard Merrill / DIRECTOR: Jerry Paris

Supporting Cast: Millie—Ann Morgan Guilbert, Dr. Phil Nevins—Ross Elliott, Tony Daniels—Ken Berry

Filmed on December 31, 1963.

Laura is convinced that Rob's recurring back pain is a subconscious sign that he doesn't want to spend the weekend alone with her.

Behind the Scenes: Ken Berry's choreographer character would return for a second appearance in the show's ninety-sixth episode, "My Mother Can Beat Up My Father." A few years later, Berry would assume a central role in the cast of *The Andy Griffith Show* and its spin-off series, *Mayberry, RFD.*

Episode 82, "The Brave and the Backache."

83) The Pen Is Mightier Than the Mouth Airdate: 2/19/64
WRITERS: Bill Persky and Sam Denoff / DIRECTOR: Jerry Paris

Supporting Cast: Mel—Richard Deacon, Stevie Parsons—Dick Patterson, Bernie Quinn—Herb Vigran, Dave—Johnny Silver, Announcer—Carl Reiner (uncredited voice-over), Announcer—Jerry Paris (uncredited voice-over)

Filmed on January 7, 1964.

Sally considers leaving her job on *The Alan Brady Show* after she makes a splash on a late-night talk show.

Behind the Scenes: The first of two parts.

84) My Part-Time Wife Airdate: 2/26/64
WRITERS: Bill Persky and Sam Denoff / DIRECTOR: Jerry Paris

Guest Stars: Mel—Richard Deacon, Millie—Ann Morgan Guilbert, Jackie—Jackie Joseph

Filmed on January 14, 1964.

Rob reluctantly agrees to hire Laura as interim secretary during Sally's unexpected absence.

Behind the Scenes: This episode was inspired by writer Bill Persky's memories of casting his then-wife as an actress on a show he'd written. "My wife wanted to be an actress," he recalls, "and we actually put her on a show. And it was a nightmare for me. It was just the worst—like having your mother around."

85) Honeymoons Are for the Lucky Airdate: 3/4/64
WRITER: Carl Reiner / DIRECTOR: Jerry Paris

Supporting Cast: Millie—Ann Morgan Guilbert, Sam—Allan Melvin, Capt. E. Lebost—Peter Hobbs, Mrs. Campbell—Kathleen Freeman, Alfred Campbell—Johnny Silver, Soldier—Frank Adamo

Filmed on January 21, 1964.

Rob recalls how he went AWOL from Camp Crowder in order to spend a honeymoon night with Laura.

Behind the Scenes: Captain Lebost was named after Reiner's wife, whose maiden name was Lebost.

86) How to Spank a Star Airdate: 3/11/64
WRITERS: Nathaniel Curtis and Bill Idelson / DIRECTOR: Jerry Paris

Supporting Cast: Paula Marshall—Lola Albright, Mel—Richard Deacon, Alan Brady—Carl Reiner (uncredited voice-over)

Filmed on January 21, 1964.

Laura is jealous when Rob receives an unexpected promotion to the post of producer at the behest of *The Alan Brady Show*'s beautiful guest star.

87) The Plots Thicken Airdate: 3/18/64
WRITER: Carl Reiner, Bill Persky, and Sam Denoff / DIRECTOR: Jerry Paris

Guests Stars: Sam Petrie—J. Pat O'Malley, Clara Petrie—Isabel Randolph, Alan Meehan—Carl Benton Reid, Mrs. Meehan—Geraldine Wall

Filmed on February 4, 1964.

The Petries try to avoid getting caught up in the debate when their in-laws wage a battle of wills to determine where Rob and Laura will take their eternal rest.

Behind the Scenes: Though this episode's three writers would leave their collective fingerprints on virtually every script written for the show during its final three years, this would be one of only five episodes to bear their joint scriptwriting credit. "I think it was just for a change of pace," recalls Bill Persky. "We actually sat in a room and said, 'Well, let's write this one together.'"...Sam Petrie's penchant for grand toasts was a character trait borrowed from writer Bill Persky's own real-life father. "My father," says Persky, "if you gave him any form of liquid, he would make a toast. I mean, if he took a tablespoon of medicine, he would use it as an opportunity to make a toast. He'd hold up the spoon and say, 'May none of you ever be sick!' I called him Harry Persky—the automatic toaster. You put a glass in his hand and he pops up. So we incorporated that into the show."

88) Scratch My Car and Die Airdate: 3/25/64
WRITER: John Whedon / DIRECTOR: Howard Morris

Guest Stars: Mel—Richard Deacon, Millie—Ann Morgan Guilbert

Filmed on February 11, 1964. Songs: "On the Sunny Side of the Street" (McHugh, Fields)

Rob's obsession with his new sports car doesn't make it very easy for Laura to confess after she brings it home from a trip to the market with a scratch.

Behind the Scenes: This episode was inspired by Dick Van Dyke's own weakness for fancy sports cars; shortly after he signed to star in his own series, the actor had indulged himself with the purchase of an expensive British import. "I'd had Corvettes back in the fifties in New York," he recalls, "but at the time the Jaguar E type had just come out—I think it was about '60 or '61. And I ordered one, and it came in off the boat down in San Pedro. I think I had one of the first ones in L.A.—and I protected that car with my life."

89) The Return of Edwin Carp Airdate: 4/1/64
WRITER: Carl Reiner / DIRECTOR: Howard Morris

Supporting Cast: Edwin Carp—Richard Haydn, Mel—Richard Deacon, Arlene Harris—Herself, Bert Gordon—Himself, Mrs. Carp—Amzie Strickland, Announcer—Carl Reiner (uncredited voice-over)

Filmed on February 18, 1964. Song: "You Need Feet" (R. Irnin, arranged by Sid Colin)

Rob attempts to coax a legendary radio star out of retirement for a guest spot on a TV special.

Behind the Scenes: The show's storyline reflects Carl Reiner's own effort to stage an affectionate tribute to the golden days of radio with an episode that features three well-known stars from the medium's heyday: Bert Gordon, Arlene Harris, and Richard Haydn.

90) **October Eve** Airdate: 4/8/64
WRITERS: Bill Persky and Sam Denoff / DIRECTOR: Jerry Paris

Supporting Cast: Serge Carpetna—Carl Reiner, Mel—Richard Deacon, Henry—Howard Wendell, Henry's Wife—Genevieve Griffin, Sketch Artist—Frank Adamo

Filmed on March 3, 1964.

Laura encounters a long-forgotten skeleton from her closet when a nude oil portrait bearing her distinct resemblance surfaces at a prominent New York gallery.

Behind the Scenes: Dick Van Dyke's priceless reaction upon hearing Laura's pained explanation of the circumstances that led to her appearance in the portrait still stands as one of the show's all-time funniest moments. He waits until she leaves the room and then, in his pent-up anger, clenches the rings on top of the kitchen range with such force that he practically can't let go of them, even after it dawns on him that they are very, very hot. "Whenever I talk about Dick's genius," says Bill Persky, "I point out that stove take. There's no way you can write that, you know? It just happened." And though most Van Dyke show staffers cite the ovation that greeted Greg Morris's entrance in "That's My Boy???" as the show's all-time longest single laugh, film editor Bud Molin awards that singular distinction to Van Dyke's classic stove take in this episode. "*That*," claims the editor, "was a bigger laugh."

91) **Dear Mrs. Petrie, Your Husband Is in Jail** Airdate: 4/15/64
WRITERS: Jerry Belson and Garry Marshall / DIRECTOR: Jerry Paris

Supporting Cast: Benny Joey—Herkie Styles, Maureen Core—Barbara Stuart, Alberta Schweitzer—Jackie Joseph, Arnold—Art Batanides, Nick—Johnny Silver, Policeman—Henry Scott, TV Car Salesman—Carl Reiner (uncredited voice-over)

Filmed on March 10, 1964.

Rob ventures into a steamy honky-tonk to catch an old buddy's nightclub act, only to wind up spending the night in jail.

Behind the Scenes: According to Sam Denoff, this episode's opening scene—an extended monologue in which Rob Petrie does little more than mutter to himself in his living room—was devised to capitalize on one of the actor's lesser known talents. "Dick was the best mumbler in the business," observes Denoff. "We used to love to put Dick alone in a room, just to hear him mumble to himself."

92) My Neighbor's Husband's Other Life Airdate: 4/22/64
WRITERS: Carl Reiner, Bill Persky, and Sam Denoff / DIRECTOR: Jerry Paris

Supporting Cast: Jerry—Jerry Paris, Millie—Ann Morgan Guilbert, Waiter—Johnny Silver

Filmed on March 17, 1964.

Laura and Rob suspect the worst when they spot Jerry having dinner at a fancy restaurant with a beautiful blonde.

93) I'd Rather Be Bald Than Have No Head at All Airdate: 4/29/64
WRITERS: Bill Persky and Sam Denoff / DIRECTOR: Jerry Paris

Supporting Cast: Mel—Richard Deacon, Irwin—Ned Glass

Filmed on March 24, 1964.

Worried that he might be going prematurely bald, Rob consults a quack whose miracle hair restoration formula bears a peculiar resemblance to salad dressing.

Behind the Scenes: Co-writer Sam Denoff insists that the springboard for this episode came from a conversation he and Bill Persky had with the show's star one morning before a reading. "Dick," recalls the writer, "who has this marvelous head of hair, came in one day and said, 'I think I'm losing my hair.' And I said, 'Get out of here.' And he said, 'No, no. I'm serious. I think I'm losing my hair.'" Naturally, the writers wasted little time translating the actor's insecurities into the basic premise for this memorable episode...The sight gag that arrives at the episode's climax—where Rob wakes up to discover that his scalp has been transformed into an actual head of lettuce—was a special effect that makeup man Tom Tuttle achieved by ingenious means, employing a standard theatrical bald cap and other items obtained at the local grocer. "I found an old cabbage," explains Tuttle, "and then I took a needle and thread and just sewed it through. Leaf by leaf."

94) Teacher's Petrie Airdate: 5/13/64
WRITERS: Jerry Belson and Garry Marshall / DIRECTOR: Jerry Paris

Supporting Cast: Mr. Caldwell—Bernard Fox, Millie—Ann Morgan Guilbert, Miss Prinda—Cheerio Meredith

Filmed on March 31, 1964. Song: "Blue Danube" (Strauss)

Rob is unable to share Laura's enthusiasm for a creative writing course once he begins to suspect her attentive instructor's true motives.

95) My Two Show-Offs and Me Airdate: 12/16/64
WRITERS: Sheldon Keller and Howard Merrill / DIRECTOR: Jerry Paris

Supporting Cast: Mel—Richard Deacon, Lorraine Gilman—Doris Singleton
Filmed on April 3, 1964.

The attentions of a visting reporter transform Alan Brady's writing staff into a trio of bickering grandstanders.

Behind the Scenes: This would be the final Van Dyke show script from writers Sheldon Keller and Howard Merrill... Although produced at the end of the show's third year, this episode would not be broadcast until the following December, when it would be aired as the thirteenth episode of the show's fourth season.

Episode 94, "Teacher's Petrie"; Dick Van Dyke, Bernard Fox.

1964–1965
THE DICK VAN DYKE SHOW
Season Four

The series enters a fourth year of popular and critical acclaim, with Carl Reiner continuing as the show's producer. Reiner and his newly appointed story consultants, Bill Persky and Sam Denoff, write the majority of the season's scripts, with notable contributions from Garry Marshall and Jerry Belson, and Joseph C. Cavella, among others. Once again, Jerry Paris would direct the majority of the season's episodes.

Fourth-Season Credits:

Created and Produced by	Carl Reiner
Associate Producer	Ronald Jacobs
Music	Earle Hagen
Director of Photography	Robert DeGrasse, A.S.C.
Art Director	Kenneth A. Reid
Film Editor	
(episodes #107–108)	Beryl Gelfond
(episodes #96–106, 109–127)	Bud Molin, A.C.E.
Assistant Director	
(episode #105)	Edward M. Hillie
(episodes #96–104, 106–127)	John C. Chulay
Prop Master	Glenn Ross
Camera Coordinator	Robert Sousa
Casting	Ruth Burch
Script Continuity	
(episode #127)	Gloria Morgan
(episodes #96–126)	Marjorie Mullen
Set Decorator	Ken Swartz
Rerecording Editor	
(episodes #96, 98–103, 105, 107, 109–118, 120–26)	Dick Maier
(episodes #97, 104, 119)	John Hall
(episodes #106, 108)	Robert Reeve
(episode #127)	Sid Lubow
Story Consultants	Bill Persky and Sam Denoff
Hairstylist	Donna McDonough
Makeup	Tom Tuttle
Costumes	Harald Johnson
Sound Engineer	Cam McCulloch
Music Coordinator	Walter Popp
Recorded by	Glen Glenn Sound Co.
Executive Producer	Sheldon Leonard in association with Danny Thomas
Production Supervisor	Ronald Jacobs
Production Manager	Frank E. Meyers

Mr. Van Dyke's Wardrobe Furnished by Botany 500

Women's Fashions by Ann Arnold; Mancini; Catalina, Inc. Swimwear; Nardis; House of Gold; Suivante; Michael Anthony; Dorothea Beatty; Gibi Knits; Mannis of Hollywood

96) My Mother Can Beat Up My Father Airdate: 9/23/64
WRITERS: Bill Persky and Sam Denoff / DIRECTOR: Jerry Paris

Supporting Cast: Cavendish, the Drunk—Paul Gilbert, Tony Daniels—Ken Berry, Miss Taylor—Imelda de Martin, Ed Wilson—Tom Avera, Vinnie—Lou Cutell

Filmed on August 4, 1964.

Laura reveals a previously unknown talent for self-defense when she defends Rob against an unruly drunk in a Manhattan bar.

Behind the Scenes: Effective with this episode, the show's closing titles begin to list each character's name along with the actor who played them...Guest star Tom Avera had been in the original cast of *Your Shows of Shows* in the early 1950s...According to co-writer Sam Denoff, the script for this episode was inspired by little more than the availability of an actor who could pull off a convincing judo flip. "Somebody said, 'Paul Gilbert can do a great flip,'" recalls Denoff. "So we said, 'Gee, it would be fun to have him do it on the show.' And that was the start of that—the fact that we knew an actor who could do a funny fall."

97) The Ghost of A. Chantz Airdate: 9/30/64
WRITERS: Bill Persky and Sam Denoff / DIRECTOR: Jerry Paris

Supporting Cast:
Mel—Richard Deacon,
Mr. Little—Maurice
Brenner, Caretaker—
Milton Parsons

Filmed on August 11, 1964.

Rob and Laura share an unsettling night in a haunted cabin with Buddy and Sally.

Episode 97,
"The Ghost of A. Chantz."

98) The Lady and the Babysitter Airdate: 10/7/64
WRITERS: Bill Persky and Sam Denoff / DIRECTOR: Jerry Paris

Supporting Cast: Roger McChesney—Eddie Hodges, Man in Library—Frank Adamo

Filmed on August 18, 1964. Song: "The Thing "(Grean)

The Petries' teenage babysitter develops an adolescent crush on Laura.

Behind the Scenes: This episode was designed to showcase the talents of former child star Eddie Hodges, who'd made his first splash some seven years earlier as the lisping juvenile lead in the original cast of Broadway's *The Music Man*...Never a fan of this particular show, co-writer Bill Persky nevertheless cites the scene where Rob playfully chides Laura for having the temerity to offer him a slice of chocolate cake—*without* a companion glass of milk!— as one of the most fondly remembered moments of the entire series. "That was really a kind of lame show," confesses Persky. "But people still come up to me and say, 'I love the milk cake show!' Only it wasn't about milk and cake at all. But it had that two-page exchange that people always remember." "When Rob says, 'Chocolate cake is *milk* cake,'" observes Sam Denoff, "the audience howled. Because they recognized that as a true moment. And it became a very human moment, all because we were willing to leave the story for a few minutes so they could talk about cake."

99) A Vigilante Ripped My Sports Coat Airdate: 10/14/64
WRITER: Carl Reiner / DIRECTOR: Peter Baldwin

Supporting Cast: Mel—Richard Deacon, Jerry—Jerry Paris, Millie—Ann Morgan Guilbert

Filmed on August 25, 1964.

Rob and Jerry lock horns after Rob refuses to join a vigilante group that's been organized to protest a neighbor's unruly crabgrass.

100) The Man From Emperor Airdate: 10/21/64
WRITERS: Carl Reiner, Bill Persky, and Sam Denoff / DIRECTOR: Jerry Paris

Supporting Cast: Drew Patton—Lee Philips, Coffee Girl—Nadia Sanders, Laura #2—Gloria Neil, Florence—Sally Carter, Miss Finland—Tracy Butler, Sam, the Secretary—Mary Tyler Moore (uncredited voice-over)

Filmed on September 1, 1964.

Rob is tempted by an offer to join the editorial staff of a glossy men's magazine, though Laura has other ideas.

Behind the Scenes: Mary Tyler Moore contributes an uncredited voice-over as Drew Patton's sultry off-screen secretary, Sam—a sly reference to the actress's early role as the unseen receptionist of the same name on the *Richard Diamond* series in the late fifties.

101) Romance, Roses, and Rye Bread Airdate: 10/28/64
WRITERS: Gary Marshall and Jerry Belson / DIRECTOR: Jerry Paris

Supporting Cast: Mel—Richard Deacon, Usherette—Jeri Lou James, Actor—Frank Adamo, Bert Monker—Sid Melton

Filmed on September 8, 1964.

Sally discovers that she's got an unlikely admirer when the deli man starts dropping off flowers along with her pastrami sandwich.

102) 4 1/2 Airdate: 11/4/64
WRITERS: Garry Marshall and Jerry Belson / DIRECTOR: Jerry Paris

Supporting Cast: Lyle Delp—Don Rickles, Mel—Richard Deacon

Filmed on September 15, 1964.

Rob recalls the story of Lyle Delp—an inept stick-up artist who once tried to rob the Petries in a stalled elevator.

Behind the Scenes: The first of two parts...Story editors Persky and Denoff had contributed material to guest star Don Rickles's nightclub act during their early days in New York.

103) The Alan Brady Show Goes to Jail Airdate: 11/11/64
WRITERS: Bill Persky and Sam Denoff / DIRECTOR: Jerry Paris

Supporting Cast: Lyle Delp—Don Rickles, Boxer Morrison—Robert Strauss, Warden Jackson—Ken Lynch, Harry Tinker—Arthur Batanides, Guard Jenkins—Allan Melvin, Convict—Vincent Barbi, Guard—Alfred Ward

Filmed on September 22, 1964. Songs: "Vienna, Vienna" (Amsterdam); "Camptown Races" (Foster); "Cotton Fields" (Ledbetter); "I've Got Your Number" (Coleman, Leigh)

Rob and the gang are all set to perform a prison benefit show when Rob is mistaken for one of the inmates.

Behind the Scenes: Alan Brady's name was inadvertently misspelled—with two *l*'s—in this episode's opening titles, an error that has been carried into all surviving syndication prints.

Episode 103, "The Alan Brady Show Goes to Jail"; Dick Van Dyke, Vincent Barbi, Arthur Batanides, Rogert Strauss.

104) Three Letters From One Wife Airdate: 11/18/64
WRITERS: Bill Persky and Sam Denoff / DIRECTOR: Jerry Paris

Supporting Cast: Mel—Richard Deacon, Millie—Ann Morgan Guilbert, Alan Brady—Carl Reiner, Miss Thomas—Valerie Yerke, Jack Sullivan—Jerry Paris (uncredited voice-over)

Filmed on September 29, 1964.

Against Laura's better judgment, Millie wages an ill-fated write-in campaign to bolster Rob's professional standing with Alan Brady.

Behind the Scenes: This episode marks Carl Reiner's first full-fledged appearance as Alan Brady—as well as the first time the producer would receive an on-screen credit in the show's closing titles for playing the role.

105) It Wouldn't Hurt Them to Give Us a Raise Airdate: 12/2/64
WRITER: Jay Burton and Ernest Chambers / DIRECTOR: Peter Baldwin

Supporting Cast: Mel—Richard Deacon, Doug Wesley—Roger C. Carmel

Filmed on October 6, 1964.

Rob enters the labyrinth of corporate finance when he tries to squeeze a raise for Buddy and Sally from Alan Brady's tight-fisted accountant.

106) Pink Pills and Purple Parents Airdate: 11/25/64
WRITERS: Jerry Belson and Garry Marshall/
DIRECTOR: Al Rafkin

Supporting Cast: Millie—Ann Morgan Guilbert, Sam Petrie—Tom Tully, Clara Petrie—Isabel Randolph

Filmed on October 20, 1964. Songs: "I Dream of Jeannie With the Light Brown Hair" (Foster); "Monkey Doodle Polka" (Bagley, Horton)

Rob recalls the disaster that resulted when Laura hosted a dinner party for his parents after accidentally taking an overdose of Millie's prescription pills.

Behind the Scenes: Mary Tyler Moore's "drunk" scene in this episode recalls Dick Van Dyke's comical inebriation in the show's thirty-sixth episode, "My Husband Is Not a Drunk," which was—by odd coincidence—one of only three other Van Dyke episodes also directed by Al Rafkin.

Episode 106, "Pink Pills and Purple Parents."

107) The Death of the Party Airdate: 12/9/64
WRITERS: Bill Persky and Sam Denoff / DIRECTOR: Al Rafkin

Supporting Cast: Millie—Ann Morgan Guilbert, Uncle Harold—Willard Waterman, Cousin Margaret—Jane Dulo, Cousin Grace—Patty Regan, Paul—Pitt Herbert, Frank—Frank Adamo

Filmed on October 27, 1964.

Despite a raging fever and a bad case of the chills, Rob is determined to get through Laura's family gathering without anyone suspecting that he's deathly ill.

108) Stretch Petrie vs. Kid Schenk Airdate: 12/30/64
WRITERS: Garry Marshall and Jerry Belson / DIRECTOR: Jerry Paris

Supporting Cast: Neil Schenk—Jack Carter, Bill Sampson—Peter Hobbs, Headwaiter—Albert Carrier, Second Model—Lynn Borden, First Model—Judy Taylor, Girl—Sally Carter

Filmed on November 3, 1964.

Rob finds it next to impossible to stand up to Neil Schenk, an opportunistic old friend who comes around fishing for a job in return for an ancient favor.

109) The Impractical Joke Airdate: 1/13/65
WRITERS: Bill Persky and Sam Denoff / DIRECTOR: Jerry Paris

Supporting Cast: Mel—Richard Deacon, Phil Franklin—Lennie Weinrib, William Handlebuck—Alvy Moore, Guest #1—Johnny Silver

Filmed on November 10, 1964. Song: "Battle Hymn of the Republic" (Steffe)

Wary of being taken in by a practical joke, Buddy refuses to heed a visit from an agent of the Internal Revenue Service.

Episode 109,
"The Impractical Joke";
Lennie Weinrib, Dick Van Dyke,
Mary Tyler Moore.

110) Brother, Can You Spare $2500? Airdate: 1/6/65
WRITERS: Garry Marshall and Jerry Belson / DIRECTOR: Jerry Paris

Supporting Cast: Mel—Richard Deacon, Main Hobo—Gene Baylos, Harry Keen—
Herbie Faye, Hobo #3—Jimmy Cross, Hobo #2—Tiny Brauer, Woman—Sheila
Rogers, Cop—Larry Blake, Warren—Brian Nash

Filmed on November 17, 1964.

A lost *Alan Brady Show* script is recovered by a vagrant who demands $2500 in
exchange for its safe return.

Episode 110, "Brother, Can You Spare $2500?"; Dick Van Dyke, Gene Baylos.

111) Stacey Petrie—Part I Airdate: 1/20/65
WRITER: Carl Reiner / DIRECTOR: Jerry Paris

Supporting Cast: Stacey Petrie—Jerry Van Dyke, Herman Glimsher—Bill Idelson, Dr. Lemler—Howard Wendell

Filmed on November 24, 1964.

Rob talks Sally into coaching his withdrawn brother Stacey through a practice date at her apartment.

Behind the Scenes: The first of two parts.

112) Stacey Petrie—Part II Airdate: 1/27/65
WRITERS: Carl Reiner, Bill Persky, and Sam Denoff / DIRECTOR: Jerry Paris

Supporting Cast: Stacey Petrie—Jerry Van Dyke, Millie—Ann Morgan Guilbert, Julie Kincaid—Jane Wald, Lou Temple—Herbie Faye, Tinker, the Butler— Kendrick Huxham, Willie Cook—Carl Reiner

Filmed on December 1, 1964. Songs: "I Dream of Jeannie with the Light Brown Hair" (Foster); "Hello Dolly" (Herman)

Rob and Laura help Stacey recover from a rejection by the woman of his dreams.

Behind the Scenes: Listen closely and you'll hear Julie Kincaid's butler referred to as Tinker, a joshing reference to Grant Tinker, who was at that time married to Mary Tyler Moore...The show's comic high point arrives in the slapstick confrontation that ensues after Herman Glimsher discovers the hapless Stacey lounging in Sally's apartment without his pants on. But despite the apparent mayhem that follows, guest star Idelson insists that director Jerry Paris made certain that conditions on the set were anything but chaotic when the sequence was filmed. "Jerry Paris choreographed that entire fight," says Idelson. "It's a wild bit. But if you watch it, you'll see that that thing is choreographed down to a gnat's eyelash. We went over that, and over that, and over that. Jerry Paris loved doing that kind of physical comedy. That was fun."...Co-writer Bill Persky describes how he had the pleasure of rediscovering this episode not long ago. "One morning I got up around four-fifteen or something like that," he recalls, "and I couldn't fall back to sleep. So I flipped on Nickelodeon and the Van Dyke show was on. It was the one with Dick's brother, with the Cyrano de Bergerac plot. It was so great. I said, 'Jesus, this is so brilliant!' I couldn't remember who'd done that one. And then when I saw the credits, I saw that *we* had written it!"

113) The Redcoats Are Coming Airdate: 2/10/65
WRITERS: Bill Persky and Sam Denoff / DIRECTOR: Jerry Paris

Supporting Cast: Mel—Richard Deacon, Millie—Ann Morgan Guilbert, Ernie—Chad Stuart, Freddie—Jeremy Clyde, Richard Karp—William Beckley, Marge—Trudi Ames, Estelle—Ellie Sommers, Phoebe—Mollie Howerton, Janie—Wendy Wilson, Girl #1—Shelley Cochran, Girl #2—Linda Cochran

Filmed on December 8, 1964. Songs: "No Other Baby" (Stuart, Clyde); "My How the Time Goes By" (Stuart, Alquist)

The Petrie residence becomes the site of a mob scene after Rob offers asylum to a pair of English teen idols called the Redcoats.

Behind the Scenes: This lighthearted send-up of American teenagers' response to the Beatles and other British rock groups of the era offers another example of one of the show's infrequent stabs at topicality—and, predictably, the comedy suffers as a result...The Redcoats were played by the real-life British folk-rock duo, Chad & Jeremy, who must have had very good agents—just a few weeks after they filmed the Van Dyke show, the pair would repeat their performance, almost beat for beat, on an episode of ABC's *Patty Duke Show.* The singers also logged an appearance on the Western series *Laredo* during that same period, as well as an episode of ABC's *Batman* in which they played themselves.

Episode 113, "The Redcoats Are Coming"; Dick Van Dyke, Jeremy Clyde, Chad Stuart, Mary Tyler Moore.

114) Boy #1, Boy #2 Airdate: 2/3/65
WRITER: Martin A. Ragaway / DIRECTOR: Jerry Paris

Supporting Cast: Mel—Richard Deacon, Jerry—Jerry Paris, Millie—Ann Morgan Guilbert, Freddie Helper—Peter Oliphant

Filmed on December 15, 1964.

Millie and Laura become stage mothers after Ritchie and Freddie are chosen to play small parts in a TV commercial.

115) The Case of the Pillow Airdate: 2/17/64
WRITERS: Bill Persky and Sam Denoff / DIRECTOR: Howard Morris

Supporting Cast: Judge—Ed Begley, Jerry—Jerry Paris, Millie—Ann Morgan Guilbert, Wiley—Alvy Moore, May—Amzie Strickland, Bailiff—Joel Fluellen, Man #1—Johnny Silver

Filmed on December 22, 1964.

Rob fancies himself a crusading lawyer when he takes an unscrupulous pillow salesman to small claims court.

Behind the Scenes: Another eccentric Van Dyke show storyline inspired by real life. "That happened to me," swears coauthor Bill Persky, describing a scenario that's almost a carbon copy of Rob Petrie's plight. "I bought these pillows from this guy who came to my apartment when I first got married. And I said they smelled like ducks. He said, 'No they don't!' Then my wife said, 'Yes, they do. It's two against one.' So then he went down to his car and got *his* wife. And she said, no, they didn't. So, I went next door and knocked on my neighbor's door—people I'd never met before. They said, 'Hi, welcome! Come on in, have a drink.' I said, 'No. Come into

Episode 115, "The Case of the Pillow"; Ed Begley, Dick Van Dyke.

our apartment.' And I said, 'Smell this. Don't these smell like ducks to you?' It was hysterical, and we put it all in the show."

116) Young Man with a Shoehorn Airdate: 2/24/65
WRITERS: Jerry Belson and Garry Marshall / DIRECTOR: Jerry Paris

Supporting Cast: Mel—Richard Deacon, Millie—Ann Morgan Guilbert, Lou Sorrell—Lou Jacobi, Sid Feldman—Milton Frome, Laughing Woman—Amzie Strickland, Woman Customer #1—Jane Dulo; Sexy Girl—LaRue Farlow, Male Customer—Irving Bacon

Filmed on January 12, 1965.

Rob and Buddy sign on as not-so-silent partners in a discount shoe store operation.

Episode 116, "Young Man with a Shoehorn."

117) **Girls Will Be Boys** Airdate: 3/3/65
WRITERS: Jerry Belson and Garry Marshall / DIRECTOR: Jerry Paris

Supporting Cast: Ogden Darwell—Bernard Fox, Doris "Dolly" Darwell—Doris Singleton, Priscilla Darwell—Tracy Stratford

Filmed on January 19, 1965.

Laura is understandably concerned after Ritchie arrives home with a bruise inflicted by a bully named Priscilla.

118) **Bupkis** Airdate: 3/10/65
WRITERS: Bill Persky and Sam Denoff / DIRECTOR: Lee Philips

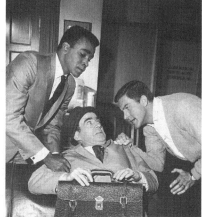

Episode 118, "Bupkis"; Greg Morris, Robert Ball, Dick Van Dyke.

Supporting Cast: Frank "Sticks" Mandalay— Greg Morris, Buzzy Potter—Robert Ball, Sheila, the Secretary—Patty Regan, Songwriter—Tim Herbert, Mr. Doldan—Charles Dugdale, Traffic Announcer—Carl Reiner (uncredited voice-over)

Filmed on January 26, 1965. Songs: "Weather Jingle" (Persky, Denoff); "Bupkis" (Persky, Denoff) (sung by Dick and Deedee); "Sergeant Foley" (Persky, Denoff); "Attila the Hun" (Persky, Denoff); "The Only Girl I Ever Loved" (Persky, Denoff)

Rob is delighted to hear a novelty song he penned with an old army buddy pop up on the radio, until he discovers that his former partner has taken all the credit.

Behind the Scenes: Persky and Denoff's "Bupkis" is sung by Dick and Deedee— Dick St. John Gosting and Deedee Sperling—a pop singing duo whose modest string of hits in the early 1960s included "The Mountain's High" and "Thou Shalt Not Steal"...Coauthor Sam Denoff recalls that he borrowed his fictitious pop song's title from an old Yiddish expression he picked up from his mother, which he'd always been told meant "nothing." But he didn't discover that the word had more subtle shades of meaning until the night the episode was filmed. "My mother and father came to see the show," recalls Denoff, "as they very often did on Tuesday night. And my mother laughed like everybody else. But afterward, she says, 'Sammy, you can't put that on the air!' And I said, 'Why not?' And she said, 'Don't you know what bupkis means?' And I said, 'Sure, it means "nothing."' And she says, 'No. "Nothing" is the loose translation. The literal translation for bupkis in Yiddish is "goat shit." Goat shit is worth nothing, so bupkis is goat shit.' We decided to leave it in anyway—but we didn't tell the guy from network standards and practices."...Curiously, coauthor Bill Persky retains somewhat less agreeable memories of this particular episode. "The worst show we ever did was 'Bupkis,'" he insists. "Oh, I hated it. Just hated it."

119) Your Home Sweet Home Is My Home Sweet Home
Airdate: 3/17/65
WRITERS: Howard Ostroff and Joan Darling / DIRECTOR: Lee Philips

Supporting Cast: Jerry—Jerry Paris, Millie—Ann Morgan Guilbert, Mr. Parkly—Stanley Adams, Mr. Steele—Eddie Ryder

Filmed on February 2, 1965.

Rob recalls the day he and Laura decided to buy their dream house, even after they discovered that it came fully equipped with a massive rock jutting out of the basement floor.

Behind the Scenes: In the episode it's revealed that Rob and Laura's dream castle carried an asking price of of $27,990...The script also establishes that before they moved to New Rochelle, the Petries and the Helpers lived in a city identified as Willetown, which was almost certainly a reference to the maiden name of Dick Van Dyke's real-life wife, the former Marjorie Willett.

120) Anthony Stone Airdate: 3/24/65
WRITER: Joseph C. Cavella / DIRECTOR: Jerry Paris

Supporting Cast: Anthony Stone—Richard Angarola, Delivery Boy—Frank Adamo, Waiter—Bob Hoffman

Filmed on February 9, 1965.

Rob and Buddy make the startling discovery that Sally's mysterious new boyfriend is a mortician—and a married one, at that.

121) Never Bathe on Saturday Airdate: 3/31/65
WRITER: Carl Reiner / DIRECTOR: Jerry Paris

Supporting Cast: Millie—Ann Morgan Guilbert, The Detective—Bernard Fox, Bruce, the Bellboy—Bill Idelson, Maid—Kathleen Freeman, Engineer—Arthur Malet, Waiter—Johnny Silver

Filmed on February 16, 1964.

Laura finds herself in an embarrassing fix when she gets her toe stuck in the water spout of a fancy hotel bathtub—with the door locked from the inside.

Behind the Scenes: According to story editor Bill Persky, Dick Van Dyke's decision to switch shoulders in midrun during his assault on the bathroom door was the result of an inspiration that hit the actor the night of the performance. "That was another great move that Dick did spontaneously while he was filming."...Carl Reiner's script for "Never Bathe on Saturday" would earn the writer his fourth consecutive nomination for an Emmy Award in the writer's category, though he would not win the award in that particular category that year.

122) 100 Terrible Hours Airdate: 5/5/65
WRITERS: Bill Persky and Sam Denoff / DIRECTOR: Theodore J. Flicker

Supporting Cast: Mel—Richard Deacon, Mr. Van Buren—Fred Clark, Alan
   Brady—Carl Reiner, Mr. Waring—Dabbs Greer, Mr. Chambers—Howard
   Wendell, Dr. Gage—Harry Stanton, Photographer—Johnny Silver, Dr.
   Adamo—Frank Adamo

Filmed on March 2, 1965.

Rob recalls the time he attempted to broadcast a radio show for 100 hours
straight mere hours before he was scheduled to meet Alan Brady for the very first
time.

Behind the Scenes: Like his on-screen persona, Dick Van Dyke was also raised
in Danville, Illinois...Though Van Dyke also had held down an early job as a disc
jockey, writers Persky and Denoff drew most of their inspiration for this episode's
script from their own experience as reluctant deejays at New York's WNEW-AM
in the late fifties. "I was the assistant program director," recounts Persky, "and Sam
was the head of the commercial continuity department. And there was a strike.
Because we were management, Sam and I had to go on the air for eight hours a day
until it was settled. So we did the Sam and Bill show in the afternoon. Then we had
like an hour off before we had to come back, when we'd do the Bill and Sam show
at night. We were exhausted, but we just kept it up, doing our regular jobs and
doing these eight hours a day of broadcasting, too. By the end of that week, we
were pretty punchy."...Supporting actor Frank Adamo retains his own name in his
cameo as Dr. Adamo.

123) A Show of Hands Airdate: 4/14/65
WRITER: Joseph C. Cavella / DIRECTOR: Theodore J. Flicker

Supporting Cast: Mel—Richard Deacon, Millie—Ann Morgan Guilbert, Chairman
   Rodney Johnson—Joel Fluellen, Vice-Chairman Joe Clark—Henry Scott, Delivery Man—Herkie Styles

Filmed on March 9, 1965.

Rob and Laura are forced to wear gloves to a prestigious awards banquet after
they accidentally dye their hands an indelible shade of black.

Behind the Scenes: Yet another episode torn from real life, as Carl Reiner
explained to a 1988 gathering sponsored by New York's Museum of Broadcasting.
"When we'd get together with new writers," said Reiner, "we'd always ask the question, what happened to you lately at your house? Don't give us any fantasy ideas.
But if you've got anything that really happened, we'll build a show around it. And
the guy was fussing around all day—it was Joe Cavella—and he said, 'The only
thing that happened, my wife was dying some clothing in black dye, and her hands
got black and she couldn't get it off.' We said, 'That's it!' So he wrote it."

124) **Baby Fat** Airdate: 4/21/65
WRITERS: Garry Marshall and Jerry Belson / DIRECTOR: Jerry Paris

Supporting Cast: Mel—Richard Deacon, Buck Brown—Richard Erdman, Lionel Dann—Sandy Kenyon, Harper Worthington Yates—Strother Martin, Alan Brady—Carl Reiner

Filmed on March 16, 1965.

Rob agrees to doctor the script for Alan Brady's Broadway debut, only to have second thoughts about performing such a thankless task without recognition.

Behind the Scenes: "That was a story out of Garry's life," observes co-writer Jerry Belson, recalling the inspiration for this classic episode. "He was brought in to ghostwrite a play like that—I think it was summer theater with Jack Carter. I don't know if they made him hide in a closet, but I think he did have to hide in the next room."...Strother Martin's flamboyant playwright Harper Worthington Yates is clearly modeled after Tennessee Williams; the script doctor who finally ends up ghosting Brady's play is identified as Dave Murrows, an obvious reference to the real-life Pulitzer Prize–winner and well-known real-life script doctor, Abe Burrows...One of Carl Reiner's all-time favorite Van Dyke shows, the producer would be particularly proud of his work as an actor in the episode. Says Reiner, "I'd put that in my bank as one of the best things I ever did."

Episode 136, "Go Tell the Birds and Bees"

125) **Br-rooom, Br-rooom** Airdate: 5/12/65
WRITERS: Dale McRaven and Carl Kleinschmitt / DIRECTOR: Jerry Paris

Supporting Cast: Policeman—Sandy Kenyon, Jolly—Jimmy Murphy, Mouse—Bob Random, Gus—Carl Reindel, Doris—Linda Marshall, Counter Man—Johnny Silver

Filmed on March 23, 1965.

Rob takes his new motorcycle out for a spin and unwittingly falls in with a gang of unruly bikers.

Behind the Scenes: The first Van Dyke show script from newcomers Carl Kleinschmitt and Dale McRaven, the teleplay would go on to win a Writer's Guild of America Award as Best Episodic Comedy script for the year 1965...Van Dyke reportedly improvised much of his own dialogue in the solo scene that takes place in Rob's garage, some of it during the actual filmed performance—a circumstance that, according to Van Dyke's friend and stand-in, Frank Adamo, was not all that rare during the show's later days. "A lot of that stuff," recalls Adamo, "they would never even rehearse. They'd say, 'Dick does X number of minutes here. And then they'd block the area where they thought he'd be, and they'd just let him loose to do what he wanted.'"...A prop billboard used in this episode advertises the fictional soft drink Calvada, an in-joke reference to Calvada Productions, the legal name of the partnership that produced the Van Dyke show.

126) **There's No Sale Like Wholesale** Airdate: 5/26/65
WRITERS: Garry Marshall and Jerry Belson / DIRECTOR: Jerry Paris

Supporting Cast: Millie—Ann Morgan Guilbert, Nunzio Vallani—Lou Krugman, Opal Levinger—Jane Dulo, Emil—Peter Brocco, Mr. Garnett—A. G. Vitanza

Filmed on March 30, 1965.

Rob decides to save a few bucks on a new fur coat for Laura by letting Buddy order it wholesale—a decision that Rob soon comes to regret.

127) **A Farewell to Writing** Airdate: 9/22/65
WRITERS: Fred Freeman and Lawrence J. Cohen / DIRECTOR: Jerry Paris

Supporting Cast: Millie—Ann Morgan Guilbert, Horace—Guy Raymond

Filmed on April 2, 1965. Song: "The Caissons Go Rolling Along" (Gruber)

Rob hopes a few days of seclusion in a mountain cabin will motivate him to complete his novel—instead, it very nearly drives him stir-crazy.

Behind the Scenes: The final show in the series' fourth production season, this episode was filmed on a Friday—four days earlier than the show's customary Tuesday night performance—after a mere three days of rehearsal...As in the show's two previous seasons, this final episode of the year would be held back for broadcast until the following season...Ann Guilbert first met future husband Guy Raymond on the set during the filming of this week's episode.

1965–1966
THE DICK VAN DYKE SHOW
Season Five

After four superlative seasons, *The Dick Van Dyke Show* draws to a close in its fifth and final year on the air. Season five would see Carl Reiner trade off producing chores with Persky and Denoff, who would also continue as the show's story consultants through the remainder of the season. Other memorable fifth-year scripts are contributed by a wide array of freelancers, including the ever-redoubtable teams of Garry Marshall and Jerry Belson and Dale McRaven and Carl Kleinschmitt, as well Joseph C. Cavella, Jay Burton and Ernest Chambers, Fred Freeman and Lawrence J. Cohen, Art Baer and Ben Joelson, John Whedon, Rick Mittleman and Joseph Bonaduce, among others. And, for the third year running, Jerry Paris would again serve as the show's primary director.

Fifth-Season Credits:

Created by	Carl Reiner
Produced by	
(episodes #128–133, 145–158)	Carl Reiner
(episodes #134–144)	Bill Persky and Sam Denoff
Music	Earle Hagen
Associate Producer	Ronald Jacobs
Story Consultants	Bill Persky and Sam Denoff
Production Assistant	Joel Swanson
Director of Photography	Robert DeGrasse, A.S.C.
Art Direcor	Kenneth A. Reid
Film Editor	Beryl Gelfond
Assistant Director	
(episodes #128–154)	John C. Chulay
(episodes #155–158)	Stanley J. Brooks
Prop Master	Glenn Ross
Camera Coordinator	Robert Sousa
Casting	Ruth Burch
Script Continuity	Marjorie Mullen
Set Decorator	Ken Swartz
Rerecording Editor	
(episodes #128–129, 131, 133, 157–158)	Dick Maier
(episodes #130, 132)	Sid Lubow
(episodes #134–156)	Reg Browne
Hairstylist	Donna McDonough
Makeup	Tom Tuttle
Costumes (episodes #128–149)	Harald Johnson
(episodes #150–158)	Margaret Makau
Sound Engineer	Cam McCulloch

Music Coordinator   Walter Popp
Recorded by   Glen Glenn Sound Co.
Executive Producer   Sheldon Leonard in association
with Danny Thomas
Production Supervisor   Ronald Jacobs
Production Manager   Frank E. Meyers
Mr. Van Dyke's Wardrobe Furnished by Botany 500
Women's Fashions by Suivante; Nardis of California; Nardis of Dallas; Gibi
Knits; California Girl; Michael Anthony, Inc.; Bridallure, Inc.; Torino Imports;
Glenhaven, Ltd.; House of Gold

128) Coast-to-Coast Big Mouth Airdate: 9/15/65

WRITERS: Bill Persky and Sam Denoff / DIRECTOR: Jerry Paris

Supporting Cast: Mel—Richard Deacon, Millie—Ann Morgan Guilbert, Johnny
Patrick—Dick Curtis, Alan Brady—Carl Reiner

Filmed on August 3, 1965.

Laura faces Alan Brady's wrath after a fast-talking game-show host goads her
into admitting that the star wears a toupee.

Behind the Scenes: This script would earn Persky and Denoff their second Emmy
Award for Outstanding Writing Achievement in Comedy...According to Bill Persky, he and partner Sam Denoff were inspired to write the show one morning after
watching Carl Reiner fret over having to buy a new hairpiece. "The toupee was a
pain in the ass for him," says Persky. "So we decided to do an episode about it."

129) Uhny Uftz Airdate: 9/29/65

WRITERS: Carl Kleinschmitt and Dale McRaven / DIRECTOR: Jerry Paris

Supporting Cast: Mel—Richard Deacon, Dr. Phil Ridley—Ross Elliott, Lady—
Madge Blake, Karl—John Mylong; Hugo—Karl Lukas; Sound Effects—Carl
Reiner (uncredited voice-over)

Filmed on August 10, 1965.

No one seems to believe Rob's claim that he saw a flying saucer hovering outside the office window.

Behind the Scenes: The versatile Carl Reiner provided the sound effects for the
show's gurgling water cooler, as well as most of the other miscellaneous vocal effects
that are heard on the episode's soundtrack...Writers Kleinschmitt and McRaven
wrote this episode's script in response to the then rampant UFO-sighting fad of
the early sixties. "Everybody was seeing flying saucers at the time," notes McRaven,
"but it was usually a guy somewhere in Indiana. We thought it would be funny for
an urban writer living in New York to see a flying saucer."

130) **The Ugliest Dog in the World** Airdate: 10/6/65
WRITERS: Bill Persky and Sam Denoff / DIRECTOR: Lee Philips

Supporting Cast: Mel—Richard Deacon, Rexford Spaulding—Billy De Wolfe, Mrs. Rocky Spaulding—Florence Halop, Mr. Mack—Michael Conrad, Berkowitz—George Tyne, Customer—Barbara Dodd

Filmed on August 17, 1965.

A homely mongrel becomes the temporary ward of the Petries after he's cut from a scheduled appearance on *The Alan Brady Show.*

Behind the Scenes: Persky and Denoff's script for this episode would earn the writers their second Emmy nomination of the year, though the award would go to their script for the show's 128th episode, "Coast-to-Coast Big Mouth"...Dog groomer Rexford Spaulding was named after a pair of prominent boulevards in Beverly Hills.

131) **No Rice at My Wedding** Airdate: 10/13/65
WRITERS: Jerry Belson and Garry Marshall / DIRECTOR: Lee Philips

Supporting Cast: Millie—Ann Morgan Guilbert, Clark Rice—Van Williams, Sam Pomerantz—Allan Melvin, Heckler—Bert Remsen, Humphrey Dundee—Johnny Silver

Filmed on August 24, 1965.

Rob recalls his only serious competition for Laura's hand, a charming army corporal who won a date with her in a USO charity raffle.

Behind the Scenes: Guest star Van Williams would return to prime time the following season in the title role on ABC's *The Green Hornet.*

132) **Draw Me a Pear** Airdate: 10/20/65
WRITERS: Art Baer and Ben Joelson / DIRECTOR: Jerry Paris

Supporting Cast: Millie—Ann Morgan Guilbert, Valerie Ware—Ina Balin, Missy—Jackie Joseph, Agnes—Jody Gilbert, Doris—Dorothy Neumann, Sebastian—Frank Adamo

Filmed on August 31, 1965.

Laura suspects that Rob's comely drawing instructor may be interested in something other than her husband's artistic abilities.

Behind the Scenes: Amateur cartoonist Dick Van Dyke contributed the caricature of Mary Tyler Moore that figures prominently in this episode.

133) The Great Petrie Fortune Airdate: 10/27/65
WRITERS: Ernest Chambers and Jay Burton / DIRECTOR: Jerry Paris

Supporting Cast: Leland Ferguson—Dan Tobin, Mr. Harlow—Forrest Lewis, Luthuella Detweiller—Elvia Allman, Alfred Reinback—Herb Vigran, Rebecca—Amzie Strickland, Ezra—Howard Wendell, Ike Ballinger—Tiny Brauer

Filmed on September 9, 1965. Songs: "Me and My Shadow" (Dryer, Jolson, Rose); "Dixie" (traditional)

Rob discovers he's the heir to a mysterious fortune that's hidden somewhere in his Uncle Hezekiah's rolltop desk.

134) Odd But True Airdate: 11/3/65
WRITERS: Garry Marshall and Jerry Belson / DIRECTOR: Jerry Paris

Supporting Cast: Mel—Richard Deacon, Millie—Ann Morgan Guilbert, Tetlow—James Millhollin, Lady with Dog—Hope Summers, Potato Man—David Fresco, Freddie Helper—Peter Oliphant, Upside Down Man—Bert May, Receptionist—Rhoda Williams, Stagehand—Ray Kellogg

Filmed on September 21, 1965.

Rob becomes a reluctant candidate for the *Odd But True* newspaper column after Ritchie connects the freckles on his father's back and discovers a reasonable facsimile of Philadelphia's Liberty Bell.

Behind the Scenes: The first of eleven consecutive Van Dyke show episodes that would be produced by Bill Persky and Sam Denoff, who stepped in after Carl Reiner departed the show for an extended leave of absence to appear in *The Russians Are Coming, The Russians Are Coming*.

135) Viva Petrie Airdate: 11/10/65
WRITER: John Whedon / DIRECTOR: Jerry Paris

Supporting Cast: Manuel Luis Rodriguez—Joby Baker, Doctor—Jack Bernardi

Filmed on September 28, 1965. Song: "La Virgen de la Macarena" (Monterde, Ortiz, Calero)

Rob and Laura attempt to find work for a newly landed immigrant whose only occupational skill is professional bullfighting.

Behind the Scenes: This show is a sequel to episode 73, "Turtles, Ties and Toreadors"...Joby Baker would also appear—as a different character—in the show's 156th episode, "Love Thy Other Neighbor." The light comic actor would also figure prominently in the cast of Persky and Denoff's 1967 series, *Good Morning World*.

136) Go Tell the Birds and Bees Airdate: 11/17/65
WRITER: Rick Mittleman / DIRECTOR: Jerry Paris

Supporting Cast: Dr. Gormsley—Peter Hobbs, Miss Reshovsky—Alberta Nelson

Filmed on October 5, 1965.

After Ritchie regales his schoolmates with a colorful description of where babies come from, Rob reluctantly faces the challenge of telling his son the real facts of life.

137) Body and Sol Airdate: 11/24/65
WRITERS: Carl Kleinschmitt and Dale McRaven / DIRECTOR: Jerry Paris

Supporting Cast: Sol Pomerantz—Allan Melvin, Capt. Warwick—Ed Peck, Bernie Stern—Michael Conrad, Referee—Garry Marshall, Norma—Barbara Dodd, 1st Soldier—Burt Taylor, Boom Boom Bailey—Paul Stader

Filmed on October 12, 1965.

Rob recalls his short-lived career as "Pitter Patter" Petrie—middleweight champ of the U.S. Army special services division.

Behind the Scenes: Writer Garry Marshall has a cameo as the boxing referee in this episode.

138) See Rob Write, Write Rob, Write Airdate: 12/8/65
WRITERS: Lawrence J. Cohen and Fred Freeman / DIRECTOR: Jerry Paris

Supporting Cast: Ollie Wheelright—John McGiver

Filmed on October 19, 1965.

The Petries find themselves locked in a reluctant literary rivalry after Rob volunteers his help on a children's book that Laura's writing.

139) You're Under Arrest Airdate: 12/15/65
WRITER: Joseph C. Cavella / DIRECTOR: Jerry Paris

Supporting Cast: Millie—Ann Morgan Guilbert, Detective Norton—Phillip Pine, Detective Cox—Sandy Kenyon, Joe, the Bartender—Lee Krieger, Mrs. Fieldhouse—Bella Bruck, Policeman—Ed McCready, Taxey—Johnny Silver, Man in Line-up—Tiny Brauer, Off-screen Voice—Jerry Paris (uncredited voice-over)

Filmed on October 26, 1965.

Rob has difficulty coming up with a plausible alibi after the police accuse him of taking part in a barroom brawl.

140) Fifty-Two, Forty-Five or Work Airdate: 12/29/65
WRITER: Rick Mittleman / DIRECTOR: Jerry Paris

Supporting Cast: Mel—Richard Deacon, Dawn McCracken—Reta Shaw, Joe Galar-
di—James Frawley, Herbie Finkel—Jerry Hausner, Johnson—Alfred Ward,
Truck Driver—John Chulay, Mr. Brumley—Dabbs Greer

Filmed on November 2, 1965.

Rob recalls the financial strains that forced him to take a job writing copy for
an electronics catalog during his first summer hiatus from *The Alan Brady Show.*

Behind the Scenes: Among the tidbits that Rob reveals in his unemployment
interview are his middle name—Simpson—as well as his home phone number, NE
6-9970...The show's assistant director, John C. Chulay, turns in a short cameo as a
truck driver in this episode.

141) Who Stole My Watch? Airdate: 1/5/66
WRITER: Joseph Bonaduce / DIRECTOR: Jerry Paris

Supporting Cast: Mel—Richard Deacon, Mr. Evans—Milton Frome, Jerry—Jerry
Paris, Millie—Ann Morgan Guilbert

Filmed on November 9, 1965.

When Rob's brand-new watch turns up missing at his birthday party, he's forced
to confront the possibility that it may have been stolen by one of his closest friends.

142) Bad Reception in Albany Airdate: 3/9/66
WRITERS: Garry Marshall and Jerry Belson / DIRECTOR: Jerry Paris

Supporting Cast: Forrest Gilly—Tom D'Andrea, Wendell Henderson—Robert
Nichols, Sugar Henderson—Chanin Hale, Sam—John Haymer, Fred—Joseph
Mell, Bartender—Bert Remsen, Chambermaid—Bella Bruck, Edabeth—Lor-
raine Bendix, Newlywed Man—Ed Rice, Newlywed Girl—Candace Howard,
Lou—Tiny Brauer, Organist—Joyce Wellington

Filmed on November 23, 1965. Songs: "Who Cares "(G. & I. Gershwin); "All or
Nothing at All" (Altman); "I'll Remember April " (Raye, Depaul, Johnston)

Rob encounters endless difficulties when he tries to find a functioning TV set
in an Albany hotel during the annual convention of the Seals lodge.

143) I Do Not Choose to Run Airdate: 1/19/65
WRITERS: Dale McRaven and Carl Kleinschmitt / DIRECTOR: Jerry Paris

Supporting Cast: Mr. Howard—Philip Ober, Doug—George Tyne, Bill Schermerhorn—Arte Johnson, John Gerber—Howard Wendell, Man—Peter Brocco, Woman—Helen Spring

Filmed on November 30, 1965.

Rob's stirring speech at a citizens' meeting brings him an unexpected nomination for a seat on the New Rochelle City Council.

Behind the Scenes: The first of two parts...The episode was inspired by writer Carl Kleinschmitt's real-life bid for local office in Los Angeles...Arte Johnson, one of the future star's of NBC's *Laugh-In*, has a featured role as Rob's high-powered media coordinator.

144) The Making of a Councilman Airdate: 1/26/66
WRITERS: Carl Kleinschmitt and Dale McRaven / DIRECTOR: Jerry Paris

Supporting Cast: Lincoln Goodheart—Wally Cox, Doug Miller—George Tyne, Mrs. Birdwell—Margaret Muse, Martha Goodheart—Lia Waggner, 1st Lady—Kay Stewart, 2nd Lady—Holly Harris, 3rd Lady—Marilyn Hare, Herb—Arthur Adams, Samantha Merriweather—Lorna Thayer, Duke—Remo Pisani, Booth Mitchell—James Henaghan, Jr., Election Night Announcer—Bert Remsen (uncredited voice-over)

Filmed on December 7, 1965.

Rob has second thoughts about his bid for a city-council seat after he meets his eminently more qualified opponent.

Behind the Scenes: Rob's well-versed competitor is played by Wally Cox, who also played the title role in the early-fifties TV classic, *Mr. Peepers.*

145) The Curse of the Petrie People Airdate: 2/2/66
WRITERS: Dale McRaven and Carl Kleinschmitt / DIRECTOR: Jerry Paris

Supporting Cast: Sam Petrie—Tom Tully, Millie—Ann Morgan Guilbert, Clara Petrie—Isabel Randolph, Mr. Mark, the Jeweler—Leon Belasco

Filmed on December 14, 1965.

Laura single-handedly destroys generations of Petrie family tradition when she accidentally crunches a garish heirloom brooch in her kitchen's garbage disposal.

Behind the Scenes: Carl Reiner returns to his post as the show's producer with this episode.

146) The Bottom of Mel Cooley's Heart Airdate: 2/9/66
WRITER: John Whedon / DIRECTOR: Jerry Paris

Supporting Cast: Mel—Richard Deacon, Alan Brady—Carl Reiner

Filmed on December 21, 1965.

Mel loses his job after Rob convinces him to stand up to Alan Brady's bullying.

147) Remember the Alimony Airdate: 2/16/66
WRITERS: Dale McRaven and Carl Kleinschmitt / DIRECTOR: Jerry Paris

Supporting Cast: Sol Pomerantz—Allan Melvin, Bernie—Lee Krieger, Gonzales—Don Diamond, Juan—Bernie Kopell, Maxine—Shelah Hackett, Mariachio—Jose Nieto, Mariachio—Guillermo DeAnda

Filmed on January 4, 1966. Songs: "Novillero" (M.T. Lara); "Alla en el Rancho Grande" (Ramos, Del Moral)

Rob and Laura recall a hectic trip to Mexico that almost spelled the end of their marriage.

148) Dear Sally Rogers Airdate: 2/23/66
WRITER: Ronald Axe / DIRECTOR: Richard Erdman

Supporting Cast: Mel—Richard Deacon, Stevie Parsons—Dick Schaal, Herman Glimsher—Bill Idelson, Announcer—Bert Remsen (uncredited voice-over)

Filmed on January 11, 1966. Song: "Swanee River" (Foster, arranged by Hagen)

Sally's televised plea for a husband on a late-night talk show yields unexpected results—including a letter from a suitor who could be Mr. Right.

Behind the Scenes: A sequel to the third-season episode "The Pen Is Mightier Than the Mouth," in which Dick Patterson essayed the role of talk-show host Stevie Parsons...Sharp-eyed viewers will note that in the earlier episode, the character of Stevie Parsons was modeled after then-reigning talk-show champ Jack Paar; however, as played by Dick Schaal in this installment, the talk-show host seems to be patterned after Johnny Carson, who had by then risen to prominence as host of NBC's *Tonight Show.*

149) Buddy Sorrell, Man and Boy Airdate: 3/2/66
WRITERS: Ben Joelson and Art Baer / DIRECTOR: Richard Erdman

Supporting Cast: Mel—Richard Deacon, Dorothy—Pippa Scott, Leon—Ed Peck, David Feldman—Sheldon Golomb, Cantor—Arthur Ross-Jones, Mrs. Sorrell—Maria Sokolov

Filmed on January 18, 1966. Song: "Sheyibone Beis Hamikdosh" (Schorr, arranged by A. Ellenstein, English lyrics: S. L. Lefkowitch)

Buddy's strange behavior has Rob and Sally puzzled until they discover he's been nervously preparing for his belated bar mitzvah.

150) Long Night's Journey into Day Airdate: 5/11/66
WRITERS: Jerry Belson and Garry Marshall / DIRECTOR: Jerry Paris

Supporting Cast: Jerry—Jerry Paris, Millie—Ann Morgan Guilbert, Artie, the Delivery Boy—Ogden Talbot, Herschel, the Mynah Bird—Carl Reiner (uncredited voice-over)

Filmed on January 25, 1966.

Laura and Millie spend a terrifying night with only a mynah bird to keep them company after Rob and Jerry go off on a weekend fishing trip.

Behind the Scenes: Though Millie stands shoulder to shoulder with neighbor Laura throughout most of this episode, actress Ann Guilbert remembers that her character hardly figured at all in the script's earliest draft, which was apparently conceived as a solo piece for Mary Tyler Moore. "Originally the script had Mary talking to this bird," says Guilbert. But, ironically, notes the actress, it was the star herself who scotched that plan. "Mary said, 'I can't just do that. That doesn't make any sense.' So they brought me in to be the bird. But it was fun for me, because I really had something to do in that one." Not surprisingly, this episode remains one of Guilbert's own personal favorites.

151) Talk to the Snail Airdate: 3/23/66
WRITERS: Jerry Belson and Garry Marshall / DIRECTOR: Jerry Paris

Supporting Cast: Mel—Richard Deacon, Alan Brady—Carl Reiner, Claude Wilbur—Paul Winchell, Doug Bedlork— Henry Gibson

Filmed on February 1, 1966.

Fearing that network budget cuts might cost him his job, Rob interviews for a position as staff writer for a talking snail.

Behind the Scenes: As Sally's forlorn date, Douglas Bedlork, Henry Gibson recites "Keep a-Goin'," the poem that would be his trademark on NBC's *Laugh-In*, and would later provide the basis for the actor's showcase song in director Robert Altman's 1975 feature film *Nashville*...Jellybean the Snail is brought to life by real-life ventriloquist—and amateur medical inventor—Paul Winchell.

152) A Day in the Life of Alan Brady Airdate: 4/6/66
WRITER: Joseph Bonaduce / DIRECTOR: Jerry Paris

Supporting Cast: Mel—Richard Deacon, Millie—Ann Morgan Guilbert, Jerry— Jerry Paris, Hi—Lou Wills, Girl—Kim Ford, Cameraman—John Chulay, Blanche—Joyce Jameson, Alan Brady—Carl Reiner

Filmed on February 8, 1966. Song: "Some of These Days" (Brooks)

Pandemonium results when Alan Brady arrives at Millie and Jerry's anniversary party with a documentary film crew recording his every move.

Behind the Scenes: The show's assistant director, John C. Chulay, has a cameo as the director of Alan Brady's documentary crew.

153) Obnoxious, Offensive, Egomaniac, Etc. Airdate: 4/13/66
WRITERS: Carl Kleinschmitt and Dale McRaven / DIRECTOR: Jerry Paris

Supporting Cast: Mel—Richard Deacon, Mac—Forrest Lewis, Alan Brady—Carl Reiner

Filmed on February 22, 1966. Song: "How Dry I Am" (traditional)

Rob, Buddy, and Sally try to retrieve a script that contains less-than-flattering descriptions of their arrogant boss before he has a chance to see it.

Behind the Scenes: Late in the episode, Mel establishes that Alan Brady's wife's name is Margaret, despite the fact that the off-screen character had been identified as Barbara in one of the show's earliest episodes.

154) The Man from My Uncle Airdate: 4/20/66
WRITERS: Garry Marshall and Jerry Belson / DIRECTOR: Jerry Paris

Supporting Cast: Harry Bond—Godfrey Cambridge, Wendall P. Gerard—Steve Geray, Mr. Phillips—Biff Elliott

Filmed on March 1, 1966.

A dull weekend at the Petrie house is enlivened by the arrival of an unlikely secret agent who plans to conduct a stakeout from Ritchie's bedroom.

155) You Ought to Be in Pictures Airdate: 4/27/66
WRITER: Jack Winter / DIRECTOR: Jerry Paris

Supporting Cast: Leslie Merkle—Michael Constantine, Lucianna Mazetta—Jayne Massey, Headwaiter—Frank Adamo

Filmed on March 8, 1966.

When Rob is cast opposite a voluptuous Italian in an underground film, Laura keeps a very close watch on the star chemistry.

Behind the Scenes: Writer Jack Winter was awarded the 1966 Writer's Guild Award for this script...The episode's fictional Italian starlet, Lucianna Mazetta, was named after Rose Marie, who was born Rose Marie Mazetta.

156) Love Thy Other Neighbor Airdate: 5/4/66
WRITERS: Dale McRaven and Carl Kleinschmitt / DIRECTOR: Jerry Paris

Supporting Cast: Jerry—Jerry Paris, Millie—Ann Morgan Guilbert, Mary Jane Stagg—Sue Taylor, Fred Stagg—Joby Baker, Actor—Carl Reiner (uncredited voice-over)

Filmed on March 15, 1966.

Jerry and Millie grow increasingly jealous after Rob and Laura begin spending much of their spare time with a new couple on the block.

157) **The Last Chapter** Airdate: 6/1/66

WRITERS: Carl Reiner, Bill Persky, and Sam Denoff / DIRECTORS: Jerry Paris and John Rich

Supporting Cast: Mel—Richard Deacon, Jerry—Jerry Paris, Millie—Ann Morgan Guilbert, Chaplain—Dabbs Greer, Vendor—Herbie Faye, Delivery Boy— Frank Adamo, Cabbie—Tiny Brauer, Mr. Peters—Greg Morris, Mrs. Peters— Mimi Dillard, Alan Brady—Carl Reiner

Filmed on March 15, 1966.

Laura excitedly reads the completed manuscript of Rob's book, an autobiography that affords a comical look at the life and times of a TV comedy writer and his loving wife.

Behind the Scenes: Broadcast out of order as the series' final episode, "The Last Chapter" was comprised largely of choice clips from the classic Van Dyke show episodes, "The Attempted Marriage," "Where Did I Come From," and "That's My Boy???," rounded out with a few minutes of new footage that was shot on March 15, the same night that the cast filmed their 156th episode, "Love Thy Other Neighbor"...In the episode, Alan Brady announces that he's retained Leonard Bershad to executive produce the series he plans to film from Rob's memoir—a teasing reference to the Van Dyke show's real-life executive producer, Sheldon Leonard, who was born Sheldon Leonard Bershad.

158) **The Gunslinger** Airdate: 5/25/66

WRITERS: Bill Persky and Sam Denoff / DIRECTOR: Jerry Paris

Supporting Cast: Mel—Richard Deacon, Jerry—Jerry Paris, Millie—Ann Morgan Guilbert, Gun Drummer—Allan Melvin, Big Bad Brady—Carl Reiner

Filmed on March 22, 1966. Songs: "I Don't Care" (Sutton, Lennox); "Every Little Movement" (Hoschna, Harbach); "Oh, Susannah" (Foster).

Under Jerry's anesthetic, Rob dreams that he's a sheriff in the Old West—the only man who can save the town from the threat of Big Bad Brady.

Behind the Scenes: The last episode of *The Dick Van Dyke Show* ever filmed, "The Gunslinger" features unbilled cameos from most of the show's writing staff, including Garry Marshall and Jerry Belson—who are featured prominently in the show's barroom sequence—and Bill Persky and Sam Denoff, who are instantly recognizable as the two cowpokes who glance disapprovingly at Sheriff Rob's stoic entrance, where the hapless lawman dismounts his horse, only to discover he's left his boot in the stirrup...That particular scene also marked the only occasion where the show's crew moved outside for an exterior shot. It was filmed on the old CBS Western lot in Studio City, on the same street that had provided the backdrop for countless episodes of *Gunsmoke* and other horse operas of the era. By sheer coincidence, that same lot would later serve as home to Mary Tyler Moore's MTM Productions throughout most of the seventies and eighties...The remainder of the episode was filmed on soundstages at Desilu Cahuenga, where the cast would later gather for their well-deserved closing night celebration.

NOTES

In almost every case, the reader may assume that any direct quote appearing in this text that is attributed to its subject in the present tense originated in an interview conducted by the author especially for this book. The sources for previously published quotes—including quotes drawn from seminars and panel discussions with the show's principal players—are as follows:

CHAPTER 1: ONE MAN'S REALITY

1. "...I was what we called..." Carl Reiner. 1959 MGM studio biography.
2. "I was never comfortable..." Carl Reiner. "Let's Put Another Laugh Here." *Travel and Leisure Magazine,* March 1974.
3. "I fell right into the work..." Ibid.
4. "He used to call that..." Ibid.
5. "I took her to dinner..." Sidney Skolsky. "Hollywood Is My Beat." Syndicated newspaper column, November 28, 1959.
6. "I created my own theater..." Carl Reiner. "Let's Put Another Laugh Here." *Travel and Leisure Magazine*. March 1974.
7. "Even though I acted..." Carl Reiner interview: "Dialogue with Carl Reiner," *American Film Magazine*, December 1981.
8. "David Kokolovitz is a fictitious character..." Carl Reiner. From the author's introduction to *Enter Laughing*. New York: Simon & Schuster, 1958.
9. "I intended to record..." Patterson Greene. "Comical Versatility." *Los Angeles Herald Examiner*, March 29, 1964.
10. "... decided it was time..." Ibid.

CHAPTER 2: SIFTING THROUGH SAND

11. "My wife, in her infinite wisdom..." Carl Reiner, quoted at a symposium on *The Dick Van Dyke Show* convened by the Academy of Television Arts and Sciences at the Directors Guild of America, November 1986.
12. "Sally was a combination..." Ibid.
13. "It was an easy way to make a good living..." Dan Jenkins. "He Puts Words in His Own Mouth." *TV Guide*, May 14, 1960.

CHAPTER 3: HEAD OF THE FAMILY

14. "Carl Reiner has written eight of the first thirteen..." Burt Boyar. News item. *TV Guide*. September 20, 1958.
15. "This was the first situation comedy where..." Carl Reiner, quoted at a panel seminar convened by New York's Museum of Broadcasting—now the Museum of Television and Radio—at the Los Angeles County Museum of Art, March 12, 1988.

CHAPTER 4: A BASKET FULL OF SCRIPTS

16. "I thought that basketful of scripts..." Sheldon Leonard, quoted at a panel discussion on *The Dick Van Dyke Show* convened by the Academy of Television Arts and Sciences at the Directors Guild of America, November 1986.
17. "How do you tell an actor..." Jerry D. Lewis. "Carl Reiner: Laughs for Stage, Screen and Dick Van Dyke." *TV Guide*, January 4, 1964.
18. "He showed me the expensive shoes..." Joe Hyams. "Just a Hyphenated Cut-up." *New York Herald Tribune*, March 25, 1962.
19. "Where are you going as an actor?" Ibid.
20. "While I was sitting there..." Ibid.
21. "I never saw anybody take that kind of blow..." Jerry D. Lewis. "Carl Reiner: Laughs for Stage, Screen and Dick Van Dyke." *TV Guide*, January 4, 1964.
22. "I'll always be grateful to Sheldon..." Carl Reiner, quoted at a symposium on *The Dick Van Dyke Show* convened by the Academy of Television Arts and Sciences at the Directors Guild of America, November 1986.

CHAPTER 5: FALL GUY

23. "I've reworked the scripts to fit..." Dan Jenkins. "He Puts Words in His Own Mouth." *TV Guide*, May 14, 1960.
24. "He did a bit that fractured me..." Uncredited. "What's a Dick Van Dyke?" *TV Guide*, December 9, 1961.
25. "I did a monologue and sketches..." Uncredited. "Fall Guy." *TV Guide*, May 29, 1965.
26. "In which...I fell a lot, too..." Ibid.
27. He had a natural stage presence..." Uncredited. "What's a Dick Van Dyke?" *TV Guide*, December 9, 1961.
28. "They bought us the ring..." Uncredited. "*Redbook* Readers Talk with Dick Van Dyke." *Redbook Magazine*, November 1966.
29. "I had finally achieved what I figured was my ultimate success..." Ibid.
30. "Byron Paul brought me to New York..." Ibid.

CHAPTER 7: THE GIRL WITH THREE NAMES

31. "We knew she would be too strong for Dick..." Carl Reiner, quoted at a symposium on *The Dick Van Dyke Show* convened by the Academy of Television Arts and Sciences at the Directors Guild of America, November 1986.
32. "I gave up college to learn to become a star..." "Who Is That Cutie Playing His Wife?" *TV Guide*, June 2, 1962.
33. "I was getting scale..." Leslie Raddatz. "They've Got No Kick Coming." *TV Guide*, March 27, 1965.
34. "Other shows seemed to want to use the girl who played Sam..." Ibid.
35. "She had the wrong nose..." Danny Thomas, quoted by Carl Reiner in a September 26, 1992, interview with the author.
36. "Honey...people just won't be able to believe..." Uncredited. "Who Is That Cutie Playing His Wife?" *TV Guide*, June 2, 1962.
37. "I'll have it fixed..." Ibid.
38. "If I were a dirty old man..." Jane Mosely. "Carl Reiner Does Just Everything," *Hollywood Citizen-News*, October 16, 1967.

CHAPTER 8: NERVOUS WRECKS

39. "I woke up the next morning and knew I was in love..." Richard Gehman. "Mary Tyler Moore Is Laura Petrie—Or Is She?" *TV Guide*, May 23, 1964.

CHAPTER 10: SOFT SOAP

40. "But then I noticed that he made a little 'okay' sign..." Carl Reiner, quoted at a symposium on *The Dick Van Dyke Show* convened by the Academy of Television Arts and Sciences at the Directors Guild of America, November 1986.
41. "After six or eight months..." Hedda Hopper. "Hedda Hopper's Hollywood." Syndicated newspaper column, February 10, 1962.
42. "With TV...there's a new script each week..." Ibid.

CHAPTER 13: COURTSHIP

43. "Producers all over town..." Uncredited. "Who Is That Cutie Playing His Wife?" *TV Guide*, June 2, 1962.
44. "With Dick and Rose Marie and Morey Amsterdam..." Ibid.

CHAPTER 14: CAPRI PANTS

45. "A...highly strung worrier..." Uncredited. "What's a Dick Van Dyke?" *TV Guide*, December 9, 1961.
46. "When [Rob]was about sixteen..." Carl Reiner, quoted in "Playboy Chat: Carl Reiner—A Nice Talk About Rob's Problems with His Dad" (Sidebar to "A Candid Conversation with Rob Reiner"), *Playboy*, July 1985.

CHAPTER 15: WEDNESDAY NIGHTS

47. "How d'ya like that..." Cecil Smith. "Van Dyke: Oz Wasn't Like This." *Los Angeles Times, TV Times Magazine*, December 10, 1961.
48. "He apparently didn't mind..." Uncredited. "So This Is Who Ann Morgan Guilbert Is." *TV Guide*, December 4, 1965.
49. "Before I started it..." Hedda Hopper. "Hedda Hopper's Hollywood." Syndicated newspaper column, April 15, 1965.
50. "Joan's husband forbids her..." Program listing for December 3, 1952, episode of *I Married Joan. TV Guide* (New England edition), November 30, 1952.

CHAPTER 17: ON THE BANKS OF THE OHIO

51. "I went back East..." Sheldon Leonard, quoted at a symposium on *The Dick Van Dyke Show* convened by the Academy of Television Arts and Sciences at the Directors Guild of America, November 1986.
52. "One of the few freshman shows to be renewed..." Uncredited. "Van Dyke Show Renewed." *Daily Variety*, March 21, 1962.
53. "Procter & Gamble...will have Lorillard..." Ibid.

CHAPTER 18: NEVER NAME A DUCK

54. "I've found movies the hardest..." Hedda Hopper. "Hedda Hopper's Hollywood." Syndicated newspaper column, February 10, 1962.
55. "I seemed so stiff..." Louella O. Parsons. "A Rubber Faced Comic." Syndicated newspaper column, October 14, 1962.

CHAPTER 21: NUTS

56. "I was 100 percent wrong..." Jerry D. Lewis. "Carl Reiner: Laughs for Stage, Screen and Dick Van Dyke." *TV Guide*, January 4, 1964.
57. "I called him as soon as the show went off..." Bob Thomas. "Laurel and Hardy Special to Be Emceed by Van Dyke." Associated Press wire story, August 16, 1965.
58. "25 minutes of notes..." Ibid.
59. "I did everything I could to get a flat brim..." Ibid.

CHAPTER 25: PICTURING MARY NAKED

60. "Every other Friday night I tape two shows..." Hank Grant. "On the Air with Hank Grant." *Hollywood Reporter*, April 9, 1964.
61. "Sometimes when I'm home at night..." Leslie Raddatz. "They've Got No Kick Coming." *TV Guide*, March 27, 1965.

CHAPTER 26: TEMPEST IN A BATHTUB

62. "I wanted the audience to think of Milton Berle..." Carl Reiner, quoted at a symposium on *The Dick Van Dyke Show* convened by the Academy of Television Arts and Sciences at the Directors Guild of America, November 1986.
63. "I remember in writing it..." Carl Reiner, quoted at a panel seminar convened by New York's Museum of Broadcasting—now the Museum of Television and Radio—at the Los Angeles County Museum of Art, March 12, 1988.

CHAPTER 28: CURTAIN CALLS

64. "Carl says there is no possibility..." Cecil Smith. "The TV Scene." *Los Angeles Times*, December 28, 1964.
65. "They're breaking up that gang..." Dave Kaufman. "On All Channels— Analyzing the Van Dyke Click." *Daily Variety*, December 28, 1965.

CHAPTER 29: SHENANIGANS

66. "A charming town with one theater..." Hedda Hopper. "Hedda Hopper's Hollywood." Syndicated newspaper column, December 11, 1965.

EPILOGUE

67. "At one point...some of us did think..." Uncredited. "The Van Dyke Signature Is Unmistakable." *Los Angeles Times, TV Week*, April 1, 1968.
68. "It was like going to a lovely party..." Morey Amsterdam, quoted at a symposium on *The Dick Van Dyke Show* convened by the Academy of Television Arts and Sciences at the Directors Guild of America, November 1986.

SELECTED BIBLIOGRAPHY

Andrews, Bart. *The "I Love Lucy" Book*. Garden City, N.Y.: Dolphin/Doubleday, 1985.

Brooks, Tim. *The Complete Directory to Prime Time TV Stars: 1946–Present*. New York: Ballantine Books, 1987.

Brooks, Tim, and Earle Marsh. *The Complete Directory to Prime Time TV Network Shows: 1946–Present*, 5th ed. New York: Ballantine Books, 1992.

Brown, Les. *Les Brown's Encyclopedia of Television*, 3rd ed. Detroit: Visible Ink Press, 1992.

Eisner, Joel, and David Krinsky. *Television Comedy Series: An Episode Guide to 153 TV Sitcoms in Syndication*. Jefferson, N.C.: McFarland & Company, 1984.

Halliwell, Leslie, with Philip Purser. *Halliwell's Television Companion*. 2nd ed. London: Granada Books, 1982.

Inman, David. *The TV Encyclopedia*. New York: Perigee Books, 1991.

Katz, Ephraim. *The Film Encyclopedia*. New York: Perigee Books, 1979.

McNeil, Alex. *Total Television: A Comprehensive Guide to Programming from 1948 to the Present*. 3rd ed. New York: Penguin Books, 1991.

Mitz, Rick. *The Great TV Sitcom Book*. Expanded ed. New York: Perigee Books, 1983.

Sanders, Coyne Steven, and Tom Gilbert. *Desilu: The Story of Lucille Ball and Desi Arnaz*. New York: William Morrow, 1993

Terrace, Vincent. *Encyclopedia of Television Series, Pilots and Specials*. New York: Zoetrope, 1985.

Weissman, Ginny, and Coyne Steven Sanders. *The Dick Van Dyke Show: Anatomy of a Classic*. New York: St. Martin's Press, 1983.

FOR FURTHER RESEARCH

Classic Sitcoms: A Celebration of the Best in Prime Time Comedy by Vince Waldron (Silman / James Press) remains the most useful single reference to the episodes and behind-the-scenes stories of TV's most groundbreaking comedies, including *I Love Lucy, The Honeymooners, The Dick Van Dyke Show, The Mary Tyler Moore Show,* and *Cheers,* among others. Available at your local bookstore, or on-line at www.classicsitcoms.com.

The Museum of Television and Radio offers television scholars and casual viewers alike access to an extensive and ever expanding collection of classic radio and television programs. For membership and screening information, write or visit the Museum at 25 West 52nd Street, New York, NY 10019, or 465 North Beverly Drive, Beverly Hills, CA 90120.

The Walnut Times is a quarterly newsletter that provides fans of *The Dick Van Dyke Show* with a wealth of news items, interviews, and updates on all things Van Dyke. For subscription information, contact David Van Deusen at The Walnut Times, PO Box 622, Slingerlands, NY 12159, or on-line at TheWalnutTimes@aol.com.

And don't forget to visit *The Official Dick Van Dyke Show* Book on the World Wide Web at www.The Dick Van Dyke Show.com.

ACKNOWLEDGMENTS

It seems only fitting that I begin these acknowledgments by expressing my gratitude to the founding fathers of *The Dick Van Dyke Show*, Carl Reiner, Dick Van Dyke, and Sheldon Leonard, whose recollections and insights— both personal and professional—provided the foundation for all of my subsequent investigations into this remarkable saga. I suppose it goes without saying that this volume would have been far less interesting work had it not been for the early support and ongoing encouragement I received from these three distinguished gentlemen. I'm equally indebted to the Van Dyke show's long time associate producer, Ron Jacobs, who answered each of seemingly endless queries with a degree of patience that can only be described as heroic.

I'd also like to offer an extended round of applause to the surviving members of *The Dick Van Dyke Show*'s original acting ensemble: Morey Amsterdam, Ann Guilbert, Rose Marie, Larry Mathews, Mary Tyler Moore—and, of course, Dick Van Dyke himself—all of whom generously volunteered to share their memories of the show, and in doing so, enriched the value of this book immeasurably. Thanks also to the other members of the Van Dyke show family, whose insights and anecdotes helped breathe life into this story, including Frank Adamo, Art Baer, Jerry Belson, Harvey Bullock, Ruth Burch, Sam Denoff, Ross Elliot, Earle Hagen, Jerry Hausner, Bill Idelson, Harald Johnson, Sheldon Keller, Norm Liebmann, Dale McRaven, Garry Marshall, Rick Mittleman, Bud Molin, Marge Mullen, Jim Niver, Bill Persky, Arnold and Lois Peyser, Alan Rafkin, Ken Reid, John Rich, Jay Sandrich, Doris Singleton, Frank Tarloff, and Tom Tuttle. And for offering their unique perspectives on the show's many behind-the-scenes dramas, I'm indebted to Lee Rich, Grant Tinker, Sol Leon, Tony Thomas, Andy Paris, Julie Paris, Tony Paris, Guy Raymond, Michael Ross, and George Shapiro. I'm also grateful to Sylvia Miles for sharing her account of the circumstances surrounding her involvement in Carl Reiner's embryonic *Head of the Family* pilot; and to Bob Newhart, who provided me with the benefit of his own perspective on the early sixties comedy scene from which *The Dick Van Dyke Show* blossomed.

Thanks also to Barbara Scher of Carl Reiner's office, and to Ruth Englehardt of the William Morris office, both of whom opened plenty of doors that might otherwise have remained closed to me, and who, between them, provided most of the photographs that appear in this book. Others who offered unstinting assistance and other kindness too numerous to mention include Steve Albert, Bart Andrews, Cheryl Blythe, David Bonner, Don Croll,

Kevin Dilworth, Paul Dougherty, Howard Frank, Diane Frazen, Tom Gilbert, Pam Jones, York Knowlton, Shirley Mitchell, Annette Petelle, Wally Podrazik, Howard Prouty, Andrew Ramage, Steve Saunders, Vicki Siamas, Anne Slitcher, Randy Taraborelli, David Van Deusen, Katy and Elizabeth Waldron, and Lewis S. Wechsler. Thanks also to Andy Greenberg, Benita Silverberg, and Dana Miller at Good Times Home Video; Caroline Ansell, George Faber, Lynn Fero, and Betsy Vorce of Viacom International; and Kevin Cordero and Paul Ward at the *Nick at Nite* network.

I'm also particularly beholden to all the tireless research librarians and curators who perform their unsung labors behind the scenes at the many outstanding facilities devoted to the study and preservation of film and television arts, including the Margaret Herrick Library of the Academy of Motion Picture Arts and Sciences, The UCLA Motion Picture and Television Archives, The UCLA Theatre Arts Library, The Lincoln Center Library for the Performing Arts, and the reference departments of the Beverly Hills and Hollywood public libraries. And a very special salute to Ron Simon of New York's Museum of Television and Radio, for his many years of continued encouragement.

Special thanks are also due Mary Ann Naples, David Casmion, Hyperion, who saw the first edition of this book through the labyrinthian channels of publishing with unfailing diligence and patience; to Dona Chernoff, who set those wheels in motion in the first place; and to Glenn Young and the staff at Applause Books for offering this work a permanent home at last. And, for efforts that truly extended far beyond the call of duty, I'd like to single out Diane Albert, Gordon Flagg, Jane Fujishige, David Goodman, and Greg Williams—each of whom took the time to read this manuscript in various stages of its evolution, and whose comments, criticisms, and collective wisdom went a long way toward shaping the book that you now hold in your hands.

Finally, my warm regards to all those friends whose enthusiasm for my efforts proved such an invaluable source of inspiration during the long months I spent writing and researching this book, an honor roll that includes Amy Brooke Baker and Peter Osterlund, Cynthia Berry Meyer and David Meyer, Dan Castellaneta, Rick Copp, Siobhan Fallon and Peter Hogan, Brunhilde Goodman, Peter Johnston, Jill Kirchner, Richard Kuhlman, Tom McKern, Rich Reetz, Steve Sheridan, Dan and Mindy Staley, Ammaraporn Stapornkul, Montri Stapornkul, Karen Wagner, and Robert Waldron.

To all of you, and anyone I may have inadvertently left out, I offer my deepest and most heartfelt thanks.

Vince Waldron
Los Angeles, California

PICTURE CREDITS

INDEX

NOTE: *DVDS* for *Dick Van Dyke Show*

ABOUT THE AUTHOR

Vince Waldron is the author of *Classic Sitcoms: A Celebration of the Best in Prime Time Comedy*, which has been widely hailed as the definitive study of the genre. He has served as a comedy consultant to the BBC, and was a special program adviser on The Museum of Television and Radio's ABC-TV special, *Great Television Moments: What We Watched*. A noted playwright and director, Waldron's *American Splendor: The Life and Times of Harvey Pekar* played to sold-out houses in Los Angeles for more than a year. A graduate of Antioch College, Waldron has also worked as an improvisational writer and performer with Paul Sills's Story Theatre in Chicago. He's also the co-author of the internationally acclaimed rock and roll autobiography *Be My Baby*, a collaboration with pop legend Ronnie Spector. He lives in Los Angeles.